THE FRUGAL
ALPACA FARMER

ALSO BY INGRID WOOD

A Breeder's Guide to Genetics—Relax, It's Not Rocket Science
The Alpacas of Stormwind Farm
Hiking with the Boss

INGRID WOOD

authorHOUSE®

AuthorHouse™
1663 Liberty Drive
Bloomington, IN 47403
www.authorhouse.com
Phone: 1 (800) 839-8640

© 2017 Ingrid Wood. All rights reserved.
The book's author takes no responsibility and assumes no liability for any injuries or damages alleged or otherwise attributed to any material appearing in The Frugal Alpaca Farmer—A Holistic Approach to Success. Readers should always consult their veterinarian in regards to all care protocols on their own farms.

No part of this book may be reproduced, stored in a retrieval system, or transmitted by any means without the written permission of the author.

Published by AuthorHouse 08/07/2017

ISBN: 978-1-5462-0152-6 (sc)
ISBN: 978-1-5462-0151-9 (e)

Library of Congress Control Number: 2017911527

Print information available on the last page.

Any people depicted in stock imagery provided by Thinkstock are models, and such images are being used for illustrative purposes only. Certain stock imagery © Thinkstock.

This book is printed on acid-free paper.

Because of the dynamic nature of the Internet, any web addresses or links contained in this book may have changed since publication and may no longer be valid. The views expressed in this work are solely those of the author and do not necessarily reflect the views of the publisher, and the publisher hereby disclaims any responsibility for them.

In memory of my grandmothers, Helene Igel and Maria Görgen. They were both hard workers, frugal, and incredibly tough.

Table of Contents

Illustrations xiii

Preface xv

Acknowledgments xvii

Introduction xix

Chapter 1
The Frugal Farmer 1

Chapter 2
Commonly Asked Questions 7

Chapter 3
What Is an Alpaca? 19

Chapter 4
Pastures 29

Chapter 5
The Barn 53

Chapter 6
Barn Supplies 67

Chapter 7
Farm Equipment and Tools 81

Chapter 8
Fences and Gates 89

Chapter 9
Feeding Alpacas... 99

Chapter 10
Natural Healing 113

Chapter 11
Reducing Stress 127

Chapter 12
Come to Your Senses!...147

Chapter 13
Medical Maintenance... 157

Chapter 14
Breeding Alpacas...181

Chapter 15
Birth and Cria Care 201

Chapter 16
Livestock Guardians 217

Chapter 17
Critters on the Farm 225

Chapter 18
Biosecurity... 235

Chapter 19
Transportation 245

Chapter 20
Shearing...253

Chapter 21
Fiber Facts and Fiber Follies 271

Chapter 22
Apple Heads and Knuckle Heads 293

Chapter 23
Marketing and Selling Alpacas.. 301

Chapter 24
Products and Services 325

Chapter 25
Healthy Owners Raise Healthy Alpacas 335

Chapter 26
How Much Hay Can One Horse Eat?... 347

Chapter 27
Purchasing Your Alpacas 353

Afterword... 385

About the Author 387

Index.. 389

Illustrations

All images without a photo credit were taken by the author or her husband, H. D. (David) Wood.

Front Cover: courtesy Christina Piscitelli (author's files)

Back Cover: courtesy Andrea Wolsfeld and Barbara Ewing (author's files)

Chapter 3: huacaya photo, courtesy Barbara Ewing (author's files)

Chapter 3: suri photo, courtesy Memory M - Acres Farm

Chapter 6: courtesy Quality Llama Products

Chapter 10: courtesy Christina Piscitelli (author's files)

Chapter 12: courtesy Christina Piscitelli (author's files)

Chapter 13: courtesy Benjamin Wood

Chapter 16: courtesy Kristin Joyce

Chapter 18: courtesy Barbara Ewing (author's files)

Chapter 20: courtesy Jane Marks (author's files)

Chapter 21: courtesy fellow hiker (author's files)

Chapter 22: courtesy Barbara Ewing (author's files)

Chapter 25: courtesy Benjamin Wood

Chapter 27: courtesy Christina Piscitelli (author's files)

Preface

For many years, *The Frugal Alpaca Farmer* was a work in progress. I began writing in 2004 with a coauthor. When it became obvious that time-consuming family commitments did not permit my coauthor to devote the long hours needed to work on the manuscript, we parted ways with great sadness but remained friends. A little discouraged, I shelved the project and wrote two other books.

When I finally resumed work on the manuscript, I was forced to delete as well as re-write entire sections. For example, in 2014, the two major alpaca organizations—*Alpaca Owners and Breeders Association* (*AOBA*) and *Alpaca Registry, Inc.* (*ARI*)—merged to form the *Alpaca Owners Association* (*AOA*). The alpaca industry had changed in other, drastic ways. Prices for alpacas dropped considerably during my ten-year-long hiatus from writing. At the same time, feed and farm equipment became much more expensive. The main premise of my book—to practice frugality on the farm—has to be adopted by all alpaca farmers if they wish to make a profit.

The reader will notice that, at times, specific information is discussed in more than one chapter. Because several sub-topics can and should be addressed from various angles, these repetitions serve a purpose.

I mention several supply companies in the book. With the exception of one company, I have no business relations with any of them except as a customer. *Quality Llama Products* sells *A Breeder's Guide to Genetics—Relax, It's Not Rocket Science*, a book I wrote and published in 2004.

There are those who believe that all livestock farmers are evil and contribute to the destruction of our environment. Although I could counter that opinion with compelling arguments, I don't think that this book is the appropriate forum to do so.

You will not find the current agricultural buzz word—sustainable—in any of my book's chapters. I believe that only homesteaders—people who produce virtually everything that they consume—are entitled to describe their farms as sustainable. My husband, David, and I are not homesteaders but work hard to maintain our small farm to be as ecologically sound and economically viable as we can make it. Aside from the agricultural practices discussed in the book, we heat and cool our house with a geothermal system and generate electricity for all our buildings from solar panels placed on the roof of one of the barns. We conserve energy any way we can, buy local, recycle, repurpose, and try hard not to be wasteful.

I would have liked to have added many more photos to the text. Because the book is self-published, this was not an affordable option.

There are many farming as well as business models that can be applied to managing an alpaca farm. Novice farmers often view differences in opinion as frustrating and confusing. If you are one of them, please think about how families raise their children. No two families provide identical environments and care for their offspring. Livestock farmers are no different, and that is the way it should be.

Raising livestock successfully is a very complex occupation. Although *The Frugal Alpaca Farmer* does not cover all or most of what you need to know to raise alpacas, I hope that the book will serve its purpose as a basic blueprint and valuable resource.

Acknowledgments

Many people contributed to *The Frugal Alpaca Farmer*. Most are not known to me personally. They are the members of what I call my silent support group, and their books and articles have helped me to successfully own and manage our small farm and farm store. My cherished group includes fellow alpaca farmers, other livestock producers, research scientists, veterinarians, mill owners, fiber artists, herbalists, hay farmers, USDA staff members … the list is endless. They have my gratitude.

Several people permitted me the use of their photographs. Friends, fellow alpaca farmers, and family members contributed brief as well as extensive and meaningful quotes that should give my readers food for thought. I thank them for their time and effort.

My appreciation extends to the editorial readers of *The Frugal Alpaca Farmer*. It is not easy to find qualified people. Candidates have to be willing to spend the time, have the knowledge to read with critical eyes, and not be reluctant to voice their opinions.

Caroline Johnson is a fellow alpaca farmer who did a terrific job editing the first draft. Thank you, Caroline.

Although Pat Dranchak does not own alpacas, she loves to spin, knit, and weave with alpaca fiber and yarn. Pat read the text through the eyes of a fiber artist—a valuable addition to my group of volunteer editors. Thank you, Pat.

Diann Mellott and Jane Marks manage their farm (*Cedar Lane Alpacas*) despite physical challenges that would defeat less hardy and determined women or men. They took time out of their busy lives to review the manuscript and thoughtfully suggested corrections and additions. Thank you, Diann and Jane.

Every author should have an editorial reader like Hugh Masters, someone who gives positive feedback but is also not afraid to clearly express an opposing opinion. Hugh and his wife, Carol, owned and managed a full service alpaca farm overlooking the beautiful Musconetcong Valley in the Skylands region of New Jersey. Over the years, Hugh cared for hundreds of alpacas. Always putting the welfare of the animals ahead of his own comfort and financial gain, he has a wealth of knowledge in breeding and raising alpacas. Hugh's quotes in *The Frugal Alpaca Farmer* reflect the care he gave the animals on his farm as well as the meticulous attention he paid to my manuscript. Thank you, Hugh.

And Carol, who shared in the work on *Serenity Alpacas*? Well, I would have to add a paragraph to each chapter if I wanted to properly acknowledge Carol's contributions to *The Frugal Alpaca Farmer*, the third one of my books that she expertly prepared for publication. She typed the handwritten manuscript, patiently worked through many changes and corrections with me, and formatted the completed text as required by the publisher. Carol encouraged me many times to expand my own knowledge of modern technology. Despite her success as my teacher and mentor in that area, *The Frugal Alpaca Farmer* would never have seen publication without her. Thank you, Carol. Your talents—in so many diverse areas of life—are amazing.

I can't forget the man whom I call the farm mechanic. My husband, David, has little interest in farming. Nevertheless, he mows, builds, repairs, adjusts, designs, saws, welds ... in short, he maintains our small farm's infrastructure in good working order.

When our oldest granddaughter, Grace, was only four years old, she told me," Oma, you and Opa are a team."

Yes, we are. Thank you, David, for being the frugal farm mechanic to your wife, the frugal farmer.

Finally, credit must be given to the animals. The alpacas taught me patience, humility, and to live in harmony with nature. They continue to touch my heart and enrich my life in many ways.

Introduction

The tiny alpaca cria stood perfectly still. The bright morning sun lightened the reddish tint in its black tui fleece to the color of burnished copper. A few feet away grazed Clarissa, the baby's mom, quite content with her world. She was obviously unconcerned about the red halter worn by Annie, her first offspring.

With my back turned toward the cria, I quietly held the matching red lead rope in my hand. Although the air was cool on this wintry day, I felt the sun's warming rays on my face and tired body. The week had been tough—my energy drained by demanding students, numerous parent conferences, and late night phone calls to comfort an unhappy friend. Sighing wearily, I suddenly felt a velvety soft, little nose touch my motionless hand. Prompted by the boundless curiosity so typical for animals with a strong flight instinct, my turned back had encouraged little Annie to cautiously investigate the two-legged creature who held her captive.

Slowly, I took a small step forward. After some hesitation, Annie followed. Two steps, three steps—a quick sideways glance confirmed that Clarissa's daughter was walking calmly behind me. Her ears were up; her nostrils did not flare with the nervous energy typical of a frightened alpaca. This alpaca baby had confidence yet respectfully maintained the physical and emotional distance so important for a good future relationship with human beings. Focusing intently on the task at hand, I felt all tension leave my body. After several more minutes had passed, I gently approached Annie. Initially shying away from my outstretched arm, the little alpaca eventually stood still while I scratched its downy soft chin and finally released it. Satisfied with the weekly lesson, I watched the cria leap away to catch up with its dam.

My husband and I adored this little, fluffy huacaya alpaca. The fact that Annie was boarded on *Stormwind Farm*, and therefore not owned by us, did not diminish the pleasure we felt in her presence.

Annie's mother, Clarissa, came to us from a farm in Pennsylvania. She had been bred during the previous fall. Despite several matings, her owners did not believe her to be pregnant and decided to allow her another season to mature. The following spring, Clarissa was bred again. Her vigorous protests, not unusual for a maiden, were finally overcome by a determined male. Several months later, she arrived at *Stormwind Farm* with her traveling companion, a gelding. Calm, sweet-tempered, and incredibly athletic, Clarissa captured our hearts.

Imagine my surprise when, only weeks after she joined our herd, my husband called me at work. "We have an alpaca baby in our pasture."

"That's impossible!"

"I know what an alpaca baby looks like, and this is an alpaca baby," David protested indignantly.

After spending the remainder of my workday on pins and needles, I rushed home to find a beautiful, black female cria nursing contentedly. What a delightful surprise! But what had happened? Obviously, Clarissa had become pregnant in the fall.

When she had protested the repeat breeding in the spring, she had tried to give the previous owner a message: "Please leave me alone, I am pregnant!"

Clarissa's tall, athletic frame and fiber coat had successfully hidden an advanced pregnancy from our inexperienced eyes. This miracle baby—so utterly adorable—came at a time when my mother's death and crushing disappointments had brought much sadness in my life. Annie's birth reaffirmed my belief that we must accept life in all its rich nuances.

Since that day, quite a few years have gone by. My husband and I are both retired now and no longer have to leave the farm each morning. Our lives are not as stressful and hectic as they used to be when we worked off the farm and had to attend to farm chores before leaving for work, in the evenings, and on weekends. Nevertheless, our small farm keeps us busy, physically active, and challenges us in many ways. That's all good. I have more time to write, and —fortunately for me—my friend, Carol Masters, remains willing to decipher my handwritten manuscripts.

1

THE FRUGAL FARMER

"A frugal farmer must have a frugal spouse or partner. That's more important than anything else." H. D. Wood

Romance and Reality

There are many people—particularly women—who are drawn to what I call the romance of farming. Waking up to a rooster's crowing, seeing a hawk sail above green pastures in an endlessly blue sky, working quietly with animals that have come to trust your presence in their midst, the glittering of thousands of fireflies in a meadow at night ... yes, there is romance in farming. There is also sweat, and blood, and an aching back after mowing, and the fear of losing the fruits of your labor during the next storm. There are government regulations that make no sense, and—increasingly in many farm communities—there are neighbors who "love" your farm but not always the actual farm activities.

For the farmer, the romance of farming must be rooted in reality. I feel passion and love for my work; I have never worn the rose-colored glasses of self-deception. I advise my readers to do likewise. The book's title serves as a mission statement in very broad terms. In this chapter, I define the title's terminology. I think it will help you, the reader of *The Frugal Alpaca Farmer—a Holistic Approach to Success*, to better understand and appreciate the information that follows.

Are We Farmers?

The word farm can be applied to a great variety of infrastructures. There are farms that extend over thousands of acres, and there are farms—no larger than one acre—where the farmer earns a profit from the sale of carefully nurtured specialty vegetables. There are dairy corporations where thousands of cows are milked each day, and there are dairy farms where a couple—husband and wife—milk and care for forty pastured cows with the help of their small children. There are farms where a mono-culture produces only one crop, and there are farms where an astonishing variety of products are grown. Some farms are managed and maintained by huge staffs; on others, only a single man or woman—the family farmer as envisioned by the non-farming public— works the land. If farms are so diverse, it follows that the men, women, and children who live and work on these farms are a diverse group, and their approach to farming differs from one person to the next.

My old dictionary described a *farmer* as *a person who earns his living by farming*. This definition is outdated. Few farm families these days are able to cover all their living expenses by selling or bartering the agricultural products that they produce on their land. Many farmers—possibly the majority—have a full-time job off the farm. In other families, one partner—usually the woman—holds a job off the farm but helps with the farm work on evenings and weekends. The definition of a farmer as *a person who operates a farm or cultivates land* (*Random House Webster's Dictionary*) applies to all farmers, including those who rush home from their day jobs to plant their crops in the dark with the help of their tractors' lights. It also applies to the alpaca farmers who rise at 4 a.m. to take care of their herds before they head out to earn the money that will pay the mortgage.

Because the alpaca industry reflects the diversity found in the greater agricultural community, one small book on alpaca farming cannot address all possible business models as they apply to raising alpacas. I write about what I know best: raising a small herd of alpacas on small acreage for a supplemental income. I don't, for example, discuss the issue of employees. My husband, David, and I are the only workers on our farm. David is the farm mechanic, is responsible for construction projects, mows the pastures, and shears the alpacas. I do all the daily farm work, maintain the farm's landscaping, and keep a small vegetable and herb garden. I also help with the fiber harvest and assist with projects that require a second person to, for example, lift or carry heavy objects. In addition, I manage our farm's retail business, marketing programs, and sales of breeding stock. David and I share the housework and work together to stack each year's hay supply after it's been delivered.

I don't think much about my work load until other people ask me about it. A recent farm visitor questioned me three times about our employees. Did she think I was lying when I told her the first two times that we have none?

A group of knitters toured the farm, and the women all asked, "How do you do it?"

I laughed. "I put one foot in front of the other each day and just start working," I said.

Will my book be helpful to readers who plan to farm on a much larger scale? Yes, I believe so. For example, the chapters on pasture management, fences, natural healing, and biosecurity—among others—will provide meaningful information to all prospective alpaca farmers.

Frugal Farmers

In many ways, farming with alpacas is quite different from when we first inquired about camelids in 1995. The industry has changed over time. That was to be expected. Sales prices for alpacas have dropped drastically since David and I brought our first two alpacas home to *Stormwind Farm* in 1997. Most farmers must be *frugal—not wasteful*—if they wish to make a profit from their labor. Alpaca farmers are no longer exempt from this financial reality.

"So you are writing a book for alpaca farmers who have little money?" a friend asked me when she heard about my project.

Not necessarily! *The Frugal Alpaca Farmer* should appeal to anyone who values financial stability and believes that money should not be spent foolishly. Being frugal, however, does not mean cutting costs on, for example, a sound nutritional program for the animals. Frugality is not defined by purchasing poor quality products. There are many ways to save money without compromising the health and comfort of the herd.

What Is a Holistic Approach?

You may wonder about the holistic approach mentioned in my book's title. My old dictionary—purchased in the seventies—doesn't even carry this term.

When I shared the book's title with a fellow alpaca owner, the always diplomatic Alice Brown said, "You know, Ingrid, holistic has become a fashionable buzz word." This was, I am sure, her gentle way of saying, "There should be some substance to this claim. I hope you're not going to blow smoke to give the book a catchy title."

One of the definitions for *holistic* in *Random House Webster's Dictionary* is: "*Of or using therapies that consider one's total physical and psychological state in the treatment of disease.*"

In *Life at the Zoo* (2004), author and zoo veterinarian Phillip T. Robison quoted the medieval Jewish physician Moses Maimonides, who wrote eight hundred years ago: "The physician should not treat the disease but the patient who is suffering from it. Treating problems in isolation from their inciting causes and their hosts amounts to insensitive medicine."

The concept of a holistic approach to healing is obviously not new. It's been forgotten in our misguided trust and worship of modern wonder drugs. This book is not about treating disease. If anything, it is about *preventing disease*, so I've broadened the definition quoted above. I define a holistic approach to farming as ensuring the physical and emotional well-being of all creatures on a farm, including those of the two-legged variety. It includes the condition of a farm's infrastructure, especially the pastures' soil health. Human beings, animals, and the environment they live in are viewed as a single system.

A holistic approach to alpaca care and breeding practices recognizes that each small part—each tiny cog in the wheel—must work smoothly for the entire system to function well. Far from being a trendy and clever marketing slogan, the concept of holistic farm management is practical, sensible, and a common sense approach to raising livestock.

Defining Success

The term *success* is, of course, open to interpretation. As a future or present farmer, you should clarify your personal definition of success. What aspect of alpaca ownership will make you feel satisfied and successful? Reading *The Frugal Alpaca Farmer* should help you to set realistic objectives. Although a farmer expects to make a profit, success does not need to be measured exclusively in financial terms.

Experience Counts

You may question, as you should, my qualifications—other than a small budget—for writing this book. I have owned and bred one litter of Afghan Hounds and several litters of Whippets since the late sixties. We no longer have Afghan Hounds. We still own one Whippet, but I've stopped breeding. David and I moved to our small farm in 1995 and welcomed our first two huacaya alpacas in 1997. Very few of our animals have seen a veterinarian due to illness. While that can be attributed to luck, I believe that my sound management practices played a big role in this. Over the years, I have been involved in many aspects of alpaca farming and have a wealth of experience and practical advice to share with my readers.

Last Chapter

You may wonder why I chose to write about the purchase of alpacas in the last chapter. In my opinion, there is a valid reason for this placement. After reading what I have to say about such issues as nutrition, pregnancy, and fiber, you should have a much clearer picture of what is important to you. Your vision of quality will include the traits of the alpacas that you plan to purchase as well as those of the farmer who will sell them to you.

Do I Have Opinions?

I have occasionally been described as opinionated by other people. After more than three decades of breeding and raising dogs and livestock, it would be laughable if I did not have strong opinions on many subjects concerning animal husbandry and breeding programs. Some are based on personal observations. Most were primarily formed after extensive research. Although I am not a trained scientist, articles and textbooks on veterinary medicine, genetics, and pasture farming are my reading materials of choice. The study of species other than alpacas educated me as well and shaped my thinking about selection for genetic traits, breeding practices, and husbandry issues. I also freely seek the advice and opinions of other farmers with experience when the situation merits it. The farmer who thinks he or she knows everything is a foolish person. Additionally, I like to think that a good amount of common sense has often led me to the source of a problem or to make the right choice when faced with a decision. I have a healthy mistrust of methods and products used by others without thought or clear objectives. "Everybody is doing/using it" is not a good enough reason for me to follow suit. To the contrary, I am not afraid to march to the beat of my own drum.

I didn't write *The Frugal Alpaca Farmer* to convince readers that my farming practices are the best in the industry. Each reader, after thoughtful consideration, should apply or ignore my practices to fit the unique circumstances on his or her farm.

The Desk Drawer

Please indulge my one small request, though. Write your vision of the kind of farm and alpacas you plan to own on a small piece of paper. There is no need to go into great detail; a few sentences will suffice. Now put the paper in a desk drawer and promise not to look at it again until you've finished reading the book. Thank you.

2

COMMONLY ASKED QUESTIONS

"My farm, to me, is not just land,
Where bare, unpainted buildings stand;
To me, my farm is nothing less
Than all created loveliness."
Unknown Author

Are Alpacas a Good Investment?

As I watched my alpacas graze in their pastures today, my thoughts turned to how often the very first questions posed by a buyer concern the healthy profits the person hopes to realize from his or her venture. That's not surprising. Nobody starts a new business with the expectation of losing money. Many industry marketing brochures and e-mail messages advertise farming with alpacas as a good investment and a positive lifestyle change. They promise financial prosperity amidst a stress-free, bucolic rural environment—the ideal life for those who wish to lower their blood pressure and escape pollution, crime, and a hectic pace.

Years ago, a colorful brochure produced and distributed by the *Alpaca Owners and Breeders Association* (AOBA) stated: "No other farm animal can equal the alpaca in offering sound investment returns from easily managed animals on a small acreage."

Should anyone give a prospective buyer assurance that alpacas are definitely a good investment? Not anymore than one can be sure that stocks, bonds, gold, or real estate are the roads to wealth. There are plenty of pitfalls that can turn your "sound investment" into a financial disaster. I can't help but think of the distraught farmer who, one sad morning, found a female cria dead in its pasture. His children cried, and his wife refused to go to the barn for a week. A good portion of that year's potential profit had to be buried in the back forty.

When David and I purchased our first two alpacas, I felt confident in my capacity for hard, physical work and endurance. I knew more than the average person about farming and animal genetics. My confidence extended to David's mechanical and problem solving abilities. Other than that, I wasn't at all sure that I would be able to successfully sell alpacas.

Anxious and worried, I remember asking Carol Masters of *Serenity Alpacas*, "Do you think we'll be able to make this work as a business?"

"I don't have a crystal ball," Carol dryly responded.

It's the only answer my foolish question deserved. The bottom line is that farming with alpacas is no different from other farming ventures in that many variables determine either financial success or failure. Breeding and selling alpacas can certainly provide income along with attractive tax deductions. Over the last several decades, a few farmers have probably seen profits well into six figures. Many, like myself, have made modest profits. Unfortunately, alpaca farming has impoverished or even bankrupted a number of families. Too many people plunged into debt and financial disaster because nobody took the time to show them cost-effective ways of alpaca farming. Farmers and animals paid a bitter price. In some cases that I am aware of, people apparently invested well beyond their means. They tried hard to emulate the farmers who have considerable financial resources at their disposal. They failed to realize that many wealthy alpaca owners accumulated financial wealth long before they laid eyes on their first camelid. Farming with alpacas did not generate the money to purchase and support the opulent estates admired by the hapless dreamers. There is nothing wrong with following your dream, but a big dose of realistic thinking and planning better be part of your travel kit. The successful farmers whom I know are—without exception—smart, frugal, and very hard workers. Without a doubt, there is a symbiotic relationship between a farmer's financial solvency and the animals' health and comfort. Not surprisingly, sound husbandry practices equal profits. Such practices need not be costly and elaborate. Thoughtful care creates a cycle of wellness.

Raising alpacas is not a path to quick wealth. Despite exercising frugality in all areas of farming, it may only lead to a small income. Don't count on being able to quit your non-farming job, and don't incur debt that —as reality follows euphoria—you see no way to ever pay off.

"My husband and I can't sleep at night," one farmer told me. "We've borrowed a ton of money. I don't know what we are going to do if things don't work out."

David and I did not borrow a ton of money, and it took almost eighteen years for us to complete my original site plan—one careful planning step at a time.

Here is what I tell all prospective alpaca farmers who visit *Stormwind Alpacas* and ask questions about profits: "Contrary to what you may have heard, raising alpacas is not a very lucrative business for most farmers. If you expect to farm full-time without other income, you will need to expand your farm's products and activities beyond the sale of alpacas and their raw fiber. If you plan to farm with your primary focus on making a lot of money, don't do it. There are easier ways to make money than farming. If financial profit is your only motive to farm, you will come to resent the work and the animals. Rather than viewing farming as a sound investment in your health and family's lifestyle, you will judge the farm chores as backbreaking drudgery and the farm as a prison where the animals hold you captive."

Over the years, I analyzed why I have been successful with my farm business while many others with more extensive resources have failed. I believe that one big reason is my passion—my love and enjoyment—for the *work* that is required to make a small farm a thriving enterprise.

What Are Start-up Expenses?

This book examines the many components of alpaca farming with a focus on frugality. It should appeal to farmers and owners on small budgets as well as individuals who have plenty of money but see no reason to spend it frivolously. For many farmers, the expenses for the farm's infrastructure—land, buildings, equipment, and supplies—will far surpass the purchase price of a starter herd. Most authors who give advice on the subject tell their readers to spend their money on the very best breeding stock that they can afford. I ignored that advice and focused my energy and limited funds on first creating the best—that meant the healthiest and safest—environment for both alpacas and farmers. In the early days, our modest resources were primarily spent on fencing, building functional barns, and the development of outstanding pastures. This strategy has served us well, including from a financial viewpoint.

If you've skimmed the book's pages, I'm sure you now have this question: "Why aren't there any hard numbers listed in the book, including a sample budget?"

Prices differ from one area of our huge country to the next. New Jersey hay prices, for example, will hardly be relevant to a farmer living in Arizona. Requirements for infrastructure vary with climate, terrain, area predators, and other variables. A farm is not like a restaurant franchise where one business is a predictable copy of all others. To quote specific dollar amounts for the minimum starting capital doesn't make much sense.

A budget should include a cushion for emergencies. I turned away our first potential customers when the young couple debated the affordability of a water bucket with a heater element. In their case, the budget for start-up expenses didn't include the funds for bare necessities. Even without presenting actual dollar amounts, I think that the information in *The Frugal Alpaca Farmer* will be helpful to many novice farmers.

What Is a Fair Price for an Alpaca?

Unfortunately, that is another question that cannot be answered with the simple quotation of a dollar amount. Alpacas are not cars. They are not manufactured on an assembly line, where each one is produced to the exact same specifications of a particular model.

My late mother-in-law, Madeleine Wood, would have said, "An alpaca is worth whatever someone is willing to pay for it."

On average, alpaca prices have come down considerably since the first days of the North American alpaca industry. Those of us who are realists expected this. The effect of supply and demand on price is a pretty simple concept to understand. The overall state of the economy also has an impact on almost any business. Because prices are more in line now with those paid for other livestock, it is more important than ever that alpaca farmers practice frugality if they plan to make a profit. Let me assure you that alpacas are here to stay. They produce a viable, agricultural product.

Isn't It a Pyramid Scheme?

In a pyramid scheme, each buyer is part of a financial chain. Only the people at the top of the pyramid stand a chance of making considerable profits. To apply this concept to farming with alpacas is wooly thinking. Once farmers have paid for their alpacas, they are no longer financially beholden to the sellers unless they agreed to special clauses in their contracts. This is no different than farming with sheep or cattle, and I've never heard the pyramid concept applied to any other livestock species. I don't know where this silly idea originated. It's time to put it to rest.

Can I Keep One In My Backyard?

In 2008, the U.S. government officially designated alpacas as livestock. You will not be permitted to keep alpacas in a residential zone even if your backyard covers several acres. Some people impulsively purchased alpacas only to find out that zoning didn't so much as permit them to keep a chicken—never mind alpacas—on their property. One man found out that he could have dozens of alpacas on his New Jersey property but township's laws forbid their sale or that of their offspring. Welcome to the wacky world of zoning regulations!

Some officials are clueless about farming practices. In Pennsylvania, a farmer was cited for allowing "unsightly weeds" to grow on his property. It was a hay field. A New Jersey man lost his farm assessment for his ten-acre hay field. "It's in front of his house, so it's a lawn," the tax assessor ruled.

My husband and I paid attention to these issues when we looked for farm property. We bought land in a community that is firmly committed to farming, preserving farmland, and seeing its farmers prosper. New residents must sign a statement that informs them that farm activities such as spreading manure are considered vital to the community, and residents' complaints about normal farm practices will be ignored.

State governments have programs that give property tax relief to farmers. They vary widely from state to state. Township officials enforce the eligibility requirements for these programs to various degrees. Educate yourself as to what it will take to qualify for and then maintain such tax status. You will most likely be asked to show proof that you are actively farming by producing sales records in a certain amount. Townships may have additional rules and regulations that govern raising, marketing, and selling livestock. For example, for marketing and sales activities on our farm, we must provide adequate off-street parking. That is a reasonable and sensible request.

Can I Keep Alpacas With My Horse?

A kick from a horse or donkey could severely injure an alpaca. My friend, Jane Marks, has owned horses for fifty years. I asked her to comment. Jane said: "There is no way that I would ever consider putting a horse in a pasture with alpacas. In my opinion, it would be too dangerous for the alpacas."

Sheep and goats deposit their manure anywhere. With a little planning, alpacas can be trained to keep their barn free of manure and urine. Finding sheep or goat manure in the barn will not encourage the alpacas to deposit their own, tiny "beans" outdoors. Although I know of one farm where horses, donkeys, goats, and alpacas graze together on one large pasture, I think it's best to assign alpacas their own living space.

Are Alpacas Easy to Manage?

What most people probably should ask instead is this: "Is an *alpaca farm* easy to manage?" That depends on many things, one being your definition of "easy." For example, I handle the daily chores of feeding, clean-up, and routine care such as giving vitamins, dewormers, and inoculations. I also accustom our crias to wear a halter, walk on lead, and enter a trailer. Additionally, I trim nails by myself and manage our farm's breeding program, including behavior testing to determine pregnancy status. I am strong for my age and am accustomed to hard, physical work. So yes, I find it easy to manage *the alpacas*. Taking care of the animals, however, is only a segment of a livestock farmer's workload. Prospective alpaca farmers are often so focused on the animals that they forget the work and skills required to build and maintain the farm's infrastructure. Although I use a shovel and a wheel barrow better than many men half my age, I readily admit that I would not be able to farm without my husband's help. Many women lack the mechanical skills to take care of the hundreds of things that need to be built, installed, changed, or fixed on a farm. I am one of them. If I had to hire someone to perform all these services on our farm, our profits would be reduced to zero.

Of course, women can learn to take care of machinery as well as any man can. Some women, like my friend, Barbara Ewing, surpass most men in knowledge and expertise when it comes to the trades. There are men who don't know any more than I do about fixing a motor or installing a light switch. The bottom line then is this: It doesn't matter who performs these necessary chores—man or woman—just be sure *one* of you either knows how to install a gate, fix a light, mend a fence, or is extremely motivated and willing to learn.

It's not impossible for a single, competent person to raise alpacas, but it would be very hard. Often, you need two pairs of hands to carry, lift, push, and pull—no, not the alpacas—the many things that are needed on a livestock farm. Sometimes, one person can do the job, but it's so much easier to have a helper.

Early on in my life as an alpaca farmer, I visited a llama ranch after meeting the owner at a camelid event. I had been in total awe of the tiny woman. How did she *do* it? Well, I found out. Upon arrival, I was greeted by the ranch manager, met the teenage helpers, admired the handiwork of the two gardeners, and observed the two maids exit the spotless house. The alpaca farmers who tell you how easy it is to raise alpacas often enjoy a similar lifestyle.

Are They Hardy?

Visitors to Stormwind Farm often say, "I was told that alpacas are hardier than other livestock."

All livestock species are hardy if bred and cared for properly. If you provide alpacas with proper housing, excellent nutrition, respect their temperament and instincts, use correct reproductive management, and practice the minimum of medical maintenance as outlined in this book, you should have few or no problems if you purchase healthy stock. Unfortunately, just like sheep, goats, and cattle, alpacas become ill and die every day in this and other countries due to their owners' neglect, ignorance, or sheer stupidity. A farm's profits disappear quickly when routine medical maintenance turns into routine medical intervention. A financially productive operation can absorb occasional veterinary treatments of ill alpacas. When you see your veterinarian as often as your best friend, your budget is in trouble. Yes, my alpacas are hardy, and my management practices keep them healthy and robust. I do not believe that alpacas are inherently hardier than other livestock species.

Do They Spit?

Yes, they do. All species have defense mechanisms that help to protect them. Alpacas kick and spit when they feel threatened. Because alpacas don't have hard hooves, kicking and stomping is only effective to fight off or kill small predators. Alpaca spit—slimy and with a nauseating smell—makes a great weapon. Males spit at one another during a fight. Pregnant females spit at males that try to copulate with them. A female alpaca with a nursing cria at its side will spit at the crias of other mothers should they come close. In the animal world, protecting one's milk supply for one's own offspring is prudent behavior. Alpacas that have been imprinted on human beings will eventually spit at them and become aggressive. These improperly raised—constantly petted, hugged, and otherwise handled—crias will become potentially dangerous adults. Being spit on will be the least of your problems with such a camelid rogue. Properly raised, handled, and trained alpacas do not spit on human beings.

Can You Ride Them?

Alpacas have neither the conformation nor the temperament to make them suitable candidates for a riding program. Underneath that heavy fiber coat, they are much smaller than the public suspects.

Over the years, I have been asked questions that were amusing as well as disturbing because they revealed an astonishing lack of knowledge in basic science and farming practices.

"Do they lay eggs?" "Are they a cross between a goat and a sheep?" "Do they ever sleep?"

Some people judge without asking questions. Teenage girls once hissed, "Killer!" at me at a festival because they assumed that I slaughter my alpacas to harvest their fiber.

It's all in a day's work, and it's good to deal with all questions and comments with a sense of humor.

Do Alpacas Require a Lot of Time?

I am frequently asked whether alpacas require a lot of time or care. If you are a horse owner, you may consider alpaca care a walk in the park. If all you've cared for so far in your life is a hamster, you may come to think of alpaca farming without employees as an intolerable burden on your time and energy. I have already pointed out—and it bears repeating—that it takes more time to maintain the farm's infrastructure than to care for the animals.

Is It Fun?

My definition of fun: *To care for livestock and perform hard, physical work under all kinds of weather conditions, working in quiet solitude in the peaceful environment of my small farm.* What is your definition?

Alpaca farming is often marketed as a lifestyle without stress. The husband and wife who almost came to blows over whether their new cria should wear a warming coat may have a few things to say about stress. The husband—worried about what he perceived to be a fragile, little creature—lovingly dressed the cria in a brand-new, quilted cria coat. Impressed with the newborn's sturdy appearance and precocious behavior, the wife removed the protective garment. He put it back on. She removed it again. By the end of the day, husband and wife were no longer speaking. Most definitely, they felt stressed.

Of course there is stress involved in farming! Farmers who must rely on farm profits as their sole income experience enormous stress in their lives. David and I don't belong in that category. Fortunately, we don't have to worry about not being able to pay our bills if we don't sell alpacas for several months or even longer. That doesn't mean that we live in a state of continual bliss. I appreciate that I can control my farm's destiny through hard work, knowledge, skill, and creative thinking. Not everything can be controlled though. Our hay farmer's harvest may be in jeopardy due to relentless rain—big stress! A storm destroyed one of the barn doors, a pregnant alpaca is long overdue to give birth, the feed store's delivery schedule got bollixed up, a wild animal is scratching like crazy in the attic at night—all minor stuff in the greater scheme of things, but all problems that need to be faced and taken care of. Farming with alpacas is a wonderful occupation, but it's not without stress.

How Did You Get Started?

Our alpaca farming adventure started with my informal search for an interesting book at the local library. While browsing through the livestock section, I found a book on raising llamas. A visit to a local llama farm led to my discovery of alpacas. The small size and the beautiful fiber of the alpacas appealed to me. Despite my repeated pleading over the years to buy a farm, my husband, David, had always refused to get involved in any kind of farming venture. To my great surprise, he agreed to join me in satisfying a lifelong desire to own and breed livestock. He occasionally reminds me of my promise that his part in alpaca farming would consist of gently rocking on the front porch. There hasn't been much time for rocking. We purchased eight acres that had been planted in soybeans. To save money, we acted as our own contractor while building our house. What a learning experience that turned out to be! There were many times when I felt like giving up and escaping the nightmare of dealing with all our subcontractors. In contrast, working with a local farmer who planted our pastures for us was a very positive experience.

We started with a small barn and two small pastures. Two barns and fencing for two more pastures—paid for with profits from alpaca sales—were added several years later. We did much of the work ourselves. It was very hard at times, but I often thank fate for leading me to the book on the library shelf that changed my life.

One of my customers recently asked, "Has there ever been a time when you regretted getting into alpaca farming?"

As of this writing, I can state truthfully: never! The only regret that I have is that we did not discover these wonderful animals long before I took my fateful trip to the library.

3

WHAT IS AN ALPACA?

"An alpaca is a four-legged creature. It is long-necked, fluffy, and cute." Rioghnan, Grace, and Kaitlin Wood (ages 9, 7, and 4)

Camelid Species

In *Medicine and Surgery of South American Camelids,* Murray E. Fowler, DVM tells the reader that "the classification of SACs (South American Camelids) has been controversial." The classification refers to a system that scientists use to group members of all species. For the purpose of this book, a few basic facts will suffice. There are two types of camelids—Old World and New World. The first group includes the Dromedary camel and the Bactrian camel. The second group includes the llama, the alpaca, the guanaco, and the vicuña—collectively identified as lamoids. Llamas and alpacas are domesticated. Although the majority of guanacos and vicuñas are wild, in South America, vicuñas are rounded up and shorn in biannual intervals. All SACs have an identical chromosome count. This makes it possible for them to interbreed and produce fertile offspring. A few years ago, a crossbreeding program with a formal registry was initiated by North American farmers. The crosses—Paco-Vicuñas—are between alpacas and vicuñas.

Llamas and alpacas have been crossbred to various degrees by South American pastoralists. This practice became prevalent after the Spanish virtually destroyed the sophisticated breeding programs adopted by the

Incas. In *Lamas – Haltung und Zucht von Neuwelt-Kameliden* (8.Jahrgang, Heft 2), Dr. Marina Gerken reports on a presentation made at the Second World Congress for camelids held in Cusco, Peru, in November 1999. A genetic study proved that hybridization "was a far greater problem than anyone had suspected" (Heather Pringle, *Discover Magazine,* 2001). Since hybrids usually enjoy great vigor and vitality, we may question why anyone would consider the camelid crosses a problem. Unfortunately, the llama influence coarsened alpaca fiber. An argument can also be made that using alpacas in a llama breeding program reduces size and with it the llama's suitability as a pack animal. By now, selective breeding has created several varieties of llamas—classic, light wool, heavy wool, suri, and mini—on the North American continent.

Eric Hoffman writes about the comprehensive genetic study in *The Complete Alpaca Book* (revised edition, 2006). According to Hoffman, zoologist Dr. Jane Wheeler, her husband, Dr. Raul Rosadio, and British geneticist Helen Stanley sent blood samples from 2,000 South American camelids to the Institute of Zoology in London, England. Research was extensive and eventually a DNA test to determine hybridization was developed.

In any case, geneticists Dr. Miranda Kadwell and Dr. Michael Bruford confirmed with their research at the Institute of Zoology in London, England, what Dr. Wheeler had long suspected after working with camelid skeletons: "The vicuña are the most likely ancestor of the alpaca, and the guanaco are the most likely ancestor of the llama" (Bruford, *Discover Magazine,* 2001). The research resulted in reclassification of the alpaca from *Lama pacos* to *Vicugna pacos.* The four SACs are therefore classified and referred to as *species* rather than breeds in much of current camelid literature. This can be confusing when we consider that fertile offspring result from crosses between camelid species as well as the extensive hybridization that has already taken place.

Huacayas and Suris

Additionally, there are two breeds—we can also classify them as varieties—of alpacas. The huacaya has springy, crimpy fiber, giving the animal a teddy bear like appearance. Some authors use the term spongy to describe the typical huacaya fiber phenotype. The suri's fiber is longer, has no crimp, and hangs down in dreadlock type ringlets, often referred to as pencil locks. Due to the way their fleeces part along their spines, suris need a little more protection from cold and rain. The suri is the rarer of the two varieties. The trait for suri fiber is believed to be under dominant genetic control. I explain in *A Breeder's Guide to Genetics* why genetic dominance does not necessarily translate into a larger population of the variety that carries the dominant gene(s).

This is a typical huacaya alpaca.

Do the temperaments of the two alpaca varieties differ?

Here is what a Swiss farmer had to say: "The suri is somehow different than the huacaya. It is livelier, more active, more charming, but also more tractable, tamer" (*Lamas,* 9.Jahrgang, Heft 3).

An American farmer for whom I translated this article—and who owns both varieties—laughed out loud. "And what is the title of this little piece?" she inquired. "A suri fantasy?" She described her own suris as more aloof than her huacayas.

This is a typical suri alpaca.

The truth is probably that suris, like their huacaya cousins, have strong individual differences in temperament, and much of their behavior depends on how they are handled and trained. The Swiss farmer's description may very well paint a true picture of his own alpacas.

Alpaca Anatomy and Physiology

The size of individual alpacas varies considerably within the greater population, and adult weights range from approximately 100 to 200 pounds. Like all South American Camelids (SACs), alpacas have soft footpads with toenails. Most of the skin that covers their bodies is thick and tight. Each alpaca produces an annual fiber harvest of one to ten pounds, with a few animals producing a higher quantity. Colors span the full spectrum from white to black as well as a variety of patterns.

SACs are sometimes referred to as modified ruminants. True ruminants have four stomach compartments. Although SACs only have three, Dr.

Fowler is very clear on the fact that camelids are functional ruminants and describes the first two compartments of their stomachs as "anaerobic fermentation chambers." Alpacas, like the other lamoids, chew their cud. Feed is mixed with saliva to form a bolus. This is initially swallowed and brought up later to be chewed more thoroughly. Bloat is rare in camelids.

Alpacas are induced ovulators and copulate in a prone—cushed—position. After a gestation that lasts about one year, the alpaca gives birth to a single baby called a cria. Live twins are rare. A cria may nurse for up to eight months or longer if its dam permits this.

The scope of information presented in *The Frugal Alpaca Farmer* is a small fraction of what farmers need to know about the unique physical characteristics of the alpaca. Owners of fiber herds should know the basic facts. More detailed knowledge of alpaca reproductive anatomy and physiology is essential for farmers with a breeding program. This will be the key to proper husbandry techniques. For example, once you find out that sweat glands are poorly developed in alpacas, much less so than in sheep, you understand the urgent need for cooling devices during hot days. Dr. Fowler tells us that lamoids have sweat glands distributed over much of the body, but only the belly and inside of the upper legs act as a major thermal window. Fiber coverage should therefore be sparse on that part of the body to allow for maximum comfort of the alpaca. Money may be spent on unnecessary tests and treatments if a farmer is not familiar with normal values for thyroid levels or blood glucose levels. Dr. Fowler reports that T_3 and T_4 levels for alpacas "are higher by 6-10 times than those reported for any other species in which values have been determined." Levels also vary at different ages.

Alpaca Temperament and Behavior

Behavior is the result of temperament—an individual's natural disposition—being influenced and shaped by the animal's environment. Among individual alpacas, there are great differences in temperament. This is often already obvious right after birth. Nevertheless, there are specific behavioral traits that are typical of all alpacas.

Alpacas are herd animals and require the companionship of other alpacas. Within a herd's hierarchy, they have rich social lives. Alpaca females normally bond quickly with their newborn crias and are protective of their offspring. Males fight for dominance in their herd, particularly in the close presence of open—not pregnant—females.

As an herbivore, an alpaca is vulnerable to attack by many species of predators. Years ago, when one of the first visitors to *Stormwind Farm* seemingly did not grasp the predator/prey concept, I thought she was mocking me for pointing out the obvious. I was dumbfounded when I realized that the woman truly did not comprehend the potential danger that her dog, a predator, posed for my alpacas, and why they reacted with fear to its presence. A prey animal has no defense but to be extremely alert and suspicious of novel stimuli in its environment and go into flight mode rather than risk being attacked and killed by one of its predators. This instinct is hardwired in the alpaca. The animal is not stubborn or stupid when it refuses to cooperate in situations it perceives as dangerous. That is normal alpaca temperament and smart alpaca behavior. If a frightened alpaca is prevented from taking flight, it will either "freeze" and mentally shut down, or it will kick and spit. It has no other defenses. Fear is a huge stress factor for prey animals and has many negative consequences for their physical health.

Like other grazing species, alpacas have long memories. Dogs will often quickly forgive humans, their fellow predators, for treating them harshly. As typical prey animals, alpacas are slow to forget and forgive lapses in human patience and kindness. Likewise, they are quick to remember gentle handling and training techniques. *Properly raised* alpacas do not spit at their human caretaker. None, including sexually mature males, will attack or challenge human beings at any time. I can enter our farm's male pastures—sometimes when it's pitch dark—without any concern for my safety. It's a nice feeling.

Alpacas that trust their caretakers are a pleasure to work with. It takes time and patience to develop such trust. The most trusting alpaca, however, will not be interested in the kind of relationship that a dog has with its respected master. As a dog owner, I initially felt disappointed when confronted with the aloofness of a typical alpaca. After some soul searching, I finally realized that I must respect this aspect of their temperament. Over the years, I have come to appreciate and enjoy what my friend, Alice, describes as "the essence of the alpaca."

Alpaca Emotions

We've had visitors to our farm cry out, "Look at them! They have such human expressions."

It's true. I have seen a spectrum of emotions in our herd: fear, happiness, rage, sadness, contentment, and more. They're all there if we just take the time to observe. Many people, especially scientists, feel uncomfortable with the notion of assigning what they consider human emotions to animals. Not everybody agrees with this group. In her book, *In Service to the Horse,* Susan Nusser describes the care and training routines of famous Olympic Gold Medalist winner, David O'Connor. David and his wife, Karen, participate in a grueling sport called Three Day Eventing. Nusser marvels that when O'Connor talks about his horses, he uses words like "personality" and "like a person." He described a particular favorite horse of his as "just a nice person to be around." In her very moving book *Songs of the Gorilla Nation,* author Dawn Prince-Huges, Ph.D. describes her intense struggle growing up as an autistic child. Observing and working with the gorilla population at a zoo finally taught her how to interact with her fellow human beings and how to function as a member of her community.

I know that my alpacas are not human beings. When I tell my Whippet, Diesel, that she is a good girl, I do not think of her as a little person in a fur coat. Nevertheless, I am acutely aware that the alpacas as well as Diesel have feelings and a range of emotions. The alpacas are not mere fiber machines. After Mariah, our temperamental redhead, lost her first baby to a sudden, unexplained death immediately after giving birth, she looked angry during the following pregnancy. One year later, she had a beautiful, chocolate colored girl. As I watched Mariah graze proudly next to her daughter, she wore what can only be described as a smile on her face. It was so pronounced that I could not stop staring at her in total wonder. I also often think of an incident that happened after I had made my first sale as an alpaca farmer. We started our herd with a pregnant female named Soft Breeze and a gelding. After I had sold and taken away Breeze's first two daughters and a grandson, she picked up a heavy feed dish with her mouth and deliberately and—with amazingly accurate aim—threw it at me. She had never done anything like that before. It is easy to understand why South American pastoralists call llamas and alpacas their *speechless brothers*.

"How can you stand to sell any animals then?" you may ask now. "Don't you feel guilty?"

No, I don't. Human children also leave their parents and other family members. All must strike up new relationships. That's part of life. Although I don't feel guilt, I don't arrogantly refuse to acknowledge that animals have emotions and that relationships matter to them.

The frugal alpaca farmer is aware of the unique physical, emotional, and behavioral traits of the animals under his or her care and works diligently to meet their needs. For example, I try hard to keep alpacas together that enjoy an unusually strong bond with one another. Animals that are maintained in harmony with their natural needs are usually healthy, robust, and reproductively prolific.

Resources

Very few visitors to our farm have inquired about suitable reading materials for prospective alpaca farmers. In my opinion, four books that all offer *alpaca specific* information are essential components of a successful alpaca business. These books are costly, but in light of their scope and depth of information, they are absolute bargains. Sometimes, the most frugal course of action is to spend money to save money.

The late Murray E. Fowler, DVM published *Medicine and Surgery of South American Camelids* first in 1989; a revised, second edition became available in 1998. I assume that a third edition would have included minor revisions and additional information. To ignore Dr. Fowler's work because of the last revision date would, in my opinion, be a very foolish thing to do for the serious alpaca producer. The wealth of information, the numerous photos, and the clarity of language make *Medicine and Surgery of South American Camelids* a masterpiece.

The second, revised edition of Eric Hoffman's *The Complete Alpaca Book* was published in 2006 prior to the merger of the two major alpaca organizations. Eric Hoffman's excellent book remains, in my opinion, the most comprehensive guide for alpaca owners at the present (2017) time.

In *The Camelid Companion*, Marty McGee Bennett focuses on handling and training with emphasis on recognizing and utilizing alpaca temperament and instinctive behavior. If you wish to live in harmony with alpacas, reading this book will teach you to "talk with camelids."

The fourth book is only important for those who plan to breed alpacas. I discuss *Llama and Alpaca Neonatal Care* (Bradford B. Smith, DVM, PhD et al.) in more detail in a future chapter.

There will come a time when the extensive knowledge you will gain from reading *The Complete Alpaca Book, Medicine and Surgery of South American Camelids, Llama and Alpaca Neonatal Care,* and *The Camelid Companion* will save you a veterinary bill that would far surpass the combined price of the four books.

4
PASTURES

"I can't imagine raising alpacas on dry lot. It would create a lot more work, increase expenses, and decrease quality of life for the alpacas." Kristin Joyce

No Pasture, No Profit!

If you wish to raise healthy alpacas with as few annual expenses and problems as possible, think of their pastures—rather than the barn—as their "home." Your animals should be outdoors in fresh air and sunshine as much as possible. Our alpacas, including the crias, enter the barn only during severe storms, hot summer days, when pastures are covered with snow, and occasionally at nightfall. This is as it should be. Hay and pelleted supplements are expensive. With rare exceptions, it is impossible to make a profit if alpacas are kept on dry lot. Excellent pastures and year around grazing should be the frugal alpaca farmer's priority for his or her animals.

Alpacas Need to Graze

Ruminants have a physical as well as an emotional need to graze. You can raise alpacas on a dirt lot with hay and grain. You will not make them truly healthy and happy by doing so. I believe passionately that herd health starts with healthy pastures. The longer a ruminant's expected life span, the more important it is to pay attention to that component of raising livestock.

Dr. Fowler makes the point that "even though the lamoids have become evolutionarily adapted to survival in their harsh environment, it is important to recognize that they may grow better and be more fertile if given optimal nutrition, at least for a major portion of the year."

I am sure that our farm's pastures do not duplicate the assortment of native grasses and forbs found on the South American Altiplano. Our alpacas thrive on the large and rich variety of pasture grasses, legumes, herbs, shrubs, and tree leaves that grow well in this particular area of New Jersey. Compared to South American alpaca pregnancy and cria survival rates, those on our farm are amazingly high. This supports the validity of Dr. Fowler's statement.

Grazing Resources

Frugal alpaca farmers usually have considerable sweat labor invested in their farms. We are often short on time and money. Acquiring the knowledge to establish and maintain pastures can be time consuming. Seed and fertilizer are expensive. You don't want to spend money where it's not necessary or will have negative results.

A visit to the nearest USDA (*United States Department of Agriculture*) office is a good starting point. You will probably be directed to an employee of the NRCS (*Natural Resources Conservation Service*). Staff members will come to the farm and help you formulate a program to either create new pastures or overseed existing ones. They can also recommend and show you how to apply for grants to plant windbreaks, fix drainage problems, and any other practices that will create a better grazing environment. The NRCS staff will make you aware of grazing conferences, workshops, seminars, and pasture walks in your area. Request advice from USDA employees who own farms where they've gained practical experience with grazing livestock.

The grazing community is passionate about providing pasture for livestock, and members are eager to share their knowledge. Reach out to farmers who use organic practices! They don't have to be livestock farmers. What you learn about soil health from, for example, a vegetable farmer, can be applied to pasture management.

The articles and books written by scientists on the subject are often not comprehensible to a lay person. The information seems overwhelmingly complicated. Fortunately, there is an author who writes about grazing with clear simplicity, in depth, with great humor, and based on practical experiences on his own Ohio farm. In *All Flesh is Grass,* author Gene Logsdon explains how to manage a grazing farm. While Gene Logsdon primarily produces animals for human food consumption, alpaca farmers can benefit from his experience and that of other graziers. Although subtle differences exist among grazing species, the basic concepts discussed by Logsdon apply to all of them.

Know the Soil

A friendly hay farmer once tried to educate me about soil and said, "Dirt is dirt." I understood what he meant by that and heartily disagreed. His hay was of poor quality.

When Amish farmers came to this country to escape religious persecution in their native land, they tended to settle on fertile farmland where they built substantial and sturdy houses and barns designed to last for centuries. In Pennsylvania, where these old world farmers tilled, sowed, and harvested crops, their descendants still work the very land that their ancestors so laboriously wrested from the forest many generations ago. In contrast, other immigrants often moved several times during one farmer's lifetime, leaving depleted soils and tumble-down dwellings behind. The difference? Those who arrived with centuries old farming skills proved to be astute judges of soil. On the East Coast, knowledgeable agriculturalists appropriated the best limestone soils for their families, and then worked their land with expert care. Farmers with little knowledge about soil selection and conditioning often were unable after only a decade of farming to feed their large families, let alone have enough farm products left for barter or sale.

If you are contemplating alpaca farming and have not purchased land yet, start off by educating yourself about soils most suitable for pastures. In other words, don't adopt the slogan "Dirt is dirt." Pastures are much easier to establish and far cheaper to maintain when soil conditions favor vigorous growth for grasses and legumes. There are many different types of soil on the North American continent. Soil consistency and quality can vary within a state, a county, a township— even on an individual farm. For example, the soil on our land is fertile but heavy clay. Avoiding soil compaction and working around drainage issues is tricky at times, but basic, good fertility and suitability for pasture more than compensates for our property's shortcomings. In contrast, a friend of ours—only living five minutes away—has soil so sandy that parts of her property resemble a beach. Sandy soil, while often providing good drainage, is low in humus and nutrients. Creating and maintaining pastures under such conditions takes careful planning and regular injections of cash. You will need to budget for irrigation and frequent fertilizer treatments. The stocking rate per acre must be kept very low. Sandy soils are a money pit for grazing operations. As a frugal alpaca farmer, I would not attempt to graze alpacas under such conditions.

Soil Testing

Long before laboratory tests were available, farmers had their own methods of testing. They touched, smelled, and even tasted the soil. Additionally, they observed what kind of plants already grew on it naturally and drew conclusions as to fertility and other soil properties from their laboratory of senses. Although you can do so as well, the novice farmer is well advised to take soil samples and send them to a laboratory for testing. Your local farm extension agent can supply you with an inexpensive testing kit. The kit includes detailed instructions on how to obtain samples. The results will be mailed to you. Your agent can then offer advice on the specific nutrients that must be added to the soil.

I use an independent laboratory—*A & L Eastern Laboratories, Inc.*—in Virginia. After analyzing the sample, the company sends a detailed soil analysis report along with soil fertility recommendations. The report is easy to understand. It breaks down soil minerals into ppm (parts per million), and—easier to comprehend for a lay person—the rate at which these minerals occur from VL (very low) to VH (very high). Organic matter is expressed in percent/rate. Soil pH, so important for plant growth, is also given.

Once the results of the soil sample have been returned, assess the situation. If a property that has been abused and neglected has soil highly suitable for pasture, it is worth investing money and labor to bring it back to health. If the soil sample shows a severe lack of humus (decomposed organic matter) and minerals, you are possibly looking at an exercise in futility. Managing such a farm as a grazing operation can not be done with frugality unless your stocking rate is ridiculously low.

The *Agri Dynamics Company* provides a soil report analysis in their catalog. It compares an ideal soil with one needing recommendations.

Organic Matter and Humus

I learned from an article written by well-known and respected soil fertility specialist Neal Kinsey to differentiate between the terms *organic matter* and *humus*. Although many authors use the terms interchangeably, I think Kinsey's definitions clarify the issue of soil fertility.

> "Organic matter is considered any formerly living, growing type of organism that has been produced and consequently made available for incorporation back into the soil. This can be whole green plants, crop residues, ground up parts of plants and/or animals, etc., including any useable combinations thereof. Humus, on the other hand, results from the proper decomposition of the residues of living organisms. Humus occurs when the complete decomposition of organic matter is accomplished." (*Increasing Organic Matter and/or Building Humus*)

In a nutshell: We must add organic matter to the soil to build humus. The cheapest way to build up humus in pastures is with free organic matter. Because landfills often charge hefty fees, some towns or landscape companies are only too happy to deliver huge piles of leaves, wood chips, and grass clippings to farmers for free. If you're really lucky, you may even negotiate a payment for receiving their "trash." Check with your own municipality about environmental laws first. You may be directed to plow the mountain of leaves under as soon as it is delivered. Decaying plants, while adding organic matter and nutrients, may change the soil's pH level. Building humus is a slow process.

Minerals and Vitamins

Aside from a high humus content, the minerals in your soil will determine growth and health of your pastures and ultimately the growth and health of your alpacas. Why are minerals so important? According to the late Jerry Brunetti, who was a popular and dynamic speaker at agricultural conferences:

- Minerals provide structural materials for bones and connective tissue.
- Minerals allow electrical impulses to be transmitted across nerves.
- Minerals act as catalysts, initiating numerous physiological processes.

"Calcium is the locomotive for other minerals," Brunetti emphasized when he talked to graziers. "It mobilizes the other minerals in the soil."

In his presentation: *The Soil, Forage, Livestock Connection* (2005), he also pointed out that boron is necessary for calcium absorption and helps maintain magnesium as well as testosterone and estrogen levels.

Dr. Fowler's book includes a chapter on feeding and nutrition with a comprehensive list of minerals and vitamins needed by alpacas to grow and thrive. Each mineral and vitamin is listed with function, interactions, and signs of deficiency, signs of toxicity, diagnosis, treatment, and prevention. I have heard several farmers complain about ocular (eye) discharge in their alpacas. Dr. Fowler lists this symptom as one occurring with Cobalt deficiency. Cobalt is an important component of vitamin B_{12}. Another interesting fact I gleaned from his chapter is that "copper deficiency in sheep causes wool to lack normal crimp, have less tensile strength, and lose color in those breeds having dark wool."

Requirements for minerals and vitamins can vary from species to species. The symptoms of either deficiency or toxicity, however, are often the same for all mammals, including human beings. Lack of iodine, for example, produces arrested fetal development in all species of domestic animals that have been studied by scientists. Severe deficiencies in minerals or vitamins can result in physical defects. Low levels of copper, zinc, and cobalt correspond with high levels of parasites. Minerals and vitamins are a huge issue with fertility. Green pasture, with its high levels of vitamin A precursors (carotenes), assures high levels of fertility in alpacas. Mineral or vitamin levels that are too high may be harmful. In some cases, such as Selenium and Vitamin D, signs of toxicity and deficiency mimic each other.

On a perfect farm with perfect soil, animals would be able to meet all their mineral and vitamin requirements by simply grazing and browsing. Such soils are rare. Many soils are deficient in minerals. For example, virtually the entire East Coast is deficient in Selenium. Of course, the opposite problem occurs in other areas of the country. Although you can—and should—provide a loose mineral mix or kelp, a grazier's emphasis should always be on restoring and then maintaining soil health on the farm so the animals consume all necessary minerals and vitamins with their forage.

Feed the Soil

Have you heard home owners talk about fertilizing the grass? Have you discussed fertilizing the lawn with a neighbor and only thought of the grass growing above the soil's surface? As a livestock farmer, it's best to lose the image of feeding the grass. It's the soil that should be fed.

For every living thing on our earth, there exists an ideal environment that allows it to thrive—not merely survive—and reach its genetically programmed potential. You don't have to be a farmer to know this. Any good gardener knows that shrubs or perennials will only grow well under certain soil and climate conditions. Grasses and legumes are no different. For example, cool season grasses thrive under an ideal soil pH of 6.0 – 6.5 whereas warm season grasses do best if the pH is around 5.5. For optimal pasture growth, the soil's mineral content must be in balance. When you establish and maintain your pastures, focus on the health of your soil. Healthy, vigorous plants will be the result. This is identical to the approach you should take if you wish to produce superior alpaca fiber. Beautiful fiber begins with a healthy animal, not with potions and other treatments applied to the fiber itself. Health from the inside out is a concept that can be applied to all growing things.

Lime

The standard solution of many homeowners to a poor lawn is an annual application of lime. Novice graziers are also often under the impression that lime is always a good thing. Lime is good—but only if your particular soil requires it to promote optimum plant growth. Otherwise, the application is counter-productive and a waste of money. The frugal farmer does not apply lime or other soil enhancements without the previously discussed soil analysis.

When we needed large amounts of lime applied on our land, we were perfectly willing to perform the labor ourselves. It soon became obvious that it was actually cheaper to pay a local, commercial operator for a substantial application of agricultural lime. Buying it in fifty pound bags at the local farm supply store would have been more expensive. Now that our pastures are established and fenced in, we will use our own—much smaller—spreader should another lime application become necessary. It's best to allow rain to wash the lime off the plants and into the soil before the animals graze on the limed pastures.

At least once a year, I lime the "bathroom" areas in our pastures to neutralize acid and destroy possible parasite populations. I purchase non-caustic guide lime to prevent burning the soles of the alpacas' feet and use a rake to cover the area as evenly as possible. Never use regular lime in areas where the alpacas will come in direct contact with it. Non-caustic lime is sometimes referred to and sold as *White Athletic Field Marker Lime* because it is used to mark baseball and football fields.

Manure as Fertilizer

Centuries ago, farmers and gardeners could not purchase commercial fertilizer that was conveniently packaged in bags. The main source of fertilizer was the dung produced by livestock. Some alpaca farmers sell or give away all the dung produced by their herd. I wonder at this practice. Why would you purchase chemical fertilizer when a perfectly natural— and free!—product is available to you right at your own farm? Although I give away surplus composted manure to gardening friends—to the consternation of their non-gardening spouses—I wouldn't dream of giving away or selling my entire supply of what I call *Alpaca Gold* and spending money to buy fertilizer elsewhere.

I compost the manure from our farm in bins constructed from plastic pallets. In addition to manure, I add kitchen scraps—peels, egg shells, and coffee grinds—to the piles. My alpacas generate only tiny amounts of wasted hay, but if it's available, that is added as well. In the fall, there are leaves. After the pile has composted for one to two years, I spread the contents across a pasture. I keep the alpacas off the fertilized pasture until all signs of the spread compost have disappeared. The healthier the soil, the faster this will happen. The results of spreading composted manure on our pastures have been amazing and justify all my efforts.

There are faster and more efficient ways to compost manure. By turning the pile regularly and paying careful attention to the manure/plant material ratio to heat up the pile, I would have humus within a few weeks that would rival and surpass the quality of the best soil amendment you can purchase commercially. I don't have the equipment or the time to manage my compost piles that way.

"Don't the piles attract flies?" you probably want to know. "And how about the smell?"

Alpaca manure, as many visitors to our farm have remarked in amazement, hardly smells at all. Because alpacas are herbivores, flies are not particularly attracted to their manure. If you are concerned, there are several products that will help you to keep the fly population to a reasonable minimum. Of course, keeping that manure pile far away from the house and barn is desirable. On a very small farm, this may not be possible.

Composting and the dung's exposure to the sun help to destroy parasites passed in the dung. An effective deworming program should also put your mind at rest about using alpaca manure as fertilizer. Such a program eliminates all or most intestinal parasites before the dung is deposited on your pastures. Certain anthelmintics are not totally degraded in the animal's digestive system. There is valid concern over anthelmintic residues destroying soil life. They may also affect the alpacas' health if manure containing residues is spread on pastures. That said, let's remember that chemical fertilizer is not without its negative effects. I noticed that our farm's composted manure piles are crawling with fat earthworms, always a sign of soil health. If you are concerned, don't use manure in your vegetable garden.

Livestock producers with large herds may have to file what is called a Nutrient Management Plan. New Jersey, for example, has different requirements for three tiers of livestock farms. Assignment to a tier depends on how many animal units (AU) produce manure. One animal unit is 1,000 pounds of live animal weight. A mature goat buck, for example, counts as 0.2 AU. Farms with up to seven animal units—7,000 pounds—are in the Tier I group. With approximately forty adult alpacas, your operation would still qualify as a Tier I farm in New Jersey. Regulations may change over time and also differ from state to state. There is, of course, a filing fee and, for Tier III producers, an application fee. Although Tier I producers need not file a plan or pay a fee, they must follow general requirements. For example, farmers must control access of livestock to waters of the state, and manure cannot be stored in a flood plain. The local conservation district office will be able to assist you. Penalties for violations are steep.

Green Manure

There is another natural fertilizer. The plants themselves—called green manure if used for this purpose—fertilize the soil. Specifically, legumes such as clover add nitrogen to the soil. The green plants therefore fulfill a similar function and purpose as animal manure. My experience has been with frost seeding white clover on our farm's pastures, and it has worked well. The 2012 *New Jersey Grazing Calendar* (NRCS) lists frost seeding as the "easiest and most economical way to improve pasture yield with minimal disturbance to the soil" and "minimal equipment needed." I agree. Frost seeding, as the word implies, should be done when the soil freezes overnight but thaws during the day. This cycle produces tiny cracks—fissures—in the soil. The seeds fall into these cracks and germinate when temperatures become favorable. It's best, in my opinion, to wait until right before a good snowfall. You don't need fancy equipment. I seed the way my ancestors did for many generations, with a cloth bag filled with seed hanging around my neck and casting the seed by hand. The nitrogen provided by the clover quickly produces results. Very soon, grasses once again dominate in the pastures. Some farmers attribute the success of frost seeding to the tiny size of clover seeds and do not believe that it works well using grass seed. I've had good success with the latter as well. Of course, weather conditions play a role, and we certainly don't have control over that.

Clover Warning !?

According to *The Merck Veterinary Manual*, there are "some strains of subterranean clover" that can cause temporary and, due to prolonged exposure, permanent infertility. These clovers contain phytoestrogens—plant compounds with estrogen–like activity. An *excess* of phytoestrogens reduces ovulation rate, lowers the incidence of estrus, and impairs sperm transport.

When Hugh and Carol Masters of *Serenity Alpacas* delivered the first two alpacas to our farm, Carol was quite concerned about the amount of clover she saw in our newly established pastures. As a former horse owner, she was worried about bloat or colic. Dr. Fowler points out that bloat from legumes is somewhat rare in alpacas, but it can happen. Other farmers reported that their alpacas foamed at the mouth after grazing clover in pastures. My alpacas never experienced any problems with the white clover they consume. We mow a pasture when the animals can't keep up with its growth. The alpacas also have unlimited access to good quality Orchard grass hay.

Synthetic Fertilizer

When most people talk about pasture fertilizer, they think about the standard fertilizer sold in bags. Synthetic fertilizers—because they feed the plants directly—give great, immediate results. The long-term effects are less desirable. An application of such fertilizer kills microbes in the soil, has an adverse effect on earthworm activity, drives up salt concentration in the soil, and pollutes ground water and streams. Farmers who insist on applying standard fertilizer should exercise caution. For example, "anhydrous ammonia and nitrate fertilizers and solids naturally high in nitrogen tend to increase nitrate content in forage" (*The Merck Veterinary Manual*). Hot, humid weather or prolonged cloud coverage can increase nitrate concentrations in plants. Severe nitrate poisoning can result in death. I learned in my research that ruminants are especially susceptible to the effects of nitrate and nitrate poisoning. According to *The Merck Veterinary Manual*, effects such as retarded growth, vitamin A deficiency, and abortions may be "subacute or chronic."

Should you decide to apply commercial fertilizer, your alpacas should not graze on that pasture until it has rained on the application several times. If you apply it yourself, beware of large amounts that may inadvertently pour out of the spreader on a small patch of ground. That brief moment of carelessness may cost an animal its life.

By the way, anhydrous ammonia is used by drug addicts and sellers to "cook" methamphetamine. Farmers with large stores of this fertilizer know better than to leave their storage areas unlocked. In some areas of the country, it has become a serious problem. For example, western and southern New York counties received more than 300 reports of anhydrous ammonia thefts in a one year time span.

Organic Fertilizer

Organic fertilizer may include fish meal, cottonseed meal, kelp, bone meal, seaweed, and liquid animal manures. Compared to synthetic fertilizer, organic products bring slow results because they feed the soil rather than the plants. They promote the proliferation of the microorganisms that release the nutrients for vigorous, healthy plant growth. Neal Kinsey calls it "increasing life in the soil." Feeding the soil is the only sensible approach to creating and maintaining excellent pastures. It's not a quick fix, and the initial expense may be higher than the few bags of synthetic fertilizer you'll buy at the local feed store. I agree with Neal Kinsey: "There are those who maintain that feeding the soil costs too much, but in the course of time, anything and everything is far more costly!"

When a lawn specialist who only uses organic products examined my pastures to see if they needed aerating, he laughed and told me. "Your pastures show so much earthworm activity that aerating them would waste your money. The earthworms are your acrators."

Drainage and Canada Geese

One prospective alpaca farmer admitted to me that much of her land destined for pastures stood under water for several weeks or sometimes even months of the year. The remaining dry portion didn't offer enough space for a few rabbits, never mind alpacas. If you inspect such a farm during a dry spell, you'll get a nasty surprise once the rainy season starts. Such a disaster can drain—no pun intended—your limited resources before your alpaca business is barely off the ground. In some areas of the country, it's not a bad idea to shop for land after a heavy rainfall. Good drainage is a very important component of creating excellent pastures. Drainage should also determine the location of a barn and other farm buildings.

Small or overstocked pastures with poor drainage quickly turn to mud. Although alpacas normally don't suffer from foot rot so common in sheep, I can't imagine that constantly standing in mud will not affect the health of their soft footpads. The sight of an alpaca herd mucking around a muddy compound certainly is not attractive to buyers and other farm visitors. Standing water can harbor the common liver fluke (*Fasciola heptica*), one of several varieties of flukes that exist in North America. Ingested flukes destroy liver tissue, damage the bile ducts or rumen, and can be fatal in domestic ruminants, including alpacas.

In this area of the country, ponds and drainage catch basins unfortunately attract Canada geese. These northern birds have taken to over-wintering in New Jersey. Their droppings contaminate parks, playing fields, and pastures to the point where, in some cases, you're hard pressed to find a single square foot of grass without at least one pile of goose poop. Once there, the geese are hard to get rid of. You will get little sympathy from the general public. Totally ignorant of the realities of farming, the local non-farming population will visit their wrath upon you if you use draconian measures—such as shaking the eggs—to rid your farm of the unwelcome feathered visitors. Not exactly a public relations coup!

In my opinion, it is not wise to allow alpacas access to ponds or streams. Prolonged exposure to water—standing or sitting in it—will rot fiber off the submerged body parts. Aside from the hazard of liver flukes and giardia, unfenced ponds may pose a danger while covered with ice. Alpacas like to urinate and defecate while standing in water. This could become an environmental as well as a legal issue on your farm. Livestock farmers everywhere are encouraged or ordered to fence off streams to cattle and other grazing animals.

Deep drainage ditches dug around the perimeter of your farm are another option to drain excessive water from farmland. A neighboring farmer manages his fields this way. The quality of his Orchard grass hay is unsurpassed in this area. Drainage ditches can be a safety problem. The alpacas should not have access to them. Drainage tiles are effective if the water can be directed to a low area on the property. Tiles can become clogged from tree roots. Their installation will be more difficult once fencing is in place.

Planting Season

Choosing the right season in which to plant your pasture seed may make the difference between success and failure. On the East Coast, late summer is generally most successful. Fall rains and cooler temperatures provide a good environment for germination and growth of grasses and legumes. Check with your local agricultural agent to determine the ideal time to seed pastures in your location. Care must be taken not to till the soil when it is too wet. Tilling wet soil results in severe soil compaction which reduces water movement through the soil and hinders root development. It is important to allow newly seeded pasture plants plenty of time to take root before alpacas are permitted to graze. Although you may be impatient to stock your farm with animals, it will be worth it in the long run to hold off until pastures are properly prepared and pasture growth is well established. Waiting one year is not unreasonable.

Overseeding

Ideally, a pasture's plant growth should be so dense that it is not possible to see bare soil. On many livestock farms, neglect and overgrazing leave bare spots on what should be a green, lush pasture "carpet." These marginal pastures can often be saved by overseeding, fertilizing, and regular mowing. Overseeding means that seeds are planted into an existing stand of grasses and legumes. Seeds may be spread on top of the ground or drilled into the soil. A third and very effective method is to thinly spread old hay on top of the pastures. Refurbishment of abused pastures takes time. It will not happen in one growing season.

Plant Diversity

When I was a child, my father showed me how plants, animals, and man can live to mutually benefit one another. He believed that nature has much to teach us and we better heed these lessons. "I don't want a lawn," my father always insisted, "I want a meadow."

What is a meadow? The German publication *Lamas* featured an article on feeding camelids in its winter 2001 edition. The author, Walter Egen, told readers that a good meadow (pasture) will grow at least fifty different plants suitable for camelid consumption. Helene Dreisbach, a longtime dairy farmer, wrote in *Grazing—Our Way* (Lancaster Farming): "Over a period of time we settled on a "salad"—several species, even several varieties of the same species, in a pasture produced the best yield over the entire grazing season."

Don't create a mono-culture by choosing only one particular grass. Kentucky Blue Grass may be pleasing to the eye, but—as the only grass in a pasture—does not meet the nutritional needs of a grazing animal. Because alpacas love Orchard grass hay, some alpaca farmers think that Orchard grass is the only plant species that they should grow in their pastures. Orchard grass, Orchard grass hay—it's like feeding your family a diet exclusively made up of spinach. Although spinach is nutritious, it can't meet all nutritional needs. Land seeded only in Orchard grass will make a good hay field; it's not a pasture.

What should you plant? Because soil and climate vary greatly across the country, there is not one right answer for this question. You should seed with a pasture mix suitable for the soil and climate in your own area. In some climates, a good mix ensures almost year round grazing. A pasture is never static. It responds to changes in temperatures and precipitation, grazing pressure, seeds dropped by birds or brought to the farm by gusts of wind, and other variables.

As pH changes, it may favor cool (6.0 - 6.5) or warm (5.5) season grasses. A pasture soil starved for nitrogen may explode in legumes such as white clover during one season. Grasses will take over again once a favorable nitrogen level has been established.

In any case, both Eric Hoffman and Dr. Fowler feature tables in their books that list the composition of pasture grasses and legumes. For example, crude protein and digestible energy are two of the categories whose values are given by the authors.

There's a Fungus Among Us

An organism called fescue fungus or fescue endophyte lives within the tall fescue plant. Animals that consume it may suffer from a host of problems such as dystocias, abortions, lack of milk production, retained placentas, and reduced pregnancies. You can't see the organism with the naked eye. Ryegrass can also be infected. The fungus actually helps grass to resist insects and produces environmental tolerance such as drought resistance. *Turf producers* therefore view it as a *desirable* feature. This is one subtopic where Gene Logsdon and I part company. In *All Flesh is Grass*, he mentions using turfgrass seed and does not consider its use in pastures to be a problem. I prefer to pay the higher price for endophyte free pasture seed. My comments here should not discourage anyone from reading Logsdon's book. It is packed with valuable information.

The pasture mix we've been using for two decades includes almost 40% endophyte free perennial ryegrass. We have not experienced any problems.

Appreciate Those Weeds

Americans have a fetish for weedless lawns not shared by the rest of the world. One of our alpaca customers, a sod farmer, paled visibly when I advised him to cultivate dandelions, wild onions, plantain, and other nutritionally important "weeds" in his pastures. Allowing alpacas to graze on pastures treated with weed killer is asking for trouble and financial losses. Generally, there is no reason for such treatments. To the contrary, a large variety of herbs—mixed in with planted grasses and legumes—will promote glowing health in alpacas.

Juliette de Baïracli Levy, the great natural healer of all species of beasts, wrote in *Herbal Handbook for Farm and Stable* in great detail about the importance of herbs growing in pastures and hedgerows.

Weeds can be as nutritious as deliberately cultivated and seeded grasses and legumes. *Agri Dynamics Company,* a business that sells a natural and holistic product line for livestock, includes an interesting chart in their sales catalog. Compiled by Jerry Brunetti in 2000, it compares the nutritional value of many "weeds" with alfalfa.

The dandelion, a plant described by Juliette de Baïracli Levy as "one of the most valuable known to the herbalist," is higher in protein than alfalfa, has a higher TDN (Total Digestable Nutrients), boasts close to four times the amount of iron, and has a slightly higher zinc level. "Zinc may be the most critical mineral for male sexual function, supporting sperm formation, sperm motility, and hormone metabolism" (*Taste for Life,* June 2004). In Europe, people to this day pick fresh, young dandelion leaves from their—chemically untreated!—lawns to add to a healthy salad mix. In *The Big Horse,* (2004), author Joe McGinnis describes how the successful trainer Allen Jerkins spent some time every afternoon digging dandelion roots behind his barn. "He was a great believer in feeding dandelion roots to his horses," McGinnis stated. If you can purchase a commercial supply of dandelion seeds, mix in a pound or so with the grass seeds. Of course, in many parts of the North American continent, a healthy stand of this much-maligned herb will develop on its own. Years ago, I was delighted to see hundreds of dandelions sprout and bloom on our newly planted pastures. When our alpacas aggressively grazed on dandelions, the plants completely disappeared from our two original pastures. Our animals had grazed these beneficial herbs with such enthusiasm that eventually not enough growth remained to support their renewal. When we enlarged pasture space—we added several acres—the dandelions fortunately made a reappearance.

Another common "weed," plantain, is comparable to alfalfa in protein, higher in calcium, and also higher in zinc. It is called the white man's foot by Native Americans because of its shape and the fact that European settlers brought plantain seeds to this continent along with their grass seeds. Juliette de Baïracli Levy describes it as a cure for ulcers and praises its ability to bring down a fever.

Alpacas show preference for specific pasture plants. For example, although my alpacas eat wild garlic and thistles with great appetite, they've ignored the German chamomile. This herb has a calming effect on people as well as animals. Having escaped from my perennial gardens, it grows along our pasture fence lines. It is a natural blood thinner and contains coumarins, similar to the chemicals found in a popular prescription drug. Interestingly, I have never observed an alpaca eating a chamomile plant. Animals pick and choose if given the opportunity to do so. It is important to remember that a large *variety* of grasses, legumes, and herbs—let's stop thinking of them as weeds!—is what's best for the animals. I will address herbal medicine again in a future chapter.

"If all these plants are so great for the animals, why do other farmers try to get rid of them in their pastures?" a visitor to *Stormwind Farm* once asked me.

One reason is the taste of their end product. Heavy consumption of certain herbs can add flavor to milk or meat that consumers find distasteful. Additionally, the lawn care industry has brainwashed people to think of herbs as ugly and undesirable in an expanse of grasses. I think this mindset is sometimes still adopted by livestock farmers. Unless you identify toxic plants, there is simply no reason to use chemical weed killers in your pastures.

Toxic Plants

Wild animals can easily avoid toxic plants. On pastures, domesticated livestock will usually do so if there are plenty of non-toxic grasses, legumes, and herbs available to them. If pastures are bare of beneficial plants, hungry animals will eat toxic plants in desperation. Depending on the toxicity of the plant and the amount consumed, the animal may die within a very short period of time or not show effects of disease for days.

The effects of toxic plants on a fetus can be devastating. For example, research proved that ingestion of false hellebore (*veratrum*) by ewes during gestation caused severe deformities in their offspring. Locoweed and lupines are two other plants that cause problems, ranging from brain lesions to cleft palates.

The Merck Veterinary Manual has a comprehensive section on toxic plants as do Eric Hoffman and Dr. Fowler's books. Under all circumstances, it is always prudent to remove plants that have proven to be poisonous to grazing animals.

Don't only think of *live* plants in terms of toxicity. Last summer, a heartbroken Pennsylvania man called me. He was interested in buying a gelding and shared with me how one of his alpacas had suddenly died. The man had ordered a load of mulch for his farm. When it arrived, he had spread it on a walking path where the long necks of the alpacas could easily reach it. The mulch partly consisted of ground-up yews, a highly toxic evergreen.

Size of Pastures

Alpacas love to run and pronk, especially at dusk. The latter gait, also called stotting, is interesting to watch and requires considerable strength and athletic ability. All four legs leave the ground as the alpaca leaps up and forward at the same time. Crias and weanlings love to pronk around dusk, but healthy adults—including pregnant females—also pronk daily when cool temperatures favor such a strenuous activity. Ideally, the size of your pastures should be large enough for them to indulge in and enjoy these activities. Small paddocks and pens are not suitable for alpacas. You cannot properly assess correct conformation and health on a farm where alpacas can neither pronk nor run at full speed.

Rotational Grazing

Rotational grazing is not a new concept. Animals practice it in their natural habitats by moving on once an area has been grazed down and returning to it when plant growth has sufficiently recovered. On a livestock farm, the term applies to a system where animals are rotated to another pasture after grazing for a specific amount of time on the previous one.

For several reasons, rotational grazing is smart pasture management. For one thing, the farmer can better control grazing pressure on the plants. If a pasture is grazed down to a nub, it loses its ability to regenerate sufficient growth. Under extreme conditions, the land becomes barren or one giant weed patch—and not necessarily with the type of weeds that are beneficial or palatable. In a good rotational system, the herd is moved out of a pasture while there is still plenty of growth above ground to support a strong root system. As an added bonus, rotational grazing prevents build-up of heavy parasite loads. It also allows for extensive maintenance such as liming, frost seeding, and spreading composted manure. Last but not least, grazing animals enjoy entering a "new" pasture. They kick up their heels in happy excitement and pleasure when the opening of a gate signals rotation.

How often do you rotate your herd to a new pasture? There is no true and tried formula. Each farm is different. The time frame varies from hours to days or even weeks—depending on size of pasture, soil conditions, weather, and stock density. A rotational grazing plan cannot be directed from a desk. The farmer has to walk the pastures being grazed each day and make his or her decisions based on observations.

A grazing farm should have a minimum of two pastures for each group of animals. On farms with small acreage, this can be a problem, but—if at all possible—try to apply the concept of rotational grazing no matter how small your herd may be initially. Let's say you only have six acres of pastureland. Instead of dividing the land into two three-acre parcels, you would be well advised to create four smaller sections. If you can't afford that much fencing in the beginning of your alpaca farming venture, design the pasture layout in such a way that additional division is easily accomplished at a later time. Producers of other livestock species routinely use specially designed movable fencing. I don't know how well such fences work with alpacas and therefore am reluctant to make recommendations.

Stocking Rates

Although we'll never know how many angels can dance on the top of a pin, people often ask how many alpacas can comfortably graze on an acre of pasture. The number usually given in the alpaca industry is five alpacas per acre. Now, which acre would that be? The acre with a dense stand of diverse forage plants? The acre with marginal growth of any forage? Or the acre grazed down to a nub, with substandard soil and little rain supporting only a few stands of scraggly grasses and shrubs? Stocking rates should depend on soil conditions, how hard you're willing to work to create and maintain superior pastures, and how much money you're ready to invest. Nobody should give a standardized answer to the question: "How many alpacas per acre?" I can't help but view farmers who answer, "Five per acre," as poorly informed and thoughtless in their approach to raising livestock.

Mowing

The pastures are the alpacas' breakfast, lunch, dinner, and in-between snacks. Although the animals help themselves to their meals, it is the farmer's job to maintain the grasses, legumes, and herbs in a palatable form. Like most grazing animals, alpacas prefer the plants they eat to be soft and fresh. In theory, a well-managed rotational grazing program should make it possible for the farm's mower to remain in the shed. That's theory! In reality, pastures will require at least occasional mowing. If the stocking rates are not adequate to keep up with plant growth, the pastures must be mowed. Additionally, alpacas will rarely graze close to the areas where —due to urine and dung deposits—plants grow particularly vigorous. Mowing also eradicates some species of toxic plants—milkweed, for example—in pastures.

Set your mower so roughly six inches of growth remain. Pasture grasses that are cut very short have a hard time generating new growth. Scalping your pastures during hot weather will only allow the most drought resistant plants to survive. In the fall, you want to time your last mowing so the alpacas will have plenty of grazing to last them through the winter. I find this to be quite tricky. Mow too late, and the pasture will be grazed to a nub well before spring growth. Stop mowing too early, and the alpacas will find many grasses to be unpalatable by December. Because a livestock farmer can't control the weather, pasture management will never be an exact science. There's a little bit of guessing and luck involved.

Clearing Land for Pasture

I wish I had 100 dollars for every visitor to my farm who told me, "We are planning to buy alpacas, but we'll have to clear the land first for pastures."

I would only recommend such a program under two conditions. The first one calls for the soil to be favorable for that purpose. The second is your age. Converting a woodlot with fertile soil to excellent pasture takes several years. Is it wise to follow such a plan if you're already in your sixties? Just asking! If you are indeed my age and plan to convert a wooded property that has sandy soil and grows scrub pines into pastures—well, what can I say? There are always people who love to make their lives as difficult as possible. That's O.K.; just don't expect to ever break even—never mind make a profit—on raising and selling alpacas.

Alpacas Like to Browse

Shrubs and trees, due to their deep roots, have a higher mineral content than the much shorter pasture grasses. Browsing on the leaves of non-toxic shrubs and trees is therefore a healthy forage habit for alpacas.

In the German publication *Lamas*, I read with great interest about a study done in 1994 in southern France. The subjects were twelve llamas. The animals had access to a wide variety of plants. Their favorite munchies on this natural pasture were ginster, oak, and juniper, while they ignored rosemary and thyme (Spring 2000, 8. Jahrgang, Heft 1).

Juliette de Baïracli Levy points out the benefits of establishing a hedgerow for grazing animals. Stray dogs are less likely to enter your pastures and it provides privacy. Best of all, hedgerows are home to many insect eating songbirds, not a small bonus when you live in mosquito country. On our farm, I decided against cultivating hedgerows but planted a few forsythias close to the fence for the alpacas to browse on. Judging by their good pruning job, the animals like the taste of the stems, branches, and leaves.

Shade Trees

Your alpacas must have shade. It will be healthier for them to spend hot days grazing under a nice shade tree rather than sitting in the barn. Research which trees are not toxic and, just as important, which ones will thrive in your climate and soil conditions. The tree trunk should be protected with fencing material to prevent the alpacas from destroying the bark.

Beware of trees that are advertised as growing several feet a year, such as certain types of poplars or the popular ornamental pear trees. Sure, they'll grow fast, but the wood is soft, breaks easily, and the tree dies at a young age. As with many species, if you want longevity, you must be content with slow maturity. It pays to go to a reputable nursery and follow advice. Plant trees while they're dormant.

Our eight acre parcel of land was a soybean field and did not have a single tree growing on it when we purchased it. We planted a sycamore, a Norway maple, and a sugar maple in three of the four pastures. They give plenty of shade, and the alpacas love munching on the leaves. Agricultural supply companies sell cloth that supplies shade to grazing livestock. I think a tree is a better, permanent solution.

Final Thoughts

As a final thought, I'd like to leave you with a sentence from *A Herd Health Overview,* by Jerry Brunetti.

"Herd health is no coincidence, or a matter of good luck!"

What promotes alpaca herd health? What provides optimum physiological and metabolic activity? Grazing on good pasture!

5
THE BARN

"Your farm's location and climate should dictate the design of your barn." Jane Marks

Site Plan

Over the years, I visited farms that were poorly designed. Some were quite fancy and employed staff to do the heavy work. As a frugal farmer, you will be reluctant to spend money on salaries. It will be to your advantage to design a site plan—the layout of your pastures and outbuildings—that is conducive to efficient management of your time and resources. Ideally, your mentor should be willing to help you establish a functional, healthy environment for the animals. Keep this in mind while you are shopping for alpacas. Visiting other farms can be helpful—if only to learn from the mistakes made by their owners. If you do, please be honest and state the purpose of your visit. Don't pretend that you are there to buy animals if you're not, and don't feel insulted if your request for free education is denied.

If you are on a modest budget, plan the final dream design of your farm's layout *on paper*. Then work backwards and delete what you can't afford to build at the present time. Design the location of your barn, fences, and gates in such a way that it will be easy—and therefore less costly—to add pastures and outbuildings at a later time. Be prepared to make compromises. I have never seen a farm property that lends itself to a perfect site plan. All seem to have one or several undesirable features.

Terrain, closeness to neighbors, drainage, and quite possibly other considerations will dictate the location of any outbuildings. Good drainage is very important. The floor of your barn should remain dry during heavy and prolonged rainfall. You want easy access to each barn with a vehicle. On our farm, that isn't possible. I sacrificed easy access for more pasture space and maximum drainage for the barn floors. Foolishly, I did not plan for the installation of solar panels when I sited the second barn. Fortunately, we were able to site the third barn to serve multiple purposes—equipment storage, animal housing, a farm store, and the installation of solar panels.

One or Several Barns?

"Several barns? We can barely afford one!" some of you probably think after reading this subtitle.

When we started raising alpacas, a second barn wasn't even a blip on our farming radar screen. Our first barn is thirty-two feet long and twenty-four feet wide. After a few years, I felt that our growing business required a second barn. Although it would have been less expensive if we had built the first one larger, if given a choice between one large barn or two smaller ones, I'd choose the latter. Why? As induced ovulators, open—not pregnant—female alpacas are ready to be bred at any time. Housing sexually mature males and open females in one barn can therefore be a problem. I managed this quite well for a few years, but I was happy when we were able to build the second, larger barn—forty feet long and thirty feet wide—some distance away from the first one. Visitors to our farm often comment on its calm, peaceful atmosphere. Although I realize that other management techniques— we'll discuss them later—contribute to this, I am convinced that housing males and females in separate barns is one of the main factors. If necessary, I can expand the separation with livestock panels or by leaving the pasture between two of the barns closed off to either group. With two or several barns, there's more walking, of course, and carrying of tools and supplies, but isn't exercise in fresh air part of the reason you wish to become an alpaca farmer? Our second barn not only offers more space for each alpaca, it also solved a hay storage problem and made room for a shearing table.

If you decide to eventually build a second barn, you must factor in the expenses of running additional water lines and conduits for electricity. There are also two building permits to pay for rather than one. Heavy snowfalls and lashing rains may find you happy to own one large barn rather than two small ones. Climate may therefore impact your decision. An excellent compromise, in my opinion, is one barn with a solid wood wall and a service door dividing the male and female sections. This wall need not reach the roof line. A height of eight feet should be sufficient to accomplish the goal of "out of sight, out of mind," meaning that sexually mature males will not be constantly aroused by the sight of open females cushed next to the dividing panels when weather conditions confine the animals indoors.

Plans for Expansion

A full addition of a second barn to the first barn with a shared dividing wall will also be less expensive than a second, freestanding structure. Due to the location of our first barn, this was not an option for us. At the time the smaller barn was built, our site selection was based on an extremely cautious approach to investing in alpacas. I don't have regrets though. We have no debt and own infrastructure and all animals outright. Nevertheless, I urge you to make long-term plans for eventual expansion.

Overhangs

I have several friends who own barns with large overhangs. The alpacas love to cush there to chew their cud. They're great—both the friends and the overhangs. Unfortunately, our first barn isn't quite high enough to add any kind of overhang extensions. Poor planning! Our second barn is ten feet high, and David installed a header on one side. This will allow us to easily add an overhang if we ever feel the need for it. Overhangs can be closed in when herd expansion calls for more barn space.

Size of the Barn

After seeing our male barn, a visitor remarked, "Gee, you could easily pack thirty of them in here."

This man knew little about alpacas. The size of a barn is important in relationship to climate and the number of animals you plan to keep. Although alpacas are herd animals—even more so than llamas—and cannot bear to be separated from their herd mates, they do not like to be within touching distance of another animal. Occasionally, you'll see a cria and its dam touching each other while they're cushed. Sometimes, two or three crias will rest together. Adult alpacas, particularly mature males and pregnant females, prefer to keep their distance from other adults. "Packing them in" should not be considered by ethical and concerned farmers. What impact can disregarding this management practice have on your finances? Plenty! Stress and parasite problems caused by crowded living condition have been the financial ruin of more than a few alpaca farmers. Advice here is simple: Build each barn as large as you can afford and stop breeding or buying alpacas before the animals are crowded. Careful consideration should also be given to the height of each barn. If height is not fully utilized—hay storage and large equipment come to mind—it is wasted space. A building with a relatively low height may be more user friendly, practical, and possibly cheaper to build and maintain.

Pole Barns

Although a barn need not be fancy, alpacas require a safe, dry, and draft-free shelter. If you're young and ambitious, scan farm papers for offers of *Free barn—you dismantle*. They're not as rare as you may think. If you're past the age when working fifteen hours a day seems like a piece of cake, look into pole barns. These barns are built without a foundation. Large poles are sunk into the ground. Walls and a roof are added. On fairly flat land, there is no need to carefully level the barn site, saving you money on heavy equipment rental. Pole barns are sturdy, safe, and less expensive to build than conventional barns. I think they're attractive as well and a sensible choice for a frugal alpaca farmer. The dirt floor inside the barn can easily be left as it is or leveled out. Although I don't recommend it, you can add a concrete floor. Don't think of a pole barn as settling for second best. Close to our farm, a beautiful bakery and café were constructed from a pole barn skeleton.

The Barn Floor

Not only is the construction of a pole barn cheaper than a conventional barn with concrete floors, the natural floor is also healthier and more comfortable for the animals. If you doubt that, spend one night trying to sleep on a concrete floor. Standing on concrete is hard on legs for both people and animals. Safety is also an issue. A wet concrete floor is dangerous for alpacas as well as their caretakers or farm visitors.

Do you have other options? Wood shavings or sawdust will make alpaca fleeces only suitable for garden mulch. Sand is comfortable for the alpacas but may destroy your fleece harvest and dull shearing blades. Stone dust looks nice. Unfortunately, not only is it uncomfortable for the alpacas, but it is also absolute hell on fiber and shearing blades. Abrasive floor coverings make fleeces feel much coarser than they are in reality. You may lose the sale of an animal if you can't convince a buyer that the handle of the alpaca's fleece has been compromised because the animal rolled in stone dust. These are also not the best choices if you are counting on the income from your farm's fiber.

Dirt is alpaca and people friendly. During bitterly cold weather, you can cover it with straw. During hot days, a dirt floor can be wet down and is cooler than any other surface. There are several drawbacks. If fans are used during hot weather, they will blow dirt around and out of the barn. As the dirt becomes compacted, the level of the floor sinks. Eventually you may have rainwater flowing into the barn. Raising the floor with loads of dirt and installing rain gutters to insure better run-off can prevent this. Beware of what kind of dirt you bring in. Make sure it wasn't soil removed from toxic waste sites or heavily sprayed orchards. Free soil is not a bargain when you must deal with health and environmental issues later on.

As much as I liked the dirt floors in our barns, the problem of the disappearing dirt described above convinced me to purchase rubber horse mats. They can be placed on top of dirt, concrete, or other surfaces. Horse mats are readily available, durable, and easy to clean. Because they saved the expense of adding dirt at regular intervals, the mats payed for themselves. Our farm supply store sells mats with small defects at a much lower price than their perfect counterparts. The defects are barely noticeable. If your animals urinate and defecate in the barn and you want to avoid a strong urine smell, I recommend mats as the best solution. You'll need an absorbent material to place in the communal "bathroom" area to soak up urine.

As far as the alpacas' comfort is concerned, the floor is a barn's most important feature. This is especially true if you live in a northern or very rainy climate and your alpacas are confined to the barn for long periods of time. Your choice of barn flooring may also impact your choice of the barn site and building materials and style.

Conventional Barns

I can't imagine why a frugal alpaca farmer would choose to build a conventional barn with a concrete foundation and can't think of a single feature that would be an improvement over a pole barn. You may nevertheless want to check out one or two conventional barns yourself, if only to make an educated decision. If you own or purchase a farm with an existing barn and it has a concrete floor, cover it with the thickest, most comfortable horse mats that you can find.

Fabric Structures

Fabric structures are very popular with horse owners who appreciate the abundance of natural light in a riding arena. Of course, as with everything, there are considerations aside from the basic purchase price. One company gives a fifteen-year warranty on their "premium white rip-stop fabric." Does the warranty apply to the structure as well or only to the fabric covering it? Will the fabric be very expensive to replace if it becomes damaged beyond repair after the warranty has run out? How much does it cost to erect the building? Will your township give you a permit to do so? If you live in a climate with violent windstorms, will the structure hold up under such pressure? Will the building be suitable for alpacas in very warm climates?

Run-in Sheds

Three-sided run-in sheds are popular with many alpaca farmers. You can have one or several delivered all ready to be occupied—instant barn! A portable run-in shed works well as shelter in a quarantine area or a permanent home for a tiny group of alpacas. Please consider that it offers little storage space and not as much protection from inclement weather as a barn. The climate and your farm's location will dictate the suitability of a run-in shed. Frequent high winds and lack of a protective shelter belt of trees—rather than cold temperatures—make a three-sided run-in shed an undesirable substitute for a barn. You can add a front wall once the shed has been delivered.

Carports, Calf Hutches, Garden Sheds

Creative and frugal alpaca farmers can find a variety of solutions to housing their animals. As long as the alpacas are sheltered from snow, torrential rains, and icy drafts, the appearance of the shelter does not matter to them. It may matter to potential buyers. A farm that features a hodgepodge of ramshackle buildings is a turn-off to many people. You must also remember that alpacas are herd animals. Five females with their babies at side will not be happy inside five individual calf hutches or garden sheds. All will want to cush together inside one shelter. Movable shelters may not remain anchored in very high winds and become a safety hazard.

Barn Siding

Years ago, my husband's co-workers made him feel guilty that he had never given me an engagement ring. Because we were never engaged and I don't care much for jewelry, this did not bother me one bit. When David arrived home one day—grinning sheepishly—with an expensive ring, I made him return it immediately. In exchange, he had a combination shed/dog kennel built for our Whippets. He chose Atlantic white cedar for the siding as well as the roof shingles. It's a beautiful, little building and has hardly cost us a penny to maintain since it was built. After roughly thirty years, we replaced the roof. When we moved to our farm, we paid a professional house mover to transport it to the new location.

I will never know what possessed us to use textured plywood on our first barn. We must have been temporarily brain-dead. Although the cedar clapboard would have been more expensive to purchase, it would not have to be treated with an expensive preservative to prevent rotting. Cedar has the added benefit of repelling insects. It takes on an attractive silvery gray color as it ages. When my husband built a small pole construction addition on the existing barn, he sided it with cedar left from another job. We selected cedar for our second and third barns as well and are allowing the siding to age naturally. Another nice feature of cedar: You can touch it with your bare hands and need not worry about splinters.

I prefer a wooden over a steel barn, especially if a site does not have natural shade. A steel barn can heat up to very uncomfortable temperatures during a typical New Jersey summer. That's an issue with animals that prefer cool or even cold weather. Unfortunately, a wooden barn can be quite expensive. We did much of the work ourselves. When we hired the man we call the Barn Czar to erect the basic structures and put on the roofs, we essentially acted as his laborers. We carried all the building materials to the sites and neatly stacked them. My husband also carried the shingles up on the roof and helped with other construction tasks that required another pair of hands. He put on the siding and built the sliding barn doors. This work made our choice of wooden barns affordable.

There are other options for siding a barn. Because you more than likely will have to live with your choice for a long time, it's wise to study the issue carefully.

Roofing Material

Two of our barns have the same shingles as our house. For the third barn, we selected a metal roof. A solar panel installer told a friend of mine that his company's employees would not be able to install panels on her barn's metal roof. Our installer had no problems doing just that. Regardless of your choice, make sure a ridge vent is installed to allow heat to escape. A ridge vent does not take the place of fans, but it's another component in a good alpaca management plan. Depending on temperatures, humidity, choice of flooring, and possibly other variables, a metal roof may collect condensation. Water will drip down. That's especially bad if it drips on stored hay bales. Insulation must be installed to prevent that. It's best to work with insulation installers who are familiar with insulation materials suitable for agricultural buildings.

Barn Doors

If your climate includes cold, blustery winters as well as hot summers, place the location of your barn doors with both temperature extremes in mind. During the winter, barn doors must be closed toward the prevailing winds. Because the northern door in the barn that shelters the female alpacas and crias doesn't close flush with the dirt floor, I push straw bales against the open spaces. This prevents any cold breezes from whipping through the barn between December and May. Low temperatures—below freezing—have never bothered our alpacas, and I've never closed them in or provided them with any heat. During the summer months, cross-breezes are extremely important. Except for a service door, the barn doors should therefore be wide. Ours slide open to a width of close to eight feet. This also allows equipment to be driven into the barn. I'll address the last—and possibly most important—reason for having wide barn doors in the next chapter.

Windows and Skylights

Although a barn looks friendly with light shining through clear windows, your alpacas don't need windows. It is true that alpacas don't like to enter a dark space. I told you in a previous chapter: Alpacas belong outside in their pastures. The barn is for inclement weather only. Why encourage them to become barn potatoes by making the barn a bright and inviting place? When it snows, hails, or rains cats and dogs, they will run for shelter in a second. When medical procedures require brighter light than overhead barn lights can provide, use a movable industrial light—much cheaper than paying for the purchase and installation of several windows. Given a choice between windows and skylights, I would choose the skylights. In a small barn, windows complicate storage and partition plans. If you live in a climate where your alpacas will be confined inside the barn for long periods of time, you may want to give them more light during their many snowbound days and install both windows and skylights. We have neither in our barns but installed a service door with a built-in window in our smallest barn.

Electricity

In a barn, access to electricity is extremely convenient. Is it an absolute necessity? No, but be prepared to work a lot harder without it. Lack of electricity will be a problem during heat waves, when cooling fans help keep the alpacas comfortable. During freezing temperatures, constantly breaking up ice in water buckets is not a pleasant chore. If your house is located close to the barn, you may be able to handle emergency situations with extension cords until your finances allow you to make an improvement. Make sure to use heavy grade industrial twelve gauge extension cords. They should only be used temporarily, and the outlet should have GFI protection. A generator is another—albeit very expensive and noisy—solution. Improperly installed generators are a fire safety hazard. There is another option. Urban and suburban dwellers are often totally unaware of how many North American citizens live "off the grid"— without water or electricity supplied by outside sources. A company in Deford, Michigan offers what they call a Power Wagon. It's a solar powered system mounted on a wagon and supplies 12,000 watts of electricity without running a generator.

Water

I must admit that—hardy as I am—I would not be willing to be an alpaca farmer without easy access to drinking water for the animals. Although I initially resisted their location, I am now grateful that my husband insisted on installing the water hydrants inside the first two barns. It's a welcome location during inclement weather and saves me extra steps. The small animal area in the third barn will never house more than two or three alpacas and those only for short periods of time. I elected to have the hydrant servicing that barn outdoors where it also serves as a water source for my vegetable garden. When you choose locations for your hydrants, keep multiple purposes in mind: drinking water, cooling alpacas, watering gardens, or any other purpose that will become important to you. Hydrants can be installed from an extension to your existing well. We rented a machine and dug the ditches for the pipes ourselves. Keep in mind that all waterlines need to be located below the frost line.

Electricity or Water?

If I had to make the choice between electricity or water in the barn, I would choose easy access to water. A powerful flashlight is easier to carry than heavy water buckets. Except for an emergency during total darkness and the use of fans, having electric lights in a barn is not a necessity. Your decision will depend on the climate you live in and the proximity of your house to the barn. Ideally, it's best to have electricity and a water hydrant.

Male Euphoria

I will be very happy if I never see a ditch witch or any other large piece of equipment on our farm again. One or two of my editorial readers are sure to censor what will come next, but gosh darn it, it's the truth, and it's staying in.

Many men seem to be overcome with a sense of euphoria after climbing on or guiding a big piece of machinery. A few years ago, trenches for water, electric, and a cable for faster computer dial-up service left our small farm looking like a disaster area. When—in unbridled enthusiasm—a helper busted an existing waterline, I ran into the house and called my friend, Nancy. She listened with sympathy to my longshoreman's vocabulary. You need to be emotionally prepared for such devastation. Don't worry, it can all be fixed. Don't try to restore your lawn or pastures to their former glory immediately after the job is done. Fill in the ditches and give the dirt time to settle. Depending on rain fall, this may take a few months.

Permits

On a general note: Please look carefully into zoning laws and permits before putting up any structure, including your farm sign! Building codes for agricultural structures differ from those written for residential buildings. Blatant disregard for township and state laws may cost you a fortune at a later time.

Old Barns

If your property has a previously used barn on it, you will have to modify the building to suit the alpacas. Most old dairy barns have concrete floors. If it is too expensive to remove the floor, cover it with enough mats and straw during the winter to give each alpaca a more comfortable resting place. If the barn was used for horses, remove several stall dividers to open up the space for your herd.

Old barns can be very beautiful, and many were built with materials and a level of workmanship that can only be duplicated by extremely wealthy people in this day and age. Consider yourself lucky if you find such a gem. There are, however, some serious concerns you should have about any barn previously occupied by livestock. For example, I read in *The Merck Veterinary Manual* that the papilloma virus can contaminate premises well after the last animal with a wart has left and that "stalls, stanchions, and other inert materials can be disinfected by fumigating with formaldehyde." Papilloma virus is common in many species. The barn treatment suggested in *The Merck Veterinary Manual* sounds, in my opinion, environmentally very harsh and unhealthy to the applicator as well as future barn occupants. Environmentally friendly products such as lime and vinegar come to my mind. Because this is such a potentially serious problem, I suggest you consult with experts from the organic farming community. One organic farmer I spoke to advised using a mixture of water and peroxide. Unfortunately, he was vague about the ratio. Another concern is the misleadingly named ringworm. The spores of ringworm, *T. verrucosum* and *T. mentagrophytes*, a fungal infection, "may remain viable for up to 4.5 years in hair and cellular debris scraped off the animal and left attached to barn walls, fence posts, trees, feed bins, halters, blankets, packs, brushes, and combs" (Fowler).

Hay Storage

Even farmers who own abundant acreage for pasture will need to feed hay. Although alpacas, compared to cows or horses, consume very little hay, you should have a generous supply stored prior to the winter months. Hay consumption can vary greatly from farm to farm. Variables are, of course, the size of your herd, pasture growth, type of feeding station, and the weather.

One of our storage areas for hay—in what is now our male barn—measures roughly four by eighteen feet. We are able to stack fifty bales in that space. To prevent dust and sunlight from ruining the hay, we hung a large, plastic tarp to separate the hay area from the rest of the barn. This works quite well. The bulk of the annual hay supply is stored in the much larger female barn. We have it delivered but do all the stacking ourselves to save money. In both barns, hay is stored on wooden pallets to keep it dry. Because moisture from a dirt floor will penetrate the lowest layer of hay through cracks between the pallet slats, I cover the pallets with sheets of plywood or very heavy cardboard to keep the hay dry and safe to eat. Building a barn with a hayloft is also an option. A roof made from trusses, although cheaper to build, makes installation of a conventional hayloft impossible. A friend of mine built a freestanding loft in his barn. He stores hay on top and small equipment below it. I like it a lot.

Insufficiently dried hay is prone to spontaneous combustion. Many a barn has gone up in flames due to this problem. A separate building for hay storage prevents loss of equipment and possibly saves lives. Because our alpacas are never confined to the barn, building a separate hay barn would not make financial sense.

6

BARN SUPPLIES

"Supplies can be costly. Ask your mentor for advice before you make purchases." Diann Mellott

A Tidy Sum

Although barns, fences, and purchased animals swallow up the largest portion of an alpaca farm start-up budget, it doesn't end there. Alpacas don't require anywhere near the supplies and gadgets that horses do, but even their modest needs can add up to a tidy sum. As with all other aspects of alpaca farming, the frugal farmer can find ways to save money.

Livestock Panels

On *Stormwind Farm*, we initially housed intact males and females in the same barn. Metal livestock panels separated the boys from the girls and also the service area from the animals. Now that we have three barns, the panels only serve the latter purpose. Additionally, panels are used as catch pens, as corrals during visits to farm fairs, to temporarily divide a pasture, and to protect young trees from alpaca nibblers. Our livestock panels are approximately nine feet long and five feet high. They are fairly expensive; prices vary depending on size and materials. If you're handy, you can build panels from wood or PVC pipes. For safety, I prefer the metal panels because of their weight. I would not want to take a chance with, for example, determined males pushing over flimsy barriers to breed females at random. I view livestock panels as indispensable for handling and training. At a minimum, an alpaca farm should have four panels to build a catch pen. You can sometimes purchase used panels at greatly reduced prices from a farmer who is closing his or her business or from an alpaca show organization at the conclusion of the show.

Rubber Mats

I already mentioned rubber mats in a previous chapter. They are normally purchased by horse owners and are available in most farm stores. I don't know how they stand up to horses. With alpacas, they are virtually indestructible. If you're lucky to find used ones in good condition, be sure to disinfect them carefully before installing them in your barn. Here's another plus for rubber mats: Hay does not get ground into the dirt by busy alpaca feet. Less waste means a smaller feed bill.

Hay Feeders

Alpacas can be very wasteful with hay. You'll get these "Come on, this stuff is four hours old already; it's time to replace it with a fresh supply!" looks. It's all too easy to give in to the demands of those big eyes. The plan therefore calls for a feeder that is both safe and discourages waste.

Let's first discuss what not to use. Do not install hanging hay feeders designed for sheep! A friend of mine found her first cria, a beautiful female, hanging dead by its neck between the slats of the hay feeder. There are freestanding, portable feeders advertised as suitable for alpaca farms. A fellow farmer witnessed such a feeder topple over in high winds and severely injure one of his pregnant females. Alpacas also have been injured by getting their heads caught in the very popular hay bags. These bags are great while the animals eat under constant supervision, for example at a show. At home, they're a danger and an unnecessary expense. Large plastic buckets are a waste of money because the alpacas pull the hay out anyway.

There are two designs that I like. One is a very low, shallow box with a metal or wooden grid placed on top of the hay. The grid squares prevent the alpacas from pulling large amounts of hay out of the feeder. The other is a hay feeder constructed from four livestock panels. Each panel is five feet long and four feet high. On our farm, we use the latter model in each barn. The panels are placed on rubber mats. Additionally, a wooden pallet covered with a sheet of plywood keeps the hay off the ground. I can fit four to six bales—each weighing roughly forty to fifty pounds—inside a feeder. I have found this design to be very economical and extremely safe. The alpacas still manage to pull out small amounts of hay and leave it on the ground. Each day, I sweep it up with a rake and put it back inside the feeder.

Grain Dishes

Grain dishes need not be expensive. Although almost any shallow pan will do, I remember dog breeders complaining years ago that their dogs developed dermatitis while eating out of cheap, plastic dishes. I have not found this to be a problem with the sturdy, high quality plastic feed bins that can be hooked over the livestock panel bars. Stainless steel dishes would be best. Very cheap, stainless steel dishes of high quality can often be found in thrift shops.

Grain Storage

I can't emphasize enough the importance of making it impossible for the alpacas to help themselves to large amounts of grain supplements. A friend of mine incurred a huge veterinary bill when all her female alpacas managed to bust into her barn's storage area, removed the lid on the grain bin, and gorged themselves on pelleted feed. A garbage can with a lid will store grain just as well as an expensive grain bin. I leave pellets in the bag that they come in and put the entire bag in the can. Unopened bags are stored inside another, securely latched container to prevent rodents from gaining access to the feed. All feed containers should be located in a barn area that is always dry and out of direct sunlight.

Mineral Containers

You will also need a container for the loose mineral mix. Because some temperamental alpacas like to overturn feed dishes, I recommend a plastic pig creep feeder that you can attach to the barn wall. That way, the expensive minerals will not be dumped on the ground. I read years ago that salt blocks are commonly offered to horses and various livestock species, but that most alpacas will not use them. I keep a salt block in a feed dish inside the barn. The alpacas consume the salt sparingly. Contrary to what I read, I observe them licking the block.

Water Buckets

Unless you have a strong back and are willing to carry warm water out to the barn several times a day, buckets used during cold weather should contain a heater element to prevent water from freezing. The combination of some types of plastics and heat can unfortunately be very unhealthy. Research has shown that plastics shed xenoestrogens when they are heated. Since the water in heated plastic buckets stays rather tepid, I am not sure this needs to be a concern. Xenoestrogens, by the way, are foreign substances that have "a profound impact on hormone balance" (John R. Lee, M.D.). Any recycled bucket can be utilized as a summer water bucket. I wouldn't advise using one that once contained harmful chemicals, but there's nothing wrong with scrubbing out a laundry soap bucket and using it. The healthiest—but not the cheapest—choice is a stainless steel bucket. Of course, one can make the argument that the healthiest choice is always the cheapest in the long run. If you plan to be in this business for decades, this may be your best choice for summer buckets. I still own and use the original stainless steel dog dishes and buckets that I purchased thirty years ago. No cracking, no discoloring, and no worry about leaching chemicals. I find the stainless steel buckets easy to clean and consider them more sanitary than the plastic ones. If you're shopping for stainless steel supplies, do so in stores or catalogs that sell to livestock owners.

Muck Buckets

I have used recycled paint buckets to collect dung for years. The buckets will last longer if you drill a few holes in the bottom for drainage. Other alpaca farmers prefer a bucket/cart combination.

Hugh Masters, one of the editorial readers, added these important considerations:

> "Some people may use a muck cart with associated bucket which runs around the cost of a wheel barrow. We used these for daily cleanup in the barn as well as around the outside of the barn and nearby pastures for years. We then placed the bucket into our Utility Vehicle for transport to a compost area. A note from experience: Single handle muck carts are safer than full handle carts. I've had alpacas place their heads and neck through the full handle carts, panic and take off through the barn or pasture wearing the muck cart. Trying to catch a panicked alpaca (or any animal) can be dangerous for all. I've also seen this happen with water buckets that aren't securely fastened. It should be kept in mind that any equipment used around animals must be carefully inspected to insure safety. As you have indicated in a previous chapter, alpacas are a very curious animal and, as you know, when your back is turned anything can happen!"

On *Stormwind Farm*, we had a little drama unfold once when, in the middle of one alpaca's birth, a cria put its head and neck through a plastic lawn chair. With one baby dangling half way out of its mom's body, the older cria went crashing wildly around the pasture, breaking the chair but thankfully not injuring itself. Needless to say, lawn chairs have not been left in the pasture since that nerve-racking incident.

Automatic Waterers

Automatic waterers are available in a variety of models. Some are quite expensive and require special installation. Others—buckets with a float valve that are connected to a hose—do not cost much more than a standard, good quality water bucket. If alpaca caretakers must leave the farm for many hours each day, I think automatic waterers are a good choice.

Hydrant Insulation

Although hydrants should be installed to allow water to fall below the frost line, severe cold or other circumstances—OK, I admit it, I left the hose attached to the spigot—can cause a freeze-up. If you're unlucky, you'll find your pipes have burst and your barn floor will be under water just at a time when the alpacas really need their shelter. A special heat tape wrapped around the hydrant and plugged into an electric outlet will prevent any calamities.

Fans

During high temperatures and humidity levels, fans are not a luxury. The safest options are fans especially designed and built for use in barns. These commercial fans come with encased motors. *It should tell you that on the fact sheet that comes with the fan.* Fans with encased motors are expensive. Rebuilding a barn is more expensive. The alpacas should not be able to reach and touch a fan while the motor is running. Hang the fans off the ground or cover and store them in your garage or attic during the winter. The less dust they're exposed to the better—another reason to have rubber mats. Overhead fans greatly add to the comfort level of a barn's environment during the summer months. Choose models that are appropriate for barns. Don't take chances with safety: Replace any fan as soon as the noise of the motor sounds the least bit strange.

A Scale

If your schedule doesn't allow for extended visits to barn and pastures for the purpose of observing and handling your alpacas, a scale should definitely be part of your barn inventory. If your herd is small and your power of observation very strong, visual cues and body scoring will tell you if an animal is not doing well. Body scoring is simply a farmer's term for touching the animal, especially along the spine. Does the alpaca feel fleshed out or is it very bony? If you do this on a weekly basis, you'll be able to tell if an animal drops a lot of weight. Minor weight loss is normal for nursing females.

Of course, a scale can tell the story more accurately than the human hand. Resist the temptation to acquire a commercial scale not designed for livestock use unless you can get it virtually for nothing. Yes, there's a little story here—

If you haven't read *Moving Up Country* and *Living Up Country*, you should. The author, Don Mitchell, moved to Vermont, bought land, built a house, and started to raise sheep. When Mitchell built his home, he hit upon the idea of having an indoor swimming pool serve the dual purpose of a solar heat sink. To save money, he bought a septic tank to use as the swimming pool. Cleverly, he also contracted a builder of manure lagoons to excavate a pond on his farm.

"What," you may ask now, "does this have to do with alpaca scales?"

Mitchell is my husband's secret twin. My husband, a descendent of generations of frugal New England residents, bought an antique, commercial stockyard scale. In a moment of insanity, I agreed to this caper. The scale was huge. To protect its mechanism, David insisted that it be stored in the garage. It was a lot of hassle to lead the animals across our stone driveway. The garage was not familiar to them; the scale was neither as flat nor as steady as a modern livestock scale. Although you'll never catch my better half admitting it: Buying this scale was a poor decision. Sometimes, an object can easily be adapted to other uses. Other times, it's just not a good idea.

In fairness, I will alert you to another adaptation. The February 2002 *GALA Newsletter* featured an article by Paul Wade. He bought a platform scale—commonly used in feed stores—for $50. It has a capacity of 1,000 pounds. He used plywood to extend the platform, removed the wheels, and put spacers under each extended corner so the plywood won't dip more than ½ inch when the animal gets on it. Hmm—! Paul Wade, you may just be one of triplets separated at birth. Seriously, if your space can accommodate a scale like that and you can adapt it as per Paul's instructions, I'd say it's a great deal. Alpacas are surprisingly willing to climb onto a raised surface. I am even willing to admit that the problem with our scale was not so much the scale itself but the inconvenient location. We eventually did purchase a digital scale suitable and commonly used for alpacas and set it up in the barn that houses females and crias.

Many alpaca farmers use the popular hanging scales to weigh crias. Crias hate to be picked up and may become injured in their struggle to free themselves while dangling in the sling. I do not recommend a hanging scale. If you feel that you must weigh a cria and don't have a platform scale, use a bathroom scale. Keep a firm grip on the squirmy cria while you step on the scale.

A Chute

Another large expense is a chute. You will find that alpacas generally do better with little restraint. I train our alpacas to stand still while their nails are trimmed and for inoculations. Nevertheless, we own a chute that we bought used at a greatly reduced price. Why? Male alpacas try to assert dominance over one another by wrestling and pinning their opponent to the ground. A favorite technique is to grab the other alpaca's rear or front legs and thereby throw it off balance. Considering the male fighting style, it only makes sense that an intact, sexually mature male alpaca views a human being trying to lift its hind feet to trim nails as a threat to its very life. The alpaca is not being mean or obstinate when it fights this move with all its might and tries to escape. The chute contains the animal and makes life easier for everybody. We have also used the chute while removing fighting teeth—usually done once or twice in a male's lifetime—and trimming our gelding's front teeth.

I want to emphasize that a chute should not take the place of proper handling and training. Alpacas have been killed because their owners did not understand and appreciate the danger of forcefully restraining a frightened alpaca inside a chute. On our farm, we view and use the chute as a mini catch pen, not a restraining device. When I start halter training our male crias, I walk them into the chute each time during a training session, without actually restraining them. By the time I need to trim nails or top knots, they have lost their fear and stand quietly.

If you are handy, you can build a chute for a fraction of what it costs to buy one. Jovi Larson, who owns and manages a suri alpaca farm in Virginia, designed and built a chute using wood and PVC pipes. I've seen homemade, wooden chutes on other farms. They work quite well.

Toenail Clippers

You will need small pruning shears to clip toenails. *Quality Llama Products, Inc.*, a small company that has been in business for over twenty-five years, offers a wide array of camelid supplies. Their *Magic Toe Shears* are excellent. I oil them occasionally and once had to replace the spring—sold for less than two dollars by *Quality Llama Products*. Their *Ergonomic Toe Shears* are more expensive but are better for people with large hands. They also permit trimming nails at awkward angles. After a friend praised these shears, I made the switch and am glad that I did.

Halters and Leads

The company also offers a wide assortment of halters. Although we started out with non-adjustable halters, I now only purchase *Zephyr* alpaca halters designed and manufactured by Marty McGee Bennett. They're a little more expensive than other brands but worth every penny. When you read Marty McGee Bennett's articles on handling and training, you will realize how important proper halter fit is. Leads should be strong and well-made. Alpacas do not require leads heavy enough for a horse, but keep in mind that a large male alpaca can snap a poly lead in half. I saw it happen once. A light dog training lead is appropriate for crias.

Specialty Catalogs

New farmers often find that purchasing supplies from the big farm catalogs can be confusing and overwhelming. I have also seen items advertised in the camelid sections of certain catalogs that are completely inappropriate for alpacas, including poorly designed halters. A great place to familiarize yourself with camelid items is a specialty catalog sent out by the previously mentioned company, *Quality Llama Products*. Will you need all the items offered in the catalog? No, of course not. These folks, however, know camelids and are happy to help you choose the right products. Additionally, the catalog contains interesting information about stress reduction, shearing, a table of "physiological normals" such as respiration and heart rate. The company also sells a small selection of herbal remedies.

Serving the Alternate Livestock Industry Since 1979

Quality Llama Products, Inc.
& Alternate Livestock Supply
www.llamaproducts.com • 800.638.4689

Odds and Ends

You don't need a large tack room. A metal or old kitchen cabinet to store odds and ends as well as hooks for hanging halters and leads will do just fine. The alpacas should not have access to this area. Temperature sensitive medical supplies should not be stored in the barn.

Barn Trained Alpacas

For quite a few years, I was a lucky farmer. My alpacas, without fail, urinated and deposited their alpaca beans in their chosen bathroom areas outdoors. They did this during severe rain storms, heat waves, and blizzards. Daily manure cleanup of pasture was easy. I could not believe my good fortune. It may have helped that my late mother greeted our first alpacas upon their arrival and instructed them in all seriousness, "You have a very nice, clean barn. Keep it that way!" More likely, our wide barn doors encouraged their clean habits. Alpaca herds have a social hierarchy. If a dominant alpaca blocks a narrow barn opening, those below it in the hierarchy will be too timid to push past the herd boss or any alpaca outranking them. Eventually, their only choice will be to urinate and defecate inside the barn. Multiple, wide doors increase chances that indoor spaces will stay clean.

There are several additional strategies that you may use to keep your barn clean. When your alpacas first arrive on your farm, keep them out of the barn for at least two days. During and after a snowfall, clear a bathroom area in front of the entrance. Make sure that your alpacas are never snowed in. During one unusually heavy snowfall, I stayed up all night and ventured out every hour to shovel. Take advantage of hot weather and get your babies used to getting wet by spraying them with a hose. A baby that spent its first months in a drought and was never hosed may be too scared to go outside in a heavy rain.

Never close your alpacas inside the barn unless your climate, the terrain, or your alpacas' safety demand it. When I have to catch my animals and keep them confined for any length of time, I make sure that a large catch pen is connected to the barn. The alpacas can't leave the area to enter the pasture but still have the opportunity to leave the barn to visit the dung pile.

The area in front of a barn door tends to get very muddy when it rains. Alpacas hate walking through mud. Eventually, even those alpacas that prefer to use the outdoor dung pile will urinate and defecate in the barn to avoid the muddy mess. I solved that problem by building patios with sand and inexpensive patio blocks. Stone dust is another option. Covering the mud with straw or old hay is not a smart practice. The vegetative matter will compost and make the problem worse.

All my strategies worked for us, year after year— Then Greta arrived, and my fellow farmers could stop feeling envious of my pristine barn. On the nicest days—clear with sunshine—Greta and her cria, Mack, used the barn as their private toilet. It wasn't long before my own female alpacas followed suit.

"I would wring her skinny alpaca neck," a friend suggested callously. She lives in the suburbs and always feels that I am crazy to work so hard.

Greta had been sent to *Stormwind Farm* to be bred. Once her pregnancy was confirmed, she and Mack departed. Things improved, but on rainy days, I'd still find a mess in the barn.

Alpacas can be encouraged to urinate and deposit their dung in a designated bathroom area in a barn simply by spreading any material that will absorb fluids. Alpaca farmers use straw, sand, wood shavings, and compressed sawdust pellets. In my experience, wooden pellets sold for that purpose work best. The pellets soften and turn into sawdust once the urine has been absorbed. Unfortunately, this material is expensive. If you have access to free sawdust, it would save you quite a bit of money over the years. Make sure it does not include pressure treated wood. Straw does not work as well and may not be all that inexpensive either. Although a "bathroom" sand pit could possibly be a good solution, cheap construction sand may contain silica.

On our farm, I've worked out a system that keeps expenses to a minimum. I discovered that the alpacas are quite willing to step outside in heavy rain once they are shorn and the weather has turned warm. From the beginning of May to the first winter storm, I close off the indoor bathroom area with three livestock panels. During the winter months, it is kept open. Each day, I clean up the dung and only replace the sawdust with a fresh pile once the old one is fairly well soaked. We pick up free sawdust from a local cabinet maker. The discarded sawdust is saved as composting material for dead alpacas.

Does that last sentence shock you? If it does, you may want to rethink your plan to raise alpacas. Livestock dies, and proper composting is the most frugal and efficient way to dispose of the bodies. It's quick, and there is hardly any odor.

"They must be dying like flies on your farm," commented a visitor when I explained the purpose of the sawdust pile.

I assumed that he was referring to alpacas and answered accordingly. "No, they are not dying like flies. I simply think that it's prudent to be prepared."

Our male alpacas keep a clean barn in all seasons and weather conditions. After each rain, I tell them that they are true princes and to please continue to behave themselves.

Forget Cupolas

The prices for all these items quickly add up to a considerable sum of money. Analyze where and how you can save money without jeopardizing the health and safety of your animals. Unfortunately, I've noticed a pattern among too many alpaca farmers. They invest heavily in animals but won't spend money on infrastructure and good quality supplies. That's very short-sighted. Although it is true that alpacas can survive under less than ideal or even harsh conditions, they will not thrive. Fiber quality, reproductive performance, and general good health will suffer under those circumstances. The farmer also suffers. Catching, handling, and training alpacas without livestock panels is frustrating for the most patient person. Trimming nails with poorly functioning clippers aggravates both farmer and animals. I wish I had ten dollars for every alpaca I've seen gasping for air and its embarrassed and upset owner struggling to control it because of an ill-fitting halter. If you wish to own and raise alpacas, you should have the basic supplies to do it well.

What you can totally do without are fancy and expensive cupolas on the barn roof, barn kitchens, custom-made signs, and similar frills. A barn needs to be a functional, safe, and healthy dwelling for the animals, not an expensive status symbol. O.K., I admit it. I have a secret hankering for a cupola crowned by a copper weather vane. It'll have to wait.

7
FARM EQUIPMENT AND TOOLS

"Hand tools are as essential for the farmer as heavy equipment." Jane Marks

Tractor Buddies

In Somerset County in Pennsylvania, a group of twenty men and their wives meet every Wednesday during the summer as part of a club called the *Roof Garden Tractor Buddies*. What is their club's purpose? Its members—hold on to your Deere cap—square dance while sitting on their tractors. The group has a choreographer and a caller. Their first show was on May 24, 2003 at a farm festival.

It's plain that many men—and some women—love to play with heavy equipment, especially heavy, *new* equipment. This desire often spells financial doom for farmers on small budgets. Across the country, farms that survived drought, floods, insect pests, recessions, and deaths have come under the auctioneer's hammer because the last generation plunged into deep debt over new farm equipment.

Mechanical Skills

A frugal farmer is, by necessity, an excellent mechanic. If you have good mechanical skills or, at the least, are highly motivated to learn, you can take advantage of opportunities to buy reasonably priced farm equipment and tools. With no mechanical aptitude, it'll be hard to remain frugal and on a modest budget. Maybe you can work out a barter system with a skilled family member or friend where you exchange services. This person would have to live close enough to your farm to respond to the occasional emergency call to, for example, come fix a spreader, determine the source of black smoke coming from your tractor, or install a thingimajiggy—he'll know what it's really called—to hold your sliding barn doors tightly against the barn during a storm with predicted hurricane force winds.

Resist the Urge!

What kind of equipment you need will depend on the size of your farm. Resist the urge to buy more and bigger than what is necessary. It is neither cost effective nor necessary for the owners of most small alpaca ranches or farms to own a fleet of heavy-duty equipment. Of course, individual circumstances differ from farm to farm. For example, if you intend to install fence posts yourself, a hydraulic power auger would be a wise investment. For jobs that are done only once or occasionally, it may be more cost effective to pay someone who already owns the equipment. Additionally, just about any piece of equipment can be rented these days. Hugh Masters, one of my editorial readers, pointed out that a farmer's fitness level may dictate the purchase of a particular piece of equipment. He is correct, of course. In any case, analyze the need for each purchase carefully and remember that the expense of sheltering and maintaining the equipment has to be factored into the cost.

As a practical example, I will describe the equipment we own and use on *Stormwind Farm*. Since 1997, we've done just fine with a used diesel powered pick-up truck, a used diesel mower, a wheel barrow, two spreaders for seed and lime, a weed trimmer, and small hand tools. My husband tried to convince me to buy a manure spreader. I don't need one, and I don't want one. For years, however, I had a small skid loader on my wish list to help maintain our long driveway. We finally purchased one and have used it on several projects. With the challenges on our property, it makes financial sense to own rather than rent a skid loader.

The Truck

A pick-up truck is essential for the operation of a small farm. Ours has carried hay, barn mats, lime, straw, sand, stone, lumber, seed, mulch, and a collection of other products over the years. When we transport alpacas, it pulls the trailer. The truck looks pretty well used by now. It runs; it carries stuff—and that's all I care about.

The Mower

Our biggest expense was a mower. I don't believe that a farmer who wants well-maintained pastures can do without one. Alpacas, like sheep, prefer to graze on fresh, succulent growth instead of rank, overgrown grasses and legumes way past their prime. If a herd cannot keep ahead of pasture growth, it's best to have a mower to keep pastures clipped. Overgrown pastures also encourage the presence of ticks. A nice, expensive veterinary visit will cure an alpaca of tick paralysis, but why not prevent it?

On *Stormwind Farm*, we own eight acres. Roughly six acres are in pasture. One acre is devoted to the house, a parking area, and a spacious fenced playground for our Whippet. The grassy playground has, in times of need, done double duty as another pasture. Frontage and a small meadow in the rear of the property add up to another acre. A small residential riding lawn mower wouldn't last beyond one season under those conditions. A farm-sized tractor would be overkill on such a small property. We purchased a used six-foot front deck mower with a diesel motor and are quite satisfied with this decision. One machine mows everything: pastures, front of the property, back meadow, and lawn.

My friend, Diann Mellott, who has maintained her small farm for the past forty years, had this to say about mowers:

> "I do not use a lightweight riding mower for my pastures, but I use an inexpensive—no more than $2,500—lawn/garden tractor to do all my mowing. I searched my memory and recall that each one that I have owned lasted at least ten years. My present mower is a 26-horse power garden tractor

gasoline model with a 54-inch mower deck. It has a cast iron frame as opposed to a lawn tractor that only has a steel frame. This option may be a little cheaper than a diesel mower."

It's a lot cheaper. There are pros and cons to each choice. Assess your farm's pastures—size as well as soil fertility—and your stocking rate to make a sensible decision.

A Weed Trimmer

The large mower does not fit into all the nooks and crannies of the farm where weeds grow. We purchased a walk-behind weed trimmer, and I use it with good results.

Spreaders

You will need a spreader for liming, fertilizing, and possibly overseeding your pastures. We have two: a very small walk-behind and a larger one that must be attached to the mower. I already mentioned that we do not own a manure spreader. Unless you can pick up a used, small manure spreader very cheaply, it's not cost effective to buy one for a small herd. If you choose to fertilize your pastures with composted manure, you can pay somebody to spread it once every two or three years. An old-fashioned metal garden rake and muscle power will also do the trick. It does for me. We're not talking about the mountains of manure that horse owners usually collect.

A Wheelbarrow

For our silver wedding anniversary, David presented me with a brand-new wheelbarrow. What a guy! The romance of his gift simply overwhelmed me. No, seriously, I was quite happy with my new wheelbarrow because I couldn't farm without it. A few years later, a friend made me the present of a clever adjustment that allows me to push the wheelbarrow like a baby carriage. I use the wheelbarrow for gardening, to move a heavy bag of feed or minerals, to transport materials for small construction projects such as a patio, to move composted manure, and many other chores.

Rakes and Shovels

Alpaca manure can efficiently and quickly be raked into small piles with a stiff plastic leaf-rake. The piles are then picked up with a commercial dog poop-scoop—shovel and rake—and deposited into buckets. Fifteen adult alpacas—consuming mostly pasture plants—produce approximately two 5-gallon buckets filled with manure each day. That amount hardly warrants the purchase of heavy equipment.

Gardening Tools

Aside from the shovels and rakes used to collect manure, we also own an assortment of sturdy shovels, spades, and rakes that I use for gardening as well as for farm chores. Manual hedge clippers and a handsaw round out the collection.

A Wagon

A Gator or a used golf cart is great for transporting items such as several bales of hay from one end of the farm to the other. A small wagon hitched to a tractor or mower works on the rare occasions when a wheelbarrow is not large enough. A wagon pulled by hand is suitable for my purposes. I transport all kinds of supplies without having to rely on a machine powered by an engine. This includes the weekly trip to take our garbage can to the street.

Snow Removal Equipment

Once the lawn chairs are permanently stored in the shed at summer's end, it's almost time to bring out the snow shovels. Each heavy snowfall on the farm gives me new respect for the trials and tribulations of our northern friends, both two- and four-legged species. The heavy snow equipment for house and barns on *Stormwind Farm* consists of a few snow shovels and muscle power. The latter isn't all that great when you're in your sixties. I console myself with the knowledge that other women pay for expensive gym memberships while I get to flex my muscles for free. Alpaca farmers who live in harsh climates need to be better prepared.

Yard Sales and Equipment Auctions

Rural areas always offer auctions where farm equipment can be purchased. You must be knowledgeable about the equipment and possess auction savvy to come out a winner from such a venue. If you don't trust yourself to find good heavy equipment deals at an auction, at least look for used tools such as shovels, rakes, pitch forks, and other smaller implements at auctions or yard sales. Old tools that have always been properly cared for work as well or better than brand-new ones. My husband, David, completed one job in our new barn with a pulley lent to him by one of our farming neighbors. The pulley is over 100 years old and completely functional. Our friend, Bob, found a pitchfork in an old shed next to a building he purchased and renovated. He gave it to me. I guess that its age rivals that of the pulley. It is beautifully crafted and works better than the new pitchfork I had bought in a hardware store.

Your Hands

Finally, let's mention your most important farm tools: your hands. For many years, I did not own or wear any work gloves and thought that people who did were pampered sissies. An article in a farm publication changed my mind. The author pointed out that good farmers treat their equipment with care. She wondered why many were so careless about their most valuable equipment—their hands—and urged readers to envision a workday without the use of these essential tools. Ever since reading this article, I wear heavy work gloves while performing many farm chores. Although I would never think of wearing gloves to clean or garden, I do not leave my hands unprotected while I carry fence posts, move heavy livestock panels, or hold an alpaca male's mouth open to file down fighting teeth. Inexpensive canvas gloves will do fine for many jobs, but invest in at least one pair of heavy, good quality work gloves.

All That Glitters Is Not Gold

Just remember: All that glitters is not gold. The alpaca farmer whom you envy over his shiny, new tractor may be in debt up to his eyeballs. Two of the most successful farmers—hay, corn, vegetables, and soybeans—in our county don't own a single piece of new equipment. Almost without exception, dairy farmers who changed to rotational grazing comment on their relief after unloading expensive equipment. These are pragmatic people and my farming role models. Use common sense when it comes time to purchase equipment. Buy only what you really need. A frugal farmer does not buy expensive toys or status symbols.

Equipment Compacts Soil

There is another important reason why a farmer should never use bigger equipment than what is necessary to do the job. Any time equipment passes over farmland, it compacts the soil. The heavier the equipment, the worse the compaction. Soil health suffers, which has a direct impact on plant growth. On our farm, I never allow heavy equipment—in our case, that's our mower—on the pastures if I can do the work with my light wheel barrow and hand tools. When I read *Deeply Rooted* (Lisa H. Hamilton), I felt a kinship with the Podoll family of North Dakota, especially David Podoll who worries about soil compaction and says that working in his garden taught him how to farm.

8

FENCES AND GATES

"Investing in good quality fencing is like buying a good pair of shoes." Jane Marks

Labs and Skunks

One fall, we had an unexpected early and brutal cold snap. Not only was it cold, but the wind whipping across our pastures was so severe that my alpacas spent the entire day hiding inside the barn. Aside from the brief visits that the animals paid to the outdoor dung pile, I saw neither hide nor hair of them all day. Nightfall found them still indoors, and I assume that's where they stayed. The next day, I phoned a friend to discuss business and casually inquired how her alpacas had fared during the storm. She was very upset.

"You're not going to believe this, but I found all my females and babies huddled together outside this morning," she told me. While checking the barn, she discovered her neighbor's two big, old labs snuggled deeply in the straw, stinking to high heaven of an unfortunate encounter with a skunk. "I bet the dogs' owners wouldn't let them in the house when they came back smelling of skunk," my friend speculated.

She was upset that her alpacas, including the nursing moms, had been out in the frigid weather all night without any warm water to drink. An additional concern was how the two canine culprits had entered the pasture and how to prevent future episodes.

Fencing Out Predators

Fencing is as important, or maybe more so, than an adequate shelter. We returned the deposit on our first sale when we discovered that the buyer intended to contain and protect the alpacas with fencing constructed from flimsy chicken wire. The part of the chicken in chicken wire apparently had not given her a clue.

In areas with predators such as cougar, bear, wolves, and coyote, substandard fencing can spell doom for a breeding program before the first cria has a chance to be born. If you've lived in a city or the suburbs all of your life, this aspect of livestock farming may come as a rude awakening. For example, most New Jersey residents are totally unaware that coyotes reside in our state. They are present in all twenty-one counties. There are also bobcats, foxes, and a rapidly growing black bear population. The biggest predator threat comes from roaming dogs as well as the family pet dog that's permitted to enter pastures without training or supervision. Although deer are not predators, their presence in and around pastures poses a special health hazard to the alpacas. You will learn about that in a future chapter.

It's the Law!

Paying for the installation of livestock fencing is a strain on a modest budget. If you do it yourself, it's extremely labor intensive. Either way, you don't want to commit any resources until you know for sure that location, materials, and height of your planned fence are in compliance with township laws. I wouldn't take a clerk's word over the phone on this issue. Visit the township office and ask for a copy of the specifications. Farmers with designated wetlands areas on their property need to be particularly cautious. You may have to leave unfenced buffer zones or apply for a state permit if you wish to fence in wetlands or areas close to them. Do not be naive and think that you will stay below the radar just because your farm is in a remote location. The government agencies that enforce these laws search for offenders with the help of helicopters.

Height

Alpaca perimeter fencing should be at least five feet high. With additional features such as electrified strands, guardian dogs, thorny hedgerows, or double fencing to ensure the safety of your alpacas, a height of four feet may be fine.

Chain-Link Night Paddock

If you have considerable financial resources, your choice of fencing material is only limited by safety issues and your sense of aesthetics. For those of us on a modest budget, fencing presents a major expense. At the extreme end, I've read about farmers using twelve-foot high chain-link perimeter fencing for their pastures. The cost of such safety measures would be prohibitive for a family with limited funds. Assess the need for such expensive fencing before you commit your life's savings to purchasing property, building a barn, or putting a non-refundable deposit on alpacas. A possible solution would be a small courtyard—livestock farmers call it a night paddock—connected to the barn and secured with chain-link fencing. For maximum safety, this structure must include a chain-link top, turning it into a giant cage. At dusk and during the night, when predators are more likely to strike than during daylight hours, the alpacas can be confined inside this safety compound. This would be far more affordable than entire pastures enclosed with chain-link fencing.

There is a drawback to a night paddock. During very hot weather, grazing animals usually rest during the day and graze during the night, a reversal of their normal schedule. A night paddock will make nocturnal grazing impossible.

High-Tensile Wire

A fence constructed from wooden posts and strands of high-tensile wire is one of the least expensive options. To prevent predators from entering the pasture, the strands must be electrified. Aside from possibly zapping visitors or—horrors!—potential customers, alpacas can get caught in the wires and electrocuted. I know several farmers who lost beautiful alpacas that way. Aside from the emotional upset, the distraught owners suffered financial losses. Small predators such as dogs or coyotes can easily flatten their bodies to crawl underneath the lowest high-tensile wire. Friends of ours witnessed two pit bull terriers do exactly that. One pit bull terrier attacked a female alpaca while its companion watched. The alpaca was saved but sustained severe injuries.

Woven Wire

More expensive than the high-tensile wire system—but safer for the animals—is woven wire fencing, specifically two-inch by four-inch non-climb fencing. Welded wire is less expensive but, once the strands separate, is not safe. Trying to save money on that would be false economy. When you install the fence, attach the fencing material to the side of the post that faces the pasture. Should the animals lean or rub against the fence, the posts will help to keep the wire in place. This adds stability to the installation. Woven wire can also be attached to already existing rail fences that are often found on horse farms.

Anyone with strong muscles can use a post hole digger; stringing many feet of woven wire is not all that easy if you don't have the proper tools and experience. Be careful that you don't leave gaps anywhere in the fence for nosy crias to squeeze through. The wire mesh should be as close to the ground as possible. A very determined dog can dig under the fence, but why give predators easy access?

Electrified Strands

Another option is to install a woven wire fence and run electrified strands along the top and bottom. If you put the latter on the outside, it's also the safest installation for the alpacas. Alpacas rarely challenge a fence; there is no reason for them to receive electric shocks to teach them not to try to escape. The purpose of the electrical system is to shock and deter intruders.

Cattle Panels

Some alpaca farmers use the popular wire cattle panels as fencing. I don't like the fact that each square is large enough for an alpaca to stick its entire head through the opening. A panicked alpaca could sustain a severe injury if it tried to pull the head back and wasn't immediately successful.

"If it went in, it'll come out," you may think now.

Not necessarily or not always easily. We once had to use wire cutters on the chain-link fence of our brand-new kennel run to free a hysterical Whippet puppy.

Fence Posts

Your choice of fencing material may impact the selection of fence posts, another big budget item. Their purchase and installation will need to be carefully considered. Friends of ours used cedar posts cut from trees growing on their own property. This not only saved a lot of money, it was also a healthy choice for their alpacas. What about posts if cedar trees are not conveniently growing on your property? Many livestock farmers use pressure-treated lumber. At one time, such lumber was treated with arsenic. If you come across it in your search for fence posts at bargain prices, educate yourself about its negative aspects. Chemicals from the posts may leach into the soil where they are absorbed by plant roots—one reason why you should never use pressure-treated lumber as borders for a vegetable bed. Pressure-treated lumber is also not suitable anywhere bare skin can come in contact with it, for example decks or playground equipment. During Victorian times, women ingested arsenic to promote hair growth— with deadly results. Unscrupulous dog breeders have fed arsenic to grow better coats on their show dogs and doomed their unfortunate canines to ill health and death. My husband talked to carpenters who suffered from arsenic poisoning as the result of working with pressure-treated lumber. Former neighbors of ours have a niece who almost lost a leg when a splinter from a deck built with pressure-treated lumber became imbedded below the skin and her leg swelled to grotesque proportions. Wear gloves and safety goggles while handling the posts and wash clothing in a separate load.

Several years ago, the federal government demanded changes in the manufacturing of pressure-treated lumber. Nevertheless, careful research into present requirements is advisable.

The healthiest choice—for humans and animals—is untreated lumber such as cedar, locust, or Osaga orange (sometimes also spelled Osage orange). We used locust posts on our farm. Although the leaves of a live black locust tree are toxic to animals, the posts are safe. The untreated posts will outlast us; they weathered to a nice, soft grey and are perfectly sturdy and functional.

I talked to a Mennonite farmer who told me about locust posts on his family farm that were put in the ground close to a hundred years ago. A woman from Pennsylvania mentioned that one of her uncles recently sold his PA farm and moved to upstate New York. The buyers of his PA property had to allow the seller to pull all the locust posts out of the ground to take with him to his new farm.

"They thought he was crazy," she laughed.

"Yeah, crazy like a fox," I agreed.

The old-time farmers were very much aware of the real value of natural hardwoods. Judith Summer wrote in *American Household Botany* (2004): "Black locust resisted wood fungi and was used to craft fence posts and railway ties." On cedar: "White cedar provided abundant wood for shingles, some of it collected from submerged logs that had resisted decay for centuries."

Temporary Fencing

Many livestock farmers use temporary fencing, especially those who practice rotational grazing on their farms. There are all kinds of different models available. I would not consider any of them safe enough for our alpacas as perimeter fencing, not even with an electrical charge.

Gates

Quality, installation, and location of your farm gates can all impact the safety of your animals and the efficient management practices on your farm. Our gates are standard metal farm gates with wire fencing material attached to them. I insisted on using the so-called kiwi-latches on all of them. They're not expensive and are probably one of the more secure latches you can find. Installed properly—the length of chain should not be very long—it is impossible for an alpaca to unlatch them. One day, I observed one of our female alpacas trying to do just that with its nose. The animal was not successful. Neither are most two-legged visitors who attempt the task and are not familiar with this type latch. That's good.

Safety Issues

My husband often gets annoyed with me for being overly cautious, but even he will admit that my obsession with safety and attention to detail prevent accidents on the farm. Improperly installed fencing can injure animals. So can the hardware that's often dropped and left after the job has been completed. If a work crew installs your fencing, impress on them the importance of not leaving nails or pieces of wire on the ground. Better yet, follow their path after the job has been completed and pick up dropped debris. This precaution can save you a costly veterinary bill. All fencing—but particularly perimeter fencing—should be inspected frequently if you wish your herd to remain safe.

Toxic Plants

An poorly groomed fence line will quickly invite vegetation to grow on both sides of the fence. It may include toxic plants. On our farm, I am always looking for and removing milkweed along the fence lines. We have no problems with this toxic plant in the pastures where regular mowing has eradicated milkweed as well as the non-toxic thistles. Because both plants are beneficial to pollinators, we promote their growth in our farm's wildflower meadow.

Hedgerows

Some livestock farmers allow plants along fence lines to grow and even plant trees and shrubs close to an already existing fence. Over the years, the plants form an impenetrable, natural fence. These hedgerows serve as windbreaks but also help to contain livestock and keep out predators. Hedgerows are—literally speaking—edible fences. The owner of a neighboring llama farm, for example, tells me how her llamas love to eat the wild rosebushes that form a natural hedgerow along her pasture fences. Rose hips are extremely nutritious.

Herbalist Juliette de Baraïcli Levy mentions the curative power of honeysuckle, raspberry, and hazel as well as blackberry and juniper. She calls the hedgerows "rich sources of natural vitamins, minerals and roughages," and describes "a most successful organic farmer" who "never trims his hedges other than the little required to keep them stock-proof."

Jerry Brunetti, in his presentation *The Soil, Forage, Livestock Connection* advocates the planting of hedgerows on livestock farms. His list of suitable plants includes Osage Orange, Persimmon, Kentucky Coffee Tree, Common Paw Paw, and Filbert.

There are several negative aspects to developing living fences. Hedgerows may substantially increase the number of ticks on your property and therefore the chances of ticks latching on to your alpacas. Leaf litter attracts snails. A future chapter will discuss the possible health threat to alpacas if the snails are ingested. You would have to be vigilant about checking for toxic plants. Additionally, densely growing vegetation will destroy the wire fence and possibly cause fence posts to rot. Of course, the ultimate goal is for a natural hedgerow to eventually replace a man-made fence. It may take several years to establish a hedgerow that can actually take the place of a conventional fence. Don't think that a hedgerow doesn't need care and maintenance. It needs to be checked, possibly trimmed in places, and occasionally may need sections replanted. The entire issue is a judgment call, and there is obviously no definitive answer as to what is best—hedgerow or a cleared path—behind the fence line. Very few issues with raising livestock are clearly either black or white.

Creative Solutions

There are other creative solutions to containing alpacas. For example, I visited one farm where the owners had nailed wooden pallets to fence posts. They had been able to obtain the pallets at no cost. The fence is unconventional but sturdy and functional. Whatever materials and methods you use, make sure the fence is safe and the job looks neat and presentable. Few things make a farm look more ramshackle than a haphazard, poorly planned, and sloppy fencing job.

9

FEEDING ALPACAS

"Acidosis is simply the upsetting of the ruminant's digestive system by feeding too many seeds or grains."

Paul Dettloff, D.V.M.

Alpacas Feed Themselves

We already discussed that pasture should be the mainstay of a good nutritional program. In essence, the alpacas feed themselves. Great pasture will also cut down considerably on the annual feed bill. Better yet, alpacas that feed themselves reduce the workload for their farmer. There are times, though, when weather conditions and possibly other variables make it advisable—and sometimes necessary—to bring and offer other feed to the animals in our care. Most alpaca farmers feed a combination of hay, a pelleted supplement, grain, and a commercial mineral mix. Several scientists have presented research on alpaca nutrition. It is highly technical information. The good news is that, with adequate pasture, an alpaca nutritional program is easy to manage. There is no need to comprehend complex nutritional formulas and scientific terminology.

Hay

The digestive system of the alpaca is superbly designed to digest forage. Next to pasture, hay—cut and dried grasses and legumes—is an important component of an alpaca nutritional program. Unless you grow your own hay, it's best to make arrangements to buy it before you plan to bring your alpacas home. Good hay is not easy to find under adverse weather conditions. Excellent hay is rare at all times and usually spoken for before it's even harvested. Many books and articles on nutrition advise livestock producers to test hay for protein content and moisture. With great pasture and year around grazing, there is no need to know the exact protein content of your hay. The hay supply in some areas is such that, while you're waiting for test results, somebody else comes along and buys every bale you have been looking at out from under your nose. Some hay farmers resent being questioned about the quality of their product.

"What the heck," one of them told me, "I've been farming for fifty years. This gussied-up dame comes along and wants to break apart one of my bales and have it tested." He snorted in disgust. "I chased her right down the lane. A blind man can see that this is top quality stuff. Let her break another farmer's bale apart."

It may be more diplomatic to buy ten to twenty bales and have them tested without saying so. Once you've established a relationship with a hay farmer, ask if you can purchase one bale. If the alpacas approve its taste, buy enough hay for a year or, at the very least, as much as you can store.

Good hay should be green, leafy—that is not "stemmy"—and dry. Second and third cuttings are usually softer and of a higher quality than the first hay harvest taken off any given field. The smell of fresh, high quality hay is aromatic and pleasant. When we receive or bring home a fresh supply, our alpacas start snacking it right off the truck. Alpacas should never be fed moldy hay because it can make them very sick. High moisture content creates mold and is a fire hazard.

Weather has a huge impact on crop quality. During extremely wet or dry years, even the best farmer has a hard time producing an outstanding product. Cut your hay supplier some slack and don't complain about conditions that he has no control over. Don't blame the hay farmer if you find pieces of trash in your bales but rather the idiots who littered. During cutting and baling, it's entirely possible for a flattened beer can or a popped balloon to escape the harvester's notice. It's your job to check each bale as you break it open.

Prices can vary considerably depending on regions of the country and individual sellers. If given a choice, go with the higher quality hay, even if it is more expensive. The alpacas will waste a lot of poor quality hay, so in the long run, you won't have saved anything. Old alpacas with worn teeth will not be able to eat rough, stemmy hay. Don't be alarmed, though, if your alpacas occasionally nibble on straw. It's good roughage and won't hurt them.

"Your pastures are so great. Why do you feed hay?" visitors sometimes ask me. I find that my alpacas crave and apparently need a certain amount of the roughage provided by hay. Maybe our pastures are more lush than what alpacas are accustomed to in their native countries. In any case, I make Orchard grass hay available to them at all times, and they may eat or leave it as they see fit. How much hay will a *pastured* alpaca consume? The standard—and somewhat thoughtless—answer is often: "Ten bales per alpaca per year." The amount fed per animal on a farm varies from year to year. The two main variables are always weather and pasture condition. Out of curiosity, I kept exact count over twelve months for one group of our alpacas.

From January 1, 2014—December 31, 2014, the three adult male alpacas on our farm consumed a *total* of nineteen bales of hay. Each bale of Orchard grass hay weighed approximately forty pounds. Pasture conditions were excellent, including during the summer months. Most of the hay was consumed during the winter, when grazing stopped for several weeks due to heavy snow cover on the pastures.

My alpacas prefer to be outside except during severe weather conditions. They enjoy eating their hay outside as well. Sometimes, I place several flakes right on the pasture grass but always a good distance away from any dung areas. Putting large amounts of hay outside is wasteful. The sun quickly bleaches it—thereby destroying important nutrients. Rain leaches nutrients out of the hay as well.

Minerals

Ideally, pasture and hay should cover the mineral needs of a grazing animal. Unfortunately, even pasture and hay that look picture perfect may not supply all nutrients for optimum health. Because so many North American soils are depleted of important minerals, the crops that grow on them are missing these minerals as well. A good quality mineral mix should therefore be made available at all times.

In addition to a salt block, we offer kelp free choice—meaning the animals eat as much as they want. The kelp is kept in a pig creep feeder mounted on an inside barn wall— well away from any door. No matter which direction rain or snow is coming from, the kelp is protected from the weather. I've noticed that our alpacas consume more of it when weather conditions make grazing impossible. That makes sense because even the best hay can never completely match the nutritional value of good pasture. The pregnant females consume more than the males. Animals visiting from other farms sometimes consumed huge amounts of minerals the first few days after their arrival—almost as if trying to make up for a deficiency. I would not sell an alpaca with a fertility guarantee to a farm where free choice minerals are not a main component of its nutritional program.

Supplements

When most alpaca farmers say that they are feeding grain to their alpacas, they are not talking about feeding corn, barley, and oats. What they should say—and what they mean—is that they are feeding supplements in the form of manufactured pellets, chow, sweet feed, or crumbles. I define *supplements* as any feed that consists of or includes grain or grain by-products in any form.

I will not pretend that I don't have strong opinions on the subject. I believe that, on a well managed alpaca farm, feeding supplements is—nutritionally speaking—neither necessary nor desirable. Alpacas evolved over thousands of years as extremely efficient foragers. Their digestive systems are not designed to deal with grains, at least not large amounts. This is true of all ruminants. Dr. Fowler, widely acknowledged as an authority on camelids, makes it very clear that feeding supplements can lead to gastric problems, which in turn can lead to other health problems.

Candid quotes from several sources:

- "The over ingestion of highly fermentable carbohydrates, usually concentrates, may lead to acidosis, dehydration, and depression" (Fowler).
- "If the pH of the first compartment of the stomach of a SAC drops below 5.5 as a result of either Ketoacidosis or grain overload, microorganisms cease to grow" (Fowler).
- "Simple indigestion due to excessive feeding of grain results in anorexia and ruminal stasis" (*The Merck Veterinary Manual*).
- Feeding high-grain diets to ruminants can predispose them to polioencephalomacia (polio) because it slows thiamine production in the rumen ... (*Sheep Industry News*).

A grain overload can become life threatening if it destroys the natural bacteria in an alpaca's digestive system. In mild cases, giving the alpaca a microbial product containing live, naturally occurring microorganisms will cure the problem. In severe cases, an animal will die unless the mass of undigested grain is removed by a skillful veterinarian and the stomach is "re-seeded"—this medical procedure is called transfaunation—with the stomach contents from another animal, preferably a camelid. This can become very costly. Alpacas should not have free access to grain, either accidentally or on purpose. Changes in diet should proceed gradually to allow new microorganisms to slowly establish themselves.

"Other livestock species are fed large amounts of grain. Why don't they have problems?" you may ask now.

They *do* have problems! *The Merck Veterinary Manual* has entire sections devoted to their diagnosis and treatments. Alpaca farmers need to be aware that ruminants which are fed large amounts of grain to efficiently fatten them for slaughter are also administered medication to prevent or treat acidosis caused by such a grain overload.

Jerry Brunetti, in his presentation on soil and forages, stated at the 2005 N.O.F.A. conference held at Rutgers University in New Jersey that "the architecture of ruminants is not designed to consume grain." He warned that "grain is the best harbinger of mycotoxins and mold, while grass cleanses the digestive system." That wasn't all. "Respiratory problems actually start in the gut," Brunetti explained. He added, "The combination of grain and poor pasture results in liver problems." Brunetti's power point presentation included a graph of what happens when healthy pH levels in the rumen are destroyed. Lactic acid rises to levels that are toxic to ruminants. Brunetti suggested the use of apple cider vinegar "to prime the digestive pump."

Judging by the farming publications that I read, the movement for all livestock rearing is away from formulated feed and back to the natural forage these animals thrived on for thousands of years before man started to meddle with their natural lifestyle.

In additional support of my views, it is perhaps best to describe the feeding program on *Stormwind Farm*. Our alpacas enjoy abundant pasture throughout the year. I work very hard to find and purchase high quality and palatable Orchard grass hay. Pasture, hay, salt, and kelp are never restricted and the alpacas consume as much as they desire.

Females and weanling alpacas are fed one to two ounces of a supplement once a day throughout the year.

"I understand. That's because they are pregnant and nursing." A visitor to our farm was sure she knew my reasons for feeding the daily supplements.

She was wrong. I believe that pregnant and nursing alpaca females can do very well on the three major nutritional components—pasture, hay, and minerals. During most months of the year, I feed the tiny amounts of supplement only for one reason: It helps to get the animals off the pastures and into the barn or the area that I call the dining parlor. From there, I can herd them into a small catch pen for medical maintenance, clipping nails, breeding, behavior testing for pregnancy status, and halter training crias. On days when there is no specific reason to move females and crias into the barn, the feeding routine helps to reinforce the alpacas' sense of security and trust in my presence.

"But isn't developing trust in you equally important with your male alpacas?" my visitor asked after my explanation.

Yes, it is, but with males, it's easier to do so. I explained that hormonal changes during pregnancy and the presence of a cria often make an alpaca female nervous and hyper alert in the presence of its human caretakers. The daily feeding session continuously proves to my females that I enter their midst without predatory intentions. In contrast, alpaca males have no crias to protect, and most males are therefore relaxed around people they know and trust.

Why do I feed daily supplements to the male alpacas? Animals, like small children, thrive—physically and emotionally—on a daily routine. They crave predictability more than change and novel experiences. Every morning, the male alpacas follow me into the barn where each animal is given its small daily treat: one ounce of pelleted supplements. This gives me the opportunity to detect any obvious problems. When it comes time to have their nails trimmed or to receive inoculations, being brought inside the barn is not a novel and stressful experience for the animals.

Grain

Unprocessed grains are far healthier for a ruminant's digestive system than the processed kind. My choice is crimped oats. The alpacas like the taste. Additionally, oats are an immune system booster. Juliette de Baïracli Levy recommends them as a remedy for rickets and an important food that promotes "strong teeth, hooves, horns, nails and hair." The only drawback to feeding crimped oats is that it's messy. The alpacas drop pieces on the ground. If not removed, the oats will attract rodents into the barn.

I feed oats to an elderly female alpaca—Breeze is twenty-two years old—that has trouble digesting hay. When snow covers pasture, I supplement Breeze's diet with a mixture of crimped oats and a feed formulated for old horses twice a day. The equine senior feed is *high in fiber* and has 14 percent protein. During these supervised feeding times, she can eat as much as she wants. Breeze does very well on this program. Fortunately, snow does not cover pastures in our area of the country for long periods of time.

Choke

Many farmers experience *choke* with their alpacas. It is awful for the animals and can cause major problems such as inhalation pneumonia. During the rare occasions that it happened on my farm, I was able to dissolve the obstruction with vigorous massaging of the neck and another special technique that I describe in a future chapter. An inexperienced farmer should learn both techniques prior to ever feeding supplements to alpacas. As a precaution, I stay in the feed area and supervise consumption until the last animal has finished eating. Pasture and hay do not cause choke in alpacas.

Hay—Not Grain—Equals Heat

A great misconception exists about when and how much grain to feed depending on the weather.

"During the summer, I feed grain late in the evening," one fellow alpaca farmer told me. "It's better for them to eat light during the heat, you know?"

No, I didn't know. To the contrary, I learned from reading about other species—mostly dairy cows—that the digestion of grain generates less heat than that of hay or pasture.

Dr. Fowler confirms this: "A paradox occurs in feeding herbivores. A high-fiber diet yields more heat for warming the body. A high-concentrate diet provides more energy, but it is not as efficient in warming the animal."

In other words: Feeding hay to alpacas is not comparable to people eating "light" meals of salad, vegetables, and fruit on hot days. If you are worried about keeping your alpacas cool, you should feed their grain portion in late morning, right before the worst heat of the day. Grain portions can be increased a little during very cold weather, but it is more important that hay is of high quality and offered in unlimited quantities. A healthy, well-fleshed-out alpaca that is sheltered in a barn with straw bedding will hardly suffer from loss of energy and weight during extreme weather conditions. I am more concerned about digestive upsets due to a forced lack of mobility.

Alpaca Cafeteria?

Alpacas vary greatly in their metabolisms, not unlike their human caretakers. Some remain slender on the richest pastures while others seemingly can live on air. There are authors who advise feeding a different type of supplement to various individuals or groups in a herd: the thin ones, the fatties, the pregnant ones, the nursing mamas, the weanlings, and the working studs. The farmer is supposed to calculate the amount fed to each group or individual with a complicated formula. I think this is unrealistic and unnecessary. Pasture and plenty of exercise are more important than cafeteria-style feeding programs. As I mentioned earlier, I make exceptions only for very old alpacas that can no longer grind up hay with their worn teeth and would starve when weather does not permit grazing.

Dry Lot Feeding

Many alpacas in North America are kept on dry lot. That means that there is no pasture, and the animals depend entirely on the feed that is brought to their dry lot each day. Can alpacas exist under such conditions? Yes. Do they thrive in a dry lot? Not likely. Will a farmer see a profit on alpacas bred, raised, and maintained on dry lot? I don't believe that it is possible except under very unusual circumstances. A frugal farmer would despair over the expenses/profits ratio. A detailed program on dry lot farming has therefore no place in this book.

Mom's Milk Bar—It's Best

Dr. Fowler states: "Neonates have a higher surface to body weight ratio and thus have a greater insensible fluid loss than adults. Fluid and energy requirements are linked to an all-milk diet."

It has been proven in human infants that introducing solids at an early age promotes lifelong allergies. Bitches whose puppies are forced to eat solids lose interest in nursing them. Maybe this happens with alpacas as well. We create problems when we meddle with systems fine-tuned by natural selection over thousands of years. Mom's milk bar provides better stuff than any feed harvested and processed by humans. I never encourage crias to consume grain or pelleted supplements while they are still nursing. If a cria in my herd ever showed an unnaturally early interest in grain, I would question the mother's milk supply. I like to see crias nurse until they're at least six months old. I don't care at what age the crias start to consume supplements after weaning. All do eventually in imitation of their mothers or others in the herd. Of course, they start grazing and nibbling on hay long before weaning time.

Feeding Nursing Alpaca Mothers

Herbal mixes that promote milk production in a lactating female sell like hot cakes. Why? It has never made sense to me that so many alpaca farmers experience problems with lack of milk production with their animals. Although it is true that agalactia—failure to produce milk—can be due to an inherited trait, I refuse to believe that this is the case with many alpacas. They have been raised for thousands of years by dirt poor South American farmers. These pastoralists were in no position to coddle poor milkers, and survival of the fittest was and still is the order of the day for many alpacas on the South American continent. Such selection pressure does not produce high numbers of poor milkers. North American farmers are doing something wrong if many females exhibit poor milk production. Nutrition has to play a role. Either the mothers are undernourished or too fat. The animals may carry a heavy parasite load. Farmers who are breeding for super heavy fleeces are asking these mothers to "burn the candle at both ends." The protein to make milk *and* produce an unusually heavy fleece has to come from somewhere. Add to that poor or no pasture (dry lot), marginal hay quality, emotional stress, and acidosis from grain overload, and it is no wonder that the milk supply is deficient. All these conditions can and should be addressed. A nutritional program for nursing alpaca mothers should be based on excellent pasture. On our farm, they are fed the same as always: unlimited amounts of pasture, hay, minerals, and one to two ounces of supplements offered once a day. Nothing more, nothing less. I never had an alpaca on our farm that did not produce enough milk to raise a cria. Nursing mothers usually lose a little weight. If they're lively (pronking, running), graze eagerly, consume hay, and calmly chew their cud—relax!

"You talk like pasture is the answer to everything," a fellow farmer once complained. "When we're talking about livestock, it is," I said.

Growth and Maturation

Several alpaca farmers have stated that "early development" is an objective in their breeding program. A company that produces alpaca feed supplements states in an advertisement: "Don't take a chance with slow weight gain!"

I believe that this concept is borrowed from other livestock industries where slaughter weight is the primary consideration. In South America, where alpacas are slaughtered around the age of seven to eight years and meat and pelts are used, selection for early maturity may be an economically smart choice. Under those management practices, it is also not critical that animals are selected and fed for long-term health.

Why are North American alpaca farmers promoting accelerated growth and weight gain? Most of us are not breeding to reach maximum slaughter weight in the shortest possible time. Alpacas that mature early may be able to reproduce at a younger age than we normally expect. Does that translate into more successful pregnancies over a female's lifetime? It would be interesting to see scientific research conducted on this subject.

Dog breeders arrived at the conclusion that feeding high protein, high calcium puppy chow to large breed puppies was actually harmful. Rapid growth and weight gain put too much strain on a developing body, stressing muscles, ligaments, bones, and internal organs.

Dr. Fowler has this to say: "An interesting sidelight for North American breeders is that a high plane of nutrition (particularly excess energy) just prior to puberty results in lower mammary secretory tissue weight and is associated with low milk production in subsequent lactation."

My observations and opinions are not an invitation to provide low quality hay, pasture, and grain to your animals. The alpacas certainly should not be undernourished. All I am saying is this: Don't push the envelope. Give the animals a chance to develop according to their own, genetically programmed time schedule. On my farm, I prefer slow, steady weight gain over rapid growth.

The Other Extreme

In contrast to those who overfeed, there are farmers who deprive their alpacas of necessary nutrients—to save money, from sheer ignorance, or to produce fiber with a lower micron count. The first reason is foolish because emaciated alpacas become ill and reproductively unsound. The second reason is sad, but education can fix that problem. The third reason is both foolish and—from a moral standpoint—despicable. Although starvation produces fiber that is finer than what is normal for the individual alpaca, the fiber becomes weak and brittle and is therefore worthless. Unfortunately, not all buyers have the knowledge and expertise to detect starvation fiber fineness, and farmers who engage in such a morally corrupt practice are sometimes financially rewarded.

Safety

A few years ago, several hundred alpacas fell ill and died after being fed a supplement formulated and mixed by a well-known supplier of livestock feed. My friend, Alice Brown, who researched the issue thoroughly, was informed by a competitor of this company that the ingredient that caused the death was Salinomycin, a coccidiostat used in poultry feed. This had been accidentally mixed in with the alpaca feed. What can you do to prevent such devastating losses? A woman who spent her entire life around livestock told me that many rabbit breeders have a sacrifice population. Whenever a new bag of feed is opened, the contents are first fed to a few rabbits that are of little importance to the breeding operation. This may strike you as repulsive from a moral standpoint—why are some animals more important than others?—but it makes financial sense for a livestock farmer. Better to have a gelding die than a breeding female.

Water

I can't stress the importance of offering clean, fresh water to your alpacas enough times. Drinking sufficient water promotes digestion and feed intake. A dehydrated alpaca will not eat properly. Inexperienced livestock farmers often think that water is only important during hot weather. Not so! Water consumption greatly depends on the moisture content of pastures. On a warm day, alpacas will drink very little if they are out grazing after a heavy rainfall soaked the pastures. On a cool day, but with dry pastures or consuming mostly hay, alpacas may drain the water buckets very quickly. If pastures are covered with snow and hay is the only forage available, alpacas will need to be well supplied with fresh, warm water. All too often, this component of winterizing a farm is not given enough importance. In cold weather, buckets with a heating element are not a luxury. Here is another reason for heated buckets: "Livestock losses have occurred during cold weather due to the concentrating effect of freezing, which increases nitrate content of remaining water in stock tanks" (*The Merck Veterinary Manual*).

Alpacas are finicky drinkers. They like their water fresh and clean. Sure, they'll drink enough to stay alive if dirty water is offered to them, but they won't consume enough to enjoy truly superior health. In humid, hot weather, hang water buckets out of the sun. Algae should never be seen in a bucket. During the summer months, I change water at least once, sometimes twice, and often more times a day. During cool weather, it may be sufficient to keep adding to the depleted water level and fill the buckets with a completely fresh supply on the third day. Use some discretion and common sense. I've noticed that some alpaca groups keep their water sparkling clean; others manage to get their drinking water dirty within half a day. A simple rule: If it's dirty, you change it! A large brush does a good job removing any dirt or scum. A green scouring pad used to clean dirty pots also works well. Baking soda can be used as a cleaning agent. You need not worry about leaving a residue in the buckets. Baking soda (Sodium Bicarbonate) is an antacid that relieves heartburn and acid indigestion. Tiny amounts will not harm the alpacas. It is a much healthier product for the animals, the farmer, and the environment than bleach or other harmful cleaning agents. Another excellent choice is apple cider vinegar. It cleans, and any residue left in the buckets is healthy for the animals. Vinegar is routinely used to treat indigestion, ruminal stasis—a condition where active ruminal fermentation ceases—and urea poisoning.

"Administration of weak acids in cold water returns the pH of ruminoreticular content toward physiologic levels, promotes the uptake of volatile fatty acids, depresses the absorption of ammonia, and inhibits excessive urease activity. Acetic acid (4-5%) or vinegar (cattle: 4-8 L: sheep: 250-500 ml) is the most common acidifying agent used" (*The Merck Veterinary Manual*).

Quite a few farmers believe that the addition of vinegar to the drinking water promotes the conception of female offspring. Whatever happened to little girls being made of sugar and spice?

You will occasionally find dead animals floating around in water buckets. We've found several fully-grown birds and a chipmunk so far. Your alpacas won't go near the water if that happens. The little chipmunk's suicide on a hot day could have presented serious health problems for my alpacas had I not checked the water buckets in a timely fashion.

It is not unusual for water pumped from a farm well to be contaminated by high nitrate content—run-off from fertilizer. You can choose the very best breeding stock and lavish the best care on it; if an important component such as healthy water is missing, you don't stand a chance to make a profit. It's a health hazard for people as well, especially for children. Testing water from a well every few years should be part of a farm's management plan.

10

NATURAL HEALING

"It is always wise to prevent rather than treat illness."
Kristin Joyce

Immune System

Because a healthy immune system translates into healthy adult alpacas, healthy crias, and a healthy bank account for the farmer, much is made in the alpaca industry of IgG—immunoglobulin G—testing. Farmers have reason to be concerned.

"This specific immunoglobulin is the main source of antibodies for the neonate" (Fowler).

Alpaca crias ingest the antibodies with the mother's colostrum, the sooner the better. There is roughly a twenty-four hour window for this to happen. Closure of the cria's intestinal wall to IgG is believed to begin by six hours postpartum. Of course, if the mother's own immune system is compromised, her colostrum offers very little protection to her cria. Owners of crias diagnosed with a low IgG count often elect transfusion of blood plasma or serum. According to Dr. Fowler, plasma is preferable. Much has been written about the need for such transfusions, where to obtain the plasma, the choice of procedures, and the dangers of such an invasive procedure to the cria. Diagnostic testing and treatment are costly and, *purely from a financial viewpoint*, can hardly be justified as a standard care protocol by the frugal alpaca farmer.

Arguments rage pro and con about the administration of booster inoculations given to the dam several weeks before delivery to maximize the cria's immune system response immediately after birth. A cria's own immune system starts working on its own at about one month of age and by three months old is usually fully functional. Protocols vary regarding the immunization of crias, with many farmers electing to immunize at least twice with C, D, & T (*Clostridium perfringens types C & D and Clostridium Tetani*) within the first three to six months of a cria's life.

None of this is surprising. Conventional rearing and medical practices for animals often narrowly focus on treating disease—and then only the symptoms—as well as preventing illness by a series of inoculations. Instead, the main focus of a sensible livestock program should always be on boosting an animal's immune system the natural way, with inoculations viewed as secondary, supportive measures. Livestock farmers should expect their animals to enjoy glowing health. Unfortunately, many expect illness as an inevitable part of doing business.

One of the most important books you may ever read as a livestock farmer is *The Herbal Handbook for Farm and Stable* by Juliette de Baïracli Levy. This will be an eye-opener to those raised exclusively on the wisdom of conventional medicine. In her extensive travels with European Roma and Arabian horse breeders, the author learned of the immense healing power of plants growing in abundance in the meadows and hedgerows of the countryside.

Animals Heal Themselves

Frugal farmers should take a deep interest in natural healing. It has its roots in the belief that much sickness can be prevented and cured by allowing animals to live in harmony with nature and to take advantage of Mother Earth's healing powers.

Wild animals seek out and consume medicinal plants. In *Becoming a Tiger,* Susan McCarthy described how capuchin monkeys in Venezuela rub themselves with millipedes to repel mosquitoes. Highly pregnant African elephants were observed seeking out and eating large amounts of certain tree leaves that were also used by local Masai women to induce birth.

Domesticated animals have not lost their ability to seek out what helps them if given the opportunity. By keeping alpacas in fenced pastures, we rob them of this opportunity and force them to eat what we select.

Juliette de Baïracli Levy writes about giving herbs to the farm animals "by planting them in the pasture lands and alongside the hedgerows where the animals graze."

Distrust of Natural Remedies

Many Americans still harbor an almost pathological distrust of natural remedies. A fellow dog owner—who thinks nothing of popping any prescribed or over-the-counter medicine without questions—once called me about a problem with one of her pets. The dog had been on a course of oral antibiotics and now, not surprisingly, had a severe case of diarrhea. I advised giving a large dose of probiotics. These live bacteria help keep the immune system strong and restore friendly bacteria to the digestive system. It is found in good quality, naturally cultured yogurt or can be purchased in pill form in any health food store. My friend grilled me so long and hard about possible side effects and dosage that I finally became angry and told her to make an appointment with her veterinarian.

"I think I'll give him the pink stuff," my friend said.

Not sure whether she meant her dog or her vet, I answered, "You do that," and hung up the phone.

Many young mothers give their infants prescription medicine to cure colic—without worrying a second about side effects—but look upon fennel or lemon balm as a potentially harmful substance. Fear of plants is nothing new in the history of mankind. When the potato, a plant native to the Peruvian Andes, was introduced in Europe, the people of that continent were extremely frightened. Potatoes were believed to cause tuberculosis and leprosy.

A fellow alpaca farmer wrote several years ago that little is known about using herbal medicine on animals. That is patently false. More than 2,000 years ago, educated Greeks and Romans already left written documentation of herbal healing and its practical applications. The ancient Egyptian and Chinese herbalists developed and used sophisticated and complex formulas. What the author should have written instead is this:

People in highly industrialized nations, particularly in the United States of America, know very little about herbal medicine. Many are only now starting to discover the tremendous store of knowledge their ancestors had and applied to treat disease in their livestock.

We often find out that herbs known on one continent are also cultivated and used by people in other parts of the world. Eric Hoffman mentions two herbal remedies administered by South American camelid producers that are also used by North American and European herbalists: Chamomile to treat colic and wormwood to rid the animals of internal parasites.

Patent Laws

"If herbal medicine is so great, why hasn't the conventional medical community embraced it?" you may very well ask now.

The patent laws of the United States of America do not permit patents on natural substances. Drug companies will not pour millions of research dollars into developing a product that can also be freely produced and sold by competitors.

In their book *What Your Doctor May Not Tell You About Menopause*, Dr. Lee and coauthor Virginia Hopkins do a great job explaining the difference between synthetic drugs and natural compounds. The most famous example cited by Dr. Lee is aspirin, which was originally made from the bark of willow trees. Herbalists had known of the healing properties of *salix* for centuries. In 1897, a German scientist synthesized acetylsalicylic acid, and the Bayer Company patented it as Aspirin.

Portion Control

Herbalists believe that all plants have medicinal value. What lay people need to understand is that some plants, although beneficial to living creatures in tiny amounts, are toxic when consumed in large portions. In herbal medicine, more is not always better. Think of it in conventional medical terms: Although taking one aspirin has been proven as an effective blood thinner, no doctor tells patients to swallow dozens of pills at one time.

Another good example is offered in Helen Thayer's book *Three Among the Wolves*. Thayer describes how, on the one hand, the Labrador tea plant is "used by native peoples to ease the symptoms of cold, indigestion, and food poisoning" with great results. On the other hand, excessive brewing of the leaves releases the toxin ledol and results in dizziness and even death if "drunk to excess."

Steven Malstrom, who wrote *Own Your Own Body*, praises the healing power of herbs but also cautions readers, "Herbs cannot be used indiscriminately, without knowledge, no more than food can."

Herbal remedies *are medicine* in the truest sense of the word. They are to be taken and administered with care. I can appreciate and would always advise caution. What I simply cannot comprehend are the negative attitudes of those who cheerfully swallow a pill case full of conventional medications with known, harmful side effects each day but recoil in fear at the thought of drinking an herbal tea or taking probiotics.

Grow Your Own Herbs

It is not necessary to deplete your budget by purchasing vast amounts of herbal remedies. You can grow herbs yourself and use composted alpaca manure as fertilizer and soil builder. Cultivating an herb garden need not be expensive. Many herbs are perennials and, once purchased, will continue to grow from year to year. Annual plants produce seeds which can be saved over the winter. Other beneficial plants sprout without any help from you on a seasonal basis. Chickweed, for example, can be found each spring around trees and in vegetable gardens. Thought of as a nuisance plant by most gardeners, it provides a soothing tonic for digestive upsets and is believed to act as a blood cleanser. I pull out clumps of it each spring and throw them into the alpaca pastures. Juliette de Baïracli Levy states that chickweed has properties similar to those of Slippery Elm and was praised by the Turkish Roma for its potent medicinal powers. She also suggests brewing a handful in a three-quarter pint of water to use as an eye lotion.

A Holistic Approach

Natural remedies cannot be effective in an environment that encourages disease and general poor health. The holistic approach that I've discussed in previous chapters must serve as a foundation for any treatments and preventive measures. Only then can plants, animals, and human beings remain in or return to good health.

What follows is a discussion on the plants and products that I have been using on my farm. *Disclaimer: I am not an expert in this field, and my descriptions are not to be construed as either advice or encouragement to use these particular products and remedies.*

Garlic

Individual people and animals are unique in their reactions to food and medicine. I know several people who eat great amounts of garlic daily and are in blooming good health. Others experience problems. In *Prescription for Herbal Healing*, Phyllis A. Balch describes several conditions under which it is not advisable to consume garlic.

I used to offer my alpacas fresh, finely minced garlic cloves every few weeks. Some ate them; some did not. The practice faded away when, due to the excellent condition of our farm's pastures, the alpacas now have access to grazing a multitude of beneficial plants all year.

Eyebright

Alpacas have large eyes that are vulnerable to infections or injuries. For example, a piece of hay or an insect caught under the lid may produce tearing. I keep an especially close eye—no pun intended—on our male crias. Not unlike their human counter parts, little alpaca boys want to wrestle and roughhouse. A single male cria in a herd of females will not find willing partners and will be spit on by outraged matrons and prissy little alpaca girls. There is only so much green slime an alpaca eye can take without an adverse reaction. Mild conjunctivitis can be effectively treated with the herb Eyebright. I make a tea from the leaves and flush the inflamed eye. *Agri Dynamics Company* offers a topical spray formulated from a variety of herbs to treat irritated eyes.

A chronic condition may be due to a poorly functioning immune system or blocked tear ducts. In those cases, a topical treatment will not cure the problem.

Fenugreek

I mention elsewhere in the book that I believe strongly that the problems many farmers experience with their alpacas' poor milk supply is a problem of their own making. If you fix the environment your animals live in and examine your breeding goals as to fleece density, you won't have to resort to feeding products that stimulate and improve milk production. The cria's suckling and its dam's natural hormones will be sufficient stimulation, just like nature intended them to be.

A fairly large selection of herbs has the ability to stimulate milk production in a nursing mother. Fenugreek, Blessed Thistle, fennel, borage, balm, and marshmallow root are all mentioned by herbalists as increasing milk flow. So do warm compresses, vigorous suckling from the cria, and a calm, stress-free environment. Many alpaca farmers feed prepared mixes—purchased ready-made—to their pregnant or lactating females. It is cheaper to buy these herbs separately and to mix them yourself.

A few words of caution are also in order here. Fenugreek is contraindicated for all animals with hormonal imbalances. Additionally, farmers who breed lactating alpacas—twenty days after parturition is not uncommon—need to be aware of fenugreek's special properties.

Dr. Lee and Phyllis Balch discuss, in their respective books, how fenugreek's oxytocin-like properties may stimulate uterine contractions and possibly end a pregnancy.

The herb fenugreek is available as seeds or in liquid form. The latter is easy to administer to one—non-pregnant!—female rather than putting out an herbal mix that is shared by all the females.

On our farm, I gave fenugreek on one occasion. One of our female alpacas developed an allergic reaction to a Rabies inoculation. Its head swelled to grotesque proportions within fifteen minutes after the inoculation had been administered. Medication reduced the swelling but also dried up the alpaca's milk. I fed the female's cria with a bottle for one day while feeding the dam several cups of fenugreek seeds. The alpaca's milk was back the second day. Because not all females will willingly eat the seeds, I now keep liquid fenugreek in stock should it ever be needed again.

Raspberry Leaves

Raspberry leaves and tea are highly recommended by virtually all herbalists as a toner for the female reproductive system. Again, though, caution is in order. Raspberry leaf also acts as a uterine stimulant.

Mentioning the feeding of raspberry leaves or tea to pregnant bitches will ignite a firestorm on virtually any dog breeder Internet forum or chat room. Feelings run pretty high pro or con on the subject, with success stories followed by tales of horror. When I shared this with Elaine Ferry, an accredited independent inspector of organic farms, she felt that an animal would have to consume large amounts of leaves for it to be a problem. Other organic livestock farmers at the conference where I met Ferry concurred with her opinion.

I had wonderful results with feeding raspberry leaves to my Whippet bitches during the last month of their pregnancies. I have not used raspberry tea or leaves with the alpacas.

Lemon Balm

This aromatic herb grows in profusion in the rich soil of our farm's perennial beds. The herb has antibacterial and antiviral properties. It also has—among other benefits—a mild sedative effect. Phyllis Balch writes: "This herb is gentle enough for babies and children." I dry the leaves and brew a tea that my husband and I drink during the winter months. I offer the fresh, cut leaves to the male alpacas. On a farm with females—pregnant or open—present, male alpacas can always use a calming herb.

Apple Cider Vinegar

I already presented information about vinegar. It is well worth your time to learn more about its benefits. Its medicinal purposes were recognized and appreciated thousands of years ago. During the time of the Roman Empire, soldiers were forced to drink a prescribed amount of vinegar each day to ensure their health.

Aside from benefits to the digestive system, there is another reason to feed apple cider vinegar, especially to male alpacas. Urinary calculi (urolithiasis) occur in all mammals but are common in ruminants. These calculi are small stones that block the urethra and therefore stop the flow of urine. The common folk name for the condition is water belly. *The Merck Veterinary Manual* describes it as primarily a nutritional disease. High-grain diets, dietary mineral imbalances, and insufficient water intake all contribute to this extremely painful disease.

Castration of very young males can also put animals at high risk. Male hormones are necessary for the penis and urethra to develop normally. Early castration—removal of the testicles—disrupts this natural process. Interestingly, Dr. Fowler reports that "in lamoids, it is frequently the intact, breeding males that are most commonly affected." Surgery to remove urinary calculi is complicated, not always successful, and will be expensive. Prevention is obviously the goal for the frugal alpaca farmer.

In *Alternative Treatments for Ruminant Animals,* author Paul Dettloff D.V.M. states: "This problem is not seen real often in growing dairy young stock that are receiving a good amount of forage in the ration."

In other words: Pasture and hay should make up the bulk of the young animals' diet if you want to avoid urolithiasis.

Pat Colby, who wrote the very interesting and informative *Natural Goat Care,* advises the administration of a "drench of cider vinegar." She thinks "it will certainly prevent a recurrence." She writes: "I kept up to seven bucks for many years with only a mineral bore for water. They all received cider vinegar and there were no problems with calculi."

I purchase apple cider vinegar in one-gallon jugs at the supermarket and add approximately half a cup to each bucket of water. There is no need to measure carefully. Until the alpacas become accustomed to the taste and smell, start out with tiny amounts and increase gradually. My animals prefer it over straight water.

Probiotics

On the rare occasions that I give antibiotics to my animals, I follow up with Probiotics given in powdered form or as a paste. The powder is mixed with a small amount of water. The paste is easier to administer to alpacas. The product that I prefer includes vitamins. I also give a weekly dose to all crias from October to the beginning of May.

Paravac™

Coccidiosis is a very serious problem in many livestock populations, including many alpaca herds. Although animals with strong immune systems develop a natural resistance to this parasite, stress caused by overcrowding, travel, change in herd mates, shearing, or birth trauma can bring on an outbreak of coccidiosis. Quite a few farmers administer popular drugs prophylactically at regular intervals. I am opposed to this practice. Sulfonamides are not without side effects. Prolonged treatment can cause bone marrow depression, disturbance of normal microfloral balance, and depression of vitamin B synthesis.

It is comforting to know that a natural and effective remedy is available during an outbreak. Our very own camelid community offers a wonderful example of the powers of natural healing. *Eagle Peak Herbals* is a company located in Eagleville, California. It is owned by the Hodge family who also has been raising llamas for many years. The company offers a product called Paravac™, which contains, among other ingredients, Black Walnut green hulls, Wormwood leaf, Clove buds, and Ginger root.

Their sales brochure states: "Paravac has been officially tested on llamas and alpacas at *Ohio State University* (emphasis mine). It was found to be most effective against coccidia, even surpassing current drug therapies. It was also found to be safe during pregnancy and lactation."

I have administered Paravac™ to alpacas that joined my herd with good results. Cleanliness of your premises goes a long way in preventing an outbreak of coccidiosis.

Hoegger's Original Herbal Wormer

The *Hoegger Supply Company* compounded this natural dewormer for goats. Their catalog includes the conclusions from an independent study that was reported by *United Caprine News*. The product comes in powdered form. I put it on top of pelleted feed and crimped oats. Despite its bitter taste, the male alpacas on my farm consume the dewormer with great enthusiasm. The female alpacas all refuse to eat it. Because they are usually pregnant, I have not pressed the issue.

Rescue Remedy

Homeopathy is "a method of treating disease by minute doses of drugs that in a healthy person would produce symptoms similar to those of the disease" (*Webster's Dictionary*).

These minute doses must be given at regular and prescribed intervals to be effective. That makes, in my opinion, alpacas poor candidates for homeopathic treatments. Catching an alpaca several times a day to administer the treatment would greatly increase the sick animal's stress levels and therefore be counterproductive.

I keep one homeopathic remedy in stock. It is the famous Bach Flowers Rescue Remedy. If an animal experiences anaphylactic shock, homeopaths advise administering a dose of Rescue Remedy every fifteen minutes while waiting for a veterinarian to arrive.

Fly Spray

Another product I keep on hand is a natural spray repellent. Its ingredients include citronella and lemon grass oils. The spray is highly effective in keeping pesky gnats and flies away from the moist and tender ears of newborn crias. It works for adults as well. You can make your own spray by mixing half of a cup witch hazel, half of a cup apple cider vinegar, thirty drops of lemongrass oil, and thirty drops of lavender or peppermint oil.

Resources

This chapter is far from a comprehensive guide on herbal medicine. View the information presented here as merely an introduction. It was important to me that my readers initially embrace the wisdom of a natural approach to health and healing. I hope that it will motivate you to explore the subject in more depth. There is quite an extensive collection of literature available in this country that deals with a holistic approach to healing and preventing disease. If you are eager to learn, you may feel confused about where to begin.

To begin your studies, read the previously mentioned *Herbal Handbook for Farm and Stable*. The author presents such powerful arguments in support of her philosophy on caring for farm animals that it should be required reading for all veterinarians and farmers. Paul Dettloff D.V.M. wrote *Alternative Treatments for Ruminant Animals*. The book is full of good information and fascinating examples from Dr. Dettloff's large animal veterinary practice in Wisconsin. Pat Coleby is the author of *Natural Goat Care*. Her book includes practical advice on goat care, much of which is also pertinent for alpaca farmers. Another book I added to my library is *Prescription for Herbal Healing* by Phyllis A. Balch, CNC. This is an excellent choice if you are worried about negative side effects of herbal treatments. Each herb is given a general description—including its Latin name— followed by evidence of benefits and considerations for use. For example, the author tells you that garlic can counteract the effects of Lactobacillus cultures and should be avoided if you take blood-thinning drugs or have issues with your blood not clotting properly. The allicin in garlic can irritate the digestive system. That being said, the benefits of eating garlic are so tremendous that—unless allergies or special conditions exist—only a foolish person ignores nature's wonder drug.

Prescription for Herbal Healing was not written for livestock producers. None of the books mention alpacas. All are valuable resources for alpaca farmers. Those who keep a very narrow focus on alpaca specific informational materials are turning their backs on a wealth of resources.

I repeat the words of caution that I mentioned earlier: Herbal and other natural remedies are medicine in the true sense of the words. Before you administer any to your alpacas as part of a treatment plan, consult a professional and make sure that you are aware of correct dosage and contraindications, especially as they apply to young or pregnant animals. Using natural remedies (specifically a wide assortment of herbal pasture plants, apple cider vinegar, and probiotics) as part of a holistic approach to *prevent* illness, is, in my opinion, the easiest and also the most cost-effective plan for the frugal alpaca farmer.

11

REDUCING STRESS

"What stress? They eat, they pee and poop, they sun themselves...I'd like to be an alpaca on our farm sometimes." H.D.Wood

Stressed Alpacas

"Aha," you say, "we're finally getting to the point. I knew you'd eventually tell me how I can become happy and wealthy by selling alpacas. A life without stress, that's part of my plan."

Hold it, not so fast! The stress we're talking about is the alpacas' stress—often caused by their well-meaning, loving owners. Once, when I asked Hugh Masters of *Serenity Alpacas* for his input on a management concept, he told me, "I am more convinced than ever that many, maybe most, maladies suffered by alpacas are the result of stress." For quite a few years, Hugh and his wife, Carol, owned and managed one of the largest boarding facilities on the East Coast. I value their opinions.

Not all stress can be avoided, and a healthy alpaca is certainly equipped to deal with carefully planned procedures and interactions with humans.

Stressed Owners

The stress experienced by the animals has a direct effect on your finances. Stressed alpacas become ill and require costly veterinary services. Bought as a "huggable investment," your sick animals don't want to be hugged—actually, they never did—and their care will quickly turn any dream of earning money into a financial fiasco. Additionally, taking care of sick alpacas is a lot of work. The time that must be devoted to diagnosing a medical problem and nursing a sick animal back to health can play havoc with an alpaca farmer's schedule and energy level. A sick alpaca often does not want to be caught, confined, and treated. Its instincts tell it to stay with the herd and pretend that everything is all right. This can make nursing alpacas much more difficult and frustrating than, for example, nursing a sick dog back to health. Talk about stress!

Physical Effects of Stress

Producers of market animals are increasingly catching on to the fact that stress experienced by the animals diminishes their profits. Studies are commissioned, workshops are presented, and livestock producers are learning a gentle and soft approach to handling. Of course, cynics will tell you that their motivation is not the welfare of the animals but concern for their profits. Does it matter if the end result is the same?

For example, in one study a group of pigs was handled aggressively, the other group gently. In the first group, 20.4 percent of the pigs were classified as "downers" (sick), while the percentage of sick pigs in the gently handled group was zero (*Lancaster Farming Reference Guide*, 2003).

In mammals, adrenal glands are responsible for producing a precursor to hormones. They help to make and repair protein. They also make corticosterone and cortisol. These chemicals regulate glucose and energy balance, reduce responses to inflammation in the body, and regulate the immune system. What happens to the body during times of stress?

Stress has been proven to produce an excess of cortisol in mammals. The alpaca farmer who chooses to ignore scientific research results in regard to alpacas as well as their human caretakers is foolish. Dr. Fowler points out that, for example, blood glucose levels in llamas may be elevated due to restraint "stimulating catecholamine release."

While stress can cause illness over time, a severe stress factor can have immediate, devastating results. Gay L. Balliet presents an unfortunate example in *Lions, & Tigers & Mares…Oh, My!* Her veterinarian husband purchased a single llama baby for his wife as a Christmas present, a poor decision under any circumstances. When the petrified llama baby was released into an indoor riding arena, it "went berserk" (author's words). Startled at feeding time, Larry the llama bolted, crashed into a wall, and broke a leg. Balliet admits, "We felt terrible and responsible."

Stress Factors

An authority in the field of camelid medicine, Dr. Fowler devotes an entire chapter to stress. *It may just be the most important chapter you will read in his book.* He presents a long list of conditions that may trigger a stress response. A few examples are thirst, parasites, overcrowding, and restraint.

I believe that the majority of health problems can be avoided with proper management. The frugal alpaca farmer continuously evaluates the farm's environment as to its impact on the alpacas' stress levels.

Species Specific Instincts and Behavior

An animal experiences stress when its human caretakers refuse to use management practices that are aligned with the animal's instincts and what it considers reasonable behavior. This seems obvious to me yet many people—several generations removed from living on a farm—have a hard time understanding it.

All species—or breeds within a species—have unique needs. Wolves differ in their behavior from cats. Cows experience a sense of comfort and contentment from environmental conditions that would leave a herd of elephants bewildered and frustrated. A dog owner gets the best results when he respects his dog's natural instincts and the purpose the dog was bred for. For example, I would no more expect my Whippet to function as a Livestock Guardian Dog than I would hope for my alpacas to wag their tails when they see me enter the barn. Not confusing intelligence with obedience also helps to understand animal behavior.

What are an alpaca's natural instincts? We already discussed that the instinct of a prey animal is to flee from real or perceived danger. Because alpacas know that lack of mobility is a death sentence, they are strongly motivated to protect their legs. Like all prey animals, alpacas are suspicious of novel objects and experiences.

Instinct also governs reproductive behavior. In South America, wild camelid males—vicuñas and guanacos—fight one another over the right to breed. A dominant male protects and breeds a herd of females until a stronger challenger defeats it and either kills it or drives it off. All other males travel in bachelor herds. Like their wild cousins, male alpacas are attracted to open—not pregnant—females through smell and sight. Fighting among males escalates if open females are housed in their vicinity. A male alpaca that tries to wrestle its rival to the ground and slice open the other male's testicles with its fighting teeth is not mean but acting on instinctual behavior. The female alpaca's brain is hardwired to help it successfully raise its offspring. It protects its own baby's colostrum and milk supply by chasing other crias away should they come close. Although the alpaca is fiercely protective of healthy offspring, a strong survival instinct urges it to abandon a sick and weak cria that may jeopardize the safety of the herd with its inability to flee from predators.

For several thousand years, alpacas have been bred for superior fiber. Human selection pressure did not favor behavioral character traits such as getting along well with human beings. Llamas had to "play nicely with the other children"—human beings and other llamas—to efficiently perform their job as pack animals. Alpacas had to be good at producing fiber and making crias. Being docile and nice to human beings were not important traits. If anything, alpacas that trusted their caretakers often ended up as charqui—dried strips of alpaca meat. They were much easier to lasso than their skittish counterparts.

Because stragglers are more likely to be killed by predators on open grazing land, natural selection pressure took care of those that refused to stay close to the herd. Staying close to the herd was good. It meant safety and survival. Alpacas that are raised in countries where they are protected by fences and livestock guardians nevertheless still feel a strong urge to remain close to other members of the herd. Being separated from the herd is cause for alarm and fear.

As their caretaker, remember and respect the alpaca's original purpose and don't expect the impossible. Don't demand compliance with behavioral expectations your animals can't possibly understand. Make it a cardinal rule not to try to make your alpacas or your spouse into something they're not. Enjoy them the way they are. That said, you'll be surprised how alpacas respond favorably to patient and skilled handling and training. When we consider the alpaca's long history as to its primary purpose, we should be amazed at its willingness to form any kind of bond with people.

Animal Emotions

I recently read about the history of wolves in the United States. Talking about the animal stories written by Ernest Thompson Seton, the author described how "hunters, biologists, and naturalists cringed at the sentimental schlock and anthropomorphic fluff that oozed from Seton's short stories" (Jon T. Coleman). In one story, Seton described how a wolf died from "a broken heart" after it searched for and found its mate, Blanca, slaughtered and staked out to lure the male into a hunter's trap. Wolves enjoy rich social lives and form close relationships with their mates. Is it really "sentimental schlock" to assume that a male misses and pines for its dead mate? Is it anthropomorphic fluff when we talk about alpaca emotions? Why are human beings so reluctant to acknowledge that species other than *Homo sapiens* feel a spectrum of emotions? Is it arrogance, or are there possibly feelings of guilt we do not wish to face up to?

Alpacas are not human beings in fiber coats. Their emotions do not always mimic those felt by human beings, but the animals nevertheless feel—in the true sense of the word—emotions: alpaca emotions!

Dr. Temple Grandin, who advocates tirelessly on behalf of all livestock species, has this to say: "I believe that the best way to create good living conditions for any animal, whether it's a captive animal in a zoo, a farm animal or a pet, is to base animal welfare programs on the core emotion systems in the brain." (Read Dr. Grandin's book *Animals in Translation* (2005) for extensive information on core emotions.)

Don't Impose a Human Moral Code

We must be careful not to impose human moral standards of behavior on animals. To yell at a bitch for eating each puppy's placenta would be as ignorant as punishing her for killing a deformed or sickly puppy. These acts are neither "disgusting" nor do they make her a "bad" mother—they make her a dog. Likewise, as I already pointed out, an alpaca normally devoted to its crias may leave a cria if it senses that the baby is sickly and near death. In herd animals that are vulnerable to predators, the survival of the group must take priority over saving one life. These instincts still exist in domesticated livestock or pets.

Herd Members

The alpaca has a strong herd instinct. It is happiest as a member of a group. Stress levels can be reduced by making sure that no alpaca is kept without another alpaca as a companion. On several farms, I saw males kept in isolation because they could not get along with other males. Sometimes, this type of behavior is created by poorly designed infrastructure or poor management protocols. Other times, the cause may be of genetic origin. Good pastures contribute greatly to a calm alpaca farm environment. Alpacas that must work for their food by grazing are too busy to fight. Other livestock species are, in my opinion, not appropriate companions for alpacas.

Rich Social Lives

People who are insensitive to the needs of animals often refuse to believe that mammals other than human beings have rich social lives. A holistic approach to owning and breeding alpacas needs to discard such an attitude. Alpacas have distinctly individual personalities. This is evident in the way they react to one another. An alpaca will like some herd members while feeling indifferent toward or even disliking others. In some cases, two individuals will be so antagonistic toward each other that their constant feuding upsets the entire herd. In that case, it's best to sell one of the combatants.

Alpacas that form close relationships and friendships grieve when those are severed due to death or sales. After close to two decades of breeding alpacas, I feel so strongly about the importance of their social lives that I offer a substantial discount in order to sell and send two animals—particularly females—together to another farm. The chosen two may not have been best friends on *Stormwind Farm*, but they will be an emotional support system for each other when they leave their old comfort zone.

The Alpaca Social Hierarchy

The concept of equal rights for all does not exist in the animal world. Accept the fact that an alpaca herd has a chain of command, with the animals on the lower rungs being ordered about by those in charge. Make it easy for the former to comply with the wishes of the latter. For example, it is important to make barn doors wide enough so individuals on the bottom of the hierarchy can pass the more dominant animals to go outside. An alpaca that is ordered by the herd boss to move but can't because of crowding and poor barn design is a very stressed alpaca.

As their caretaker, respect and acknowledge the herd's social order. Don't make the dominant animal wait to eat "to teach it a lesson." Do not interfere when the alpaca mothers discipline their crias. Although their actions may strike you as very harsh at times, the alpacas are better judges than you are when it comes to their crias' upbringing.

If you're smart, your management plan revolves around the personality and habits of the boss lady. It's wise to "make nice" with her and make her your partner. The herd boss has a great influence on how the other alpacas view you, and how willing they will be to cooperate.

Good Touch – Bad Touch

Although alpacas are typical herd animals, they like their personal space. There are some exceptions. Crias will often rest against their moms. They also "kiss" one another and explore their world by touching other babies as well as adults with their noses. They are quickly taught by older herd members, however, that prolonged physical contact is not proper alpaca etiquette. Adult females that are *not* pregnant are often somewhat tolerant of soft nuzzling from crias that are not their own babies, their female alpaca friends, or even intact males. An alpaca will often engage in a prolonged "kissing" session with its cria. Some farmers—I include myself in this group—believe that the purpose is to "seed" the cria's intestinal system with good bacteria. Aside from these exceptions, the normal reaction of a pregnant female to being touched by another alpaca is often the arched neck, the ears pinned back, and finally—should the socially inept culprit persist—a juicy volley of regurgitated cud.

Should it then come as a total surprise that alpacas do not like to be touched by people? Forget the "huggable investment" nonsense! Grabbing, reaching out to, and—unfortunately for the huggers among us—hugging your alpacas activates their flight response. That doesn't mean that you can't or shouldn't ever touch them. Regular maintenance requires you to handle, contain, and occasionally even restrain the animals to various degrees. That is not a problem if you remember that "less is more." Marty McGee Bennett advises camelid owners not to continuously reach out and touch the animals under the mistaken belief that frequent touching will desensitize them. This advice may not sound right to you now. It will after you've owned alpacas for a while. Restrain yourself, and you will be rewarded. If you desire physical closeness and contact with your alpacas, take a passive role. Allow them to approach you! Show respect for the alpacas' wishes not to be touched at every opportunity, and they will come to trust you.

The Sunshine Law

On our farm, alpacas know that they will only be touched inside a catch pen. I apply what I call the *Sunshine Law* when I work with my alpacas. There is full disclosure of all my intentions. The alpacas are very much aware of what is about to happen—haltering, trimming nails, inoculations, and other care protocols—and this awareness gives them comfort. There are no surprises. The alpacas thank me for my consideration by reacting to my presence in their midst with calm acceptance.

Give Them Space

Breeders must respect the alpaca's need for space and not force the herd to live under crowded conditions. Figure out how many alpacas can cush in your barn without touching or being very close to one another and then don't exceed that number. I believe that space requirements depend to some extent on the personalities of your animals and on the stability of your herd. Alpacas are constantly arriving and leaving? Their owners should arrange for more space per animal than those that have relatively stable populations. Climate should also dictate space requirements. In a mild climate where alpacas are rarely confined to a barn, a few hours spent in close quarters here and there should not cause undue stress. If your alpacas cannot graze, run, and play outdoors for days at a time, they need lots of barn space to feel comfortable.

Give Respect—Demand Respect

Although you are not the herd boss, failing to set boundaries and not enforcing rules will confuse the animals and cause stress. The relationship between a human being and an alpaca is a little more complicated than the one you have with your pet dog. Trying to emulate the predator/predator relationship that you have with your dog will have disastrous results with your alpacas. You cannot expect obedience from an alpaca as you would from a dog. Never attempt to physically dominate an alpaca to show it "who is in charge." Marty McGee Bennett urges farmers to work with their alpacas' instincts and not turn interactions into a battle of wills or dominance displays. Alpacas have memories like elephants! They are not quick to forgive and forget. Once you've tried to manhandle an alpaca into submission, its trust in you is gone for a long, long time. Because very few people have the strength to physically dominate an adult alpaca, it is foolish to try to do so. The smart strategy therefore is to handle and train it in such a way that the alpaca never realizes its superior strength.

Although each group of alpacas within the larger herd on a farm has its own herd boss, a caretaker must establish his or her role as a leader whose rules must be obeyed. Standing quietly for inoculations and nail trimming, leaving an area when directed to do so, quietly permitting the brief inspection of a newborn cria—these are reasonable rules that a human leader can expect to be followed. One effective strategy to establish leadership takes only a few seconds and does not require physical contact. Horse trainers discovered that forcing a horse to move and allowing the human being to occupy the vacated space emulates the behavior of the dominant herd member. Horses understand this language and accept the message. It works with alpacas. I regularly look for and find opportunities to force my male alpacas to vacate their space in the pasture for me, without so much as putting a finger on their bodies.

Ultimately, though, the issue is one of mutual respect. I respect the alpacas' unique emotional needs and behavioral characteristics; they respect my leadership role, and that I direct and structure certain aspects of their lives.

Body Language

Prey animals are extremely observant and are masters in reading body language. It is important to relax your posture and breathe evenly while working with the animals. Test yourself! While inoculating or body scoring, you may catch yourself holding your breath more times than not. You transmit this tension to the alpacas.

"She's holding her breath," they think, "something bad is bound to happen soon."

Breathe slowly, relax your shoulders, soften your touch—the alpacas will respond in kind. It's best to initially practice this without the added complication of actually performing maintenance procedures.

Relaxing your body is not synonymous with a timid approach. An effective leader is calm yet moves with an assertive confidence. Unforeseen problems, mishaps, and difficulties? The leader remains unflappable. If a person desires to control the actions of others, be they people or animals, he or she must first be in control of him or herself. Animals give their trust and respect to those who remain in calm control of their emotions and body language.

Sing to Reduce Stress

"This sounds like so much female emotional humbug to me," one visitor to our farm scoffed.

I had told him that I sing softly to an alpaca that has not learned to trust me yet and is nervous about being handled.

Hmm, female emotional humbug? Interesting! Have you ever watched an old cowboy movie? Did you think those manly cowboys singing softly while circling the huge herds of cattle at night were just a tad ridiculous—a Hollywood producer's romantic vision of life in the saddle? Did those hardened men sing out of longing for their sweethearts, or because they harbored secret ambitions to have careers as vocalists? No, you greenhorn! The men crooned softly during those long, dark nights on the prairie to keep their four-legged charges from stampeding. Stampedes translated into stress. That meant loss of weight, drying up of milk, injuries, and deaths. Fewer cattle reached the slaughterhouses; that meant less money for the cattle barons and their employees, the cowboys.

What would my visitor have said if he had known that I also sing to my crias during halter training to reduce stress? I make up little songs as we wander together around the pasture. Singing to the crias works like magic. Who says you have to be a man on a horse to sing to your animals?

Forced Weaning

A huge stress factor is forced, early weaning. I don't approve of it—except under extremely rare, extenuating circumstances—and will discuss my reasons in detail in the chapter on cria care.

Feeding Alpacas

Feeding time offers an excellent opportunity to use smart management techniques designed to eliminate stress. In general, feeding time should be calm and scheduled at a time of the day that does not require the caretaker to rush. Animals are creatures of habit. It is easy to accustom alpacas to an orderly routine, provided you take their unique behavioral traits into consideration.

The stress felt by alpacas forced to eat in close contact with and, worse yet, directly facing another animal, must be incredible. This is especially true of intact, sexually mature males and pregnant females.

Over almost two decades, I experimented with various feeding locations and routines. My present protocol has worked well for several years. The key concept—to avoid fighting and stress—is to keep the alpacas *out of the feeding area until all feed has been distributed in their individual feed dishes.* From spring through fall, the "dining parlor" consists of an outdoor area closed off with connected livestock panels throughout the day. As a special privilege, the alpacas are permitted to enter it to eat their grain or pellets. After the grain has been consumed, all alpacas are herded out of the parlor. A small catch pen is set up next to the area. If I wish to breed, behavior test, or train an alpaca, it is easy to herd an individual animal from the parlor into the catch pen. During the winter, the feeding stations are set up inside the barn. As with the outdoor parlor, the barn doors remain closed and the alpacas outside while I distribute the feed. The winter catch pen is set up outside next to the barn.

Females and youngsters are fed in a group setting. Individual dishes are placed in such a way that no two alpacas face each other. Dishes should be placed at least three feet apart. To further avoid conflict resulting in stress, I set out one more dish than the number of alpacas. Individual females choose their feed station each day. The feeding routine for the mature males is very rigid. Feed dishes are placed as far apart as barn space will allow. Like the females, males do not enter the barn until feed has been distributed. Each male has its own, permanently assigned station. It took a few days until the males and I sorted out where each individual should be eating, but before long, they all peacefully fell into a routine. In contrast, I have never been able to assign permanent stations to the females and finally gave up trying.

Each barn has a hay feeder that measures five square feet. Although the alpacas face one another while they stand around the feeder and eat, the piled-up hay prevents direct eye contact. There is room in each barn for an additional feeder should that become necessary. It is important to provide more than one water bucket if it is possible for an animal to block access to a single bucket. In my herd, this is never an issue with the males. They drink their fill and move on. In contrast, the pregnant ladies get temperamental at times and stand by the water bucket without drinking and for the sole purpose of joyfully irritating other members of their herd.

It's best to be flexible. Feeding management plans may evolve and change as the size of a herd increases or decreases. Herd dynamics—including the temperament of the herd boss—will impact a farmer's decisions and protocols.

Herding Alpacas

The alpaca's brain is hard-wired to fear predators. Because predators chase their prey, to an alpaca, being chased means being attacked and killed. When a farmer chases alpacas around the pasture or a barn, it creates an atmosphere of fear and hysteria. Stress levels go through the roof for the chased alpacas as well as the farmer doing the chasing.

"How am I supposed to catch my alpacas then?" one frustrated farmer asked me.

There are two herding techniques that are very effective. With one, you use herding wands; with the other, a herding tape helps you to calmly move the alpaca into a confinement area. Herding wands work well, for example, when alpacas are moved from a small holding area into an even smaller catch pen. They should be light and roughly fifty to sixty inches long. There is no need to purchase special wands. Any slender, light-weight rod will do just fine. A herding tape is a flat piece of nylon or cotton webbing. It can be several inches wide and as long as you can comfortably handle. A herding tape is helpful in a large holding area or even a small pasture. One end is tied to a post in your pasture. You grasp the other end and walk far enough to effectively form a corral with your body acting as a second post. Take care to keep the herding tape stretched taut at waist level. Walking briskly but calmly, you now move forward as you herd the alpacas into the designated area. Most animals will rarely challenge this moving corral. Of course, when one does and is in danger of becoming entangled, you must immediately drop the tape. The herding tape works like magic with alpacas that are not the sharpest pencils in the box. Very intelligent individuals quickly figure out how to dive below the tape and elude capture.

As with all handling and training techniques, maximize your chances for success by working with the animals' instincts. Prey animals are reluctant to enter dark spaces. Trying to herd alpacas into a catch pen in a dark corner of the barn may be difficult. It's much easier to herd from a dark area inside the barn into a catch pen set up outdoors. For females and crias, the catch pen should be as small as possible. It should have enough room for you to walk around in, but the animals should be fairly close to one another. Very young males can be herded and confined the same way as females. In contrast, herding a group of sexually mature and active male alpacas into a small catch pen is asking for problems. To manage males, it's wise to ignore much of what you learned about herding and confining females and crias. On *Stormwind Farm*, we use a holding area that is approximately thirty feet long and twenty feet wide for three adult males. Inside this holding area is a small catch pen. Each male is individually herded into the catch pen when, for example, I plan to administer inoculations or a dewormer.

Venus and Mars

"Something doesn't make sense here," you probably think now. "First you tell me that alpacas need their personal space to be happy; now you're advising me to pack them in like sardines. And what's up with crowding the females together but not the males?"

John Gray wrote about the differences between human males and females in *Men Are From Mars, Women Are From Venus*. I agree with the author. Those of you who believe that the differences between the sexes are purely cultural and due to the way children are raised may think whatever you want about Mr. Gray's book. As alpaca farmers, you will do well to acknowledge the inherent differences between females and males. Female alpacas and male crias like to crowd closely together when they are frightened and feel threatened. That is because the adult females' instinct is to protect their offspring by keeping them close and surrounding all crias in a herd for protection. With rare exceptions, a sexually mature male alpaca is only interested in protecting itself and its own equipment and using it whenever an opportunity presents itself. Confining two or more adult males inside a small catch pen is potentially dangerous. Presenting a haltered and restrained female *or* male to an unrestrained, intact male alpaca is an open invitation for the unrestrained animal to mount and try to breed the alpaca held captive by halter, lead, and a clueless owner. A mature male alpaca will not stand or sit still for another male to mount and force it to assume a cushed position. If you persist in this handling technique, your pen may be the sight of a battle you won't believe and may very well not have the strength to stop. A fellow alpaca farmer described such a scene to me. Trying to break up the fight, she was extremely lucky to escape with bruises. It is far safer and less stressful for all participants to catch males one at a time. Occasionally, a second or even third male will enter the catch pen uninvited. The intruders should be shooed outside with the help of herding wands before you even pull the halter and lead out of your pocket. Once a male is haltered, and you plan to, for example, trim toenails, any handling should take place where herd members cannot touch or even get close to the confined alpaca. The reasons for that should be obvious to all readers at this point.

I fully believe that life in our alpaca pastures is so harmonious because I acknowledge the fact that males are from Mars, and females are from Venus, and that I address this belief in all aspects of the alpacas' lives. Interestingly, our males often like to show off and stage "play fights" to try and impress two-legged visitors. They don't fool me or the female alpacas. The latter pay no attention to this silly behavior but stand at the fence—eyes and ears wide open—when two males occasionally fight with serious intent to hurt each other. This usually only happens when females are open.

Inoculations and Dewormers by Injection

After females and crias are herded into the catch pen, I can inject a dewormer or give an inoculation. I neither halter nor actively restrain the female alpacas and crias in any way during this procedure. A carpenter's apron tied around my waist holds the prepared syringes. After an injection has been given, I dispose of the syringe by throwing it into a container placed outside the catch pen. From the time I start herding until all alpacas are released from the catch pen, I remain calm and aware of my body language. My shoulders are relaxed; I don't hold my breath while I insert the needle below the skin; my movements are slow yet decisive. A nervous alpaca jerks away from my touch? I don't react by mimicking its behavior. If anything, I relax my body and breathing even more. My message: "You may be scared, but I assure you that I mean no harm." When I demonstrate my techniques to fellow farmers, I request that they remain a few feet away from the catch pen and keep their voices down. Most stare in utter amazement while I quietly go about my business.

Males are herded into a catch pen one at a time. Depending on the alpaca's temperament, I either give injections without restraint or halter the animal and loop the lead loosely around one of the catch pen bars. If I decide to trim toenails as well that day, each male is haltered and led into a chute for both procedures.

Trimming Nails

Having their nails trimmed is a very stressful procedure for many alpacas. Grazing prey animals die without the use of their legs. It is hardly surprising that alpacas protect their legs with ferocious determination. The handler must convince them that having their nails trimmed will not jeopardize their mobility. I use the techniques outlined in the *Camelidynamics* program. My body language communicates that I am relaxed. Each foot is kept low to the ground while the nails are trimmed. I do not pull the leg toward me—this would throw off the alpaca's balance—but keep the raised foot aligned with the natural position of the shoulder or hip. The hand cradles the foot loosely. Some alpacas can be haltered and their lead lines tied to a post for nail trimming. Others may feel more comfortable and cooperate more willingly while contained in a chute. Both techniques require patient training prior to the first nail being snipped. A few alpacas may allow a single person to trim their nails without any restraint. Regardless of the technique being used, the handler should refrain from applying what I call a death grip on the alpaca's legs and feet.

Oral Dewormers, Medication, and Vitamins

The same concepts apply when we administer oral medication or vitamins to the animals. Most alpacas that put up a struggle would probably accept the procedure with calm resignation if the owners did not apply a tight strangle hold around their necks. Practice your moves on a family member, a friend, or a willing canine partner. I describe them in more detail in a future chapter.

Halter Stress

One of the biggest stress factors on many alpaca farms are poorly fitting halters. I've also seen alpacas gasp for air and thrash around at the ends of their lead ropes at shows and sales while their clueless owners wondered why their animals behaved so badly. An alpaca wearing a poorly fitted halter is literally fighting for each breath. Marty McGee Bennett refers to these terrified creatures as "drowning victims." She designed a halter that can be adjusted to fit any type of alpaca head. The *Zephyr* halter, if fitted properly, will make handling and training an alpaca a pleasure. The halter should be removed when the animal returns to grazing. It must be periodically adjusted to allow for fiber growth.

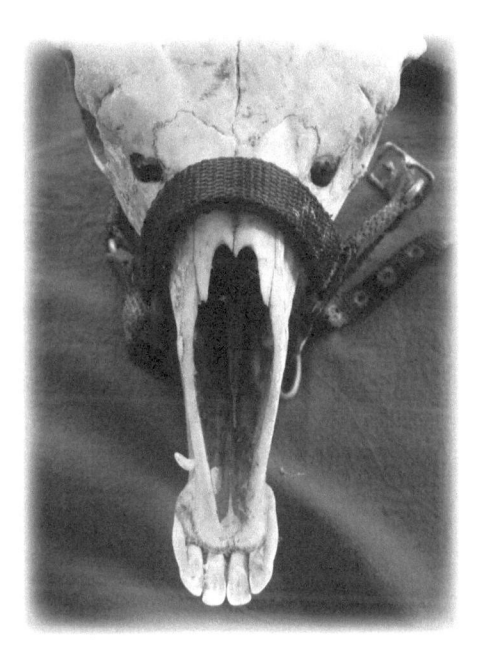

Heat Stress

Heat stress is completely preventable. Plenty of fresh, clean water, electrolytes, fans, and cooling water sprays will keep alpacas comfortable and prevent heat stress. I don't know where the myth started that you should only hose off an alpaca's belly and lower legs. Although you should *not hose a fully fleeced* animal from head to toe, you can certainly do so for several months *after shearing* when the fiber is short. One male in my herd likes only legs and belly hosed. The other alpacas demand the full treatment—a good soaking from their necks to their feet. Breeze, our oldest female, enjoys heavy water pressure. This old alpaca lady acts just like a person receiving a water massage. She absolutely loves it—the colder and harder the better! I think it's great for her circulation and gladly indulge her several times a day during the summer. Babies that are born during a hot, dry spell benefit from being sprayed in other ways as well. When it finally does rain, they're used to the water and are willing to do their toilet business out in the pouring rain. No sissies peeing in the barn because they don't like to get wet!

Total Restraint

In general, forceful restraint is very stressful to alpacas. When giving injections, for example, it's not the brief sting of the needle that causes stress but the death grip that many alpaca farmers use to restrain the animal for the procedure. There are several maintenance procedures, however, where total restraint is warranted for the safety of the animals. Quick, decisive action to restrain an alpaca—such as placing and tying it to a shearing table—does not, in my experience, lead to lingering resentment and extreme fear reactions. It's the prolonged and frequent "battles of the will" that cause lasting problems.

Does It Pay?

It pays to gently accustom alpacas to being handled. I know farmers whose animals are so unmanageable that their veterinarian has to tranquilize them for routine procedures. That's not only a health issue but a big financial burden as well. A bill for a farm visit and tranquilizing medication to trim nails? Not on my budget!

Aside from the reasons already mentioned, presenting mannerly, easily handled alpacas may help you with marketing your animals. Although you should brace yourself to meet indifference to the time you've spent handling and training your crias, this will not be true of all buyers. Your animals' high tractability will surely convince the right person one day that you are the alpaca farmer he or she wants to do business with.

Finally, let's keep my definition of a holistic approach to raising alpacas in mind. *Your* emotional health is as important as that of your animals. With proper handling and training techniques, your own level of stress will be low. You will enjoy the alpacas and your life on the farm.

Resources

I recommend that you read Marty McGee Bennett's *The Camelid Companion*. Attending one of her seminars will further help you to reduce and avoid stress on your farm.

12

COME TO YOUR SENSES!

"Forget your foolish dreams, Ingrid. Come to your senses!" Anna Görgen

Camels and Bikinis

In 1995, when I first discovered alpacas, I excitedly wrote to my family in Germany about our plan to buy a farm and raise alpacas. The response was—well, let's call it decidedly mixed. My brother, Dieter, pronounced me way too old to start such a business. I was forty-five years old! My sisters, Margit and Karin, burst into hysterical laughter and described their visions of me sitting atop an alpaca in a gold lamé bikini performing daring circus stunts. Good Lord! I think they had alpacas mixed up with camels. Aside from that, my bikini days were long past.

A very serious letter arrived from my thoroughly alarmed mother who urged, "Come to your senses!"

This I did, but not in the way she envisioned.

A Family Tradition

Literally and figuratively, I came to my senses by using them to observe the alpacas. Come to think of it, I continue a family tradition. When I was a child, our family did not need a doctor to diagnose the onset of an illness. My father only had to hold us children close and breathe in our scent. His sense of smell alerted him to health issues that often did not manifest themselves until the next day. As a young mother, I could predict a fever or general malaise in my baby son hours before he came down with it. His face would take on a pinched, drawn look.

"He looks perfectly fine to me," my husband always argued.

Fortunately, our child was seldom ill.

Squeezing Whippets

As a breeder of racing Whippets, I employed another sense to select a puppy for a specific purpose. When Whippet puppies were born on *Stormwind Farm*, I waited no longer than twenty-four hours for my famous squeeze test, developed and patented—just kidding—to predict future racing talents. Once the little ones plumped up from nursing and their dam felt comfortable and relaxed, I settled down in front of the litter box. With eyes closed, I gently kneaded and squeezed the tiny bodies. My hands roved steadily over and around the pile of snoozing puppies until my touch determined the future star: The puppy which, due to superior muscle tone, would grow up to be the best racer and courser in the litter. In five litters—two were bred by friends—my touch test correctly predicted performance achievement. The next to the last litter left me stymied. After eliminating one candidate, I was unable to choose between the three remaining litter sisters. Although they had very different temperaments, they turned out to be very uniform in physical ability. All three garnered prestigious racing titles.

This has, of course, nothing to do with alpacas, and it has everything to do with alpacas. If you want to avoid high veterinary bills, you must use your senses to daily evaluate your herd.

Use Your Sense of Sight

Are all alpacas grazing vigorously or chewing their cud? Are their eyes bright, clear, and alert? Does any herd member limp or seem to stand slightly off balance? Observe your female alpacas. Is the one near the males' fence line cushed to indicate it is no longer pregnant? Does the vulva of an alpaca look enlarged, meaning it is getting ready to give birth? Check the new cria. Does it seem energetic when walking, or is it listless and appears exhausted? Do you notice a little milk mustache when it finishes nursing? Pay attention to the older males. Do you see blood on anybody? Maybe it's time to file fighting teeth before they seriously injure one another. Do you see diarrhea or huge clumps of stool at the community dung pile? Do any of the alpacas foam at the month or drool saliva?

Use Your Sense of Smell

Does the dung have an unusual odor? The smell of normal alpaca dung from healthy animals is barely detectable, especially if the piles are removed from barn and pastures on a daily basis. A strong fecal odor can be the sign of a health problem. When you get close to an animal, does its breath have a peculiar smell? Does the hay smell musty? What about the smell of the drinking water? The pelleted feed?

Use Your Sense of Hearing

Are any of the alpacas humming? Moms hum to their crias, and that's normal. When strangers are present, humming means: "I don't know who those two-legged creatures are and what they have in mind. Let's stay alert." Humming may also be a way of expressing physical discomfort or pain. Alpacas that are ready to give birth often hum. Know your animals and learn to interpret individual reasons for humming. Do you hear wheezing, coughing, or choking sounds?

Use Your Sense of Touch

If you wish that the alpacas feel comfortable in your presence, limit touching to weekly body scoring. Familiarize yourself with what a properly fleshed-out but not fat alpaca feels like. Run your hands along each animal's spine and find the hip bones. Put your hands in the fleece. Does it feel unusually coarse compared to your last check? Coarsening fiber can be a sign of illness or parasites. Fiber coarsens naturally as the animal ages. Be aware that fiber feels much softer in high humidity.

Use Your Sense of Taste

Does the hat you knitted for Aunt Chloe look as fashionable and tasteful as you thought it did? Did you put a little too much sugar in Ingrid's apple cake recipe? O.K., just kidding! Maybe you can come up with areas where your sense of taste is important. I can only think of water. Well, maybe one other scenario. You don't own a gelding to be the sacrificial taster for a new bag of food? No problem!

"Honey, would you mind changing your breakfast cereal this morning? It's a new brand. It looks great, I just want you to taste it and tell me what you think—"

Alpacas Are Stoic

Alpacas have been described as extremely stoic. Farmers often report that when one of their animals died, they never knew it was sick. That's possible. I don't believe that it's always impossible to tell that a camelid is sick until it's too late to treat and cure it. Farmers who "never knew" simply didn't take the time to observe their herd for subtle signs or did not have the knowledge to diagnose the problem. True, alpacas are prey animals and as such try hard to disguise the fact that they are ill and therefore vulnerable to attack by stronger herd members and predators. Nevertheless, once you have lived with your alpacas for a while, you'll recognize small signs that all is not well. Of course, all of us are pressed for time some days or are occupied with thoughts about family, children, jobs, or other concerns. It's easy then to miss critical warning signals. That doesn't mean that they weren't there. If one of my females ever refused the small amount of supplements I feed each day, I would immediately be on high alert. Be aware that alpacas will usually refuse feed after a fight. The hanging lower lip—the result of a spitting contest—makes eating impossible. If that is ruled out, I would know something wasn't right. Staying cushed for unusually long periods of time, foaming at the mouth, drooling, clumped feces or diarrhea, persistent humming at unusual times, a glassy stare, not chewing their cud for extended periods of time—there are plenty of signals for the alert farmer to detect and interpret. If you're not familiar with an animal's personality, detecting first signs of trouble is much more difficult. Friends of ours, who are extremely observant and vigilant, lost a beautiful young male that they had purchased.

"This alpaca was very quiet," my friend told me. "We thought it was its natural reserve and not being used to its new surroundings."

Alpacas are, in a very real sense, individuals with many different personalities. Their emotional fabric runs the gamut from very shy to bold—not unlike those of their human caretakers—and an animal that's not rambunctious isn't necessarily ill. An attentive farmer takes the time to get to know these individual traits.

A Few Minutes? Not Enough Time!

Running to the barn and throwing a few flakes of hay on the ground once a day is not a smart management practice if you want to keep losses and expenses to a minimum. I am a very fast and energetic worker and can properly clean up dung, freshen up water buckets, put out hay and feed supplements to a small herd —let's say ten animals—in roughly fifteen minutes. This time frame, however, would not allow me to observe the herd. Good animal care requires us to slow down. People who rush through life at breakneck speed seldom make good livestock farmers.

Visits to the Back-Forty

When pastures are green and juicy, our alpacas occasionally don't bother to respond to my call for a feeding of supplements. What happens to my program of using my senses when the alpacas elect to stay out on the back-forty instead of reporting to the barn area? *I walk out to see them.* A sick or injured dog will instinctively keep its distance from the rest of the group. A sick or injured alpaca will often try to remain with the herd at all cost. That's an important difference between predators and prey animals. A sick alpaca will usually not leave the herd and stay in the barn, thus alerting you to a problem. That is precisely the reason I trek out, if necessary, to the far pasture for the daily, visual health check.

Weather Extremes

During weather extremes, herd health calls for the most attentive observations. On brutally hot summer days, I repeatedly hose down alpacas and watch for signs of heat stress. During the winter, I watch the older alpacas for signs of shivering. No matter how hot or how cold it is, I take the time to look, listen, smell, and (occasionally!) touch. I feel a special, spiritual closeness to the alpacas during those times.

Fish with Fur

A farmer once said to me, "We don't worry much about the alpacas getting sick or dying. That's why we pay insurance."

How sad for the animals. What a poor excuse for a livestock farmer this man was! When sales prices for alpacas were very high, farmers with such attitudes could do quite well financially. Those days are in the past, and I doubt that they'll return. Frugal alpaca farmers must use the power of their senses to prevent illness and death. If you view the alpacas strictly as money machines, your interest in them will quickly fade and caring for them will literally become a dreaded chore that you will come to resent. If you don't like *being* with the animals, you will not enjoy raising alpacas. I truly believe that caring for and spending as much time with the alpacas as your schedule allows will benefit your health as well. Years ago, a visitor to *Serenity Alpacas* described their alpacas as "fish with fur"—so relaxing and soothing to watch. An astute observation!

Sense of Contentment

Among your non-farming friends, few or none will possess the knowledge and observational skills to recognize a problem with an alpaca during your absence. On a limited budget, it therefore won't be easy to leave your herd to go on vacation unless family members go in shifts. Even with extra money available, you may have difficulty finding a suitable and trustworthy caretaker. You will be unhappy unless you feel a true *sense of contentment* to stay on your farm.

Common Sense

Every alpaca farmer should have the most important sense of all, and that's—tongue in cheek—*common sense*. In my experience, people who survive and *thrive* on small budgets often possess good, common sense in abundance. If you use common sense and all your other senses to purchase, care for, market, and sell alpacas, you should be well on the road to success as an alpaca farmer.

After writing the last paragraph, I asked myself, "What is common sense? How is it defined?"

Sometimes, it's easier to define a concept by explaining what it is not. The fellows who installed the staircase inside our house without checking whether the floor was level did not have common sense. The alpaca farmer who gave a newborn cria six enemas because she had not seen it pass meconium did not have common sense. Neither did the alpaca farmers who bought what they thought were two female alpacas only to discover that one was a male. We all have times when we slap our foreheads and shout, "How could I have been so stupid?" That will happen. It can't happen very often if you hope to make a profit. There are professions that reward intellectual brilliance coupled with a lack of common sense. Farming isn't one of them.

Sense of Accomplishment

Meantime, what's my family's reaction more than a decade later? My relatives adore the alpacas. Many follow the births and the events held on *Stormwind Farm* by visiting our website. I often think of my mother's warning while I am outside with the animals using all my senses. Although she never understood my fascination with and love for animals and farming, she came to appreciate the alpacas. She was visiting from Germany when Hugh and Carol Masters delivered our first two alpacas, Breeze and Harley. Looking out her second floor bedroom window every morning, my mother delighted in seeing the alpacas calmly grazing in their pasture. She was a very nervous woman, and I think she appreciated the quiet and soothing presence of the "speechless brothers." We never talked about how she had tried so hard to deter me from making my "foolish dreams" become reality. We didn't have to do so. My mother's change of mind and happiness while visiting our small farm was clearly evident. The alpacas had captured her heart. As a gifted artist who loved to work with fabrics and yarn, she would have had much to contribute to the retail side of our business. She surely would have been amazed to see me spin and knit. As a child, I hated all sedate activities except reading. I was a virtual terror in my school's home economics room. Instructed to sew an apron, I bollixed up the works on three sewing machines and was finally condemned to finish my project by hand. I still remember with dread the gloves I had to knit and never finished. It took alpaca fiber to awaken my interest in the fiber arts. Who can resist *feeling* baby soft alpaca, *looking* at the amazing variety of colors and patterns, *smelling* its clean, natural scent, *listening* to the faint, comforting whirring of the spinning wheel or the clicking of knitting needles, and *tasting* the delicious goodies your spinning friends brought to share? My guests and I look out the windows and see the alpacas graze while we're spinning and knitting their fiber.

Yes, I've come to my senses. I set out each morning eager to complete the tasks that I've scheduled for that day. Some are easy; others are hard. Several are routine, daily maintenance protocols such as cleaning pastures and scrubbing and filling water buckets. Some—trimming alpaca nails, for example—are performed only every six weeks. Others—weeding the vegetable garden comes to mind—are done daily during the growing season but not at all during the winter. All tasks have several things in common. I perform them outdoors, I see the alpacas while I work, and at the end of the day, I feel a deep *sense of accomplishment.*

That gold lamé bikini? In another lifetime!

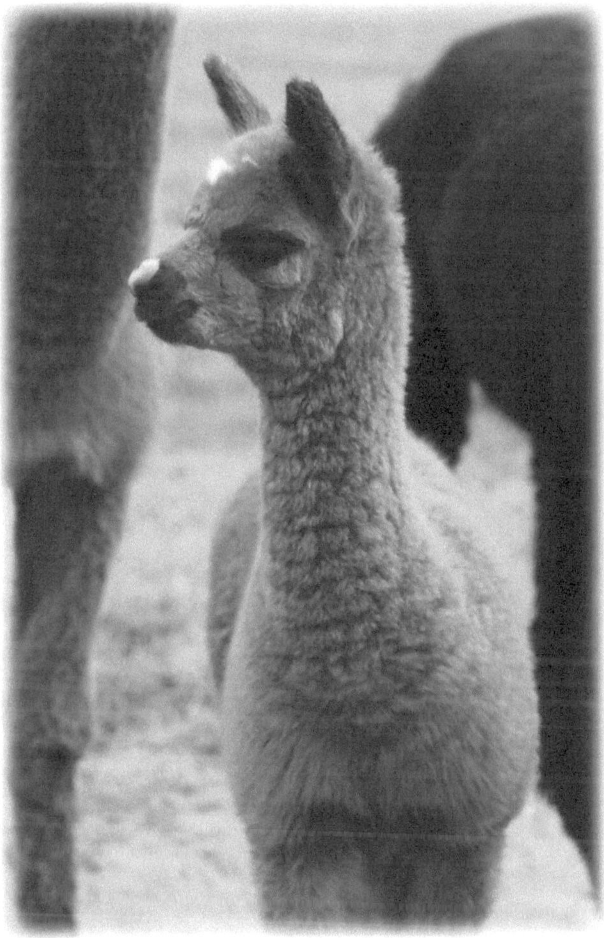

13

MEDICAL MAINTENANCE

"Keeping good medical records has helped me to enjoy low veterinary bills on my farm." Diann Mellott

Your Veterinarian

When owners of dogs and cats manage the medical maintenance of their pets, they consult with the veterinarians who care for their beloved companions. As livestock farmers, we must face several unpleasant issues. The first one is that the lack of large animal veterinarians has already taken on crisis proportions. The majority of veterinary students are women. Many prefer to treat pets rather than livestock. The men and women who elect the hard, physical work and grueling hours of a large animal practice often love and grew up with horses. Some of these equine specialists will not be interested in treating your alpacas, no matter how much cuter you think your animals are than those big ol' horses in your neighbor's barn. Depending on the location of your farm, you may have difficulties finding a veterinarian—never mind two—willing to take you on as a client. The second issue is a paradox. Ideally, you should establish a close working relationship with your veterinarian. Doing so will most likely wipe out your profits. Realistically, you must strive to see your veterinarian as little as possible. There are two ways to do that. You must prevent illness by creating a healthy environment for your alpacas, and you must take care of routine medical maintenance yourself. Of course, there are times when the expertise of a skilled and knowledgeable professional will save you money in the long run. Veterinary services are also needed for pre-purchase examinations and a *Certificate of Veterinary Inspection* for traveling to shows or other public venues with your alpacas.

Although I am not anxious to pay for unnecessary visits, I think it's sound business and simply smart to invite your chosen veterinarian out to your farm before an emergency arises. If you don't need him or her to perform a medical procedure, then extend an invitation to meet you, see the alpacas, and establish a relationship in a relaxed setting. This is a good time to share your medical record chart with your veterinarian and request his or her input. Expect to pay for this farm visit.

Years ago, few veterinarians knew much about camelids. Some alpaca farmers even purchased a copy of Dr. Murray Fowler's book *Medicine and Surgery of South American Camelids* for their veterinarian. Although alpacas have become mainstream, don't be unreasonable in your expectations. If your veterinarian has a few hundred equine clients and your alpacas are his only camelid patients, you can't expect him to read every book and article available about alpacas in the veterinary field. Don't be shy about asking questions, but please be diplomatic.

Find out what kind of procedures the veterinarian wants you to follow. When does she prefer phone calls concerning non-emergency visits? Are you expected to pay immediately or will she bill you? Would she prefer washing up in the barn or come in the house? Is she willing to draw blood without a chute? Make sure your barn is clean and picked up. Your veterinarian should not be stepping in dung piles and tripping over buckets or feed dishes. Confine the alpaca(s) prior to her arrival. Nothing upsets a busy veterinarian more than arriving at a farm at the appointed time and standing around while the owner tries unsuccessfully to corral her patients. Expect to take an active part by holding or restraining the animals. If you have a sick animal, share all your observations down to the most minute detail—even if it doesn't seem important to you. It may very well be that last, small detail that will unravel the mystery of your alpaca's medical problem.

Both of our veterinarians are knowledgeable and do not stress the alpacas with rough handling. We have their cell phone numbers. I don't abuse this privilege and take up their time calling with questions about issues that I can research myself. I respect their professional expertise. They, in turn, respect my own knowledge and power of observation. I like a call five minutes before their arrival so all is ready when they drive up our lane. I pay all bills promptly. It's very reassuring to have a comfortable working relationship with veterinarians who are caring individuals.

Have a Spare

I'm sure you noticed the plural form of veterinarian in the last paragraph. On *Stormwind Farm*, we presently have the good fortune to work with not one but two veterinarians who like alpacas and are knowledgeable about the species. Why two? Large animal veterinarians often travel long distances to various clients. They are not always immediately available in an emergency. It's good to have a back-up in case your vet is on vacation or with another client. Be honest and explain that you already have a "regular." Since all veterinarians need somebody to take over for them in a pinch sooner or later, your "spare" will be sympathetic to your concerns and arrangement. It's reassuring to have a back-up even though there is no guarantee that either will be able to come out when you call.

Take Charge

When the average alpaca female sold for $20,000 and more, it was customary for many farmers to call their veterinarians for routine maintenance procedures. At current sales prices, you will hardly see a single dollar in profit if you don't take charge of your herd's medical maintenance yourself. The frugal farmer does not call a veterinarian for routine procedures such as dispensing oral dewormers or injecting the alpacas with Ivermectin or Dectomax to protect them against meningeal worm.

Customized Management Protocols

Please take note that the title of this chapter defines it as describing *maintenance* procedures. It is beyond the scope and purpose of this book to outline and discuss treatments for serious medical problems. Additionally, please be aware that I describe protocols and practices on my own farm. Do not interpret these descriptions as advice to be followed blindly. Each farm has its unique environment, and all practices must be tailored to fit these unique circumstances. Management details depend on size of the herd, pasture conditions, climate, frequency of alpacas joining the herd from other locations, show schedules, and possibly other variables.

Each area of the country and each individual farm requires the farmer to formulate a customized vaccination program. You may not want to administer vaccinations for diseases that are highly unlikely to occur on your farm. On our own farm, for example, we've never had a case of blackleg (*Clostridium Feseri*). There is no evidence or reason for me to suspect that our soil is seeded with blackleg spores, hence my decision not to vaccinate against this clostridial disease. If you buy a farm where sheep and cattle have previously died from blackleg, discuss a vaccination program with your veterinarian. The genetic traits of the *individual* alpaca—natural resistance to parasites comes to my mind—may also play a role in a farm's medical management protocol. I am afraid that, in the future, there are nasty surprises in store for those farmers who sacrifice overall health and vitality to very narrow selection criteria such as fiber micron count. In any case, although reading about practices on my farm will give you food for thought, only *your veterinarian* should advise you on specific medical treatments for *your* animals.

Herd Health Days

You will often hear alpaca farmers say, "Tomorrow we'll have herd health day on our farm."

By that they mean the designated day each month when inoculations and dewormers are given, toenails are trimmed, and the alpacas are weighed. For several reasons, I am not in favor of using this expression. Herd health should be on a farmer's mind every single day of the year. The designated herd health day implies that emphasis on health can be relegated to a single day each month. Additionally, there is no reason to take care of medical maintenance in a single day. After my herd grew, I found it easier to devote small chunks of time to selected groups within the herd. For example, I administer Dectomax to all males on one day and perform this maintenance chore on all females and crias on another day. I trim toenails on no more than two to four alpacas on a given day. This could easily get confusing but for a very simple yet effective system of recording all health care procedures. Most important, the words herd health should bring up pictures of grazing alpacas on spacious, green pastures in a farmer's mind, not a vision of administering inoculation and dewormers.

Record Keeping

Raising livestock requires establishing and faithfully keeping records. Customers will want to see evidence of a proper maintenance program. There is no need for expensive computer programs and spread sheets. Handwritten records are perfectly fine as long as they are accurate and kept up to date. Don't rely on your memory. Make your entries immediately after inoculating, toenail trimming etc. so you won't forget.

An individual sheet for each animal should tell you at a glance when inoculations and dewormings are due. I also write this information on a wall calendar. I keep the previous year's calendar on file in case I question specific dates. Breeding records are kept on separate sheets from regular maintenance procedures. It costs only pennies to run off copies of the record sheet yet meticulous record keeping can save you thousands of dollars in corrective or emergency veterinary services. If you're more comfortable with data entry on a computer, then do that. It's not important where health records are maintained. It's important that they accurately document health maintenance procedures on your farm. Your own medical records sheet may include spaces for additional entries depending on the advice of your veterinarian.

Weights

It is normal for alpacas to lose a little weight when, for example, they can't graze due to inclement weather. A major weight loss is cause for concern. I get a baseline weight on each adult alpaca once a year. Males are weighed after shearing and females prior to being bred. Crias are put on the scale when they are one day old and at monthly intervals after that. I weigh individuals more frequently if their condition or behavior give me cause for concern. Alpaca farmers who are new to the world of livestock farming may want to weigh all animals once a month. It would also be wise for those with large herds, little time to observe the alpacas, and no experience with body scoring to adopt this management protocol.

Parasites

All livestock species and millions of human beings in countries all over the world experience disease and death from internal as well as external parasites. In the USA and Europe, most people are unaware just how prevalent parasites are in other parts of the globe. Livestock farmers, no matter where they raise their animals, cannot afford to remain ignorant on this subject.

Prevention and treatment of parasites are ongoing issues on many alpaca farms. In contrast to the myth spread years ago by a prominent farmer that alpacas are very resistant to parasites, David E. Anderson, DVM, MS, DACVS from Ohio State University tells readers of *Alpacas Magazine:* "Generally, camelids are a lot more susceptible to parasite problems than other species" (Spring, 2005). In the article, Dr. Anderson expresses his "very grave concern" and reports "many llama and alpaca deaths from this problem."

A well-informed and vigilant farmer need not fear such dire consequences. During close to two decades of breeding and raising alpacas, I have not experienced any problem with keeping parasites under control.

Resistance to Parasites

"I don't believe in deworming," one farmer told me, "I'm a nature kind of girl." Her entire herd had clumpy feces the size of horse-apples. "Wild animals live and thrive without people catching them and giving them treatments," she argued.

This is true. Wild animals, however, have access to a wide variety of plants that act as natural dewormers. Additionally, natural selection favors those individuals that have a high resistance to parasites. Those with low resistance die or are unable to carry offspring to full term. Researchers who studied a mouse population found out that females rejected breeding males with heavy parasite loads. The females' sense of smell told them to stay away from unfit partners. Domesticated animals are dependent on their caretakers to make wise choices for them. Some livestock farmers make resistance to parasites a selection criteria for breeding stock. Animals that are in poor health due to a heavy infestation are treated but are then removed from the breeding program.

Resistance to Dewormers

I am convinced that the ability to resist parasites will be judged of increasing importance in all livestock species. Why? Resistance to anthelmintics—commonly referred to as dewormers—has become a disturbing issue with all domesticated livestock species. Dr. David Anderson, DVM was one of the first veterinarians to report the emergence of "dual-resistance" alpaca herds, meaning that animals from these farms have intestinal parasites that do not respond to either avermectins or fenbendazole. Dr. Anderson blames under-dosing as one of the reasons for drug resistance. Quite simply, resistance only occurs in the "survivors" of frequent treatments of low dosages. I have found that many farmers do not understand this important concept. Combined with poor nutrition and a compromised immune system, it makes for a lethal mix. Some veterinarians advise switching products to prevent parasites from becoming resistant. Please realize that you are not changing dewormers if product X and product Y both include, for example, fenbendazole. It's important to read the fine print and not select a product based on its brand name. If you have purchased or plan to purchase an alpaca from a herd that is resistant to anthelmintics, your first step should be a visit to a holistic healer trained in herbal medicine.

Fecal Tests

Veterinarians advise regular fecal checks. Are such checks essential? How often should you submit samples? I think that, once again, a sensible management program depends on individual circumstances. One way to cut down on costs is to perform fecal tests yourself using your own equipment.

The Merck Veterinary Manual describes various techniques for diagnosing internal parasites in livestock. A centrifugal flotation procedure is advised to determine infection with nematodes as well as coccidia, lungworm larvae, and tapeworms. Without a centrifuge, certain parasite eggs may not float to the top, and you may get a false negative. *The Merck Veterinary Manual* suggests that "a saturated solution of table salt (sg 1.20) is a cheap alternative medium for diagnosis of livestock parasites."

A fellow alpaca farmer sounded apologetic after performing fecal tests herself. I don't think this attitude is warranted. If you have good equipment and are skilled, a farmer who performs his or her own fecal tests is not cutting corners but is using a smart management protocol. For example, a friend of mine was given an older female alpaca that had suffered from diarrhea and weight loss for several years. Much money had been spent on extensive tests, including numerous fecal tests supposedly run by the previous owner's veterinarian. When my friend ran her own fecal test, she detected a heavy strongyle load. After a very aggressive deworming schedule, the alpaca gained ten pounds in a single month.

If you maintain a large herd or have a steady flow of animal traffic coming and going, it should be financially beneficial to purchase the equipment and take a course on how to use it. Whether taking fecal samples to a veterinary clinic or performing the tests yourself, it's important to store the samples properly prior to testing. If the test cannot be performed immediately after taking the sample, it's best to refrigerate the dung pellets. Of course, it's not a bright idea to invite a former neighbor from the suburbs to a coffee klatsch and have her discover the refrigerated dung samples next to the whipped cream.

FAMACHA

In addition to using a microscope, farmers have a more basic tool at their disposal. The FAMACHA anemia guide was developed in South Africa to diagnose the severity of a barber's pole worm (*Haemonchus contortus*) infestation. It consists of a laminated card with color pictures showing levels from a very pale whitish pink to a healthy red. The color of an animal's inner eyelid is matched to one of the card's samples. The lighter the match, the more a farmer needs to be concerned about anemia caused by parasites. Of course, anemia can have other causes.

Inspect the Dung Piles!

Healthy alpacas produce small pellets. Change in feed, lush pastures, stress, or very rich milk may produce clumpy stools on occasion. Diarrhea is often a sign of severe parasite infestation. If alpacas stay too thin on a diet of excellent pasture and high quality hay, suspect parasites or other health issues such as infected or broken teeth. Parasites would be at the top of my list. Although you will not necessarily see evidence of parasites with the naked eye, it's of utmost importance to almost daily inspect your animals' dung deposits as they hit the ground. I think many farmers who don't do this erroneously believe that their alpacas are parasite free. If pastures are cleaned only sporadically, it's easy to miss the tell-tale signs. Small tapeworm segments, for example, can often only be detected in fresh dung. If you don't have time to wait for dung to drop, take Dr. Anderson's advice. He recommends taking fecal samples with a lubricated latex glove right out of the animal's rectum. Gross? Well, maybe, but if you're going to pay for a fecal test, you better give your veterinarian a good sample to work with. Otherwise you may be wasting your money.

Parasite Prevention

The existence of internal parasites is a reality with farm animals. "Nature Girl's" totally hands-off approach will eventually lead to trouble on most farms with small or moderate acreage, frequent animal traffic in and out of the farm, a high stocking rate, no rotational grazing, and as was the case on her farm—only sporadic dung clean-up. As I've already discussed, frequent deworming may also lead to trouble on the farm. Instead of leaning to the extreme in either direction, there is a common sense approach. Its primary focus is on prevention because it is safer and cheaper than treatment. Ideally, your parasite management program should begin with the farmer you purchase your animals from. Ask about the seller's program and interview his or her veterinarian. Make a fecal test part of your pre-purchase exam. Be present when the sample is taken and mail it off to the lab yourself to be absolutely sure that it came from the animal(s) you wish to purchase. I doubt that any veterinarian would consider very low parasite loads as a reason to reject an alpaca for purchase. A heavy load and wide assortment of parasites should raise eyebrows and have you question the farmer's competence level in general. If your property has a stream or pond, do not allow the animals access to it. Liver flukes and giardia are a concern when alpacas have access to stagnant water.

What strategies do I use to prevent infestation of internal parasites? Rotational grazing and a low stocking rate go a long way toward keeping my alpacas healthy. I pick up dung on a daily basis. Periodically, I spread non-caustic lime over bathroom areas. I keep vegetation clipped so exposure to sun kills off parasites. I deworm animals as they arrive on my farm and follow up with another treatment two weeks later. Any other dewormings are scheduled strategically based on time of the year and birth/breeding dates.

Periparturient Rise

Several years ago, I had the pleasure of interviewing Lora R. Ballweber, DVM on behalf of the *Alpaca Research Foundation*. Dr. Ballweber researched a phenomenon known very well in the sheep industry and among dog breeders: the periparturient rise of parasites. What follows is an excerpt of the *Investigator Profile* that I wrote at the request of the *Alpaca Research Foundation*.

War on Worms

Ingrid Wood interviews
Lora R. Ballweber, DVM
The Alpaca Research Foundation, sensitive to the needs of the alpaca community, approved a Grant Proposal Request submitted by Dr. Lora R. Ballweber (Mississippi State University) to research camelid parasitic issues. In collaboration with Dr. David G. Pugh and Dr. Christine Navarre (both of Auburn University), Ballweber's study is entitled "Determination of a Periparturient Rise in the Excretion of Giardia Cysts and Nematode Eggs in South American Camelids."

A Problem for Dams and Crias

Breeders of other species have long known that right around birthing, the dam experiences a temporary loss of acquired immunity to intestinal parasites. As the result of this loss, large numbers of larvae reach maturity. For example, the *Merck Veterinary Manual* talks about marked increases in strongyle eggs in sows during that time. The phenomenon is well known in sheep, where lactating ewes lose their immune response to larvae. Likewise, many puppies become infected with roundworms during the fetal stage or in the whelping box.

Larvae develop through various stages. The first two are "free living," meaning larvae can survive outside of a host. The third stage larvae are "infective when eaten by a llama or alpaca, they are the stage that ultimately develops into reproducing adults" (Ballweber).

Dr. Ballweber's research is important to breeders who wish to utilize anthelmintics at times when they're most effective. If her work establishes that a periparturient rise in parasite eggs occurs in camelids, breeders can judiciously target this specific parasitic population with appropriate treatments at the most advantageous times.

During a phone interview, Dr. Ballweber further defined the temporary loss of immunity as a "relaxation of immune response" caused by hormonal changes in the dam's system.

"Why would the mother's body create a harmful environment for the baby?" I questioned.

Dr. Ballweber's response: "The fetus obtains its genetic material from both the mother and father. Because the material from the father is different from the mother, the mother would normally make an immune response against it. If that were to happen, the pregnancy would not go to completion. To avoid this problem, several mechanisms exist that allow the fetus to escape the mother's immune response. One of these mechanisms is suppression of the mother's overall immunity in late pregnancy. This suppression helps allow the pregnancy to go to term; however, a side effect of this suppression is that normal immune responses against other organisms are also suppressed."

Camelid gastrointestinal parasites, by the way, are not ingested through mother's milk. They are picked up by crias grazing on contaminated pasture.

Dr. Ballweber's research herd did not exhibit a periparturient rise (PPR) in the shedding of nematode eggs. Dr. Ballweber reported to the *Alpaca Research Foundation* that the animals used in the study did not have *Haemonchus contortus*, typically a parasite found in the PPR phenomena, so it remained unclear whether alpaca females would show the same response as sheep.

On our farm, I treat females with *fenbendazole* (Safeguard or Panacur) within hours after parturition.

Effect of Parasites on Milk Production

One species where parasite loads and their effect on milk production is extensively studied is dairy cattle. "Deworming studies conducted in the U.S. and Canada have demonstrated lactating dairy cows may lose from 100 to 1,200 pounds of milk per lactation due to internal parasites" (Donald H. Bliss, *Lancaster Farming*, 2004). Although alpacas are not bred for milk production, females are expected to nourish their crias. Heavy parasite loads put enormous burdens on nursing moms. While poor milk production can have other causes, I would first look toward parasite infestation in my quest to find the cause of the problem.

Dosages and Treatment Schedules

There are *no* FDA approved drugs specifically for alpacas at the present time. It is highly unlikely that this will change. There are not enough alpacas in the country to justify the expense of research and drug trials. Lack of FDA approval does not mean that the drugs to treat parasites in other livestock species are not effective with alpacas. Consult with your veterinarian regarding dosages and a timetable. Do not assume that the dosage prescribed for cattle is correct for other species. One fact that alpaca farmers often fail to appreciate is that dosage recommendations for camelids are higher per pound than for horses or cattle. This is true for dogs as well. Be aware that veterinarians disagree with one another on treatment protocols. This can be enormously frustrating to novice livestock farmers. You will have to research the matter and eventually decide on a program that makes the most sense to you. Sorry, can't help you there.

Over the years, I've developed a very effective parasite management program for my alpacas. It's based on the research done by Dr. Fowler and Dr. Anderson as well as the extensive information on parasites presented in *The Merck Veterinary Manual*. Additionally, I follow the recommendations of herbal specialists and utilize the results of my own observations. A combination of conventional dewormers and herbal products has worked well on our farm. It was very tempting to outline my treatment schedule in this book. I decided against it. I pointed out earlier that parasite prevention and treatment programs must be customized to fit each farm's unique circumstances. Sharing my program in all details would only support the erroneous notion that "one size fits all" in this area of livestock management. I will, however, discuss the parasites most commonly found on North American alpaca farms.

Nematodes

Dr. Fowler lists nematodes as "the most numerous and most detrimental of the lamoid parasites." I know of one case where a heavy nematode infestation led to thousands of dollars in veterinary expenses. The totally debilitated alpaca had to be hospitalized at a clinic. Alpacas have died from heavy infestations of nematodes, including those of the much feared barber's pole worms.

Tapeworms

"Yeah, they have flare-ups from time to time," a farmer casually remarked about his alpacas' tapeworm infestation to friends of mine.

He shrugged, apparently quite unconcerned. I don't share his casual attitude. I've seen the lack of condition and loss of blooming good health caused by tapeworm infestation in both dogs and alpacas. It's with good reason that jockeys used to swallow tapeworm eggs to help them lose weight.

There are several different species of tapeworm. Alpacas will mostly likely have *Moniezia*, where mites living on grass are the intermediate host. Although mild infestations of *Moniezia* are not harmful, "heavy infestations could obviously impair nutrition and cause debility or even intestinal obstruction" (Fowler). Adult tapeworms can grow to six meters in length. For metrically challenged readers: That's roughly twenty feet. Diarrhea or clumpy feces can be two of the symptoms of infestation. Incidentally, if your dog consumes a wild rabbit, you can just about count on a tapeworm (*Taenia*) infestation. Most dog breeders I know consider *Praziquantel (Droncit)* the drug of choice for treatment. Dr. Fowler recommends it for treating *Moniezia* in lamoids.

Open Wide? Not!

Liquid anthelmintics are administered with a syringe. A long stainless steel extender makes it very easy to empty the syringe's contents into an alpaca's mouth. Be careful that the extender is screwed tightly to the syringe. I experienced a near catastrophe once when the extender separated from the syringe and came to rest on the alpaca's tongue. It was only my swift reaction—and Tasman's easy-going temperament—that prevented the alpaca from swallowing the extender. Had the animal done so, surgery would have been unavoidable. A pre-packaged tube filled with paste is safer. The manufacturer of the paste that I started using after the incident adds a component that makes the product taste like an apple. The alpacas like it and will rarely try to spit it out. Liquid as well as paste medication must be administered with care. If an alpaca fights the dosing and the medication gets into the windpipe and lungs, inhalation pneumonia may be the unpleasant result. You do *not* request your alpaca to "Open Wide!" To the contrary, you pull the alpaca's lip down at the side of the mouth and *slowly* squirt the liquid or paste into the little "pocket" found at that location. How do you accustom alpacas to having something squirted into their mouths? I start with my crias when they're only a few weeks old. During the summer, I use a 3 cc syringe—without the needle—to give each baby a weekly dose of electrolytes mixed with water. During the winter months, it's a vitamin paste. You can also simply use water or maybe an herbal tea brewed from fennel leaves. What's important is not so much the content, but that the alpaca becomes accustomed to the procedure.

Coccidiosis

Mention the word *coccidiosis* to alpaca farmers, and their eyes take on a panicked expression. I've spoken to several people who did not have a basic understanding of the scientific facts we know about this disease and worried needlessly. Others had reason to worry and didn't until it was too late.

Coccidiosis is a protozoal disease that infects and destroys the intestinal mucosa of an animal. *The Merck Veterinary Manual* lists symptoms of infection: diarrhea, fever, inappetence, weight loss, emaciation, and sometimes death. Coccidia are host specific. Dr. Fowler lists five coccidian species of the genus *Eimeria* for camelids. Farmers need to differentiate between infection rate and actual clinical disease. Just because a fecal sample shows presence of coccidia does not mean that the alpaca is sick. What's more, some species are not even pathogenic and therefore no cause for concern. When should a farmer become concerned? Any time an alpaca is subjected to conditions that cause stress such as overcrowding, travel, weaning, change in feed, poor nutrition, severe weather, poor sanitation, and illness. When these unfavorable environmental conditions are present, clinical disease can manifest itself and actually become life threatening. When you study the list above, it should become quickly apparent that farmers can easily take control of the situation or, better yet, prevent its occurrence. Cleaning up dung piles and avoiding stress goes a long way toward preventing disease. An outbreak of coccidiosis on your farm calls for intervention and treatment of the *clinically* affected animals.

I read all information published in *The Merck Veterinary Manual* about coccidiosis in various species of farm animals. The most important take home lesson was what I already stressed in the last paragraph: Treatment alone is not the answer. Farmers must address the underlying causes of a disease outbreak. This parallels the message of my book. We must view all components of raising alpacas as part of a whole system, with overlapping and interlocking pieces. If you're nervous about what you read or hear about coccidiosis: In all my years of raising alpacas, I did not experience a single case of clinical disease in adult alpacas. Despite my fastidious sanitation protocol, a few crias have experienced problems (diarrhea), but all responded quickly to treatment. The *routine* administration of medication to prevent coccidiosis makes no sense to me. If anything, I consider the practice counterproductive because the animals will not develop natural immunity.

Meningeal Worm

Injections of Ivermectin or Dectomax are an absolute necessity at regular intervals if you live in white-tailed deer country. In a nutshell: White-tailed deer carry the meningeal worm as a natural parasite, meaning it does not cause disease in that species. Passed by the deer (primary hosts) in its feces, the larvae are picked up by snails and slugs (intermediate hosts). When alpacas (aberrant hosts) ingest a snail or slug while grazing, larvae migrate to the spinal cord within ten days of being released in the alpaca's stomach. After maturation, the adults migrate to the brain. In llamas and alpacas, migration of meningeal worm larvae in the spinal cord can produce a wide range of symptoms from minor lameness to total paralysis. I know of several farms where animals became partially paralyzed due to a meningeal worm infection and never completely recovered. Scott and Kate McKelvie—fellow alpaca farmers and true animal lovers—are active in llama rescue and had to deal with the problem caused by the llama's previous, negligent owner.

"I wish all camelid owners could see poor Petey drag his hind legs around the field," Kate told me when Petey the rescued llama was being nursed back to health by the McKelvies. "After seeing him, no owner would be so lax about Ivermectin injections," Kate added.

Ivermectin or Dectomax? Please discuss the differences and timetables with your veterinarian. Opinions and recommendations vary widely among professionals. On a modest budget, you must learn to give these injections yourself. It is cost prohibitive to call out your veterinarian each time injections are scheduled.

External Parasites

External parasites are not uncommon. Alpacas may become infested with lice, ticks, or mites. Ringworm can also be an issue. Some conditions call for veterinary advice and intervention such as skin scrapings to make a proper diagnosis. Inspect your alpacas often and keep you eyes open when purchasing. Treatment must begin immediately upon discovery and must be administered without skipping sessions and applications. With proper management, external parasites can be prevented.

CD & T

The most common vaccines used for alpacas are against *Clostridium perfringens* and tetanus. Clostridial organisms are found in the soil and in the intestine. *The Merck Veterinary Manual* lists types A, B, C, D, and E. Dr. Fowler informs readers that "lamoids are known to be susceptible to types A and C" and that "type D is also highly suspect." Type A is a big problem on South American alpaca farms, with high mortality rates. There is no vaccine available, as yet. There have been outbreaks on North American farms. If your farm is located in a climate with cool, wet weather during birthing season, I strongly advise you to read Dr. Fowler's chapter on infectious diseases in its entirety. Paradoxically, both type C and type D can occur when crias are well nourished. Type D enterotoxemia is actually called "overeating disease" by producers of other species. Feeding too much grain is one of the main causes, and the disease is therefore common in feedlot cattle and sheep.

Dr. Fowler repeatedly discusses the importance of good sanitation to prevent outbreaks. He advises farmers "to keep neonates uncrowded and as dry as possible." He cites research done by South American scientists who believe that animals with severe diarrhea have a better chance of surviving. This is a concept all farmers need to understand. Diarrhea is the body's way of flushing it clear of harmful toxins. Diarrhea is symptomatic of illness, not an illness itself. When you stop it with immediate dosing of medicine, you are undermining the body's efforts to heal itself. Of course, individuals with diarrhea must be supported with fluids and electrolytes to prevent dehydration. In the case of very young crias, profuse, watery diarrhea can result in death in less than twenty-four hours even with support of fluids and electrolytes. Severe heat can promote multiplication of potentially harmful intestinal bacteria. In the United States, where so many people live in air-conditioned buildings, this fact is sometimes forgotten.

Tetanus is not nearly the problem with alpacas as it is with horses, non-human primates, and swine. Dr. Fowler cites only two cases found in lamoids in the United States. He states that camelids with "contaminated deep wounds with devitalized tissue are most at risk."

A three-way vaccine (CD&T) is available. Discuss dosing with your veterinarian in addition to doing your own research. Opinions among farmers and veterinarians differ sharply on the subject of vaccination schedules.

Rabies

Rabies is a threat to alpaca and human health. In some states, the vaccine may only be shipped to and administered by veterinarians. Please don't be unreasonable and expect your veterinarian to treat your alpacas if they do not receive regular rabies vaccinations. He has the right to protect himself against contracting a deadly virus.

Anaphylactic Shock

If you vaccinate a pregnant alpaca and it experiences swelling as the result of a severe allergic (anaphylactic) reaction, the medicine (Dexamethasone) your veterinarian may administer will most likely cause it to abort the fetus. You must therefore weigh the pros and cons of vaccinating a pregnant female carefully. Your veterinarian may advise you to keep epinephrine on hand when giving injections. This drug counteracts the effects of anaphylaxis. It is not that easy to transport an alpaca suffering from shock to a veterinary clinic. If your veterinarian can't immediately come out to your farm, you must help the animal yourself.

Learn to Give Injections

One of the best ideas I ever read for learning how to give injections was the suggestion to use raw chicken breasts. You inject the meat with a delicious barbeque sauce and then bake it in the oven. This way, you learn to "give shots" and create a good meal all at the same time.

Trimming Toenails

Although most farmers would not consider trimming nails to belong in the *Medical Maintenance* category, I do. It is an important component of a holistic approach to keeping alpacas healthy. Trimming nails once a month is not too often if your soil is soft. Overgrown toenails can compromise an alpaca's health more severely than many people realize. An animal's gait is thrown off balance by nails resembling bird claws. If walking becomes painful, the alpaca will not graze as vigorously as it should. It helps to trim toenails after a rain has softened them. During a prolonged drought, soaking feet with a hose accomplishes the same purpose.

Check the pocket between the toes of each foot for any problems. These pockets are very deep and allow little air to penetrate. The skin inside them can therefore easily become ulcerated and infected. An application of Nolvasan cream or Bag Balm works well. One time, an alpaca arrived on our farm with an already existing foot problem. Nothing I tried seemed to permanently cure the weepy sores. A single, liberal application of Desitin ointment finally did the trick. Prevention is always better than having to come up with a cure. Good drainage, especially around the barn, will ensure healthy feet in alpacas.

Filing Fighting Teeth

This ominous sounding procedure should be performed once or twice during a sexually mature male's lifetime. Alpacas have three pairs of fighting teeth, two upper pairs and one lower pair. Fighting teeth are not an issue with males that were gelded prior to sexual maturity. They are of concern once sexually mature males reach the age of two years. Occasionally, you will see a female with fighting teeth. Because females normally don't engage in brawls, their fighting teeth are not an issue. Although these teeth are tiny, they are razor sharp. Used as formidable weapons, male alpacas slash at a competitor's ears or genitals. Farmers who take a nonchalant attitude toward filing fighting teeth often face a hefty veterinary bill for minor or possibly major surgery. This is totally unnecessary because the teeth are relatively easy to file with obstetrical wire. It only takes a few seconds for each tooth to be filed off at the gum line. Some farmers use various types of nippers or even dog nail clippers to accomplish the task. There is concern that a tooth may crack using these instruments. The wire is safe and fairly inexpensive. Wear heavy work gloves to protect your hands. We use a twisted cotton "bone" made for dogs to help keep the male's mouth open. A piece of rubber watering hose also works well.

A few years ago, my husband was slightly annoyed at my insistence to file fighting teeth. "Now, not next week," I demanded. "Later," he said. News reached us that—at another New Jersey farm—a farmer arrived home to find the penis of one of her breeding males to be the size of a baseball and a bloody mess. Looking slightly green around the gills, my husband was only too happy to dig out the obstetrical wire.

"Round 'em up," he ordered tersely, "I'll be ready to go in a minute."

Trimming Incisors

Our gelding's incisors required trimming. After experimenting with various methods, we finally found one that worked for us. We used a Dremel tool with the 545 Dremel Diamond Wheel. Due to their larger size, trimming overly long incisors is more difficult than filing off fighting teeth with this particular tool. *Quality Llama Products, Inc.* sells two tools called the *Smooth-a-Matic Kit* and the *Tooth-a-Matic Complete Kit* as well as a *Protecto Guard* that fits on Dremel tools. You need not use any equipment on alpacas that have a correct bite.

Drawing Blood

Since we are discussing medical *maintenance* procedures in this chapter, I will limit this section to drawing blood from healthy alpacas. A few drops of blood are sufficient for the DNA card required by the AOA to register an alpaca. For an additional fee, farmers can also elect to have the blood sample tested for the BVD virus. That's very cost effective for the owners of small herds with two to four crias born each year. For the BVD virus test, the blood card must be received by the AOA within fourteen days. Because of medical complications and even deaths experienced by alpacas, many farmers are nervous about taking blood samples from the jugular vein. A veterinarian or an owner can draw blood from an alpaca's tail—a much safer procedure. An even safer approach is syringing a few drops of blood from a vein in the placenta. You don't have to handle the cria at all for this procedure.

Mild Conjunctivitis

Alpaca eyes are very large and prominent. Injuries can easily happen and must be dealt with by a veterinarian as soon as possible. *Do not ignore or try to treat eye injuries yourself.* A mild conjunctivitis can be handled by the farmer. I keep an Ophthalmic Ointment on hand in addition to the Eyebright tea that I suggested in a previous chapter. If conjunctivitis doesn't clear up within two days, veterinary attention is advised. Nursing males are the most likely candidates for conjunctivitis. They often annoy older females by trying to practice breeding behavior, stealing milk just to see if they can get away with it, and other high-spirited shenanigans. Their own mothers may indulge the juvenile delinquents. Other females will spit at them. If spit gets in the males' eyes, it may cause a mild infection.

Choke

A choke episode is a frightening sight, and it happens with alarming frequency on many alpaca farms across the country. Because of this frequency, I thought it wise to discuss the condition—its causes, prevention, and emergency treatment—in this chapter.

Choke is a condition where food particles obstruct the esophagus. The alpaca literally chokes. It retches, salivates, and coughs. Often, liquefied food will pour out of its nostrils. Greed or true hunger may be two reasons for frequent choking. Feeding dishes that are grouped so close together that the arrangement fosters severe feed competition can led to a choking episode. The size and consistency of supplemental feed pellets may cause a problem. Choke can often be prevented through carefully planned feeding management. If it does happen, quick action can remedy the situation. In over a decade of raising alpacas, I have only had two serious episodes with choke. One involved Breeze, our oldest female. As soon as I observed the alpaca choking, I haltered it, and vigorously massaged its neck, starting at the bottom and working my way up. I could clearly hear and feel large air bubbles working themselves up the neck and being expelled. I kept up a massage for quite a few minutes, and Breeze's story had a good ending. The second case called for additional intervention. One of the male alpacas choked. After massaging its neck, it was very obvious that an obstruction remained. The alpaca had difficulty swallowing and breathing and clearly was in distress. I remembered a technique that I had read about in Dr. Dettloff's book and decided to try it. After forcing the alpaca's mouth open, I pushed a piece of PVC pipe into the mouth lengthwise. Immediately, the alpaca clamped its mouth around the pipe and began chewing on it. Several minutes of enforced chewing dislodged the obstruction, and the animal calmly resumed eating. I don't know why Breeze and Fortune choked, and it has not happened again.

If poor management has been ruled out, and the same animal often experiences choke while others do not, a veterinarian should be consulted.

Unfortunately, there is no quick fix if the cause of choke is megaesophagus, an abnormal dilation of the esophagus.

Antibiotics

I have mentioned several times that this chapter is primarily about normal medical maintenance, not treatments for disease. There are many livestock farmers who consider antibiotics part of a regular medical program. They're quick to administer such drugs for all kinds of minor ailments. That is a dangerous attitude to take. Scientists are alarmed about how the extensive use of antibiotics has led bacteria to adapt defenses against the drugs. The emergence and spread of germs that are resistant to antibiotics has become a real problem. Additionally, antibiotics destroy the beneficial as well as the bad bacteria in the digestive tract. With big doses, the digestive action of the sick alpaca may cease to function. I can't stress enough the importance of following a course of antibiotics with a course of probiotics! I consider it almost criminally negligent when veterinarians do not urge the owners of their patients to administer this follow-up treatment. Routine dewormings and inoculations are expensive enough. Having to rush an alpaca to a veterinary clinic because nobody told you to use $5.00 worth of probiotics is ridiculous. Antibiotics are powerful medicine and can save an animal's life. Don't use them frivolously, and don't forget to counteract their negative side effects!

Purchase of Medical Supplies

I purchase dewormers and other medication from reputable mail order companies. I've done this for both our Whippets and alpacas for years and have never encountered a problem. The companies I do business with package temperature sensitive materials carefully. Delivery is always prompt and efficient. I buy products identical to those used by veterinarians and scrupulously observe expiration dates.

Emergency Kit

Although an emergency does not, strictly speaking, qualify as part of a maintenance program, the frugal farmer should assemble a medical emergency kit. Its contents should depend somewhat on access to veterinary care, products that address unique circumstances—for example, poisonous snakes—in your area, and your expertise as well as your courage to use the supplies. A suture kit isn't going to do your alpacas any good if you can't bring yourself to sew up a wound.

Read, Read, and Read Some More!

I met many alpaca farmers over the years who believed that attending several seminars and visiting many farms had prepared them well to run their own farms. Raising livestock is a complex business with a steep learning curve. In my opinion, the frugal farmer must read extensively to gather as much information as possible in the shortest period of time. This is particularly true in the case of medical issues. On one side, alpaca farmers have much to learn from the experiences and research of other livestock industries. That includes not repeating their mistakes. On the other side, the frugal alpaca farmer needs to learn about species specific conditions. For example, alpacas have T_3 and T_4 thyroid levels that are six to ten times higher than those in other species. Dr. Fowler speculates that since alpaca mothers don't lick their babies dry, such high thyroid hormone levels are necessary to prevent a cria from quickly succumbing to hypothermia. Thyroid hormones stimulate thermogenesis activity. Knowing this can save you unnecessary stress and bills one day.

I found out how important it is to educate yourself long before I started to farm and will never forget the looks on the faces of two Whippet owners when they overheard a group of us talking about canine geriatric problems. They had had their pet euthanized because they were convinced the old fellow had suffered a stroke. Dogs don't have strokes. More likely, their beloved pet had suffered from vestibular disease. It produces stroke-like symptoms. Many dogs recover completely or suffer only minor permanent damage. Medication is not always necessary or helpful. The couple's veterinarian had never even mentioned this fairly common condition to them. Husband and wife sobbed in anguish once they understood what the group was discussing. The tears rolling down their cheeks confirmed to me once again that prudent and effective health maintenance for our animals requires owners to read extensively.

14

BREEDING ALPACAS

"Don't just breed for the sake of breeding. Have a purpose and a plan!" Diann Mellott

A Guessing Game?

Although many alpacas get pregnant and give birth like clockwork year after year, others leave farmers scratching their heads in puzzlement. On some farms, reproductive success is very high; on others, farmers complain about their "bad luck." There are many aspects to getting alpacas pregnant and helping them maintain their pregnancies to the culmination of the reproductive process: the birth of a healthy cria.

Pregnancy testing can be a big budget buster. It is fruitless to discuss smart—and money saving—breeding and testing strategies unless you have a basic knowledge of the alpaca's unique reproductive system. Although it is not crucial for an alpaca farmer to comprehend every detail of alpaca reproductive anatomy and physiology, a basic understanding of what happens, where it happens, and why it happens will make it easier to plan a sensible reproductive program. With few exceptions, determining a female's reproductive status need not be a guessing game.

The Female Reproductive System

If you're not accustomed to reading scientific information, you may shy away from reading the next few paragraphs. Unless you plan to keep only a fiber herd or a few alpacas as live lawn mowers and pasture companions for your enjoyment, please make an effort to understand this topic. If building a herd and eventually selling animals is your objective, it would be extremely shortsighted not to do so. Both Dr. Fowler (the chapter on reproduction is coauthored with P. Walter Bravo, DVM, MS, PhD) and Dr. Tibary (*The Complete Alpaca Book*) present detailed descriptions with many photographs and drawings for interested readers. I will limit myself to those facts that are, in my opinion, crucial for you to understand. Let's begin with a *simplified* version of the rather complex female alpaca reproductive anatomy and physiology.

The female reproductive anatomy consists of the vulva, the vagina, the cervix, the uterus, the uterine tubes (oviducts), the ovaries, and the mammary glands.

The *vulva* is located directly below the anus and can best be described as a vertical slit. It is the external opening leading to the vagina. In my experience, swelling (edema) of the vulva is an excellent indicator that parturition (birth) is possibly only hours away.

The *vagina* is shaped like a tube. Strictly speaking, it separates into *vestibule* and *vaginal cavity*. In the maiden alpaca female, the two sections are separated by the *hymen*.

The *cervix* is located between the vagina and the uterus. While it is open in a receptive female, its two or three rings are tightly closed during pregnancy. The alpaca's cervix is very sensitive and easily damaged.

The *uterus* consists of a short section called the *uterine body* which branches out into two *uterine horns*. The entire organ is roughly shaped like a Y.

The *uterine tubes* connect the uterine horns with the *ovaries*. The uterine tubes are extremely important. The sperm swims from the uterus into either one of the tubes, and this is where fertilization takes place.

The *ovaries* serve as a storage facility for the unfertilized eggs.

The *mammary glands* of alpacas are, compared to those of many other species, fairly small. The udder has four nipples.

Alpacas are *induced ovulators*. This means that females are always receptive to a male unless they are already pregnant or were bred up to twenty-four hours prior to the attempted mating and have ovulated. They do not, in contrast to many other species, experience estrous (come "in heat"). Instead, they *ovulate* (the ovaries release an egg) between twenty-four and forty-eight hours *following copulation*.

The reproductive process begins when the male alpaca mounts the female alpaca, forces it to cush, and positions itself on top of its mate. The penis penetrates through the vagina, cervix, and into one of the *uterine horns* (usually the left one). Prompted by the breeding act, the female's brain now "turns on" the secretion of *gonadotropin-releasing hormone* (GnRH) which in turn initiates the release of *luteinizing hormone* (LH), causing ovulation within twenty-four to forty-eight hours following copulation. In some cases, orgling of the male or just an attempted mating without actual penetration may be sufficient to release LH.

I already mentioned that the unfertilized eggs are stored in the ovaries. Each egg is encased in a fluid filled sac called a *follicle* (Latin *folliculus* = little bag). Dr. Fowler tells readers that these "follicles grow and regress in an average time of 10-12 days..." in an overlapping, wavelike pattern (*follicular wave*). If a female is never mated, these follicular waves continue indefinitely. Understanding this cycle—also called a *follicular phase*—is one of the keys to sound breeding practices.

When the luteinizing hormone is released, it causes a *mature follicle* (approximately seven millimeters in diameter) to rupture and to release the egg. What happens if the follicle is not at the mature stage? If it is too small, mating will not induce ovulation.

Dr. Fowler points out that if a female is bred during the regressive stage of its follicular phase, "copulation may initiate luteinization of the follicle, without ovulation." In that case, the luteal phase lasts only five to six days. Dr. Fowler speculates that such an occurrence may explain somewhat erratic receptive behavior by the female.

Let's imagine that everything goes as planned:

The mating results in full penetration by a fertile male. The female alpaca just happens to be in a segment of its follicular phase that is favorable for fertilization: The follicle is the required seven millimeters in diameter. The egg is released from the ruptured follicle twenty-six hours after mating and is carried from there into the uterine tube. If the tiny sperm cell survived its perilous passage through one of the uterine horns, it arrives in the uterine tube and fertilizes the egg. Success! It beat the competition in its quest to reproduce.

The fertilized egg, now called a *zygote*, hangs around inside the uterine tube for several days, and then slowly meanders into the uterus. For reasons not quite understood, almost all zygotes travel to and remain in the left uterine horn. The entire process takes approximately six to seven days.

Counting from the day of copulation, it takes approximately three to four weeks for the alpaca *embryo* to firmly implant itself in the left horn.

What sustains the pregnancy? Remember the original follicle that ruptured and released the egg? The cells from this follicle reorganize and grow into a solid mass called the *Corpus Luteum* (CL). The CL produces *progesterone*, the hormone responsible for sustaining the pregnancy. *Progesterone production causes the alpaca female to "spit off" a male and refuse to cush. Gestation* is long and reported averages vary slightly from one research study to the next. On our farm, the earliest birth was on day 335. The longest gestation lasted an unbelievable 372 days.

Pink or Blue?

Chromosomes that code for the sex of a cria are either X (female) or Y (male). If the sperm cell carries the X, the cria will be a female. If it's a Y, the cria will be a male. Normal females are always XX, so the dam (mother) can only contribute an X. The sire's chromosome therefore always determines the sex of the baby.

Retained Corpus Luteum

Embryonic mortality is high in camelids during the first three months of their normally long pregnancy. If the pregnancy is terminated, the CL begins to regress. In that case, progesterone production will shortly stop. Unfortunately, sometimes the normal progression of hormonal events cease to function. If, for whatever reason, the *Corpus Luteum* is *retained* and continues to produce progesterone, it signals the female alpaca that it is pregnant even though there is no embryo. This can persist for many months. During this time, the females will not be receptive to a male. The CL eventually may regress on its own, or hormonal intervention can speed up the process.

Is She Receptive?

What exactly does *receptive* mean? Alpaca farmers have two definitions for the term. This fact causes considerable confusion.

First definition: The female alpaca wants to be bred. "Exposed" to a male, it willingly cushes (sits) and waits for the male to mount it. Some females are so anxious to be bred that they will cush for anyone who comes in close contact with them—including human beings—and refuse to budge.

Second definition: The follicle cells are at least seven millimeters in diameter. A mating will therefore trigger ovulation and, if the male is fertile, will result in a pregnancy.

These two concepts—*behavioral* versus true *physiological* receptivity—are synonymous in many farmers' minds. They believe that a female alpaca will only cush when it is in the "right" phase of its cycle, meaning when its follicles are large enough to trigger ovulation.

If a female alpaca refuses to cush within a New York minute of exposure to a male, it's not necessarily because its follicles are not mature yet. In contrast, a female that virtually drops like a stone at the sight of a male may not have follicles large enough to trigger ovulation. In any case, it's not unusual for females to play "hard to get" and initially run away. One of our maiden alpacas stood quietly but stubbornly for four minutes until its knees finally buckled and it cushed. It was successfully impregnated during this one ten-minute breeding. It bears repeating that not all females respond in an identical way; it pays to show some patience and also take mental as well as written notes on individual breeding behavior.

Are You Receptive?

Body language can vary considerably among individual females. Signals may depend on age, social status, proximity to males, and whether the alpaca likes and approves of the male you have chosen for it.

"Oh, come on, you are kidding, right?" a friend asked me once when the subject of female alpacas' likes and dislikes for a particular mate came up. My friend had called me in frustration. He owns a very beautiful, black stud and had tried—unsuccessfully—to mate it to a maiden.

"There is something wrong with that alpaca. It will not go down no matter how often we try to mate it," the owner complained about the "stubborn" female.

"Maybe it doesn't like the male," I said and suggested, "try to mate it to your fawn stud."

"It's an animal, for Pete's sake!" My friend let me know what he thought of my suggestion.

"*She* is a female," I told him and smiled. One week later, the phone rang.

"Ingrid—"

"Yes?"

"How did you know?"

The way a male looks, smells, or behaves may either attract or "turn off" a female alpaca. If given the opportunity, females will watch intently when males fight. Their preferences for a particular partner may be based in part on these observations. Dominant females with high social ranking in the herd may refuse to submit to a male that they judge to be of low rank or lacking in masculine traits. The smart farmer makes sure that he or she is "receptive" to a female's messages.

Age at First Breeding

At what age should you breed a female alpaca for the first time? The owner of a small herd is naturally anxious to breed a female as young as possible to maximize profits over the animal's life-time. In several other livestock industries, the belief is that an animal must be bred early to become a consistent producer.

It's interesting that one page in *The Merck Veterinary Manual* tells us: "If a cow is to calve consistently, she must be early with her first calf." We read a few pages later: "The expected occurrence of dystocia is about 10-15% in first-calf heifers and 3-5% in mature cattle."

Although some dystocias have happy endings, others result in the baby's or mother's death, or both may die. Trying to get a jump on financial gains may cost you a lot more in the long run. Years ago, Hugh Masters told me that he was convinced that a boarded alpaca on his farm refused to nurse its first baby due to lack of emotional and physical maturity. During subsequent pregnancies, this same female proved to be a devoted mother. I think Hugh was absolutely correct in his educated guess and think it's best to give a female the chance to grow and develop properly without the added demands that a growing fetus makes on the mother's body. I have also always questioned the conventional wisdom of deciding a first breeding based on projected adult body weight. This may make sense if a species or breed is extremely uniform in size and weight. There is a wide range of adult size and weight in the alpaca population. In genetic outcrosses, you can't predict future adult size from birth weight or even weanling size. There are alpaca farmers who linebreed to achieve physical uniformity in their herds. These farmers may be in a better position to predict final size and weight for one of their young alpacas.

Very young females will often assume a submissive crouch/flipped tail pose while walking close to a sexually mature male. Some alpaca farmers interpret that as "flirting." Although the pose can be an expression of sexual interest, I think it's often a submissive gesture and has nothing to do with reproductive receptivity. You will see young males approach a mature male using identical body language. Cushing near a male—for example, next to the fence line—is a better indication of a female's willingness to be bred. I saw six-months-old weanlings do this and simply ignored the behavior. With rare exceptions, eighteen months is, in my opinion, the earliest age to start a female's reproductive career. It's better to wait a few additional months, particularly if the herd's caretaker is a novice to farming with livestock.

Male Stuff

Understanding the unique camelid reproductive system will also work for you if you are too cowardly to refuse invitations to boring parties, weddings, and company picnics without giving a compelling reason.

"I'm so sorry we can't attend. On that day, our alpaca's follicles will be at the optimum size, and she will need to be bred. Yes, yes, I supervise this myself. We hand breed, so we'll have to be present." If your boss or relative shows even the slightest inclination to protest, throw in a casual, "I am so happy that our stud's penis is finally free of adhesions and we can use him. We have been waiting forever." A final, "His testicles are nice and large so he won't have any problems getting my female pregnant," will guarantee you a virtually empty social calendar—except for visits to and from other alpaca farmers, of course. On second thought, you better not share these observations with your boss. Political correctness is "over the top" these days and such comments may get you fired. If they make *you* blush and squirm in discomfort, breeding livestock should not be in your future.

In any case, the prepuce *does* adhere to the glans penis in all young male alpacas. Until the penis is free of adhesions, the young stud cannot extrude it sufficiently to penetrate the female's reproductive tract. Of course, many young males will go through the motions—orgling and thrusting away with the best of them—but not much happens. Some males do not lose their adhesions until they are three years old. Occasionally, it will take a few attempts to breed to loosen them. Once fully functional, the penis penetrates the cervix and is threaded all the way into the uterine horn—usually the left horn. This causes friction as well as inflammation and is precisely the reason why female alpacas should not be bred on consecutive days.

"That just sounds too weird. Are you sure that you have that right?" a farm visitor once questioned me.

Well, let's look at the facts. Although the diameter of the penis is less than half an inch when at rest and does not expand much during an erection, the erect alpaca penis is fourteen to sixteen inches long. Even more "weird": In the unaroused male, the stream of urine is projected backward between the back legs. When a male alpaca is sexually aroused, muscles pull the prepuce (the foreskin) in the opposite direction.

As has been proven in other species, testicular size may impact fertility. In a sentence: The larger the better! The testicles should also be uniform in size. If you go stud shopping, request to see the testicles of a breeding prospect. Unfortunately, alpacas have the uncanny ability to pull the family jewels up into the body. This little trick comes in rather handy while fighting with another male whose fully erupted fighting teeth can inflict serious damage to its opponent's male equipment. You may try to catch a full view of the testicles while the male is visiting the dung pile and has its tail slightly raised. Compared to other species, camelids have small testicles. A study of 158 alpacas—cited by Dr. Fowler—gave 3.6 cm x 2.4 cm (1.4 inches x 0.9 inches) as the mean size for three-year-old males. In contrast, the size of a ram's testicles is large enough to cause an accident—literally! After a sheep farmer friend of mine had her ram castrated, she slovenly failed to remove the severed appendages, tripped over them the next day, and severely twisted her ankle. How would you like to explain that little mishap to your boss? Who needs that headache when little golf ball sized testicles do the same job? No need to worry about crippling yourself should you fail to clean up after an alpaca castration.

Orgling

Before and during copulation, males "orgle"—a rather strange, almost indescribable sound. Alice Brown says it sounds like a kind of gargled hum. Years ago, when a boarded male bred on our farm for the first time, it puffed out its cheeks in a comical attempt to orgle but no sound came out. The female refused to cush until I, more as a joke than serious strategy, imitated the orgling sound. The second the female alpaca heard it, it dropped like a stone and the breeding proceeded smoothly.

Easy Does It

The novice farmer was frustrated.

"I don't know what's wrong. My male is supposed to have experience, but he's not doing anything. He's just sitting on top of my female like a bump on a log."

"Is he orgling?" I asked.

"Loud enough to bust my eardrums," the woman replied.

"Did he thrust at all when he first mounted your female?"

"Yes, but not very hard and only a few times. Since then, he's been acting like a slug."

"When you look at him from the side, do his back and rump form a rounded shape?"

"Yeah, he looks like he's slumped over a bicycle without pedaling, the lazy couch potato," the caller complained.

I smiled. "Congratulations," I said. "Your alpaca stud knows what he's doing, even if you don't. Those little sperm cells are swimming as we speak."

Once intromission is accomplished, you should observe very little movement. The most skillful studs accomplish intromission in a few seconds and then remain virtually motionless until—five to fifty minutes later—they terminate the breeding by standing up.

Prolonged thrusting is a sign of inexperience, impatience, incompetence, or a male that is so excited that it is incapable of concentrating.

The gems among alpaca studs are the individuals that are eager to breed yet calm enough to accomplish quick intromission. Additionally, a competent male will be firm in its insistence to breed but will not act like an out-of-control maniac.

The Novice Male

A young male's first attempts to breed should not include the job of behavior testing an older female alpaca that rules the roost and will literally whip the male around the barn if it is pregnant. If possible, allow several successful breedings before the youngster is spit upon and otherwise chastised. You must approach the reproductive career of a young stud with patience and skill. Friends of ours were ready to give up on a young alpaca and geld it. This male was well over three years old before it showed interest in the ladies. Last we heard, its nickname is "The Sex Machine." Several years later, it was our friends' turn to tell me to be patient. Tasman, a young male purchased by us, had never bred and seemingly showed no interest.

"Give him time to get acclimated to your farm and the other animals. He just needs to get his confidence level up," Carol advised me.

My husband was blunter. "You're standing there tapping your foot and acting all impatient. Don't you think your body language is making Tasman nervous?"

I knew this wasn't truly meant to be a question. Male insight into a male problem was obviously at work here. It was time to step back! Tasman went on to become an exemplary breeder and has sired many beautiful crias. I learned to be patient with the slow starters. Even a highly motivated young male may need a little time to figure out the details. If the first time isn't a total success, so what? Millions of mammals all over the world discover all on their own that the male's penis can be inserted into the vagina. Some alpaca farmers are concerned that an inexperienced male will initially insert its penis into the female's rectum and later on contaminate the reproductive tract. They cover the anus with a piece of tape. Judging by the tell-tale signs of seminal fluid after a breeding, I have never seen this happen. A female may interrupt a breeding by jumping up and dislodging the male. Young males often do not have the knack to prevent this. They also may become frustrated while searching for the vulva and ejaculate outside of it. Relax! Rome wasn't built in a day, and a young stud doesn't become Mr. Quick n' Easy in one breeding. Let nature take its course.

Helicopter Breeding

Animals can be sensitive to interference. Years ago, when I supervised the breeding of a Whippet bitch, the stud threw my bitch lots of shy, sideways glances but would not mount her. Using my best "Follow my orders now and don't argue" teacher voice, I threw the stud's hovering owner out of the room. Not two minutes later, we had a tie and a pregnant bitch.

Unfortunately, potential alpaca buyers are often impressed with farmers who conduct what I call helicopter breedings. These farmers hover anxiously over the animals and micromanage almost every aspect of a mating. It should be just the opposite. Be impressed with the animals that demonstrate good reproductive instincts and the farmers who allow them to do so.

There are alpaca farmers who manually break the hymen of every maiden alpaca prior to it being bred. Talk about helicopter breeding! I am opposed to this invasive procedure as part of routine reproductive management to "make it easier for the male." Sexually mature males are perfectly capable of breaking a normal hymen.

Field Breeding

In contrast to intensely managed pen breedings, some farmers prefer field breeding. A male is pastured with a group of females, and they are left alone to do their job. The advantages to this method are a reduced workload and savings on the farmer's time. This seems especially desirable for farmers who also have full-time jobs off their farms. Unfortunately, there are a few disadvantages to field breeding. Many veterinarians feel strongly that female alpacas should not be bred less than seven days apart. Shortly after starting in the alpaca business, I read an article describing the uterus of an alpaca bred on several consecutive days as looking like raw hamburger. Like the farm visitor whose comments I quoted earlier in the chapter, I found this a little hard to believe. After studying Dr. Fowler's description of camelid copulation, I quickly learned that the author's gruesome analogy had been entirely accurate. During field breeding, an overly aggressive male may copulate with an open female repeatedly on one day. It may overpower and breed a timid female that has already ovulated but its cervix has not closed yet. This is more likely to happen if you have only a few females in the pasture with a breeding male. An alpaca stud—or herdsire, as many farmers call a breeding male—that must service a large herd of females is less likely to engage in frequent, potentially damaging repeat breedings with the same female. Field breeding will leave you totally guessing as to birth dates unless you limit the herdsire's presence in the female pasture to a few weeks.

Hand Breeding

There is a compromise between the two extremes—helicopter breeding and field breeding—and it's called hand breeding. The farmer determines the time and location of the breeding. If possible, the wise farmer will bring the male to the female. The reverse will awaken strong territorial instincts in the male and eventually cause much fighting if more than one sexually mature male is kept on the premises. It may also make a young male—new to the job or at the bottom of the males' social order—too nervous to perform. What follows is a description of the breeding protocol on *Stormwind Farm*.

I halter the female alpaca and confine it in a catch pen outdoors. After checking its vulva for any signs of abnormal discharge, I slip a sock—with the foot section cut off—over its tail. The sock keeps the fiber out of the way and makes it easier for the male to accomplish a quick intromission. While the female alpaca waits in its pen, I catch and halter the male in another catch pen. I walk the male to the female pasture and into the breeding pen. While holding the stud's lead in my right hand, I quickly grasp the female's lead with my left hand. I keep both leads firmly in my hands until the male has mounted the female. Most times, I then remove both leads, leave the breeding pen, and busy myself with pasture clean-up and barn chores. A breeding can easily last up to forty minutes. During that time, I can get quite a bit of work accomplished. Usually, the male decides when to terminate the breeding. Both alpacas may want to sniff and nuzzle each other for a while afterwards. I allow them ample time to do so. The female's tail wrap and the halters are removed before both animals are released into their respective pastures.

With a maiden, I remain in the breeding pen. Although their instincts and hormones tell them to submit to the male, some maiden alpacas are frightened of a new experience. I assume that some feel pain when the male breaks the hymen. I stay to give emotional support to the female and to ensure the safety of both alpacas. When a maiden is being bred, I usually leave the lead attached to the male's halter. An experienced male will not object to this, and it gives me more control should the female hysterically resist intromission or strongly object to the male's presence at any time. In that case, it is better to cancel the planned breeding and try again the next day.

On our farm, I manage hand breeding and behavior testing without help. I have quick reflexes, am strong, and do not feel intimidated by my males. The novice alpaca farmer may want to solicit help. Although orchestrating a breeding between two sexually experienced alpacas is usually easy, a combination of inexperienced farmer, inexperienced male, and maiden female is potentially a recipe for disaster without assistance. Given a choice, I would always breed a maiden to an older, experienced male. If you leave your females to be bred at other farms, ask about their breeding protocol. Don't assume that your females will be hand bred.

Quiet! The Alpacas Are Talking!

"They really do a lot of talking," a fellow farmer told me about her alpacas. "We just have to learn their language and pay attention to what they're telling us," she concluded.

How true! Our "speechless brothers"—and sisters—are not without speech at all. Their body language speaks volumes. Pay attention to what your females are telling you. Are the supposedly pregnant girls acting like friendly pets? The term "huggable investment,"—so popular in the alpaca industry—sends me into gales of laughter. If your females enjoy being hugged, their investment value has surely plummeted: They're not pregnant. Do they treat one another politely and nicely? These "ladies" are probably not pregnant. Are they especially kind and caring toward other females' crias? They're more than likely not pregnant. Female alpacas that cush when touched by people do not want to be petted and be your friend. They are not pregnant and want to be bred! (If it makes you happy, you can always pretend that the alpaca "loves" you. There's no harm in a little self-delusion that doesn't hurt anybody.)

What about male talk? When Fortune, one of the males on *Stormwind Farm*, does not orgle and try to get a female "down" (cush)—he just stands there with a resigned look on his face—I do not question what he tells me: "That female is pregnant. You are wasting my time." When Tasman refuses to get closer than ten feet to the female he bred seven days ago, I listen. "You are the leader on this farm, but I won't take a load of spit in my face because you can't smell that this female is pregnant," Tasman says to me. Only a very inexperienced, young and foolish, or socially clueless male alpaca will risk the rather smelly rejection of a mature female. Only a very inexperienced alpaca farmer will refuse to believe what the animals are saying and order expensive diagnostic tests.

Diagnostic Pregnancy Tests

Aside from paying attention to what the alpacas so clearly communicate, the alpaca farmer has several options to confirm a pregnancy. The frugal alpaca farmer with a small herd has, in my opinion, only one. *Behavior testing* is the cheapest diagnostic pregnancy test. You will need an intact, adult male on your farm for this purpose. Most pregnant females will *spit off* a male. These messages, given with firm authority to any male alpaca that persists in trying to breed, do not translate into rude behavior toward human beings. Although my pregnant females will spit at a male alpaca at the drop of a hay flake, they do not spit at me. Because it is possible to get caught in the crossfire—particularly if the female lacks confidence in its ability to fend off the male—I wear virtual rags when I behavior test. My supremely confident, older girls stand quietly and, should the male be brazen enough to approach them, calmly take aim and hit their target—the male's face—with amazing accuracy. Some alpacas will not spit but run away. A few—usually very submissive and fearful females—may cush even though they are pregnant. Fortunately, many females are very clear in their messages as to pregnancy status. I often detect an increasing aversion to being touched for any reason as the pregnancy progresses.

Another pregnancy testing option is an ultrasound performed by a veterinarian. Although a *rectal ultrasound* can detect the embryonic vesicle as early as fourteen days after copulation, many farmers elect to have this done between thirty and forty-five days. A *transabdominal ultrasound* can be performed at a later time in the gestation. Not all veterinarians are very skilled in reading the results or own a sophisticated ultrasound machine. There are also diagnostic *blood tests* as well as *palpation*. Diagnostic tests can run into large sums of money.

The turning point in our reproductive program came when Carol Masters pointed out to me: "The ultrasound test can tell you that your female is pregnant—*that day.*"

That's the problem with all diagnostic tests in a nutshell. Your alpaca can test pregnant on Monday and lose its pregnancy two days later. More than a few farmers have paid for an ultrasound, never tested again, and then—one year later—were shocked to find that there was no baby. I exclusively use behavior testing over a period of three months—with increasing intervals—and am more than satisfied with the results.

Embryonic Mortality and Abortions

The loss of a pregnancy from conception to sixty days is called embryonic mortality. From sixty days on, it is defined as an abortion. Numbers of losses vary considerably depending on which study is cited by individual authors. Even one loss represents a major financial setback for a farmer on a small budget. What are the reasons for embryonic death or abortion? How can you prevent losses on your farm?

Alpacas that are deprived of proper nutrition may not be able to sustain a pregnancy. Grazing on good pasture as well as being fed excellent quality hay, a mineral mix, and sensible, small portions of grain will go a long way toward protecting your investment. Certain plants, if ingested in large enough amounts, can induce abortions. Needles from the Western Yellow Pine, for example, are known to cause abortion in cattle. Ponderosa pine needles, broom weed, loco weed, and moldy, sweet clover are all mentioned in *The Merck Veterinary Manual* as causing abortion in farm animals. Remove harmful plants from your pastures. Stress can cause embryonic mortality or abortion. This includes emotional as well as heat induced stress. I already discussed how such stress can be minimized or avoided. Nitrate poisoning has been implicated in abortions, especially in ruminants. Fertilizer run-off can cause dangerous nitrate levels in plants and water sources. Apply organic fertilizer. Partially frozen drinking water leaves increased high nitrate content in the remaining water. Use water buckets with a heater element during cold temperatures. Viral and bacterial infections are other causative agents for abortions. Keeping a closed herd and not exhibiting your animals at shows or fairs will reduce the likelihood of infectious diseases on your farm to almost zero. Unfortunately, a closed herd cuts off any income from stud service and boarding. Prevent infection by maintaining a strict biosecurity area and insist on testing for diseases such as Bovine Viral Diarrhea Virus for incoming animals.

Genetic defects cause embryonic death in all species. Many species have well-documented lethal genes. Animals or human beings that carry a *single* dose of a lethal gene are perfectly healthy. Those who inherit the gene from *both* parents die—depending on the defect it codes for—in utero or shortly after birth. In rare cases, such as in Huntington's disease in man, affected individuals live to adulthood. Quite a few genes coding for coat color patterns have proven to be lethal in other species. Examples are dominant white in horses, yellow coat color in fancy mice, the merle pattern in dogs, and the roan pattern in horses.

In my early days as an alpaca farmer, I once waited for hours for a veterinarian to come out for a scheduled visit. "I am sorry I'm so late," she apologized upon arrival. She looked upset. "I had to euthanize a foal at a farm close to you," she explained. "It was born without an anal opening. The owners had bred their overo mare to an overo stallion."

I nodded. After reading extensively about genetic problems in other species, I was familiar with this defect—*anal atresia*. The foal's owner had bemoaned her "bad luck." I call it lack of information and education instead.

"Yes, breeding is more complicated than mating pretty to pretty," my friend, Denise Como, coauthor of *A Breeder's Guide to Genetics*, agreed when I told her the story.

My heart went out to the owner of the dead foal and the mare. With a little research, this sad experience could have been so easily avoided. Alpaca farmers who arrogantly believe that alpacas are exempt from lethal genes need a reality check. Lethal color genes—should they ever be scientifically established in alpacas—are not a reason for hysteria.

Some reasons for early embryonic death or abortion are out of a farmer's control. In horses, "the most common noninfectious cause of abortion... is twinning" (*The Merck Veterinary Manual*). That may be true for alpacas as well. Full-term twin alpaca births are extremely rare. Roughly 95 percent of alpaca embryos implant in the left uterine horn. Implantation in the right horn may be the cause of either embryonic death or abortion.

Infertility

It is beyond the scope of this book to discuss in depth the numerous reasons for infertility in alpacas. Some, such as deformities of the reproductive organs, you can't do anything about. Others you can rectify by sound husbandry practices. For example, sheep breeders discovered long ago that extremely thin ewes had problems conceiving. This is true for any anorexic mammal including a woman. Increasing the female's weight to boost fertility is called flushing. In alpacas, flushing may consist of allowing marginally thin animals to graze on high quality pasture or have alfalfa added to their diet. As I've pointed out in a previous chapter, adding large amounts of grain or feed pellets to achieve this effect can cause severe health problems. Grossly overweight females also experience diminished fertility. Males can have weight related fertility problems as well. I know of one case where a very fat male was physically unable to breed. This male alpaca had been co-owned, and one owner allowed it to become grotesquely obese. Of course, the co-owner was furious when the male arrived at his farm unable to perform.

A male may be infertile due to age, illness, or heat stress. If the latter happens, it will take weeks for sperm count to increase sufficiently to impregnate a female. A fever will have the same effect. In severe cases, infertility may be permanent. The frugal farmer should think twice before taking a stud to a large indoor show where exposure to viruses can result in a high fever. When you are repeatedly hosing down your alpacas during a blistering hot day, you're doing more than keeping the animals comfortable—you are protecting your investment.

I have no scientific proof for my opinion, so take it for what it's worth: I am convinced that many "fertility problems" are the result of poor husbandry practices or mismanaged breeding protocols.

Embryo Transfer and Artificial Insemination

Both reproductive options are used extensively in other livestock industries. They have been practiced to a much lesser degree by camelid producers. In the USA, the *Alpaca Owners Association* (AOA) started to accept the registration of alpacas born as the result of either embryo transfer or artificial insemination on or after January 1, 2017. I question the wisdom of this decision.

Artificial insemination is sometimes used by livestock farmers who do not wish to expose their families to the dangers of housing a sexually mature male on the premises. Alpaca farmers need not have such fears. A correctly raised, handled, and trained alpaca stud shows no aggression toward people. Another reason to elect artificial insemination involves transportation. A bull, for example, requires a large trailer if it needs to be moved from one farm to the next. An alpaca stud—if no trailer is available—can be transported in the family van or similar vehicle. Over time, most livestock farmers wish to diversify their breeding programs. Proponents of artificial insemination and embryo transfer always stress how these reproductive programs will speed up genetic improvement in a herd. In theory, that is correct. Like many theories, it takes a simplistic approach to a complex issue. Additionally, alpacas are induced ovulators. Without induced ovulation, there will be no pregnancy no matter how many straws with semen or frozen embryos are purchased and used. If an alpaca male cannot be used to induce ovulation, then drugs must do the job. They do not always work the first time and maybe not the second and third time. Add up the expenses: Straws with semen or frozen embryos, drugs, veterinary farm calls and treatments, ultrasound or blood tests to confirm pregnancy—where is the ultimate *profit* for the *female alpaca's owner*?

I read several articles about alpaca embryo transfer and artificial insemination. None of the authors who so enthusiastically endorsed these programs addressed the stress these procedures impose on the alpacas. None addressed possible health issues for the farmers who are exposed to the hormones that must be used in these programs. Scientists already have grave concerns about hormones in our environment. Our industry advertises alpacas as "environmentally friendly" livestock. Does this label apply to farms where artificial insemination or embryo transfer is practiced?

Breeding Contracts

Be extremely careful when reading and discussing breeding contracts. Make sure you understand exactly what you are signing. A good contract should cover the possibility of a non-pregnancy. Set a time limit as to how many days the stud's owners have to get your female pregnant. Which pregnancy test will you agree to and who will pay for it? Will the stud fee be returned to you if the male dies before your female is pregnant? Are co-owners involved who may complicate matters? Breeding management can become very complex when you add a human factor into the mix.

15

BIRTH AND CRIA CARE

"Don't expect an emergency with each birth, but be prepared to deal with one." Jane Marks

Stormwind Farm's Best Practices

There are many different opinions and protocols on handling alpaca births and cria care. In this chapter, I give my opinions and describe my own procedures. My management style differs greatly from that embraced by most alpaca farmers. You, your veterinarian, or the seller of your alpacas may not agree with what I consider best practices. That's all right. I long ago lost any burning desire to convince others to adopt my program. Nevertheless, keep an open mind and evaluate what you learn here as to suitability for your own farm and alpacas.

Best Advice

Farmers who manage difficult births and save severely compromised crias are hailed as heroes in our industry. Fellow farmers are eager to pump them for information. If I hosted a neonatal clinic with a veterinarian who teaches how to deal with dystocias and sick crias, I would probably fill all spots. If I offered a seminar teaching prospective alpaca farmers how to *prevent* dystocias and sick crias on their farms, I would more than likely be talking to myself. That is sad. That mindset is also the reason why many alpaca farmers never see a profit.

After twenty years of raising alpacas, I am still eager to learn from the farmer who says: "I have nothing exciting to report. The births on my farm have all been easy and uneventful. I wouldn't kow a Pritchard nipple if I fell over it because I never had to use one."

In keeping with my book's mission, I will discuss how I manage births and cria care the frugal way on our farm.

Best Time of the Year

Air temperature at birth can have a huge impact on the cria's health and survival. Neither extreme cold nor extreme heat are ideal weather conditions for an alpaca birth. Alpaca moms don't lick their babies dry. If a cria is born outside— undetected by you—during freezing temperatures, it will probably freeze to death before it has a chance to follow mom into a shelter. Low body temperature also makes absorption and digestion of colostrum and milk impossible. Unusually high temperatures, coupled with lack of access to shade, can severely dehydrate a cria. Eventually, even a healthy baby will be too weak to stand up and nurse. Unfortunately, weather extremes call for intervention such as drying the cria or confining both dam and cria inside the barn. Long confinement can be the cause of many problems. Under normal circumstances, confinement is neither necessary nor desirable. The best time of the year for parturition is a season with many sunny days and moderate temperatures. On our farm, I have always avoided winter births and stop all breeding as well as behavior testing by the beginning of December.

Best Location

The best location for a birth is in the middle of a pasture. There are several reasons. A pasture is often cleaner than a barn. A smart alpaca mom would rather not be anywhere near a dung pile while giving birth. Of course, just like in the human population, not every alpaca can be the sharpest pencil in the box, but the vast majority of females will prefer clean pasture if it's available. Birth on a pasture gives a cria non-slippery footing. A pasture environment encourages it to get up on its feet as soon as possible. That's desirable behavior for the young of a prey species.

Although alpacas want their herd members to be present while they give birth, they do not wish to be crowded. A spacious pasture allows for plenty of room for mom and four-legged spectators.

All alpacas will initially cluster tightly around the newborn. Once their curiosity is satisfied, they'll move on to graze but remain in close proximity to mama and baby. The older females may assist in subtle ways to start the baby nursing. Their presence and help is especially comforting to females that gave birth to and are raising their first offspring. At times, my herd includes an alpaca that I refer to as a "baby snatcher." These females want a baby so badly that they will try to "steal" a newborn cria from its mother. An alpaca mom that is confident and ranks high in the herd hierarchy will handle this, and not too gently. A timid mother will become distraught or fail to bond with the cria. With the latter, I remove the baby snatcher from the herd until the cria has nursed several times.

If one of my alpacas chooses to give birth inside the barn, I move mom and baby outside as soon as possible—weather permitting. Crias are genetically programmed to search for milk underneath a dark space. In a pasture, that's the dam's belly. In a barn, the darkest area is often a corner. Crias will go there driven by a natural instinct that does not factor in an unnatural birthing environment like a barn. Farmers call these babies *dummy crias*. It seems fairer to me to call those who force an alpaca to give birth inside a barn without compelling reason *dummy farmers*. A pasture makes it easier for the cria to focus on its mother. Being able to focus is good for both mom and baby. Focus means bonding, early nursing, passing meconium, absorption of colostrum—and with it the all-important transfer of antibodies. Early nursing means vigorous contraction of the uterus and expelling of the placenta. This in turn means a clean uterus with no or little possibility of infection.

Best Preparations Prior to Birth

On *Stormwind Farm*, preparation for a birth—also called parturition—begins long before the event. Actually, it's an organic, continuous process that begins when an alpaca is born and culminates with the birth of its own cria. Breeding females are well nourished from the day they are born. My nutritional program promotes steady but not accelerated growth. Although I feed supplements sparingly, I presently have several alpacas in my herd that are overweight. Fat alpacas may have difficulty giving birth. They often produce less milk than their slimmer herd mates. Nevertheless, I very much disagree with the often seen advice to take overweight alpacas off pasture. In my opinion, it's better for the full-figured girls to exercise and eat plants rich in vitamins and minerals than to sit inside a barn or small dirt lot next to a hay feeder all day. Spacious pastures with an excellent variety of nutritious plants lure the alpacas out of the barn and encourage walking as well as vigorous pronking at dusk. Our females are all physically strong and toned. Hosing down the shorn alpacas from their heads to their toes encourages them to graze and exercise even on the hottest days of the year.

Keeping a pregnant female calm and content is as important as a good nutritional program. Stressing the expectant mom also harms the fetus. All farm routines are designed to remove or minimize discomfort, fear, and worry— anything that could cause a prey animal to mount a stress response.

The decision whether to shear a female alpaca in late pregnancy is a tricky one. On one side, the alpaca may abort due to the stress of being shorn at that vulnerable time. On the other side, it may abort due to heat stress caused by a heavy fiber coat. We have always opted to shear and have not lost a cria.

Most veterinarians advise inoculating the dam with a CD&T booster vaccination one month prior to the approximate birthing date. The vaccine can cause an allergic reaction. After extensive research, I elected not to vaccinate at that time. *Clostridium* disease (C and D) is usually not a problem with pastured livestock that also has access to good hay at all times and is fed little or no supplements other than minerals. The occurrence of *tetanus* (T) in alpacas is rare. Considering the low risk factor on my farm, I feel comfortable with the choice I made.

Three weeks prior to the *earliest* projected birthing date—counting 335 days from conception—I suspend the Dectomax injections. If toenails are due to be trimmed around that time, I skip the session unless a particular female has an especially placid disposition. Some females react with total indifference to the trimming of nails on the front feet but get upset if I touch their back legs late in pregnancy. In their cases, I only trim the nails of the front feet to make them more comfortable. During birthing season, I am even more fastidious about cleaning up dung piles than during other times. Although I normally remove dung once a day, I do so twice daily when I know that a cria is due to be born. I check the supplies in the farm's cria kit. Because I have little practical experience with dystocias, I review information written by various authors about emergency situations. Although it may be less costly in the long run to call a skilled veterinarian during a difficult birth, I don't count on one being available.

Best Cria Kit

Our cria medical kit contains lubricant (KY Jelly), an empty film canister (for Nolvasan), a bar of Ivory soap, a small plastic enema bottle, anti-bacterial liquid soap, Nolvasan, sterile gloves, and a thermometer. If these supplies are ever not sufficient to do the job, I would feel it wise to call our veterinarian. She will bring her own supplies and the expertise to use them. If your farm's location is a far distance from any veterinarian and farm supply store, you should be better equipped.

Best Count-Down Calendar

We learn from Dr. Fowler that "the usual length of gestation ranges from 335 to 360 days" in camelids, an *average* of 347.5 days. This wide time span is a frustrating component of breeding alpacas—if you allow it to become that way! Intense scrutiny of the pregnant females and obsessive calculations create tension in barns and pastures as well as inside the human dwelling. It's best to relax. Although I keep a calendar of the earliest expected birthing dates, I don't view a birth as a tightly scheduled rocket launch. The cria will start the birthing process when it is good and ready.

Three Stages of Labor

If you are at all observant, it will become obvious to you very quickly that many alpacas are determined to give birth in privacy, without human beings hovering closely over them and interfering. It is therefore quite possible, even for an experienced livestock farmer, to miss the *first stage* of labor. During this preliminary stage, the uterus contracts and the cervix dilates. If the dam is experienced, healthy, and in good condition, she may display absolutely no signs of the changes taking place inside her body. That is perfect behavior for the member of a prey species. Acting "normal" under any and all circumstances insures survival. Of course, not all alpacas manage to hide the first stage of labor. First time dams especially may show discomfort and express anxiety. They may hum, get up and down repeatedly, visit the dung pile numerous times, and appear restless and out of sorts. In any case, the first stage of labor lasts approximately one to six hours. The average time for first time (primiparous) dams can be expected to be longer than that of dams with several (multiparous) births to their credit.

The *second stage* of labor is the actual birth of the cria. Once you can see the cria's head and feet, the entire body should be completely expelled in approximately thirty minutes.

During the *third stage*, the placenta is expelled. In my personal experience, this happens within one hour or less. The cria's nursing stimulates the process.

Best Restraint Methods

I feel strongly that many alpaca owners are much too intrusive about handling birth and cria care. At some farms, farmers *routinely* pull crias out of their dams and vigorously manage bonding, first nursing, first pooping, and Lord knows what else. Special birthing stalls are prepared. Moms and crias are forced to remain inside the barn for hours or even days at a time. That's not how nature intended an alpaca to give birth. Much harm can be done by farmers who are not very knowledgeable and cannot restrain themselves from interfering. We must always remember that it is *normal* for the animal to take care of the entire process without help. Major human interference often leads to a first-time mother rejecting the cria. Even experienced moms may become distraught over repeated and prolonged human handling of their babies.

It's not the alpacas that need to be restrained while giving birth but their meddling owners. The best restraint method starts prior to the birth. I repress the urge to lift up a female's tail to check whether "things have started." While such an action may cause only minor stress, I don't think it's far-fetched to speculate that repeated episodes can have a negative impact on mom and baby. According to Dr. Fowler, it takes twenty-four to forty-eight hours for lymphocyte levels to return to normal after a cortisol stress response.

During and after a normal, routine birth, my role is that of observer. There is nothing, or very little, to handle. How do I restrain myself? I use binoculars to observe the birth from a distance. After the cria is born, the hardest part is to watch it try to rise and nurse. How tempting to intervene and help! I don't. Instead, I busy myself with cleaning the pastures, pulling weeds, straightening out the barns' service areas—there is always something to do on a farm. My main take-home lesson here is not to interfere *without necessity*.

Best Use of the Placenta

The placenta can be a great source for saving money. To register a cria with the AOA, you must submit a specially designed blood card with a few drops of the cria's blood dribbled inside the card's outlined circle. After the

Bovine Viral Diarrhea Virus became an ugly reality in the alpaca world, the registry offered a BVDV test. Fortunately, the laboratory uses the blood from the DNA card for that purpose. It is possible to draw blood from one of the veins inside the placenta. The AOA staff cautioned farmers that the DNA results may be compromised if the placenta somehow becomes contaminated. We were advised to only use this procedure if the placenta was caught in a plastic bag without first touching the ground.

I scoop up the placenta in a plastic bag and save it for a few hours in a container filled with ice. If there is suspicion that the cria is ill, the veterinarian will need to examine the placenta for important diagnostic purposes. Because alpacas—unlike bitches—don't show any interest in consuming the placenta, I am not depriving a female of a natural process by removing it.

Best Cria Assessment

"Ingrid, you have to come out and see my cria! It's deformed. Its legs are horribly crooked, and the ears are turned inside out. What should I do?"

I could tell that the caller was nearly hysterical and would have difficulty processing my information.

"Relax," I answered. "Wait and see …"

"Wait and see? My baby will have to be put to sleep and you are telling me to 'Wait and see'?" the distressed alpaca owner cried.

Ignoring the hostility in her voice, I calmly explained that more than likely, the cria's legs will be perfectly straight and the ear leathers will be in their correct position in a few days. Nutrition, exercise, and time take care of what many novice farmers judge to be permanent deformities. Sometimes, instant action is required to save a cria, but quite often, it is best to take a deep breath, relax, and wait. You'll see!

Best Newborn Care

Liquid Nolvasan Surgical Scrub and water are mixed in the small film canister at a ratio of 1:3. I dip the navel into the mixture shortly after birth and again two hours later. If the day is overcast or the newborn has crooked legs, I administer 3cc of a vitamin (A, D, E, and B12) and probiotics paste to the cria. That's the extent of my care for the newborn. The alpaca mama takes care of everything else.

Some farmers strip the waxy plugs from the dam's teats. A healthy, strong cria has absolutely no difficulty stripping the plugs. Because the plugs are there to prevent leakage of colostrum, I think it's best to leave them there unless the baby is too weak to stand and nurse on its own. I allow mom and cria to sort things out. I don't try to be "helpful" and push baby underneath mom. Most babies will stagger around and fumble a bit. That is normal. Of the many animals I have raised so far, I only had to show a single one how to latch on to a teat.

Best Veterinary Care for the Newborn

In a word: none! That describes my routine and choice. Inexperienced farmers who are unsure about normal cria behavior and health may want a consultation with a veterinarian.

Your veterinarian may diagnose a heart murmur in the newborn. According to Dr. Fowler, "the presence of a murmur is a frequent, perhaps normal, clinical finding in a newborn." Don't immediately hit the panic button and order expensive tests. If the murmur persists beyond a week or two, your can explore further testing.

Many farmers ask their veterinarian to routinely run IgG tests and then order plasma transfusions whenever the count is below the number they don't feel comfortable with. What is IgG? In *The Merck Veterinary Manual*, we learn that antibody molecules—immunoglobulins—fall into several classes: IgA, IgM, IgG, and IgE. The production of antibodies is necessary to help the body handle disease. Dr. Fowler emphasizes that immunoglobulin G (IgG) is "the main source of antibodies" for the camelid cria and its concentration is "a crucial component in the survival of the neonate." Crias can only acquire antibodies from their dam's colostrum within several hours after birth. When a cria is around three weeks old, the protection it gains from the dam ceases to function and its own immune system must kick in if it is to remain healthy.

I elect not to test for IgG levels for several reason:

Drawing blood twenty-four hours after birth stresses baby and mom. A transfusion is an invasive procedure that can *cause* problems for an otherwise healthy baby. I am not particularly interested in the levels of passive immunity at twenty-four hours of age. Levels of active immunity at breeding age would be more meaningful to me. I consider the cost of testing too high for the information I get from the results.

You can purchase a test kit and save money by performing the test yourself. Will you pay for the very expensive transfusion if results show low IgG levels? "That's a personal decision," a friend of mine who disagrees with my program pointed out. Of course it is! With the exception of farm management issues that are governed by local, state, or federal laws, everything any of us do on our farms is based on personal decisions.

I stated in a previous chapter that the frugal farmer cannot justify the expense as part of a *routine* reproductive management plan. Financial justification for the procedures can be found in variables such as high purchase price of the breeding stock, a projected future high sales price of a cria, proof that low IgG levels are not of genetic origin (for example, death of the cria's dam at birth), and possibly others. Decision to test and treat can also be justified purely based on an emotional attachment to the cria or the belief that all attempts must be made to preserve a life. Owners should view their choices in a realistic light. At current (2017) sales prices, routine testing and transfusions performed by a veterinarian will most likely wipe out your profits. After a few years, the IRS may have something to say about that. If your breeding program is a hobby, you need not show a profit. You can still practice frugality in other management areas of your hobby farm.

There is a situation that warrants a visit from a veterinarian to speed up the testing process. *If you have any reason to suspect that your cria is a persistently infected (PI) baby, quarantine protocols must be implemented before birth and the cria should be tested for BVDV as soon after birth as possible.* (I discuss this in more detail in the chapter on biosecurity.) Observe strict biosecurity protocols until you receive news that the test result is negative. If, unfortunately, the result is positive, immediate euthanasia of the infected cria is advisable even though it may look and act healthy at that time.

Best Imprinting Practices

Some behavior specialists and farmers advocate imprinting the newborn on human caretakers. This involves intensive touching and handling of the cria immediately after birth. *I am vehemently opposed to this practice.* In the wild, it is important for young prey animals to be up on their feet and running as soon after birth as possible. Although alpacas do not live in the wild, the instincts of their vicuña ancestors have survived over thousands of years of domestication. Why do farmers think that an alpaca is indifferent to seeing its newborn massaged, stroked, and held down by two-legged creatures? I believe it's an intense worry to the alpaca mom to see the baby stretched flat on the ground rather than learning to walk as rapidly as possible. I strongly feel that the hands-off approach is even more important with first-time mothers that may be slightly confused about their new role in life and very confused about the smell of human scent all over their newborns. These alpacas need peace and quiet to concentrate, not have their ability to think straight destroyed by worries over what the two-legged meddlers are up to. *Yes, imprinting right after birth is important, but it should be the cria imprinting on its dam —the alpaca mother—and not on a human being!* With careful, skilled handling and training begun at a much later time, my alpaca crias are just fine in their interaction with me, even without this early tour de force.

Best Cria Coat

The best cria coat is a little alpaca's own fiber coat. A healthy, full-term, vigorously nursing, and dry cria will not need a garment worn on top of its own, natural "coat." Alpacas are supremely equipped to handle low temperatures. Nevertheless, because newborns lack the ability to regulate their temperature, I have a cria coat for emergencies. If babies shiver or their body temperature dips below normal, additional protection is indicated. During twenty years of raising alpacas, the coat has been used once; I put it on a very tiny, premature cria during cold nighttime temperatures.

A cria coat can be homemade and need not be fancy. The outside should be water repellent. The coat doesn't need to be pretty or "cute," just functional. Beware that some alpacas will reject their cria if its appearance has been "altered" with a coat. Don't put a coat on a newborn baby and leave the premises immediately. Make absolutely sure that fasteners cannot come apart. You don't want to find the baby strangled in its coat.

Best Cria Care

Based on my definition, an alpaca is a cria until it is weaned. Healthy crias require minimal care. If a cria is born in the fall, I continue to give a weekly dose of vitamin paste until the beginning of May. A CD&T inoculation is given at two months of age and a booster one month later. I check dung piles and occasionally underneath a cria's tail for signs of diarrhea. If probiotics do not stop the diarrhea within two days, I administer medicine that will cure a bacterial infection. Dectomax injections begin at roughly one month of age.

Best Cria Weights

I was a speaker at a conference when I heard a fellow farmer brag: "Our last cria weighed twenty-five pounds at birth. Yep, he is a big boy."

There was pride in the man's voice. I casually inquired about the name of the sire and mentally made a note to myself *not* to breed an alpaca to this male. Cattle breeders select sires based on the low birth weights of their progeny; why was the alpaca farmer boasting about his giant cria? I don't know. Large babies account for many dystocias—difficult births—among mammals. Alpacas are no exception. I weigh healthy, lively newborn crias so I can assure a buyer that the baby's sire is *not* genetically programmed to produce offspring with abnormally heavy birth weights. Fourteen to eighteen pounds for a full-term cria makes me happy.

I weigh the cria the day after it was born and prior to Dectomax injections. Since we do not produce alpacas for meat consumption, I do not promote rapid growth by encouraging crias to eat supplements other than kelp. On our farm, weight gain is the result of each cria's genetically programmed growth rate and its dam's milk supply. I judge a cria's health by its level of activity. For example, when I observe a three-week-old alpaca baby run and pronk for ten uninterrupted minutes, I am not the least bit interested to find out how much weight it has gained since birth.

Best Weaning Practices

A healthy alpaca should easily be able to nurse a cria for six to eight months. Because most crias begin to graze on pasture and nibble on hay within a few weeks after birth, the entire burden of feeding does not fall on their dams. Initially, though, the mother's milk supply provides all nutrients.

Weaning practices vary depending on each alpaca mama's temperament and mothering skills. Some mamas, once they decide to wean, will firmly repel all attempts at nursing no matter how much the cria begs. Others will refuse during the day but will allow one nursing before the cria settles down for the night. Many mamas are more indulgent with their daughters than their sons. Pregnant females will usually wean a cria in plenty of time to produce colostrum for the new baby. Human intervention is neither necessary nor desirable. There are exceptions, of course. I intervened on several occasions when male crias made a nuisance of themselves and stressed out all the pregnant females by trying to practice breeding behavior. When they were six months old, I put them in the back male pasture under the supervision of Dexter, our oldest male alpaca. There was unhappy humming and nervous pacing for a day or two. In all cases, I believe that the mothers were relieved to see their precocious sons gone from their pasture.

Best Handling and Training Protocols

When I trained my Whippet foundation bitch for a C.D. (Companion Dog) title, her obedience trainer, my friend Barbara Ewing, taught me an important skill: patience. I still remember her reminding me again and again: "Allow the dog to *think* about what it is you are asking it to do. If it stands there in seeming confusion—wait! Give it time to sort things out in its head."

Marty McGee Bennett gives almost identical advice for training alpacas. The techniques, though, call for knowledge of species specific instincts and behavior. What works for a puppy—our fellow predator—does not work for a prey animal. Like McGee Bennett, I differentiate between handling and training. When I handle a cria, I expect it to remain calm and stand still, allowing me to give inoculations, examine its fiber, or administer vitamins. My crias are handled at weekly intervals. The sessions are brief—only mere seconds—and their moms remain with them inside the catch pen. Teaching a cria to walk on lead belongs in the training category because the cria must be an active participant. If a cria is sold and will leave the farm at six months of age, I start training a month prior to its departure. Otherwise, I am quite relaxed as to the beginning of training. Prey animals have great memories. Once learned, never forgotten! An alpaca learns very quickly if it is not worried about being separated from its mother. If early training becomes necessary for whatever reason, you will need to be very patient.

One of the biggest mistakes a trainer can make with a little alpaca is trying to push it through Alpaca Kindergarten all the way to Alpaca College in one or two lessons. People who are very goal oriented and eager to meet objectives and benchmarks will struggle with the concept of allowing the cria to set the learning pace. Some alpacas learn to accept a halter and walk on lead in two lessons. Others may need three sessions before they will take their first step. I view the training time as an opportunity to slow down—mentally and physically. Working with a cria is balm for my soul. All my movements are deliberate but calm. My body language is relaxed; my breathing evenly quiet. In *The Alpacas of Stormwind Farm*, I describe how I sing to my crias during training. It works. I cancel a handling or training session if I am tense and can't manage to relax.

Best Intervention

At the risk of sounding like a nag, I repeat: Interfering and meddling with the birth and the alpaca mother-child bonding may have very unpleasant consequences, the least of which are high veterinary bills and sleepless nights for the farmer. Occasionally, of course, things can go wrong during and after the birthing process. For example, we had one case where a first-time dam did not bond with its cria. This female showed none of the typical signs of a caring alpaca mama: nuzzling, sniffing, quick kisses, and anxious glances at the human beings in close proximity. While the newborn tottered aimlessly around the pasture, mom wandered away from the baby, totally ignoring it. This was obviously not a normal situation.

A friend advised me to sequester mom and baby in a catch pen inside the barn by themselves. I modified her advice somewhat and arranged for the two alpacas to have their own pasture adjacent to the rest of the herd. Next, I served Mariah a small amount of grain on top of Apple's back. That's right, mom had to nibble the grain right off the baby. It worked like magic. Deprived of the other alpacas' company and associating the cria now with a tasty treat, Mariah almost immediately focused on the task of being a devoted mom. Several hours later, I returned both to the pasture housing the other females and crias. This is one example where lack of intervention could have had a bad outcome for the cria.

I am not opposed to human intervention if circumstances require it. For example, I have administered an enema to an alpaca cria that, for whatever reason, was unable to pass meconium many hours after it had been born and strained at the dung pile. In my experience, alpacas often tolerate and even ask for help in a very trusting manner during times of need. Their trust in you will grow if you remain calm and in control of your emotions at all times.

It's best to have a plan in place for a major emergency. Rational decisions require thoughtful evaluation. That's hard when people are upset. On our farm, for example, we made the decision that intervention will never include treatment at a veterinary hospital. Farming with livestock sometimes requires that hard choices must be made. Not everybody feels equipped to do so.

"The constant drama with the birthings just wore me out," one alpaca owner admitted to me. "I sold all my breeding stock. Now I only have fiber boys, and I absolutely love it."

It's wonderful when a farming venture offers you choices. But why was there constant drama? Did this woman create drama because she did not provide a good birthing environment—pasture!—or use common sense? I did not ask because, at that time, it no longer mattered.

Best Teachers

One way to cut down on the drama is to familiarize yourself more thoroughly with the three phases of a birth and how you can take care of minor problems yourself. There is good reason to fear that your veterinarian will *not* be able to get to your farm within a few minutes of receiving your call for help. It is important for you to educate yourself on all aspects of alpaca care. A prepared farmer will hopefully also be a calm farmer.

In many cases, too many cooks ruin the broth, the cake, the stew—whatever. Three's a crowd, but not in this case: The three authors of *Llama and Alpaca Neonatal Care* must have worked in great harmony to produce such a valuable reference resource for novice alpaca farmers. Read it!

Best Time on the Farm

Some owners are so focused on worrying about their crias' health and monetary values that they completely forget to simply enjoy them. Their tunnel vision causes them to miss a lot of fun. The playfulness and social interactions of alpaca babies provide endless entertainment to the quiet observer. There are the bold ones, the shy ones, the future herd bosses, the prissy girls, the mama boys, the tomboys, and the partners in crime. The latter are usually a duo of males that travel the pasture and get in trouble together. Most crias enjoy a healthy mix of maternal attention and independent playtime. Dusk often finds all babies joyfully pronking around the pasture and in and out of the barn. Sometimes, the adults join in. When night falls, it's as if the herd boss rings a bell: Time to come home and go to bed! Each cria nurses one last time and then cushes contentedly next to its mom. I check water buckets one last time, make sure that all the gates are latched securely, and go in the house—with the healthy kind of tiredness felt by those who perform hard, physical work.

16

LIVESTOCK GUARDIANS

"I am fortunate to own a working Livestock Guardian Dog. My Anatolian Shepherd, Hugo, is a valued partner on my small alpaca farm. Not all dogs make suitable Livestock Guardians. The right dog, with the right owner, and the proper environment combine for a truly rewarding experience." Kristin Joyce

Alpaca Playtime

Our alpacas rarely spend time in the barn. Breeze, the female we bought in 1997, is quite the outdoor girl. After a recent snowfall, Breeze led the herd into the front pasture. While the other alpacas watched with a slightly bemused look on their faces, the old herd boss and a tiny cria ran in ever increasing circles through the deep, powdery snow. After some hesitation, most of the females and juveniles joined the wintery fun. They ran, pronked, pranced, kicked up their heels, and chased one another with joyful abandon. Eventually, several of the older alpacas stopped, looked around, and returned to the barn. Soon, the others followed. Minutes later, they were all peacefully cushed and chewing their cud. This digestive process, unique to ruminants, is quite interesting to watch. It is essential to the alpacas' health. Not chewing cud even for one day is a sure sign of a digestive problem. Once a ruminant is unable to bring up cud, it's in serious trouble. I learned from Juliette de Baïracli Levy that dripping saliva is a symptom of this condition. The cause may be—to name just a few examples—poisoning, feed inhalation, reaction to vaccination or other drugs, or even rabies.

That snowy morning, illness and disease were far from my mind. I love those quiet, peaceful times. Sitting in the barn on a bale of straw, I cherish being in the presence of creatures the South American pastoralists call their speechless brothers. Except on rare occasions, alpacas are very quiet. There isn't the usual neighing, snorting, barking, crowing, screeching, and bellowing heard from so many other farm animals or pets. Alpacas occasionally hum, mostly when they're stressed and worried. Moms hum to their crias or make clucking sounds. The wrestling matches of intact male alpacas occasionally escalate into ferocious screaming matches. If you keep two or more sexually mature males in one pasture, you may hear this sometimes daily, especially if you have an open female in your herd or recently added a new stud to your male line-up. Once the social hierarchy has been well established in a male pasture and barn, fighting and screaming are rare occurrences.

Alpaca Alert

Occasionally, alpacas produce a sound that virtually defies description. It's a shrill alarm cry meant to alert the herd and frighten off intruders, and it's completely different from any other sounds you will ever hear from your camelids. When you hear this cry, don't be surprised to find that a stranger has entered your premises. Of course, the threat may also be a strange cat, a hot air balloon flying low over your land, or a family member wearing a new hat. After living on a farm for several months, alpacas become accustomed to the sight of wildlife or pets that make regular appearances in or next to their pastures. Our alpacas no longer become alarmed at the sight of deer or the tabby cat that belongs to one of our neighbors.

As prey animals, alpacas are vulnerable to attack by predators. On the North American continent, alpacas have been injured and killed by coyotes, bears, dogs—including the family dog or a neighbor's pet dogs allowed to roam—and wild cats such as the mountain lion. Residents of urban areas in New Jersey are almost always shocked when they are told that our state has a sizable coyote population. You may very well be surprised when you investigate predator species and populations for your own location.

SSS

Farmers are usually equipped with a gun or other equipment to kill predators. Some follow the old advice to *Shoot, Shovel and Shut up* (SSS). Those who are caught killing predators illegally pay heavy fines. This includes birds of prey, a threat that usually flies—pun intended—below the radar of most novice livestock farmers. Some areas of the USA, for example, are home to American Black vultures. These powerful birds usually eat carrion. They will also pick the eyes out of newborn calves or other livestock to send the babies into shock followed by death. American Black vultures are legally protected. Without a permit, a farmer does not have the right to shoot a vulture that swoops down on a newborn farm animal with the intent to make it a meal. Ignorance of the law will not protect you.

Livestock Guardians

A farmer has many options to safe-guard his or her herd. I discussed several in previous chapters. Aside from electrified fencing, flood lights, motion detectors, night cages, and human guards, livestock producers also use animals—known as Livestock Guardians—to protect their vulnerable flocks or herds. Species used for this purpose include dogs, llamas, and donkeys. The purchase of a Livestock Guardian requires careful consideration and extensive research as to suitability for each farm's unique environment and circumstances.

Llamas

The Swiss Berner Oberland is considered a high danger zone for grazing animals. The German magazine *Lamas* features an informative article in the winter 2002 edition. Three accompanying photos show the grotesquely contorted corpses of alpacas killed and partially eaten by a lynx. In stark contrast, a fourth photo shows a flock of sheep grazing peacefully, protectively guarded by an alert llama gelding named Flip. The story? In 1999, a llama was used in Switzerland to guard a flock of forty sheep in the Swiss Alps. Not a single sheep was lost that year. In 2001, this area was stocked with 200 alpacas. Their guardian? A llama. During the summer of 2002, things changed. The alpaca herd had been sold to British farmers. As part of the preliminary quarantine requirements, the llama had to be removed. Within two months of its departure, three alpacas were killed by a lynx. The article's author, Dr. Uli Lippl, assures the readers that alpacas will never be grazed in the Berner Alps without a llama to protect them. What is particularly interesting are the observations made by Dr. Lippl that male members of the unguarded alpaca herd were more restless and prone to fighting. The guarded alpacas accepted the llama as their boss, and young males did not feel the need to fight for the dominant position in the herd. What a wonderful endorsement for the services of the larger alpaca cousins.

You don't have to travel to the Swiss Alps to find a llama guardian. Carol Reigh of *Buckhollow Llamas* in Birdsboro, Pennsylvania, is one of the North American farmers who breed and sell llamas for the purpose of protecting small livestock species. She has written about llamas guarding alpacas as well as sheep. One article described the behavior that, according to Carol, made one of her llamas, Annie, an outstanding guardian:

- Annie ran the perimeter of the field before the sheep went out in the morning.
- She didn't come in at night until *all* of the sheep were in.
- If one stayed out, she stayed out with it.
- She gave the alarm call any time a dog came on the premises.
- She was visibly upset if she thought the sheep were being hurt or distressed (especially during deworming).
- She stood and looked toward the woods—wary of predators—for extended periods of time.

Without a doubt, a well-trained female llama or gelded male llama can be the perfect choice to serve as a guardian for alpacas. A female llama should only guard female alpacas because male alpacas would want to breed it. An intact male is only suitable to guard male alpacas. The care protocols are identical for the guardian and the herd that it protects. A llama would only be slightly more expensive to keep than an alpaca. The only fly in the ointment—dung pile?—is the size of a llama. In your barn, it will take up the space of two alpacas. If your pastures are small, they will be grazed down so much faster with a llama present.

Guardian Donkeys

Although I don't know of any alpaca farmers who use donkeys in that capacity, large donkeys are effective guardians on livestock farms. They are not without problems. The author of an article in a livestock publication wrote about an experience on her farm. The donkey bonded with and protected her goats. Unfortunately, when a goat gave birth, the donkey viewed the newborn kid (baby goat) as an intruder, grabbed it with its teeth, and shook it to death. The novice alpaca farmer who is not familiar with donkeys must learn care protocols for two species. Most people struggle initially to gather and process all knowledge that is necessary to raise alpacas.

Livestock Guardian Dogs

A llama or even a large donkey will most likely not frighten large predators such as bear, wolves, and mountain lions away from your herd. A large and ferociously barking dog may stand a better chance to keep your alpacas safe under these circumstances. There seems to be a misconception among the general public that "people friendly" dogs will also like alpacas. It is the natural instinct of a predator (dog) to chase and kill prey (alpacas). Livestock Guardian Dogs (LGD)—also known as Livestock Protection Dogs (LPD)—and a few *individuals* of other breeds are the exception. (In the case of the latter, don't try to make a test case out of your alpacas.) Generations of selective breeding removed the desire to chase and kill prey animals in the LGD. Suitable breeds include: Anatolian Shepherd Dogs, Great Pyrenees, Komondorok, Maremma, Akbash, Tibetan Mastiff, and Kuvaszok.

Livestock Guardian Dogs are *never or rarely* permitted to leave their flock/herd. They do not serve dual roles as pets and guardians. Their entire lives are spent guarding the flock or herd entrusted in their care. Except for trips to the veterinarian's office for surgical procedures, they do not leave the pastures. A devoted LGD would not want to leave the animals under its protection. That does not mean that the dog should be treated like a feral creature and ignored. It should be taught its name, basic manners, and receive attention and praise from its human caretaker. The dog is—in a literal sense—a valuable farm employee and its work should be acknowledged.

A Livestock Guardian Dog is a completely different creature from what is commonly referred to as a guard dog. The latter are used to guard property such as a house or a business. When I researched LGD, I discovered that there are breeders who breed and sell LGD to people who want a dog to protect their family. These dogs may have the instinct to protect livestock, but their breeders have no knowledge of livestock and will make poor mentors. If I were to purchase an LGD, I would contact breeders who advertise in livestock magazines. I would look for a breeder whose dogs are expected and trained to guard livestock and who have the experience and facilities to assess proper Livestock Guardian Dog temperament in the individual dog. *Whatever you do, do not purchase a dog from a pet shop.*

Not all individual dogs classified as Livestock Guardians are suitable for the job. Alpacas have been attacked and killed by the dogs that were supposed to protect them. Some of those that fail may simply lack training; others—for reasons that may remain a mystery—lack the instincts that set LGD apart from other breeds. When discussing a possible canine candidate for the job of guarding your alpacas with a breeder, be sure that you are clear in what you expect the dog to do. Educate yourself thoroughly and work closely with your breeder/mentor once you have decided to go the Livestock Guardian Dog route. A well-bred LGD from proven lines will not be cheap. You will probably be put on a waiting list. If you have never owned a dog, some breeders may refuse to sell to you. Please don't interpret that as outrageous snobbery. Many ethical, caring dog breeders have been disappointed by new owners who don't follow through on advice pertaining to nutrition, parasite treatment, and training. The dogs are often returned as physical and emotional wrecks—or worse, dropped off at a shelter. That's heartbreaking for a breeder who invested thousands of hours and thousands of dollars on a serious breeding program.

Ethical breeders will tell you both the advantages as well as the disadvantages of owning an LGD. The advantages are obvious: You will not sit upright in bed each night when you hear the local coyotes yipping just beyond your pasture fences. The appearance of neighborhood dogs that frequently escape from their yards and visit your farm will no longer make the blood freeze in your veins. There are also disadvantages. In my opinion, many people lack the personality traits that are necessary for a successful partnership with such a powerful dog. Those who think of all dogs as little people in fur coats are *not* good candidates for owning an LGD and may endanger themselves, their families, and visitors to their farms. Livestock Guardian Dogs are extremely strong and fearless. A friend of mine owns three Anatolian Shepherd Dogs. The litter brother of her bitch killed a pit bull in literally seconds when it perceived its owner's child to be in danger. This true story should give my readers food for thought. If such ferocious behavior should ever be directed at a visitor to the farm by a poorly trained or mentally maladjusted LGD, the outcome would have terrible consequences. These dogs need a firm hand and owners who have insight into canine behavior and training. My friend is a young woman who is neither unusually strong nor tall. Nevertheless, on her small farm, she is the boss, the leader, the captain of her ship. Because she trained them correctly, her three Anatolians are obedient, and it is a pleasure to be around them.

LGS

"What's that?" the fellow alpaca farmer asked when I told her that I had an LGS on my farm.

"A Livestock Guardian Spouse," I laughed.

There is a positive aspect to being married to a man who doesn't enjoy travel, and it's quite appropriate to discuss the issue in our chapter on guardian animals. In addition to a four-legged guardian, your farm needs a human guardian as well. At least one family member has to be home to care for the animals. Alpacas don't need supervision around the clock. With great pasture and hay, they feed themselves. Nevertheless, a human caretaker should check that all is well on a daily basis. Not all prospective alpaca farmers understand that raising animals will curtail their freedom to travel. I know of one alpaca farmer who sold her entire herd after only one year of ownership. Why?

"When all my friends sent me post cards from Europe, I felt stuck. I couldn't stand it," she confessed to friends of mine.

On a small budget, you won't be able to pay a farm sitter to care for the animals. If you can afford to pay one, you may not be able to find a reliable worker. While I love being on the farm, I also enjoy visiting family and friends, attending seminars, and going on hikes. My excursions are usually brief—a few hours or occasionally a day carved out of my busy schedule. On rare occasions, I take a few days to visit my family in Germany. Since my husband and I moved to the farm two decades ago, I have only taken one long vacation, a hiking trip with my sister, Karin. I wrote about our adventures—they include a visit to a German alpaca farm—in *Hiking with the Boss*. The three weeks I spent in Germany required a lot of planning ahead. The only reason I was able to leave at all is the fortunate fact that I am married to a Livestock Guardian Spouse.

17
CRITTERS ON THE FARM

"Not all creatures on a farm are cute, desirable, or wanted. Get used to it!" Kristin Joyce

Barn Bunnies

My little world—the farm—comes close to the one D.H. Lawrence asks us to envision in one of his poems. Most days, there are no people but me, there are the alpacas, there is lots of grass—albeit interrupted by barns and fences—and hares are sitting up. Well, they are not hares, but plain New Jersey rabbits. The bunnies seek shelter underneath the hay pallets and have made themselves quite at home in the barn. They gnaw through electric cords, so I've learned to keep the cords off the ground at all times. Because I don't know of other safety or any health hazards that these little critters could possibly present, I leave them to their peaceful bunny existence and enjoy their presence.

All My Critters

A farm is always populated by many species. The farmer welcomes some, considers other merely a nuisance, and seeks to drive off or even eradicate those that will harm his crop or livestock. It's often a strange and interesting assortment. Some of the critters—chipmunks, for example—are appealing or look cute to most people but can do much damage on a farm. Others—bees come to mind—frighten or at least alarm non-farmers, but those of us who grow crops hail their presence. All have their place in the eco-system. Novice farmers rarely consider that they must deal with many critters other than the alpacas on their farm. This chapter may be helpful even though it covers only a few species. My readers can easily research what type of critters they may encounter at their own locations.

Rodents

No matter how fastidious you are about keeping your barn clean, it will eventually be visited by mice and rats. They are attracted by dung, any feed carelessly left about, and the shelter of a barn during winter. "Traveling" rodents will sometimes be brought to your premises inside a bale of hay or straw. The presence of rats and mice can compromise your alpacas' health. For example, rodents are carriers of leptospirosis, an infectious disease with serious consequences. They also carry the fleas that infect humans with bubonic plague. You can handle this matter in several ways. The first is rat poison. Follow the instructions on the box and make absolutely sure that the poison cannot be reached by any animals other than the rodents. Remember that alpacas have very long necks and can reach nooks and crannies that are far beyond the livestock panels that fence off the service area in a barn. The poison works well for us. I don't see a single rodent—rat or mouse—in our barn as long as I stay on top of things. I truly hate to use poison, but—without a barn cat—there are few other options. The poison we use is grain treated with warfarin. You may be more familiar with this substance as a popular blood thinner given to human beings with high blood pressure. Warfarin depletes a mammal's store of vitamin K_1. At a certain level, the animal bleeds to death internally. Accidental ingestion of high doses of warfarin by dogs or cats may take days to produce symptoms: listlessness, no appetite, vomiting, and severe bruising of the skin. Injections of vitamin K_1 or vitamin K_1 tablets will take care of the problem if administered in a timely fashion. After reading about the gruesome side effects of warfarin, I felt very guilty about using it to kill our farm's rodents. When a friend mentioned barn owls, I paid attention. By chance, the December 2004 issue of the *International Camelid Quarterly* featured information about using barn owls for rodent control. Author

Tom Hoffman presented a very well written article describing the habits and requirements of these fascinating birds. Unfortunately, owls do not seem to be a perfect solution. While they nest in a barn, they do not hunt in it.

"One explanation for this is that animals instinctively protect their young by not drawing attention to themselves at the nesting site. To the owl, this means not hunting in the immediate area around the nest box, since predators may observe the activity and follow the parent's return flight home," Tom Hoffman wrote.

There are several types of traps designed to catch rodents. We have used two of them with mixed results.

Barn Cats

Many livestock farms keep one or several barn cats. A cat may not be able to live on rodents alone but must be fed on a daily basis. Added to the food expense of a barn cat is preventive maintenance such as inoculations and regular dewormings. Shelter need not be elaborate. A cardboard box lined with blankets and tucked away in a corner of the barn will do. Barn cats—even those that are neutered and spayed—may leave the farm and roam farther afield. You may spend hundreds of dollars on a cat only to have it leave for good one week later. If you adopt a barn cat, talk to a knowledgeable person about what you can do to encourage the cat to remain on your farm and do its job. A barn cat may transmit toxoplasmosis to pregnant alpacas. If infected, the alpaca will abort the fetus.

Flies

I visited farms where horses and alpacas were driven half mad by the swarms of flies buzzing around their heads. Ruminants must eat (graze) almost continuously during the day to enjoy a healthy rumen. If not grazing, they should be chewing their cud. A heavy fly infestation will make it impossible for the alpacas to peacefully go about their digestive functions. The best pasture and the most beautifully constructed barn will not serve your alpacas well if the animals don't have a minute's peace from swarms of annoying flies. Flying insects can also transmit diseases. That doesn't mean you need to be hysterical at the sight of a *few* flies. Emphasis here is on a few!

There are many species of flies. On our farm, I deal with horseflies and common house flies. The bite from a horsefly is very painful. Mercifully, the season in our area is brief. I run fans to give the alpacas relief. House flies feel very much at home on a livestock farm. If unchecked, they will reproduce in huge numbers, annoying alpacas as well as people. They are also unsanitary. Manure removal is effective in fly control, but it will not work as a single management tool.

Over the years, I experimented with various types of flytraps. They all worked fairly well, but I was not completely satisfied. One popular free-standing model could not be left outside in very windy conditions and had to be refilled after each rain. The hanging traps were designed to be discarded after they had filled up. This offended my frugal nature. Finally, I discovered a hanging flytrap that I am completely happy with. It's a plastic dome with a screw-on lid. Flies enter the trap through one of several holes in the lid. After filling the trap with bait, I suspend it from a fence post or livestock panel. The dome should hang only roughly ten inches off the ground. When a trap is filled with flies, I unscrew the lid, submerge the dome in a bucket of water, clean it, and fill it. Rather than purchasing expensive bait, I make my own. After experimenting with various ingredients, I have finally found a very successful recipe. It makes four gallons of fly bait.

Fly bait recipe: Place four empty gallon jugs on a level surface outdoors. Pour half a cup of Fleischmann's Instant Dry Yeast and two cups of warm water into each gallon jug. Shake to dissolve the yeast and leave out in the sun for a day. To each jug, add a teaspoon of baking soda and the whites of one raw egg the next day. Shake again, put the tops on tight, and store jugs in a trash can. Fill each jug with water as needed. Shake again before you pour the bait into a trap.

I buy the yeast in large commercial packages. The leftover egg yolks are fed to our Whippet, Diesel. The bait has no ingredients that are harmful to the environment. The chore of cleaning the traps is unpleasant, but then livestock farming is not a clean occupation. After the first severe frost kills the fly population for the year, I clean and store the traps inside the barn for the winter. My only annual expenses are for the bait ingredients.

Fly Parasites

Fly parasites are another environmentally safe option. These little creatures feed on fly larvae and therefore prevent flies from hatching. There are several companies that will mail fly parasites to you on a regular schedule. They are not harmful to you or your alpacas. Please do not use insect "zappers." They kill beneficial insects along with the mosquitos and flies that plague the animals.

Wild Birds

There is another natural, free flytrap. Although wild birds do not eradicate a fly population, they help to control its numbers. The alpacas are not bothered by birds flying in and out of the barn. When birds started nesting in our barns years ago, I enjoyed their friendly chirping and welcomed their presence. With their numbers increasing each year, they have become a nuisance—not their chirping or flying but their droppings are a problem. Shiny pie plates hanging from the trusses only fooled the birds for a few days. A fake owl was effective for a few weeks.

"We need mesh bird netting installed across the ceiling of each barn," I said to my husband.

"I'll put it on my list," my husband said.

Chickens

I would love to have chickens and hope to have a little flock one day. Many livestock farmers encourage chickens scratching in their pastures because the domestic birds consume fly larvae. Chickens are also good mousers. Of course, due to their droppings, you do not want them roosting in your barn. If you're serious about keeping chickens, explore what pasture farmers call a chicken tractor. It's a movable chicken house that also serves as a fertilizing machine for your pastures. Some farms have chicken tractors so large that moving them requires heavy machinery and several hours of work. You can construct a small one for several chickens that can easily be pulled or carried to another location by hand.

Guinea Fowl

Guinea Fowl are semi-domesticated chickens that consume huge amounts of ticks and serve as noisy watch animals on a farm. You don't "own" guinea fowl the way you "own" chickens. They like to roam and may decide that the farm next to yours will make a happier home for them. At night, they roost in trees.

Mosquitos

People who live in cities and suburbs may complain about mosquitos, but they can easily escape the damage—itchy, swollen welts—by fleeing the great outdoors and staying in their homes while the pesky insects are most active. Livestock farmers don't always have that luxury. A late hay delivery, a newborn animal that needs to be checked, a pasture that needs to be mowed before a storm hits—there are many reasons why an alpaca farmer cannot hide in the house while mosquitos are looking for victims. On our farm, I work hard not to give the insects good breeding grounds. Mosquito populations thrive in standing water. With a little effort and attention to detail, it's not hard to fill in low areas in pastures and gardens and remove or empty containers that collect rain water. Purple martins are very efficient consumers of mosquitos. The birds have distinct preferences for location, height, and color of their houses. Farmers who wish to attract a colony of purple martins must fulfill the birds' wish list.

Bees, Wasps, and Hornets

Many city and suburban dwellers consider any insect that remotely resembles a yellow jacket as dangerous and to be smashed or sprayed into obliteration. This attitude does not win them friends in the agricultural community. All over the country, the lack of pollinators has taken on crisis proportions. Without bees and other pollinators, our food supply will be gone. The USDA offers a program that pays farmers to create pollinator habitats on their land. Scientists are working hard to discover what can be done to prevent the collapse of so many bee colonies. In rural communities, beekeeping is actively encouraged, and courses are easily available to people who are interested in taking up this ancient tradition. Although farmers and livestock have been seriously injured and even killed by stinging insects, honeybees—if left alone to do their job—will not attack people. Beekeepers wear protective equipment when they work with the hives.

Stormwind Farm is home to several beehives. Although the beekeeper manages the hives, I plant flowers that attract bees and butterflies.

Most pollinators are left alone to do their job. This includes the Mud Daubers that build mud nests where they lay their eggs. The only stinging insects that I eradicate on the farm are yellow jackets. I spray the nests after dark and make frequent inspections of popular nesting sites.

Dogs

As a predator, the dog is the natural enemy of the alpaca. A trained Livestock Guardian Dog is an exception. Most family pets do not fall in that category. Although we love our Whippet, Diesel, she is not permitted to enter the barns or pastures. Stray and feral dogs can be a big problem in rural areas. Research the laws for your farm's location. In some communities, you may shoot a stray dog as soon as it steps on your property. In others, your only legal option is to wait for the authorities to arrive, even if the dog is already mauling your livestock.

Deer

They look so graceful, these browsers that resemble shorn alpacas. People put out corn and hay to attract deer to their properties for the sole purpose of admiring their beauty. Who doesn't love Bambi?

City people who move to a farm often forbid their rural neighbors to hunt on their property or to use it as a passage to good hunting grounds. Review the pros and cons of such a decision very carefully. You will have to rely on your farming neighbors for many services and products. In rural communities, everybody knows everybody else. Often, everybody is related to everybody else, even if it's only around ten corners. When you stop Joe and his son from hunting where their family has hunted for the last two hundred years, you may just find that Joe's cousin, Virgil, has no time to cut and bale your hay and Virgil's brother-in-law, John, can't help to pull your mower out of the mud.

"Oh, I'll just offer them more money; everybody is for sale," a novice alpaca farmer told me when I warned her about the possible outcome of stopping hunters from walking through her property.

I thought of my relatives who farmed and smiled. "You don't know farmers," I told her.

Agriculture and deer can co-exist, but only when annual hunting seasons keep the deer population under control or natural predators do the job of thinning the herds. In areas where hunting has been banned and deer destroy crops, farmers who would not or could not put up deer fencing have gone out of business and sold their farms to developers.

Should this happen to the land next to your property, consult with employees of the United States Department of Agriculture (USDA). They have extensive experience and expertise in how to prevent or deal with complaints and lawsuits from future neighbors who may object to smells, sounds, and activities on your farm.

Earlier in the book, I discussed the impact of meningeal worm on alpacas. Deer do not have to enter a pasture to pass on the parasite. The presence of deer also attracts large predators. If you do not wish to hunt deer, then at least do not encourage their presence on your farm by growing ornamental plants that deer view as especially tasty.

Groundhogs

These furry critters dig huge holes. The holes are potential safety hazards for the alpacas and people. More than a few farmers overturned their tractors in groundhog holes and sustained severe injuries or were killed. If the groundhog population explodes on your farm and you can't bring yourself to kill (shoot) the animals, you may have to hire a professional to get control of the situation. On our farm, I had to chase a groundhog out of a pasture only once, and Diesel keeps the critters at bay in the dog yard. Nevertheless, when I walk the pastures, I keep my eyes open for groundhog holes.

Snakes

Snakes effectively keep a rodent population under control. If they are harmless to people and livestock, leave them alone. If poisonous snakes are an issue, start with preventive measures. Make sure that you do not create a favorable habitat for potentially dangerous snakes in your area.

The Yuck Factor

When the majority of people lived on farms, they were accustomed to manure, flies, snakes, rodents, and many other critters in their midst. Although farmers tried to eradicate those they deemed harmful, women did not cower at the sight of mice in their kitchens, men were not afraid of all snakes, and children did not shriek in terror if a bee or wasp landed on their piece of pie. Nowadays, with most people several generations removed from farming and their daily lives sanitized to the point of endangering their immune systems, adults and children view many species as disgusting.

"I hate spiders!" "I hate bees!" "I hate snakes!"

How often have I heard those words! Do those who "hate" bees even know the difference between a honeybee and a wasp? Do they consider that, without pollinating insects, the human race will become extinct? Life on a farm is not for people who are afraid of what I call the *yuck factor*. The only farms without insects, rodents, and snakes are the make-believe farms on the Internet. On those, you can play at being a farmer without finding a spider's net in the barn's entrance or mouse droppings in the attic. For many people, such a farm may be the only one that they should own.

18

BIOSECURITY

"We like a closed herd. It's the best biosecurity plan." Diann Mellott

Once Upon a Time

Once upon a time, in a land called the United States of America, alpacas sold for astonishingly high prices. A group of men and women—many of them wealthy—decided to become alpaca farmers. They knew lots about business plans and tax deductions but very little about farming. The newly minted livestock producers enthusiastically attended shows, auctions, and fairs with their animals.

Warnings Were Ignored

"I never heard anybody else saying stuff like this. You're the only one who is concerned. What's the problem?"

Obviously annoyed, the alpaca farmer looked at me skeptically. Without waiting for an answer or asking any questions, she curtly brushed aside my warning about attending one of the largest alpaca shows in the country with her animals. I had visited this show the two previous years and had been appalled at the total lack of biosecurity. Pens were tightly wedged together. Unless farmers put up barriers, nothing prevented the alpaca belonging to farmer A from touching noses—or worse!—with the animals belonging to farmer B. During both visits, I observed numerous alpacas reaching through livestock panels into adjoining pens to nibble on hay and drink out of water buckets. In one memorable incident, I watched a squatting alpaca shoot sprays of diarrhea into another alpaca farmer's pen. My words of caution, based on research and decades of experience with animals, were treated like the bothersome, nonsensical complaints of a querulous crank. Few of my fellow farmers listened with any real interest. None that I know of followed my advice to keep their alpacas home until the show committee made sweeping changes.

The End of a Fairy Tale

The alpaca community didn't have to wait long for the fairy tale to end. The year after I voiced my warnings, quite a few alpacas arrived back at their respective farms with raging fevers and diarrhea. The returning show animals infected those that had been left behind. On some farms, all crias became ill. A few died. Once again, I had not entered alpacas in the show. Nevertheless, upon returning to *Stormwind Farm*, I had taken a shower, washed the clothes that I had worn in the show barns, and disinfected the soles of my shoes. I had visited the show that year to look at two males owned by a friend of mine. My intention was to select and purchase one of the two. I had told their owner that the actual purchase would have to wait until the chosen male had been quarantined on her own farm for several weeks after the event. The day of the show, I remained undecided. I liked both males.

"Let me think about it. I'll make up my mind in a few days," I told my friend.

In the end, it became an easy decision to make. One of the alpacas became very ill after it returned to the home farm. A veterinarian had to be called to treat it. The other one had shared a pen and a trailer with its sick travel companion but remained fit as a fiddle. This male's immune system must be very strong, I thought. Health was the deciding factor in my choice, and one I never had to regret.

For some alpaca farmers, things went from bad to worse. Through painstaking detective work, a Canadian farmer proved that a boarded cria had introduced *Bovine Viral Diarrhea Virus* (BVDV) into her herd. Once discovered, other farm owners tested for the virus and finally found answers for previously unexplained respiratory problems, abortions, and other health problems in their herds. While many farmers were still grappling with the rather complex issue of diagnosing, treating, and preventing BVDV in their herds, a respiratory disease struck alpacas throughout the country. Labeled "the snots" by mystified owners and veterinarians, the unidentified virus raged primarily—but not exclusively—among alpacas that had been taken to shows. Caring for the sick animals became a physical, psychological, and monetary burden for many owners.

"We should have been warned that this can happen," a farmer complained to me.

I was speechless. How do you explain that supposedly intelligent people are aware of viral diseases in other species but believe that alpacas are invincible? Did this woman really think that alpacas—alone among all livestock species in the world—were special and not prone to contract the communicable diseases and parasites other livestock farmers face with disturbing regularity in their stock?

Information About Infectious Diseases

In fact, we had all been warned. Dr. Fowler's book includes a section on infectious diseases, as does Eric Hoffman's *The Complete Alpaca Book* and *The Merck Veterinary Manual*. In the latter, read *all* the information, not just the rather sparse section on camelids. You will find plenty of information about viral diseases, transmittable skin diseases, and transmittable internal as well as external parasites. There is also an informative section specifically on biosecurity.

Where and How Is Disease Transmitted?

Where are diseases transmitted? Anywhere animals gather and have contact with one another. The venue may be a show, an auction, a farm fair, or a cooperative event at a farm. Purchased alpacas can bring disease to their new home farm. Sharing trailer space adds a biosecurity risk factor. When you contract to have a purchased alpaca transported across country, be aware that your alpaca may share trailer space with others from several farms. *Certificates of Veterinary Inspection* offer some protection, but they are no guarantee against transmittal of infectious diseases.

How are diseases transmitted? The same ways they are transmitted from one person to the next. Examples are direct contact, indirect contact by human hands touching multiple animals without sanitizing hands in between individual alpacas, copulation, or—in the cases of airborne viruses—through lack of ventilation at, for example, indoor shows. Insects such as flies and mosquitos can transmit disease. Both rodents and barn cats can infect alpacas with disease. Sharing shearing equipment with other farms or hiring a traveling shearer presents a big biosecurity risk. Disease organisms can be brought to your farm on the shearer's clothing as well as equipment.

I asked Alice Brown to share a sad and costly experience with my readers.

> "My entire herd became sick after shearing one year. Some animals had diarrhea, some had fevers, others had both fevers and diarrhea. We even had one pregnant dam lose a female cria that she was carrying, at 8 ½ months gestation. The necropsy said that it died from placentitis caused by a viral infection. We have since changed shearers. The new group of shearers sanitizes everything from their mats and shoes to all their shearing equipment. They scrub everything down with disinfectant and use Clorox on their equipment. Since then, no alpacas have become ill on my farm after shearing. Thank goodness! There is nothing worse than having an entire herd come down with an illness."

Visitors to your farm can bring contagious diseases to your alpacas. Unfortunately, that includes your veterinarian. Bringing an alpaca home from a veterinary hospital also poses a risk. If your veterinarian is not available or doesn't have the resources to diagnose or treat an illness or injury, you face a difficult decision. It's best to discuss and to decide on a plan before a crisis occurs. What biosecurity risks are you prepared to take?

A Trojan Horse: the Pregnant Alpaca

It is vitally important that you educate yourself about the "Trojan horse" of the alpaca industry: A pregnant female that carries a fetus infected with *Bovine Viral Diarrhea Virus*. When an alpaca cria becomes infected with the BVD virus while in utero, its body doesn't recognize the virus as a foreign entity and does not develop immunity. After birth, the cria will shed copious amounts of the virus until it is euthanized or dies. No amount of time spent in a biosecurity area will fix that problem. *The PI (persistently infected) cria cannot be cured*. If not euthanized, PI crias usually don't live long. An alpaca that became infected *after* it was born, shed the virus, and developed antibodies to it is safe to own. That includes the dam of what is called a PI cria. This issue is quite complex. Different tests differentiate between PI status and infection contracted *outside* the dam's uterus. The wrong test will give false, negative results for a PI cria. I saw printed laboratory results that showed that the farmer's veterinarian did not order the appropriate test.

Colostrum: the Secret Danger

I don't cringe when farmers tell me that they fed their orphaned cria goat or cow colostrum. I *do* cringe when they tell me this while at the same time giving me a blank stare when I mention *Johne's disease* or *Caprine Arthritis and Encephalitis*. You will also see the latter written as *Caprine Arthritis Encephalitis*. *Johne's* is a microbacterial disease that attacks the immune system. There is no cure. *Caprine Arthritis and Encephalitis (CAE)* suppresses the immune defenses of animals. Both diseases are spread via milk or colostrum.

Dr. Ernest Hovingh of Pennsylvania State University reported on a national study at a farm management meeting in 2008 (*Lancaster Farming*, August 9, 2008). According to this study, 70 percent of US dairy farms had animals infected with *Johne's disease* in their herds at that time. Numbers varied in the reports that I read on the Internet in 2013. The disease is also found in beef cattle, sheep, and goats. Colostrum from cows has been implicated in the transmission of BVDV to alpacas. There are other diseases as well. No livestock species can be ruled out as a possible transmitter of infectious disease. Cows, goats, sheep, llamas, other alpacas—all may harbor pathogens in their colostrum. I am also leery of plasma serum transfusions. The frugal alpaca farmer considers all outside sources of bodily fluids with suspicion and as a potential threat to biosecurity. In *Natural Goat Care*, author Pat Coleby addresses the issue and offers a solution. When she prevented her CAE infected does from nursing their goat kids, Coleby fed the kids milk with cod liver oil and liquid seaweed concentrate. Would her recipe protect an alpaca cria? I don't know. Fortunately, I have not had reason to test it.

Feed Security

All feed coming to the farm should be viewed as a risk factor. A few years ago, several North American alpaca farms lost hundreds of animals when a feed mill mistakenly mixed salinomycin—an ionophore coccidiostat—in with a pelletized alpaca feed. The owners and managers of these farms had not used a designated sacrificial tester animal for each newly opened feed bag. Such biosecurity feed management should be standard practice on livestock farms. Open a new bag of feed *before* the previous one is totally empty and feed the tester animal from the new bag for several days prior to feeding the contents to a group or whole herd of alpacas.

Reduce the Risk

Prevention of infectious disease starts at home. On *Stormwind Farm*, we require all human visitors to sanitize the soles of their shoes with bleach before entering our pastures. Some farms have a foot mat designed to hold disinfectant. Visitors simply step on the mat before entering the premises. On our farm, I pour a small amount of bleach in a heavy but shallow plastic mixing pan normally used by masons, and visitors disinfect the soles of their shoes. Those who object to the procedure are offered a pair of plastic booties to wear over their shoes. The booties are discarded after each use. I also ask potential buyers to wash their hands before touching my animals. Visitors who object to biosecurity protocols are asked to leave. I am not interested in giving information about alpacas to people who show no concern for the safety of my herd. My veterinarians happily comply with my request for biosecurity. We shear our alpacas to eliminate the risk of shearers and their equipment bringing infectious disease to our farm. It is not possible to eradicate all flies and mosquitos on a farm. With a good management program, their numbers can be kept to a minimum. I described various inexpensive options in a previous chapter. I was always very cautious about allowing alpacas from other farms to join our herd, be it as a purchase, for breeding to our studs, or as boarders. I required negative test results for BVDV, Tuberculosis, Brucellosis, and Johne's, and checked incoming alpacas for any sign of skin problems. Owners had to permit me to administer an anthelmintic paste before the alpacas entered my pasture. It's not pleasant to take a hard line with other farmers who may be friends or simply likeable people. A few years ago, a fellow farmer contracted to have her alpaca sent to *Stormwind Farm* to be bred by one of our studs. After she had already paid for my required health tests, she purchased a goat from a disreputable livestock auction and allowed it to join her alpacas. The goat had not been tested for any disease. I agonized for days over my decision but finally told the woman that her alpaca would not be welcome on my farm. I explained why, but it didn't make telling her any easier.

Closed Herds

You may have noticed that I used the past tense when I described the biosecurity protocols practiced on my farm. For the last few years, I have had what livestock farmers call a closed herd. Animals never leave the farm. Those that do don't come back. No new stock is introduced. The closed status does not permit the animals to be exhibited at shows or fairs. After closing my herd, I purchased a female alpaca weanling.

"Then you can no longer claim to have a closed herd," you may say now.

In the strictest sense of the definition, that is correct. The weanling came from the farm owned by a friend. During at least one year prior to my purchase, my friend's farm had not had any alpacas from other farms join the herd. For all practical purposes, our two farms formed a closed herd at two locations. A frugal alpaca farmer may adopt this concept to his or her advantage: Two or several farms combine to form a closed herd. They remain separate financial entities but purchase—or swap—new stock and breedings only within the group. The limitations such a program will impose on each farm must be discussed in great detail and agreed upon by all participants. Although your alpacas will be protected, it will curtail your ability to market and sell animals. Even a closed herd is not protected against disease carried by insects or wildlife.

Biosecurity Area

A less restrictive but effective preventive measure is a designated biosecurity area on a farm. Such an area houses all incoming animals until they are proven to be free of infectious diseases for several weeks. Unfortunately, I have found that many farmers simply apply the label to their "biosecurity area" but don't implement necessary management practices. What are the latter?

- The biosecurity area should not share a fence line with another occupied pasture.
- Distance from the established herd should be 100 feet at a minimum.
- The alpacas in the biosecurity area are taken care of last. After feeding or medicating them, the caretaker takes a shower and puts on fresh clothing.
- Equipment is not used in other pastures. That includes but is not limited to dung removal equipment, nail clippers, shears, mowing equipment, and the shoes of the caretaker.
- Only the designated caretaker is permitted to enter the biosecurity area.

I described what I consider minimum standards. Sounds like a big hassle? It is! If a farm's owner tells you about his or her biosecurity area, ask questions and observe. You may be surprised and shocked at what you find out. If you send your alpaca to another farm to be bred, please consider that the farm's biosecurity area protects—if at all—*their* animals. It will not protect your alpaca if it shares the area with a steady stream of incoming females. Under those conditions, the word biosecurity is actually a meaningless label for both home farm and visitors. Common sense tells us that the risks of contracting an infectious disease increases with the size of a herd and the scope of animal traffic on a farm.

Taking the Risk?

Frugality as well as a small budget demand that all biosecurity risks must be carefully evaluated within the framework of each farm and its owners. How much of a risk taker are you? Will your alpacas be insured? Do you plan to make direct contact with buyers at venues off the farm your main marketing strategy? Will you more than likely be emotionally deeply connected to your alpacas, or will the death of a cria not bother you too much?

The Good News

After all this bad news, let me assure you that the issue of infectious disease in alpacas is very manageable. My advice is to educate yourself thoroughly and continuously regarding biosecurity threats to your animals. Weigh your options and be careful but don't become paralyzed with fear. Knowledge combined with common sense and appropriate protocols will go a long way to keep your alpacas protected and safe. The most important component is education. Once you understand the concepts, you can formulate a breeding program and a business plan with the safety of your herd in mind.

19

TRANSPORTATION

"Alpacas are generally cooperative and placid travelers. Nevertheless, when transporting, always keep the welfare of your animals in mind." Hugh Masters

Travel Stress

The impact of travel stress on agricultural animals such as cattle and sheep has been extensively studied. For example, in cattle destined for slaughter, stress causes weight loss called *shrink*. In one study, calves taken away from their mothers and transported to a slaughter facility lost 8 percent of their weight *overnight*. Most *shrink* occurred during the first hour of travel. Producers and haulers are concerned about it because it reduces their profits.

The *Eurogroup for Animal Welfare* (located in Brussels, Belgium) and the *Royal Society for the Prevention of Cruelty to Animals* (West Sussex, Great Britain) published a joint report in 2004. *Links Between Animal Health and Animal Welfare: The Effects of Transport on Animals* refers to the work of dozens of scientists from all over the globe. Species studied are cattle, sheep, and pigs. While similar scientific studies have not been commissioned for alpacas, only a foolish alpaca farmer would not extrapolate from other livestock studies to camelids. I have chosen to share what I consider key concepts in the report.

- Transportation generally suppresses the cell mediated immune response.
- Extensively raised breeds exhibit greater cortisol responses then those reared with more human contact.
- When weaning coincides with transportation, this will also make the journey more difficult for the animals.

It is clear that transported animals are at risk of disease as a result of the stress they experience during travel time. Livestock producers are well aware of shipping fever brought on by travel stress. One study reported a higher incidence when low temperatures were combined with high humidity. Death was caused by pneumonia and scours (diarrhea). A combination of high temperatures/high humidity is also dangerous.

The articles I have read on traveling with alpacas have primarily been concerned with the logistics of arranging transportation and practical issues such as stowing away show equipment. I believe that more attention needs to be focused on the well-being and comfort of the animals. Maybe the rare alpaca here and there doesn't mind travel or perhaps even enjoys it. For example, a male alpaca taken on numerous drive-by breedings will come to associate boarding a vehicle with the physical pleasure waiting for it at the destination. The vast majority of alpacas experience mild to severe stress when traveling. There are plenty of alpacas that arrive sick at their destination after hours of sitting in a trailer. Females may abort during or after long transit.

Plan Ahead

Residents of homes in towns and suburbs rarely transport anything other than themselves, the family pets, groceries, and various small items that make up a household. Livestock farmers must also transport hay, straw, seed, feed bags, lime and other fertilizer, topsoil, gravel, lumber, livestock panels, sawdust, farm gates, and a host of other things that are necessary to run a farm operation. Buyers may expect alpacas to be delivered. Transportation of alpacas to shows, fairs, and a veterinary clinic must be given consideration. It's smart to plan ahead because paying others to transport equipment, farm supplies, and alpacas for you will be cost prohibitive. In this chapter, I will focus on the transportation of the animals.

The Family Car

Alpacas can easily be transported in a van, SUV, or station wagon. Put a heavy tarp on the floor in case of a bathroom accident. The family car has the added bonus of air conditioning. A sturdy metal barrier as is commonly used by dog owners makes this an option for owners with small budgets. Safety must be the primary concern. A flimsy or poorly installed barrier endangers all occupants in the car. One of our alpacas was transported in a station wagon on several occasions. It took the rides in stride, curiously watching the traffic whizzing past us while complacently chewing its cud. If you plan to exhibit the alpacas at a show or fair, you may have to figure out how to transport at least four livestock panels. They must be securely fastened to a roof rack.

Trailers

An expensive livestock or horse trailer—the bigger the better—presents a status symbol to some alpaca farmers. Trailers have been showcased in national ads designed to sell alpacas. Although I would never buy an animal based on the size of the seller's trailer, maybe other people equate an expensive trailer with the quality of alpacas. In some cases, it may have the opposite effect. For example, my husband shies away from hiring contractors with new, expensive vehicles because he believes that such expenses will be passed on to customers. In any case, none of our customers or farm visitors have ever shown the slightest interest in the condition or the monetary value of our trailer. To allocate a big part of your budget to a new one is, in my opinion, a waste of money for a mechanically inclined person, especially if you don't intend to visit many shows. It's far more important to practice good traveling habits so your alpacas arrive at their destination safe and sound.

There are many used trailers on the market. Check them out carefully to make sure the floor is not rotten and that the brake system works. That's more important than a few dents and dings on the outside. Color should be a consideration. Because white doesn't absorb heat, it is the best choice for most areas of the USA. Aluminum trailers are much lighter and easier to handle than the older, heavier models built from steel. They are also a lot more expensive. A stock trailer allows good air-flow for cooling. A horse trailer has the advantage of doing double duty as temporary housing for a few alpacas or as a storage shed. Your choice of a trailer will depend on the type of vehicle you own to pull it.

Truck with Cap

A small truck with a cap is another option. Remember that you may have to lift the animals into the truck bed. A ramp can be constructed or purchased. You will have to train the alpacas so they will be comfortable using it. A permanent ramp can be installed on your property, but there remains the potentially dangerous task of lifting the alpacas off the truck at their new destination.

Fair Pens

Livestock equipment companies sell what they call fair pens. These are wire mesh livestock panels, with one panel serving as a roof. Assembled, a fair pen looks like a huge dog crate. It can be installed on a regular pick-up truck and covered with a fitted canvas top. I like this system a lot because a fair pen serves a dual purpose of transportation and exhibit pen. Once again, the drawback is the necessity of a ramp for loading and unloading the animals. If you can solve that problem and already own a pick-up truck, this may be a very cost-effective solution.

Trailer Bedding

A thick layer of clean straw is the most comfortable trailer bedding for alpacas. Additionally, it absorbs urine. Should the alpacas eat some of it during their journey, it will not harm them but simply add roughage to their diet. Another option is shredded paper. Do not use wood shavings unless you don't care about the alpacas' fiber and plan to throw it away. I haven't tried this myself, but why not use old bedspreads or quilts? They are often available in thrift shops for little money. You can also request that friends pass on such discarded items to you rather than throw them away. Soaking the quilts in cold water would add to the alpacas' comfort level during high temperatures.

Keep Them Cool

During warm weather, travel can become dangerous to the animals. If temperature is a concern, travel at night. Sometimes, the only safe choice is to postpone the trip. What's warm or too warm? I am reluctant to quote a specific temperature because humidity, travel time, distance, and fleece length as well as density all must be considered in your travel plans. People differ greatly in how they perceive and judge temperature. If you are on blood thinners or are very slender, your definition of hot may vary quite a bit from someone who doesn't fit that physiological profile.

Purchase a large garden sprayer normally used to spray chemicals and bring it along on warm days. In an emergency, you can at least cool down the alpacas' bellies. Buy a new one instead of taking a chance with chemical residues. When I used to travel with our Whippets in a car without an air-conditioner, I put ice cubes in their crates. If your alpacas are calm travelers and remain cushed, you can try that. A nervous animal may slip on the cubes while moving around the trailer.

Feed and Water

The author of *In Service to the Horse* writes about how feeding grain to horses while traveling is asking for trouble. Alpaca farmers should heed her warning. When we transport our alpacas, I place only a few flakes of hay on the trailer floor. I also bring plenty of drinking water in case of an emergency. The taste and smell of the water from your own farm will be familiar to your alpacas and entice them to drink. Animals can react with severe diarrhea to water that they're not accustomed to. Some farmers administer a probiotic paste to their alpacas prior to travel.

Bathroom "Beans"

Alpacas are often reluctant to urinate and move their bowels in new places. On long trips, they are candidates for serious impactions. Bring a can filled with alpaca "beans" with you and sprinkle them on the ground during pit stops. Supplies for several enemas should be in a medical kit for emergencies. Some alpacas are only too happy to empty their bowels as soon as they enter a vehicle. In that case, it's helpful to wait until an alpaca urinates and defecates before departure. On long trips, frequent bathroom stops will help to keep a trailer from becoming soiled.

Safety First

Safety must always be a strong consideration. Poorly trained alpacas are not good candidates for pit stops at busy interstate rest areas. Take great care while entering the trailer to prevent an alpaca from charging past you. Preferably, another person should accompany you on any trip to ensure the safety of your animals.

When Hugh Masters edited this chapter, he commented:

"Some breeders, such as myself, never take animals out of the trailer during transport stops. Even the best behaved animal can spook and break away from its handler. The exception to this, of course, would be in the case of an emergency."

This is good advice. Alpacas, like all prey species, react with fear to novel stimuli. Those that have never been transported will be very nervous. It helps to leave the trailer in your pasture for a few days prior to travel. I put a small hay supply in the trailer to encourage the alpacas to walk in and out of it. Once it's time to travel to a show or a new home, they are not so frightened when led into the moving mini-barn. If you use a van, you can also practice loading and unloading prior to departure. All alpacas should be halter trained before traveling off your farm. Of course, with very young crias, that is not possible. Check the trailer for wasps or other insects before you load anything, including the animals. The best time to remove wasp nests is after dark when the insects are not active. Don't leave anything sharp or protruding in the trailer. Put hay on the floor. A haybag does not belong in a travel trailer. An alpaca could easily become entangled in it. Dishes, buckets, halters, and leads should be stored in the truck.

Reduce Stress

Other than using the previously mentioned safety and comfort precautions, there are additional strategies that you can employ to ensure that traveling alpacas remain healthy. Use common sense for travel arrangements. For example, don't transport two mature, intact males that don't know or can't stand each other in the same vehicle. To reduce stress, alpaca farmers who sell a single animal usually bring a gelding along to keep the lone traveler company. Of course, the poor gelding then has to return home without the benefit of another alpaca's comforting presence. Owning a placid gelding is a great bonus for any farmer. Geldings are the unsung heroes of the alpaca community.

Certificate of Veterinary Inspection

Some farmers refer to a *Certificate of Veterinary Inspection* (CVI) as a health certificate. Whatever you call that important piece of travel paper, make sure that you inform yourself about its requirements (including animal identification), especially if you travel out of state. Every state has a State Veterinary Office. The staff there oversees the requirements for all livestock traveling within the state and animals coming from out of state. Sometimes, well-meaning secretaries and clerks in such offices may have no clue what they are talking about but give erroneous information with an air of great authority. I can tell you from my experiences as a show superintendent and events coordinator that it's best to request to have documents stating requirements for camelids sent to your farm or to check the office's website if it is current. This is especially important if you purchase animals from states where infectious diseases such as *vasicular stomatitis* are an issue during certain times of the year. Under unfortunate circumstances, you may find your entire farm quarantined.

If you plan on attending multiple shows or other events with your animals, analyze the schedule. What is the required time frame for the CVI? How can you schedule the veterinary exam so one visit will cover two events? Care must be taken with the scheduling of a tuberculosis test. Two tests administered too closely together can result in a false positive and a quarantine imposed on your herd. Livestock travel costs can quickly become expensive if you don't plan ahead.

Hugh Masters pointed out that some states—for example, Florida—require all livestock haulers to stop when crossing the state line. Animals and certificates will be checked.

Hiring a Transporter

You can hire a professional transporter to move alpacas. Check out the transporter carefully before you trust him or her with your precious cargo. Commercial transporters usually make many stops as they pick up and drop off alpacas across the country. When we purchased an alpaca from a farmer in California, it sat on the trailer for well over a week. I did not realize that this would happen. Fortunately, our transporter did a great job and delivered the alpaca to us in excellent condition. Several farmers whom I know have had bad experiences with their transporters. There are many risks involved in such a venture.

A Marketing Strategy

Not owning a vehicle to transport your alpacas will limit your ability to market animals. I mention in the chapter on marketing that farmers with small herds find it more difficult to attract buyers to their pastures. Small shows and co-op sales offer good opportunities for marketing and sales. To participate, you will need transportation for your animals. In my opinion, our modest trailer is not a luxury. As a frugal investment strategy, it has more than paid for itself. If you choose your marketing venues and vehicle wisely and transport with care, travel with alpacas can be an enjoyable, affordable, and profitable part of alpaca farming.

20
SHEARING

"Although it gave me great satisfaction to shear my alpacas, I consider shearing hard and potentially dangerous work." Kristin Joyce

Alpacas Have a Purpose

Alpacas are classified as livestock. We think of our properties as farms and call ourselves alpaca farmers. A true farm must produce an agricultural product, be it crops, meat, milk, pelts, wool, or fiber. For thousands of years, the primary purpose of the alpaca has been as a producer of fine, luxurious fiber. The fiber harvest should therefore be an event of great importance to an alpaca farmer. It is, after all, the culmination of genetic selection processes as well as husbandry efforts.

Reality Check

Several years ago, I read an article about a shearing day held on an alpaca farm with a large herd. It was very informative. The owners obviously had superior organizational skills and made efficient use of their shearing crews, teams of helpers, and equipment. The latter included an impressive looking vacuum system that carried dirt and debris to a disposal area outside the large building where shearing took place. Without a doubt, it was a very well managed fiber harvest. It had about as much in common with shearing day on a farm with a small herd as running a huge catering facility has with managing a small bistro.

On *Stormwind Farm*, we are also well organized, but the shearing crew usually consists of two or three people, we shear two to three alpacas on any day, and we use a small blower instead of a huge vacuum system. The end product of our harvest—clean alpaca fleeces—is the same as that harvested by the large operation. The observations and descriptions of our shearing practices presented in this chapter are based on my own experiences as a frugal alpaca farmer with a small herd. They are not meant to define a management style for all alpaca farmers.

Do It Yourself

In 1997, when my husband and I started to raise alpacas, the thought of shearing alpacas seemed a little scary to me. I knew that the techniques used with sheep would not work with alpacas. The latter are harder to restrain and have—compared to sheep—an open, dry fleece. Should we hire a shearer? I found out that, the smaller your herd, the greater the likelihood that you had to purchase and use your own shearing equipment. Sounds like a paradox, doesn't it? In those days, alpaca farming was in its infancy on the East Coast. Very few people had ever seen an alpaca let alone shorn one. There were few alpaca farms, and shearers often had to drive great distances from one farm to the next. It was not profitable for professional shearing crews to travel to farms with tiny herds. The alpaca farmer with a small starter "herd" of two alpacas therefore found it more difficult to find a shearer than the owner of two hundred alpacas. I quickly realized that David and I would have to learn how to shear.

Shearing With Handshears

My early childhood in post-war Germany shaped my attitude toward technology. Growing up with a coal stove, no refrigerator, no car, no washing machine, or any other electric appliances made me forever suspicious of anything run by a motor.

The very first time I observed an alpaca being shorn, it was done—to my delight—with handshears. The huacaya remained standing upright, and the shearer allowed it to move freely within a small catch pen. The shearer made it look easy. Years later, when I tried to handshear our gelding, I realized that the woman must have been highly skilled. I found the handshears difficult to handle with any degree of speed and competence.

There are farmers who choose to shear a fairly large herd with handshears. Jovi Larson (*Fibergenix Suris*), who breeds suri alpacas on her Virginia farm, has been successfully doing just that.

Jovi explains:

> "I handshear my suris. It certainly takes longer than using the electric clippers as others have reported (35-45 minutes for just the blanket). I prefer handshearing the suris because I like leaving a little extra length (1/2-3/4 of an inch) of fiber. I also find that I get many fewer second cuts with the handshears than with the clippers (I admit that I am a novice at using the electric clippers). In addition, other breeders that handshear report that the locks reform faster than if sheared with electric clippers or shears.
>
> I usually have a helper and a chute. The helper does anything from trying to feed the alpaca to distract, helps control the alpaca when it jumps around, and helps hold the fiber as it comes off. I have occasionally shorn by myself with a particularly well-behaved alpaca. I have a couple that will kush when put in the chute for shearing. This way you can get the blanket, but must get them up to do the belly and legs.
>
> The assistant is very helpful when we get the alpacas out of the chute – I usually do the neck outside the chute.
>
> As another respondent pointed out, just move with the alpaca and keep cutting. Give them break times. You do not have to shear the whole animal, or even the whole blanket, at one time. With particularly fretful alpacas or pregnant moms, I am very willing to shear half the blanket and then let them return to the pasture. I will try to get the other half at a later date, and then cut the neck

fiber at a third session. Sometimes my guys look a little funny out there in the pasture. Since your only equipment is a pair of shears or scissors, it is easy to halter and tie them for a short shearing session.

I have used both the traditional sheep shears (very cool looking) and scissors, but I actually prefer the Fiskars SoftTouch scissors (the ones that have a spring in the handle and one handle is elongated so you can put all four fingers in the grip).

When I tried shearing on a table, the alpaca was very calm. However, I did not like using the table for shearing suris. I had to adjust my shearing technique by starting at the belly and working my way up. I find it easier to start at the top (for suris) and work my way down. I think that if I had huacayas, I would seriously consider a table.

After several years of experience and experimentation, I have adapted my pattern of shearing. Instead of cutting in horizontal rows, which results in a "terraced" look unless one shears very narrow rows at a time, I now shear at a 45-60 degree angle (relative to the spine). I can cut a wider swath of fiber without leaving the terraced look. I think it is just a bit faster and more forgiving. As you handshear, you will develop the technique that suits you."

A fellow alpaca farmer, Sally Stacy (*Pronkers Suri Resort* in New Jersey), also handshears her suri herd. Interestingly, both women have a calm, thoughtful, and patient demeanor and are familiar and skilled with many construction tools. Because of the suri alpaca's fiber structure, it may be easier to handshear than a huacaya, but that is only speculation on my part.

Shears Versus Clippers

My husband, who likes the challenge of learning new mechanical skills, decided to use shears with a motor. Several farmers had told me that professional shears were too difficult for novices to handle. I accepted this advice without question and bought clippers instead.

The Frugal Alpaca Farmer

We—alpacas and shearing crew—were not happy campers. Clippers are not designed to shear alpacas. Nomenclature should have given me a hint. They are meant to do a finishing job once the bulk of the fleece has been shorn off. Clippers are used to trim hair off goats, cattle, donkeys, and dogs. Even a novice can tell the difference between clippers and shears. In their catalog, the folks at *Quality Llama Products* explain the difference between the two machines. If you're at all serious about shearing alpacas, shears should be your first choice. Electric clippers, as I already pointed out, do a wonderful finishing job but can go to the bottom of your shopping list.

You deserve to read another opinion on this subject. After editing the chapter, Hugh Masters wrote this response:

> "Clippers have been used for years on horses and for matted hair on dogs, llamas and alpacas. Major manufacturers (i.e. Premier) of clippers even advertise this. It's a matter of using the proper blade, keeping it sharp and cleaning it between each animal. We have used clippers over thirteen years on hundreds of alpacas and some llamas and seldom have had a problem. They are much safer for the inexperienced person. Yes, shears are faster and with 'today's' alpacas having denser fiber, shears will usually do a better job. For a beginner, I would never recommend they start with shears. I have seen and heard of too many serious accidents."

Hugh and I agree on one point: Shears are definitely the more dangerous of the two machines. You can injure your alpacas severely if you're not slow and cautious in your approach. It may not hurt to practice first on grandma's mink coat. Hugh later on followed his initial remarks with the advice that purchasing a shears-clippers combination may be a good option. I had not known that such a clever device existed.

Hugh wrote:

"Premier sells a unit that can be used as either clippers or shears by unscrewing two screws and changing heads. I have an older Lister model (no longer available) and it seems to work well. It allows the beginner to use clippers until he or she feels confident enough to progress to shears."

Purchasing this mechanical chimera is cheaper than buying one set of shears and one set of clippers. I've always been suspicious of too much cleverness in multiple purpose machines. Would you buy a washing machine that brews coffee? My husband admonished me that my analogy is totally off the wall and made the rather disrespectful remark that my giving advice on machinery is akin to an elephant giving advice on how to dance. Such crassness is best met with icy silence and refusal to use all those little machines in the kitchen that night.

Dull Blades

We embarked on a major improvement program. We started by purchasing top quality shears. Next was a reality check: We had alpacas, not sheep. Alpaca fleeces lack grease—we're not complaining!—and one pair of blades will not shear ten animals, no matter how much and how often you oil and clean them—the blades, not the alpacas! Actually, that's not true. Fast professional shearers—ten minutes per alpaca compared to our thirty to forty minutes—can shear quite a few alpacas with one blade. We learned that blades become dull by just running idle. While David mopped his sweaty brow and I tried to decide how to sort the fiber, the blades were slowly but surely losing their sharpness without cutting a single strand of fiber.

Over the years, David's shearing speed increased. He turns off the motor when, for whatever reason, I call for a brief, temporary halt to his shearing. My fiber sorting has become fast and efficient, and indecision rarely keeps the blades running idle. We know now that very fine fiber dulls blades much quicker than the coarser fiber from older animals and plan accordingly. A young alpaca is always shorn with a fresh set of blades. All used blades are sent out for sharpening prior to each shearing season.

We had been told that the shears would be difficult to adjust to the proper tightness. David did not find this to be true. Since he grew up with a refrigerator, a television, and a car in the family, he has no problems with motor-driven tools and is assured of my full admiration for his mechanical genius. If you identify with me in the technology department, keeping the shearing equipment working may be beyond your expertise. If you can tell a wing nut from a lug nut, there's hope for you.

Toil Without Oil

We also accepted advice, given by virtually everybody in the alpaca community, to put plenty of oil on the shearing blades. For years, we sheared and oiled, sheared and oiled—with oil dripping on the barn floor and leaving smelly traces in alpaca fleeces. Doug and Lori Hellman (*Hellman's Windy Hill Farm Alpacas*), good friends of ours who raise alpacas in Colden, New York State, told us one day to "shear dry." I admit that we were skeptical. No longer! We are devoted converts to the dry method. Of course, we shear only three to four alpacas per day. Doug assured me that he's sheared twice that many without putting a drop of oil on the blades. The dry method may not work for shearing a large herd in one day unless a shearer can switch shears after one set becomes too hot to work with it. In any case, it works great for us.

Safety First

Shearing takes practice. Enduring the slow fumbling of a novice shearer is hard on the animals. Don't stress out the alpacas and shearing crew by demanding a perfect job the first time. You're better off sacrificing the quality of the fiber harvest the first year. Safety should be your primary concern. This simply cannot be emphasized enough times. I have heard of cases where alpacas required hundreds of stitches to close wounds made by careless shearers. People who do not respect shears as a potentially dangerous machine do not belong in the shearing area and should definitely not be shearing. The person who harvests the fiber must be as concerned about safety as the shearer. The helper's fingers are as vulnerable near shearing blades as the skin, teats, penis, and testicles of an alpaca being shorn. I do not suffer from asthma or respiratory disease but nevertheless wear a mask and goggles while blowing out dust from the fiber. I rake and sweep the floor clean of all fiber debris and dirt after each alpaca has been shorn to prevent us from slipping and falling. We don't treat shearing day as a big party. People and animals can get hurt that way. Think twice before advertising a shearing day on your farm, with the public invited to view the activities. If you do, you will need a staff for crowd control.

Helpers

For us, the biggest problem with shearing has always been finding competent helpers. Although it is possible for two people to shear an alpaca, it's hard. The issue is not the shearing itself but the *safe* restraint prior to and during the procedure. When you are in your sixties, your non-farming friends are not clamoring to help you with physical labor. If you are young, you may have plenty of friends who volunteer to help shear because they think it's "fun." Not all will be competent. Sometimes, willing helpers prove to be physically weak or even frightened of the alpacas. There is also concern about injuries to helpers. Will your insurance cover you if your clumsy helper's nose gets broken while trying to restrain an animal? The last few years, we teamed up with friends who own an alpaca farm within a short drive of our farm's location. We travel back and forth to help one another. That's probably the best solution if you can find people who are compatible with your shearing routines.

Shearing Location

The shearing location is an important factor for a successful fiber harvest. It should give the shearer plenty of light and space to move around. Ideally, there should be no wind to blow fiber away from the shearing station. On *Stormwind Farm*, we shear in the barn. The shearing area is closed off to any alpaca still waiting to be shorn but crias can see their mamas while the latter are on the shearing table.

Shearing Supplies

I assemble and set up all supplies the day prior to shearing any alpacas. This gets our shearing season off to a calm, organized start each year.

A table holds shears, clippers, plastic bags, tags, pens, medication to treat minor cuts, equipment to file male fighting teeth, towels, dust masks, and socks. Why the socks? We usually have one or two spitters or droolers in our herd. A little spit throughout the shearing process is not a problem, but if copious amounts of the green slime pool on the floor next to the shearing table, it's a safety hazard for the shearing crew. I put a thin cotton sock over the drooler's mouth. You can also purchase a special spit mask. Two small garbage cans are lined with the plastic bags that I use for each alpaca's fleece. I make sure that a large garden rake is available for periodic clean-up of the shearing area. A thick gymnastics mat is placed in an area close to the shearing table (once an alpaca is shorn, we gently slide it off the table and onto the mat). I clean the shearing table and check the leg restraints. The blower is plugged into the electrical outlet nearest to the shearing table. An extension cord travels from the outlet through an overhead loop above the table. It will be connected to the shears or clippers.

Pre-Shearing Grooming

In comparison to sheep fleeces, alpaca fiber is very dry and the fleece is therefore described as being "open." Alpacas love to roll in the dust. This is instinctive behavior. It is healthy and should not be discouraged. Because the dust penetrates all the way to the skin, the downside is a very dusty fleece. Additionally, hay, straw, and other vegetation cling to the fiber. In my experience, the finer the fiber, the dirtier it gets and the more debris will cling to it. What can you do to minimize problems?

Alpacas should not be groomed in the traditional sense. Do not spend any money on shampoos, conditioners, or any other grooming supplies that you see listed for show llamas in various catalogs. Although we do not brush or bathe the animals, a sensible grooming program produces a superior fiber harvest.

Pre-shearing grooming begins long before shearing day. I keep our pastures free of plants that produce burrs and maintain a clean barn. One month prior to shearing, I sweep the barn floors with a broom each day. To reduce the time that the alpacas are restrained, I no longer cut nails or trim topknot and tail fiber on shearing day. Several days prior to shearing, I take care of these chores while the alpacas are in a standing position. The tail and topknot are trimmed with Fiskars SoftTouch scissors.

It's best if dust and debris are removed from the fiber immediately prior to shearing. A vacuum system like the one I described in the beginning of the chapter is ideal. When I tried our small shop vacuum, it was not powerful enough and did a poor job. For farmers with small herds, a commercial blower is a good alternative. Those offered through livestock or pet catalogs are quite expensive. They are worth every penny.

"You are destroying the fiber's lock structure with your blower," a fellow alpaca farmer pointed out to me.

Quite right, and exactly the reason why show fleeces should not be blown out but vacuumed with the vacuum's nozzle skimming along the fleece surface area. For *production purposes*—spinning or felting—the *temporary* "destruction" of the fiber's lock structure is of no importance.

"The blower drives the dirt deeper into the skin," another farmer told me.

Not true. This may be the case on farms that have sandy soil. Our farm's soil blows out of the fleeces in clouds of dust. While I wear a dust mask and safety goggles, the alpaca's head is wrapped loosely with a towel to protect its eyes. This serves the dual purpose of calming the animal. When I am done with a thorough job of blowing out a fleece, there is no dirt ground into the alpaca's skin.

The noise of the blower initially frightens most alpacas. I am sensitive to the fear that the alpacas feel when I perform any procedures for the first time. Most animals are much calmer the second time around if they had a good experience the previous year. They remember!

Vertical Shearing

Our shearing experiences have run the gamut as far as management styles are concerned. Who knows, by the time we're ready to sell the farm, the alpacas may be shearing *us*.

As total greenhorns, we decided that shearing alpacas in a horizontal position was cruel and too stressful for the animals. While alpacas accept shearing with handshears rather well in an upright position, the noise and sensations caused by electric shears adds a totally new dimension to the job. Several herd members were reasonable about being shorn while standing on four feet; others were not so accommodating. We fussed at each other and the alpacas. After getting done with the job, we left the barn aching in all joints and feeling utterly incompetent. This wasn't fun! We weren't getting any younger—something had to be done.

Shearing On the Ground

In Eric Hoffman and Dr. Fowler's book *The Alpaca Book* (1995), I searched for the photo of professional shearers expertly removing a fleece. It showed an alpaca being shorn while stretched out on the ground. The legs are tied securely with a rope and pulley system. Such a restraining system is offered for sale by companies specializing in supplies for alpaca farmers. My husband, who never had a dollar he wouldn't rather save than spend, decided that the price was too high and manufactured a neat, little machine himself. With advice from fellow alpaca farmers, we determined that a rope used by mountain climbers was the best choice. A quick glance in a specialty catalog revealed the ropes to be expensive. Fortunately, I remembered that our son's former high school wrestling coach also climbs mountains. All those evenings that I sat in crowds of testosterone crazed, screaming, and sweating males finally paid off.

"Would you mind giving us your used climbing ropes?"

"They're not safe for climbing anymore."

"We don't want them for climbing. We'll be using them to tie up alpacas so we can shear them. Hello, don't hang up, let me explain."

A few weeks later, we possessed a used, free, and perfectly functional rope. Two boards measuring 15 inches X 4 inches with one inch diameter holes drilled in each board completed the job. The whole system cost pennies and worked fairly well.

There are two commonly used ways to lower an alpaca to the ground. In the first one, three people lift the alpaca and gently deposit it on the shearing mat. Two people can accomplish this, but they better be strong and have quick reflexes. The leg restraints are applied after the alpaca has been laid down. The second method requires a pulley system. The standing alpaca's feet are placed in the leg restraints, and the animal is quickly but gently pulled off its feet and lowered to the ground. This technique works very well if two people synchronize their movements and possess speed and agility.

Shearing On a Table

After a few years, my husband felt uncomfortable either shearing bent at the waist or kneeling down. When we found a discounted, used tilt table in very good condition, we bought it. The professional models have a hydraulic system and an hourglass shape to allow the shearer easy access to the alpaca without bending over the table. The animal is strapped to the upright table with a belly band. The table is then tilted to a horizontal position, and a lock system prevents it from moving. The system has a foot pedal release to later reverse the table's position. Adjustable leg restraints prevent the alpaca from moving during shearing. Our table also has a metal ring on each corner. This allows me to secure the alpaca's head with a metal clip fastened to the halter. Cattle and dairy farmers have been using similar tilt tables for years to trim the animals' hooves and perform surgery. We are now independent and need not rely on anyone's help and schedule. Even with the table, we prefer to have a competent helper or two, but we can and have shorn quite a few alpacas by ourselves. My husband shears. I assist with securing the animal on the table and removing and storing the shorn fiber. Our alpacas tolerate being shorn on the table quite well. I think several actually enjoy it. Two of our males are so relaxed that a helper once asked me repeatedly if they had been tranquilized. They had not. The third adult male alpaca on our farm hates the table. It's easier to shear it on the ground. Animal husbandry calls for flexibility. We find that the most difficult—and the most potentially dangerous—part of the job is getting an alpaca *off* the table.

A shearing table is expensive. If you're mechanically gifted, you can build one yourself. One year, when David and I still worked off the farm, we hired a team of professional shearers. The shearers brought a table that one of them had built. Although it did not tilt, the two men had no problems lifting even the large males on and off the table. Of course, they were experienced, one was unusually tall, and both were obviously accustomed to heavy, physical labor. They pointed out that very short people may have a problem using a shearing table.

Learn By Watching

After thoughtful deliberation, I decided to omit a step by step description of the actual restraint and shearing process. Although we learned through trial and error, there are better—and far safer!—ways. One is to attend a shearing class specifically offered to alpaca shearers. Another good learning opportunity is to watch a shearing crew as a quiet observer with a notebook and pen. Do not bother and distract the crew with questions. There are also books and DVDs available that focus exclusively on shearing.

Professional Shearers

On a small budget, shearing your own alpacas is almost a necessity. Of course, the initial purchase of shearing equipment is costly, but after a few years of shearing, it will have paid for itself. If you simply don't have the stamina or skills, bartering services in exchange for shearing may be possible, but I wouldn't count on it. *Because alpacas have to be shorn each spring,* farmers who can't or don't want to shear must hire a shearer.

Most professional shearing crews work at the speed of light. The drawback to these whirling dervishes is that you need quite a few helpers to keep up with their pace. The shearers are not willing to wait between animals. When one alpaca is shorn, you better have the next one ready for them. Some crews set up two shearing stations. You won't have time to sip a drink of water in between animals. Many farmers with small herds cannot guarantee enough helpers to make it worthwhile for a crew with extreme speed to come to their farms.

A very dedicated group of men and women, working alone or with a single partner, *are* willing to service tiny herds at a reasonable pace. Their names and contact information are often only known to local alpaca farmers. Many have a loyal following. Although they are usually very patient with novice farmers, you should be well organized, follow directions, do your part to help the process along, and pay the shearer promptly when his or her work is done. Most shearers charge a fee per animal in addition to what they call a set-up fee.

Although most shearers are hardworking people who do a wonderful job, there are times a professional shearer may not work out to your satisfaction. Some shearers treat the animals roughly; some produce too many second cuts; others cancel shearing dates at the last minute. Weather conditions can play havoc with a shearing schedule. The sheep industry is experiencing problems with crews that are working in this country illegally. If immigration officials discover an illegal crew on your property, be prepared to pay heavy fines. In my opinion, the biggest issue is biosecurity. Shearers can bring infectious diseases such as a virus to your farm. Ringworm and other skin problems are a big concern with shared shearing equipment. Any infectious disease can be a potential nightmare, with many hours spent on treatments and many dollars spent on veterinary expenses.

Shearing Crias

A few words of warning about shearing very young crias are in order. A cria's mother may not recognize the baby after shearing. When this happened to us one year, it took roughly nine hours before our first-time mom allowed the shorn cria to nurse again. The cria had violently rejected all my attempts to feed it with a bottle. This little alpaca had been healthy from birth, with absolutely amazing vitality and athletic ability. Despite this, the physical and emotional stress it experienced made it sick. Luckily, I soon had things under control, but those were very upsetting days. Talk about stress! No cria, unless it's close to weaning age, will ever be shorn on our farm again. Looking back, I think the biggest mistake we made was that we did not arrange for its mom to watch the cria being shorn. There are numerous tricks one may use to prevent a problem. None are a guarantee that the alpaca won't reject its strangely transformed offspring. If you offer to shear very young crias for other farmers, I advise you to have the owners sign a disclaimer that mentions the possibility of such an occurrence.

Fleece? Fiber?

The words *fleece* and *fiber* are somewhat interchangeable. Fleece describes all the fiber when it is on the live animal; we call it fiber once it is shorn off. Things get a little blurry after that. We talk about "storing a fleece" after it has obviously been removed from the animal. We also say, "Oh, this alpaca has beautiful fiber!" when the animal is clearly still in possession of its fleece.

Some alpaca farmers insist that the shorn blanket must remain intact. The shearer and helper work together to use a technique that makes it look as if the blanket—shorn off the alpaca—is still in one piece. Is this important? If you want to enter the "fleece" in a show, it is customary to keep it intact. For production purposes, it does not matter.

Seconds and Second Cuts

There is an issue that, if ignored, *will* matter and greatly reduce the profits from your fiber sales. For the perfect fiber harvest, the ideal alpaca would have fiber of identical fineness and staple length all over its body. Such an alpaca does not exist. We find the finest and most uniform fiber in the *blanket*—the fiber covering the trunk. The fiber shorn off the neck, lower legs, and belly is coarser and shorter than the blanket and is commonly referred to as *seconds*. Some farmers differentiate further and label the fiber on the lower legs as thirds. Others separate neck fiber from the pile labeled seconds. To assure an excellent end product, an organized sorting process is a necessity. Although it is the farmer's responsibility to sort the fiber, a shearer's techniques can have a big impact on the job.

The other important issue is solely the shearer's responsibility. *Second cuts*—not to be confused with *seconds*—are produced by a poor shearing technique. When a shearer makes a pass—also called a blow—across the same section of the alpaca's body twice, the *second pass* results in *second cuts*. These are very short pieces of fiber. Mixed in with the blanket, they greatly reduce the quality of any end product. Good shearers know how to avoid making second cuts.

Separating Fiber During Shearing

It is smart to do preliminary sorting as the fiber comes off the animal. Small garbage cans that are lined with plastic bags work well for that purpose. I separate each fleece into three piles. The first pile consists of the blanket and is suitable for either handspinning or commercially produced yarn. A second, smaller pile consists of the fiber shorn from the neck. The neck fiber is usually shorter than the blanket fiber and also often has a different "feel"—alpaca farmers call it handle—to it. Crafters use it for various projects where short staple length is not a problem. For easy identification, I use clear bags for the blankets and white bags for the neck fiber. Additionally, I identify the contents of each bag with the animal's name written on a tag. Fiber from the lower legs and belly is usually coarse. It belongs in the third pile and is used as mulch in my garden or donated to the birds. I modify this basic plan depending on each alpaca's fiber quality.

For example, as the animal ages, the fiber becomes coarser and shorter. The section of fleece that I sort into the bag labeled *blanket* becomes smaller with each passing shearing season. Eventually, the entire fiber harvest from very old alpacas may have to go into the mulch pile. In that case, shearing only serves the purpose of making the alpaca feel more comfortable. In contrast, very young alpacas often have fleeces of such uniform fineness and staple length that I store all harvested fiber in a single bag.

This preliminary sorting saves me much time when I prepare my fiber for sale or to send to a mill to be spun into yarn.

My Way or...Your Way

There are many different ways to approach shearing alpacas. There is not just one right way. For example, blowing out fleeces while the alpacas are stretched out on the shearing table works so well for us that I simply marvel at the great results. A friend who tried to adopt this technique was not happy. She told me that her alpacas hated it, and she soon stopped using the blower. We are very satisfied with our shearing table and feel that it has made our job easier. Other farmers whom I have talked to disliked it enough to sell it and returned to shearing on the ground. You will find that your shearing protocols will evolve over the years. I think the most important thing is that you feel comfortable with your choices of equipment and techniques. One thing remains constant: The alpacas must be shorn annually! I get several calls each year from strangers who bought alpacas—often at auctions—and it has now belatedly occurred to them that the animals must be shorn. Sometimes, the calls come as late as August. In New Jersey, it is hard to get a shearer to come out at that time of the year. I wish people would inform themselves better before buying or adopting a living creature.

21

FIBER FACTS AND FIBER FOLLIES

"Fiber is the alpaca's canary in the coal mine." Wini Labrecque

How Complicated Can It Get?

"It's just hair. How complicated can it get?" remarked the novice alpaca farmer when I told her how much there is to learn about alpaca fiber. Her question obviously dismissed my own statement as an exaggeration of the facts. She was wrong on both counts. Alpaca fiber is not hair, and full understanding of the subject requires the absorption of a vast amount of information, much of it very technical and based on scientific testing. In *The Complete Alpaca Book*, Eric Hoffman offers a very comprehensive chapter on fiber. Every serious alpaca farmer should read this information. In my own book, I will try to address what I consider the most important, basic information. I say try because it is difficult to compress even the basic facts into a few paragraphs.

Alpaca—a Unique Fiber

Alpaca is often described as a luxury fiber. Comparable to cashmere and fine merino wool, alpaca is soft and has wonderful thermal qualities. In contrast to sheep wool, raw alpaca fiber has very little grease. After skirting, a washed fleece therefore yields almost as much weight as the raw fiber. Alpaca fiber is stronger compared to sheep wool of the same fineness.

Superfine alpaca is often described as hypo-allergenic. Its smooth handle allows people with sensitive skin to wear a garment made with superfine alpaca in comfort. Because the fiber usually coarsens as the alpaca ages, its suitability for specific end products changes throughout an animal's lifetime. Alpaca fiber is used by cottage industry fiber artists as well as in commercial applications from garments such as expensive men's suits to products such as carpets or fabrics used for furniture.

Follicles

The fiber grows out of tubelike cavities that are present in the skin. Dr. Fowler describes these cavities—the alpaca's follicles— as "tubular invaginations." Alpacas have both primary and secondary follicles. The *primary follicles* are the largest and arranged in rows in the skin in groups of three known as a trio group. The *secondary follicles* are more numerous than the primaries and usually grow finer fiber. In sheep, research showed that secondary follicles formed later in gestation than the primary follicles, and many do not produce fiber until one month after birth. I have noticed late production of secondary follicles in crias many times and learned not to judge fleece density when crias are very young. Starvation of the ewe reduces secondary follicle development in the fetus, with permanent reduction of wool growth. Is this true of alpacas? Because I do not starve my alpacas, I can't speak from experience about permanent reduction of secondary follicles.

Density

Fiber farmers are interested in producing animals with dense fleeces because density translates into a heavier fleece and presumably more income from the fiber harvest. When alpaca farmers advertise fleece weights, they rarely specify what exactly was weighed. Was it the entire raw fleece, including the rubbish that was thrown away? The washed blanket? The unskirted, unwashed blanket and seconds? Such information would be helpful for the buyer of breeding stock who makes density a production goal. Because alpacas vary greatly in size, fleece weight alone can never be an accurate measurement of density. Novice farmers often confuse coarseness with density. That's easy to do because a coarser fleece feels fuller and more tightly packed to the touch.

Skin Biopsy

A follicle count through a skin biopsy is a scientific and more accurate way to assess density. When a skin biopsy is performed, the follicle count is reported as per square millimeter (mm²). For example, an alpaca may have a fiber density of forty-five follicles per square millimeter. Even those results are subject to interpretation. Owners often don't report the age of the alpaca at the time the biopsy was performed. An alpaca will have higher density as a cria. With growth, the skin expands but the number of follicles stay the same. The same animal will have less follicles in each mm² of skin. Information about age at testing time would help to interpret the data.

On the animal, we can also judge fleece density by simply putting our hands on and inside the blanket. This takes some experience, though, and is especially difficult for novice farmers after the alpacas have been shorn.

Fineness

"This is unbelievable!" "Oh, how soft!" "I can't stop touching it!"

These are the comments I hear when farm visitors sink their hands into a bag full of baby alpaca fiber. Its silky fineness sets alpaca apart from most sheep wool. Commercial yarn producers pay premiums for superfine fiber. Why is that? It is simply a matter of supply and demand. Handspinners vary in their fiber shopping habits. Some actually prefer fiber of moderate fineness and will pass up superfine fleeces. Quite a few put emphasis on cleanliness and fiber that's devoid of second cuts. That said, let's never forget that fineness is the hallmark of alpaca fiber.

Fiber Histograms

The test for fineness does not require an invasive procedure like the skin biopsy for density. Cutting a small fiber sample from the blanket's midsection can be done prior to shearing and does not cause the alpaca any discomfort. Fortunately, fiber producers do not have to pay for expensive testing equipment. There are laboratories where skilled technicians test fiber samples. I am most familiar with *Yocom-McColl Testing Laboratories, Inc.* and find that their testing services are reasonably priced. The test results are compiled in a report called a fiber histogram.

Micron Count

"What's her micron count?" you will hear in a conversation between two alpaca farmers.

Micron count is a commonly used term to describe fiber fineness as measured by the scientific, diagnostic test mentioned in the previous section. A more accurate term would be *Mean Fiber Diameter*. Diameter is measured in microns. One micron is equal to $1/1,000,000^{th}$ of a meter or $1/25,400^{th}$ of one inch (Yocom-McColl). The mean refers to the *arithmetical mean*: divide the sum of two or more quantities by the number of these quantities—in other words, you obtain an *average*. The answer to the above question may be: "Oh, her micron count is 22.0." That means that the *Mean Fiber Diameter* (MFD) is 22.0 microns. A low micron count is considered desirable for garments that are worn close to the skin.

Standard Deviation

Obviously, no alpaca fleece is so perfect that all single strands of fiber have identical micron counts. If, in our example, the MFD is 22.0 microns, then we must assume that some fibers in the tested sample were coarser and some were finer. This *deviation* from the average is expressed as *Standard Deviation* (SD). If, for example, the SD is 4.0, it means that individual fibers in the sample deviate from the mean by 4.0 microns. Some fibers are as fine as 18.0; others are as coarse as 26.0 (based on the MFD of 22.0 microns). You want the SD number to be as low as possible because uniformity in a fleece is a highly desirable quality.

Grading and Fiber Classification

In a perfect fiber world, all alpacas would produce fleeces with identical fineness. That, in a nutshell, is the vision of many alpaca farmers and the goal they strive to reach. As of now, the fiber diameter can vary considerably from one animal to the next. In South America, skilled women—employed by commercial mills—sort huge quantities of fiber using various criteria. The women do so by hand. The fiber is sorted by color and then graded by fineness. The mills classify the graded fiber. Each grade has a descriptive name assigned to it. Unfortunately, a uniform system for classification does not exist. For example, Eric Hoffman lists two tables with different classification systems in his book. They are used by two of the largest commercial mills in South America. In the USA, alpaca farmers use grade classification from 1 – 6, with Grade 1 (<20) being the finest and Grade 6 (32.1 – 35.0) the coarsest.

Will there ever be alpaca herds with identical fiber fineness? No, because, as an alpaca ages, its fiber usually coarsens. Skilled alpaca fiber graders are in no danger of losing their jobs.

Density Versus Fineness

"It's obvious what we should set as goals for our breeding program," one farmer pointed out to me. "We combine density with fineness and ... bingo!"

It is usually easy to achieve rapid improvement when we select one genetic trait and concentrate on it to the exclusion of others. Unfortunately, such a program, while achieving the desired results, can have a negative impact on other traits. For example, when South American alpaca owners put too much emphasis on fleece density because the market at that time rewarded weight only, they sacrificed the silky fineness that the fashion world had come to expect from alpaca fiber. Years ago, when the density craze swept the North American alpaca community, many alpaca males with very fine fiber were gelded and thereby removed from the gene pool. Density was rewarded in the breeding pens and the show ring. Only one to two years after winning their ribbons, I saw show champions that had fiber so coarse that I would not have sold it as bird nesting material. Easy solutions are not in the genetic selection toolbox of a livestock farmer. Successful selection for combining two extreme fiber traits—extreme fineness and extreme density—is difficult.

What about the financial picture? Commercial companies pay a premium for very fine fiber. Although fleece weight is usually less, profits may surpass those gained from selling a heavier but coarser fleece.

Staple Length

Staple length measures the length of the fiber generated between shearings. When staple length is mentioned in the USA and Canada, it is generally assumed that shearing took place annually. A minimum staple length of about three to four inches is sufficient for all textile purposes. Huacaya yearlings and young adults often produce close to six inches of staple length. Suri fiber grows much faster, with average staple length reaching approximately eight inches. Staple length usually decreases with age. This fiber characteristic further confuses the issue when farmers try to judge fleece density by fleece weight after shearing. More is not always better when it comes to staple length. According to Wini Labrecque, commercial mills prefer to process fiber that is no longer than five inches. Suri fiber, which is often too long for processing, must be cut before it can be made into yarn.

In the USA, the alpaca industry enjoys the services of many small fiber mills. These "mini-mills" cannot process the huge quantities of fiber that the large, commercial mills in South American handle, but the good ones do a wonderful job for farmers with small or moderate size herds. Jeff and Leslie Jorritsma own and manage Autumn Mist Fiber Mill in Prattsburg, New York, USA. I asked them about desirable staple length.

Leslie answered: "Our mill can process fiber that is between two and seven inches long. Anything shorter than that tends to shed and create an unworthy yarn. Consistency in staple length is very important."

Medullation

In the fiber industry, *medullation* is normally associated with coarse guard hair. What is medullation? In botany, the spongy center of the stems of certain plants is called the medulla. In anatomy, it's the marrow of bones. In fiber, it's the hollow core inside a single strand. Compared to wool, alpaca fiber of identical fineness is more heavily medullated. The percentage of medullated fiber varies greatly from one alpaca to the next, even in some cases where MFD is identical. It was once thought that medullation occurred only in very coarse fiber and guard hair. The *Alpaca Research Foundation* helped to support research on the fiber characteristics of the huacaya alpaca. *Yocom-McColl Testing Laboratories* used a new, sophisticated method to scan for medullated fiber and found that alpacas can have such fiber in extremely low micron ranges. Current technology can only test for the presence of medullated fiber in white, light, fawn, and beige fleeces.

Comfort Factor

All fiber can be tested for *comfort factor*. In this test component, the percentage of fibers over 30 microns in the sample submitted is subtracted from 100 percent. It is clear that a fiber producer of luxurious alpaca garments would want the comfort factor to be 100 percent or as close to it as possible.

Crimp

Compared to wool, alpaca fiber has a lower resistance to compression. This is believed to be due to the lower levels of crimp found in alpaca fiber. Crimp is another term for curvature, and this fiber characteristic can also be scientifically measured. *Average Fiber Curvature*(AFC) is expressed in degrees per millimeter (mm). If you want a high level of crimp—curvature—in your fiber, you should select for breeding stock with high numbers in this category. Eric Hoffman cited a study of 600 alpacas where the *mean* (average) curvature was 32 degrees per millimeter (32 deg/mm). In contrast, vicuñas have what is called a high-frequency curvature of around 90 deg/mm.

Please read what I am about to tell you now several times:

The *higher* the curvature frequency, the *less* the naked eye is able to detect it. I'll say it another way: Alpaca fiber that has a curvature frequency (crimp) that comes close to that of the vicuña *appear* to have virtually no crimp at all. Testing equipment tells the true story. The alpaca fiber sample with the highest frequency curvature I ever saw had an AFC of 60.9 deg/

mm—incredibly high for an alpaca. The MFD was 17.6 microns. I admit that I often enjoyed some fun at the expense of prospective and novice farmers. I'd show them the sample and ask their opinion. All declared it of poor quality because it lacked "crimp." Then I would show them the male's histogram and explain his AFC numbers. There was always dead silence following this little lesson. Crimp or no crimp, I would consider a huacaya fleece with a *Mean Fiber Diameter* of 17.6 microns highly desirable.

Nature Versus Nurture

Fiber characteristics are highly heritable and make improvement for selected fiber traits easier than improving conformation and reproductive traits. Although inheritance greatly determines fiber characteristics, nurture impacts a fiber harvest. You have already learned that embryonic environment may play a role in fiber quantity. Nutrition also impacts fiber quality. Overconditioning coarsens fiber. An underconditioned alpaca's fiber will be finer than what is normal for that individual, but the fiber will be brittle, break easily, and be worthless except as garden mulch. Internal parasites ruin the soft handle of a fleece; external parasites such as lice or ticks will make it impossible to sell. Stress can ruin a fleece to an extent the novice farmer will be shocked to see. In her workshops, Wini Labrecque—a highly respected North American alpaca fiber expert—displays sample fleeces that clearly show the signs of stress: breakage and discoloration. Such fleeces are neither suitable for spinning nor for felting.

"Fiber is the alpaca's canary in the coal mine," Wini says.

Colors and Patterns

The inheritance of color genes is a science, not a crap shoot as some farmers will try to make you believe. Most people find it a little difficult to crack the genetic code, but once you understand it, you will also understand the color results of your breeding decisions.

Alpacas have two basic pigments: red and black. All alpaca fleece colors and shades must be viewed in this context. This includes white, a "color" created by genes that code for the *removal* of pigment. Genetically speaking, a white alpaca is either red or black. Sometimes, only breeding results will reveal the true pigment of the dam or sire. Often, a tiny colored spot found on a white alpaca gives a farmer the desired information. For example, a white alpaca with a small fawn spot should be thought of and described as a red alpaca with a large, white spot.

The rich variety of alpaca colors and patterns is amazing. Colors range from white to black. Patterns include various spotting patterns as well as roans. The somewhat ill advised nomenclature applied to the latter—they are called and registered as greys—does not make understanding color genetics easier for the novice.

Each year, more than a few alpaca farmers register their crias under the wrong color designation. Why? Environmental influences can lighten the outer fleece. Farmers who don't know or are too lazy to part the fleece will register alpacas by the color of their fleece tips. A visitor to our farm all but called me a liar when I told him that the "brown" female alpaca he saw in my pasture was indeed a true black. Silver greys—really black and white roans—are often erroneously registered as rose greys because of their sun bleached outer fleece tips. Rose greys are actually red and white roans. Even those of us who use the AOA color chart and use the correct method to identify color will sometimes have problems. Because fiber color can change as the alpaca ages, the original color as identified on a cria may no longer be correct after the first or second shearing.

White alpacas with blue eyes are not uncommon. Many are deaf. This is due to a lack of pigment cells which normally make it possible for the hearing mechanism to function. Keep in mind that deaf herd animals—bred for fiber—function extremely well in a protected farm environment. Their colored offspring will have perfect hearing. Not all blue-eyed, white alpacas are deaf. Not all dark-eyed, white alpacas have perfect hearing. Many blue-eyed, white alpacas are—genetically speaking—what I call *greys in disguise*. They actually express the grey (roan) pattern, but it can't be seen because other genes code for total removal of pigment. When bred, for example, to a self-colored alpaca such as a dark fawn, the blue-eyed white parent often produces a grey with a *visible* grey pattern.

Much misinformation is given out about this particular defect. Farmers who tell buyers not to purchase blue-eyed white alpacas should not have white, grey, beige, and light fawn animals in their own pastures. If they do, you may want to question them as to why they raise and sell stock that may contribute to what they perceive as a problem. If we wish to preserve the wide range of colors and patterns in the alpaca population, blue-eyed alpacas will occasionally be born and should be accepted as the inevitable result of such a program.

Lethal color genes exist in many species, including mice, dogs, cattle, and horses. In alpacas, the grey (roan) pattern may be produced by a lethal gene as is true for other species such as cattle. Hold the hysteria! This is only an issue if you breed grey to grey. If both parents pass on the grey gene (allele is the correct, genetic term), the embryo will die in utero. If only one parent passes on the grey allele, you have a healthy grey cria. If both grey parents pass on the non-grey allele, your cria will not be grey but self-colored. The latter term refers to animals that only have one color. Spotting patterns are produced by other genes and are a separate entity from the gene coding for grey (roan).

Skirting a Fleece

Alpaca fiber can be used for many purposes. I have sold raw fiber to handspinners, felters, fly fishers for lures, and crafters as padding for artificial bird nests. It has been purchased to stuff pillow cases and knitted teddy bears. A big seller is alpaca yarn, either pure alpaca or an alpaca/merino wool mix. For most applications, it is necessary to skirt a fleece to produce a superior end product. Even the most skillful shearer will generate a few second cuts. Small amounts of debris cling to all fleeces, no matter how clean. To ensure a quality end product, these impurities need to be removed. Ideally, after skirting, all the fiber stored in each bag should be free of debris, and individual strands of fiber should all be of the same length and fineness. Realistically, you are not going to achieve this level of perfection. The results should come close, though, particularly if you wish to produce or provide the raw material for a superior yarn.

There is a misconception among alpaca farmers and even shearers that the fleece must stay in one piece as it comes off the animal and also during the skirting process. For a production fleece, this is of absolutely no importance. Only fleeces that you plan to enter in a show need to remain in one piece. For the purpose of future processing, you can pick them apart during skirting, and I dare say that you'll have a better skirting job.

I remain seated while I skirt one small portion of the fleece at a time. I simply pull a handful of fiber from the fleece. This way, not the smallest piece of debris or a single second cut is overlooked.

If you recall, I already sort each fleece into two bags during shearing: one for the blanket and one for the neck fiber (I use the very coarse fiber from the lower legs and belly for garden mulch). There isn't much neck fiber, and the contents of the small bag are quickly skirted. For skirting the blanket, I now add another bag. I don't care how skillful a shearer and sorter are at harvest (shearing) time, the tendency is to try and maximize the yields of a fleece. As a result, the area of the body that shearer and sorter judge to be covered by the blanket—the prime and most desirable fiber—is usually measured too generously. The fiber at the perimeter (the "skirt") of the blanket is classified as *seconds* and must be separated from the *prime*. (Reminder: Do not confuse *seconds* with *second cuts;* the latter term describes the tiny pieces created by poor shearing techniques.) That does not mean that the seconds are worthless. I sell them but for a lower price than the prime. It's best to skirt each fleece with a fresh view and an individual approach. *Tui* (baby) fleeces and outstanding adult fleeces have blankets of such superb consistency that, at the end of the skirting session, the bag designated to hold the seconds will remain virtually empty. Many times, I skirted tui fleeces that had neck fiber with the same fineness and staple length as the blanket. As the alpaca ages, the prime fiber harvest diminishes with each year.

Initially, I found sorting the fiber difficult and extremely tedious. My early skirting sessions were studies in indecision. Prime or seconds? Seconds or prime? Since the prime fiber commands higher prices, it makes sense not to waste money by sorting it into the bag of seconds. My final decision has always been: If in doubt, put it in the bag with the coarser fiber. If you're counting on repeat business from your fiber customers, you must sell a high quality product. With each harvest, my level of competence and speed increases. Skirting is a skill that, in my opinion, can only be learned by actually doing it. Reading about it and watching others helps, but only a hands-on approach results in expertise.

The techniques described above work for me. Other fiber producers may have different ways of preparing their alpaca fiber harvest for sale or the next production process.

Skirting Tables

Instead of a solid surface, a skirting table has a mesh top. Dirt and small pieces of debris fall through the mesh when you shake the fleece prior to skirting. The supplies needed for a skirting table are not expensive, and it is a practical piece of equipment. Some farmers also use specially designed tumblers that remove the worst dirt and debris. Because of my initial, meticulous preparation, I have not found it necessary to use a skirting table or a tumbler. I skirt on a white folding table that readily shows up any irregularities and debris in colored fleeces. For white fleeces, I use our wooden dining room table. Very little dirt is left on either table after I've completed the job.

Skirting Show Fleeces

Many farmers enter their fleeces in fleece shows, either those sanctioned by the *Alpaca Owners Association*, or shows that are held in conjunction with fiber festivals. Only the skirted blanket is submitted for show judging. To optimize chances of the fleece placing in a show, both shearer and skirter must be aware of techniques that will present a fleece to its best advantage.

Cottage Fleece Shows

According to the AOA website, the Cottage Fleece Show is designed for any alpaca farmer who wants to know how his or her breeding program "competes in the area of marketable and usable fiber." Twenty-five percent of the final score consists of a separate spin-off evaluation where "fineness, uniformity of micron and length are very important in creating a quality end product." (AOA).

Spin-Offs

If the task of submitting a professionally prepared show fleece seems too daunting, the alpaca farmer has the option of entering a fiber spin-off.

Only a few ounces are submitted for judging. If you wish to be competitive, educate yourself on how to select, prepare, and submit your fiber sample.

Storing Alpaca Fiber

Fiber artists are not interested in purchasing a fleece that has been subjected to extreme temperature changes, insects, and possibly rodents. Until sales are made, the fiber must therefore be stored carefully, not simply thrown into a corner somewhere. I know fiber producers and their customers who lost hundreds of pounds of raw fleeces due to moth infestations. I would never take a chance of storing fiber without protecting it. Although there is no need to buy custom-made fiber bags, only clear plastic bags should be used for storage. I place the bags in a light, climate controlled room without direct exposure to the sun. I *loosely* close the bags with string and attach a tag listing the animal's name, weight of fleece, and price. I leave enough of an opening in the bag so the fiber doesn't "sweat." You should not see beads of moisture accumulate inside the bag. If space is at a premium, you can do exactly the opposite. Squeeze *all* air out of the bag and wrap it tightly. I learned this management option when I attended a fiber workshop presented by fiber artist and fiber judge Wini Labrecque.

I add a piece of cedar to each bag. Some fiber producers prefer a sheet of fabric softener. Moth balls are effective but unfortunately have a harsh smell, and their fumes are not healthy for humans and pets to inhale. An old time remedy is lavender. The dried flowers of this pretty, pleasant smelling plant should be placed in a porous cloth sack which in turn is put in the bag of alpaca fiber. I also place large baskets filled with fragrant lavender leaves in my fiber room.

If you notice moth infestation, you may still be able to save the fiber if it's in the beginning stages. Wash the fiber gently by hand in cold water (I use a cleaning agent called EUCALAN for all alpaca or wool garments), then rinse, dry, and store it in the freezer for a few days. Take it out, leave it in a light room without direct sun exposure for a week and freeze it again. Don't sell any fiber which has been invaded by moths, even if you think you've conquered the little beasts. Once you have a heavy infestation, you may as well throw every bit of fiber away and resign yourself to your loss.

Marketing and Selling Raw Fiber

I often hear alpaca farmers complain that they have many bags filled with fleeces stashed in their basements, garages, and attics. In contrast, I have sold every ounce of fiber that our alpacas have ever produced. Why? To begin with, I worked hard to understand alpaca fiber properties. I still read every article that I find on the subject. Although I am far from a fiber artist, I work with the fiber from helping with shearing, skirting fleeces, spinning my own fiber, and finally knitting simple projects such as hats and scarves. A farmer is usually much more successful marketing and selling a product that he or she can talk about with at least a basic level of knowledge.

I sell fiber right off the farm and at various agricultural venues. Most years, I sell my fleeces raw. They are, with occasional exceptions, clean and meticulously skirted. If, for whatever reason, a fleece is not skirted, I identify it as such and reduce the price. It takes time to establish a loyal customer base and a sterling reputation. Be honest about presenting your product. My first encounter with a handspinner was a very angry woman who told me in no uncertain terms, "You alpaca breeders can stick your fleeces…" Well, you get the picture. What had happened? She showed me. This woman had paid top dollars for alpaca fiber at another farm. The upper layer in her bag looked very nice. Once I removed it, I discovered a tangled, filthy mess. This fiber was not even suitable for felting, let alone spinning. Our industry had lost a customer due to a farmer's dishonest business practice.

Spinning and Other Fiber Arts

To truly understand and appreciate alpaca fiber, you must work with it yourself. I already mentioned that even basic knowledge and skills help to sell fiber and products. The five most popular fiber arts are spinning, knitting, crocheting, felting, and weaving.

Prospective alpaca buyers are always fascinated to learn about the spinning process. New spinning wheels are quite costly. Join a spinning guild and make it known that you're looking for a wheel. Make sure that any used wheel you eventually buy is in good condition. Learning to spin is hard enough without battling mechanical problems. Some models, for example the old-fashioned Ashford wheel, are quite attractive. The traveling wheels don't look as quaint; they are more practical if you intend to spin in several or many locations. Spinning looks like a deceptively simple craft, but it's not easy to produce a consistent product. Fortunately, many fiber artists prefer to buy homespun yarn over commercially milled skeins. Some actually look for yarn with interesting irregularities. It's wonderful to sell yarn that you have spun from the fiber of your own animals.

Knitting has become a popular craft for people of all ages. Although I have neither the time nor the interest to learn complicated and sophisticated patterns, I knit and sell scarves, cowls, and hats. I am familiar with and can discuss basic knitting terminology with my yarn customers. My yarn displays include samples of products that I knitted with worsted as well as chunky yarn. When customers ask, I can explain the difference between the woolen and worsted process of spinning fiber into yarn. In the worsted process, the individual strands of fiber are aligned in a smooth, orderly fashion with a firm twist. In the woolen process, the twist of the individual strands is less firm, and the fibers are more randomly arranged. Because of its smooth handle, worsted yarn is used for woven luxury garments such as suits; the lofty woolen yarn lends itself to knitted products such as sweaters, scarves, and mittens.

Alpaca farmers should know that the term *worsted* can also refer to the specific weight of a *woolen yarn* and not the worsted process. I find that it's a popular weight, and many knitters prefer it over bulky or lace weight yarns. When I sell yarn, I don't pretend to be more knowledgeable about knitting than I am, but my customers appreciate my sincere interest in their craft. Those who prefer crocheting over knitting also appreciate the softness of alpaca yarn. Because my own expertise in that area is limited to potholders, I asked a friend to crochet a cowl from a hank of chunky yarn for display as a sample project.

I have not tried felting but enjoy wearing a hat that Carol Masters, a friend and fellow alpaca farmer, felted and presented to me as a gift. It is warm, amazingly waterproof, and light weight. My sister, Karin, wears another one of Carol's creations on her many long hikes in Germany. She loves it! We both wore the hats while hiking together in Germany in 2012. Karin wore her hat each day, all day. I found mine too warm at times but was very grateful to have it when temperatures dropped and when it rained. The hats passed the test, no doubt about that. The front cover of *Hiking with the Boss* shows a photograph of my sister and me wearing Carol's felted alpaca hats on our hike. Coarser fiber from older alpacas is a good choice for felting projects. Two different techniques can be used: wet felting and needle felting.

Hiking with the Boss

MY JOURNEY TO THE MOSEL VALLEY

Ingrid Woo

Weaving is another ancient fiber craft. It is less popular than the others. I assume that's because of the expense and space requirements of a loom. Carol, in addition to spinning and knitting, also weaves and has created some beautiful shawls and throws with alpaca yarn. With her help, I wove a scarf—using three different colors—from worsted alpaca yarn. I found it an interesting and very challenging experience.

The general public has little understanding of the time and skills required to, for example, weave a scarf or knit a hat. It's good for people to watch fiber artists at work. Comments can sometimes be hilarious. A friend of mine took part in a spinning demonstration at an apple festival. A woman and a small boy stopped briefly to watch. As they were leaving, my friend heard the woman say to the boy, "See, now you know how they ground up meat in the old days."

Commercial Fiber Mills

If your spinning skills can't keep up with the demand for yarn, try one of the previously mentioned small specialty fiber mills that can turn your raw fiber into rovings, yarn, and felted sheets. The people who own these mills and do the processing are not miracle workers. If you hand or send them dirty, unskirted fleeces, don't expect quality end products. The processor will either return your fiber or charge you for cleaning and skirting. The latter is unacceptable for the frugal alpaca farmer. You may have to wait up to a year to receive yarn spun from your fiber. Three to six months is an excellent "turn around" time. Some alpaca farmers pay handspinners to produce yarn for them. Very few spinners are willing to process for others. The identities of those who do are often kept a well-guarded secret by those lucky to have found such a jewel.

Fiber Cooperatives

There are several fiber co-ops in the United States. Check them out carefully. Our own experience with a fiber co-op was frustrating and wound up costing us a lot of money. This was many years ago. Since that time, several cooperatives have been formed that provide their members with good products and services. Independent processors in the USA purchase large quantities of fleeces from individual farmers as well as fiber cooperatives if the quality and quantity is right for their intended end products. Specialty stores that sell fiber and yarn will sometimes work with farmers on a consignment basis. My experience with such an arrangement was not good, and I can not recommend it.

Fiber Follies

Every community of livestock producers has its Pied Pipers—people who promote crazy and often harmful "improvements to the breed" and lure scores of fellow farmers to follow their foolish schemes. Some of these schemes are financially wildly successful, but only for the Pied Pipers. By the time their enthusiastic disciples come to their senses, it is often too late. The damage has been done. I will present a few examples.

Alpacas have fairly thick, tight skin. This has served them well for several thousand years. There are farmers who promote selection for *soft skin* to reduce micron count. Do they know about the fiasco with soft, pliable skin in Merino sheep? The skin problems? The discrepancy of micron count inside the folds compared to outside the folds? Are they aware of the time it takes to shear a sheep with numerous skin folds? The effort it took for sheep farmers to remove the extreme wrinkles of the fleecy "Shar-Peis" from their breeding programs? What *are* alpaca farmers thinking who promote this concept as a desirable trait in alpacas? There are already numerous alpacas across the country with soft, loose skin. A shearer told me about the difficulty shearing them, and the techniques he must use to protect the animals from being cut with the shear's blades.

Emaciated alpacas will produce finer fiber than the MFD they'd produce if all their nutritional requirements were met. Fiber producers refer to this as *starvation fineness*. Sick and very old alpacas are often thin. A few individuals will always have a slender appearance no matter how well they are cared for and fed. When I talk about starvation fineness, I refer to alpacas that are advertised with an MFD of less than 20 microns—some as low as 15—and, within a few months of arriving on a new farm and being fed properly, show an increase of 5-8 microns. Starving fiber animals on purpose to achieve a low MFD is cruel and unethical. On your own farm, not only is it cruel, it's outright stupid. Unusually fine fiber produced through starvation is so weak and brittle that it cannot be processed. Unfortunately, a histogram will only show the low MFD. The test cannot evaluate the fiber's strength. Neither can the novice farmers who pay large sums for these animals, and then are shocked to find that their "beautiful" fleeces are worthless. I have no problem with alpacas that produce superfine fiber while properly fed. Such animals are valuable as breeding stock.

We see a rapidly increasing number of blind alpacas on our nation's farms. Oh, there is nothing wrong with their eye sight. They suffer from a condition sheep and fiber goat producers call *wool blindness*. Thick, long fiber covers the alpacas' faces. Only a thin slit indicates where the eyes are. Sheep farmers discovered that wool blindness leads to loss of condition and poor mothering skills. Is it wise for alpaca farmers to select for this trait? Do those who select for it care about the alpaca's quality of life?

Some advertisements tell prospective buyers that the seller's alpacas "have *fiber down to their toes*." Mine have it too, but I don't find it a trait worth bragging about. Fiber from the lower legs is not worth a plugged nickel, and it's a pain in the neck to shear. Not shearing it for years—as so many farmers elect to do—can cause skin problems and severe discomfort for the animals.

Should alpaca farmers set the *total removal of medullated fiber*— including guard hair—as a genetic benchmark? Some farmers think so. In the species that have guard hair, each hair acts as a tiny umbrella. Rain and snow cannot penetrate all the way to the skin, keeping the animal dry and healthy during inclement weather. Several dog breeds no longer have guard hair thanks to heavy human selection pressure. Unless these dogs are brushed almost daily, their coats become a clumpy, matted mess. The same is true for Angora rabbits. A friend of mine who sheared for other farmers saw several alpacas with what fiber producers call *cotted* fleeces. These were fleeces so matted that they had to be thrown out. Compared to alpacas, sheep fiber has little medullation but is greasy. I imagine that the grease—also called lanolin—acts as a protective coating. Is it so hard to believe that natural selection made sure that alpacas—their fleeces have virtually no grease—are protected in inclement weather? Do we really want to produce alpacas that must be forced to stay inside a shelter any time it rains or the wind blows? I should also mention here that fiber mills have machines that remove guard hair during processing.

Years ago, there were several Pied Pipers who promoted breeding for *fleece weights of twenty pounds*. Where did they plan to keep these fleecy wonders? In an air-conditioned barn? In many areas of our country, alpacas with half that fleece weight suffer—despite intervention—from heat stress. I believe such a breeding objective is inhumane.

People who are new to livestock farming should read books that discuss how farmers of other species pushed the production envelope, only to have their programs turn into health issues for their animals and financial debacles for their owners. Why are there so many advertisements to cure mastitis in dairy cows? Why do the breeders of Suffolk and Hampshire sheep need to test for *Spider Lamb Syndrome*? Why did it take two hours to shear some Merino sheep? Why are there grazing animals that would remain hungry if only kept on pasture?

Must we repeat the follies of other livestock industries and add our own into the bargain? Must our alpacas suffer so a few farmers can play Frankenstein and reap financial rewards at the expense of the animals? I hope that more and more farmers will have the courage to speak out and say to the Pied Pipers: "You are wrong, and I will not follow your lead."

Luxury Fiber?

I mentioned in the beginning of this chapter that alpaca is often described as a luxury fiber. For twenty years, I have been raising and shearing alpacas, working with raw alpaca fiber, and producing as well as wearing alpaca products. I never felt comfortable labeling and marketing alpaca exclusively or predominately as a luxury fiber. After two decades working as an alpaca farmer, I feel more strongly than ever that we limit our market by doing so.

Is alpaca fiber *luxurious*? Oh yes! The superfine fiber more than deserves that adjective. But it's more than that! The products that are made from alpaca fiber are warm, durable, and *practical*. For the construction worker or the man repairing power lines after a winter storm, alpaca socks and hats are not a luxury. I don't consider the alpaca insoles that I wear inside my farm boots a luxury but an important component of my *work* outfit.

Women who sit in cold and drafty warehouses behind their computers buy my socks and fingerless gloves. "I don't care about the color," they say. "To finally have warm hands and feet at work! I can't thank you enough."

"Thank the alpacas!" I say.

22

APPLE HEADS AND KNUCKLE HEADS

"I cannot see why they should need thick leg bones for coping with the severe environment of the Andes, when vicuñas do not seem to be heavy boned and yet cope just fine." Australian alpaca farmer

Camelid History

Based on the research of Dr. Jane Wheeler and other scientists, the wild vicuña is the undisputed ancestor of the domesticated alpaca. Under the stewardship of the Incas, captured vicuñas evolved into alpacas. Over many generations of selective breeding, the Incas managed to retain the fineness of the vicuña's fiber but added longer staple length. Domestication promoted the mutation from the uniform vicuña fleece color to a dazzling array of alpaca colors and patterns. The Incas bred alpacas exclusively for their fiber. Carrying the highly prized alpaca fiber to all corners of the vast Inca empire was the responsibility of the much larger llamas, the "ships of the Andes." The llama's ancestor is the wild guanaco. The two domesticated species—alpacas and llamas—were kept strictly separated, and each was carefully bred for its designated purpose.

After the victorious Spanish conquerors captured and executed the Inca Atahualpa in 1532, all that changed. The Spanish did not acknowledge and appreciate the value of the South American camelids. Many alpacas were slaughtered; carefully planned and maintained breeding programs were destroyed. Alpacas and llamas were allowed to mingle and freely interbreed. Occasionally, a captured vicuña was thrown into the genetic mix.

Modern South American alpaca production varies greatly. At the extreme ends, there are large farms with highly selective, sophisticated breeding programs, and there are small herds owned by poor peasants where selection consists of survival of the fittest individuals.

Do We Need a Breed Standard?

The history of the South American camelids explains why we find a large variety of alpaca phenotypes. Among individual alpacas, there are distinct differences in size, head shape, proportions of legs to body length, and fiber qualities. When alpaca farmers talk about a breed standard, they are really talking about standardized production goals. The objective of such a program is a population with cookie cutter identical conformation and fiber traits. From a commercial production standpoint, the goal of physical uniformity in livestock has merit. Consumer studies show that people are more apt to buy a product if its quality—shape, size, taste, color, etc.—is predictable. We can apply such a concept to alpaca fiber and alpaca meat. It all sounds very logical, organized, and—well, standardized. Standardized conformation does not happen in a genetically diverse population. It is achieved through inbreeding and linebreeding. In a nutshell: Genetic diversity is slowly whittled down until the entire population is *homozygous* (the same) at each *genetic locus* (genetic address). Such a program has repercussions. A fragile immune system, diminished fertility, frequency of genetic defects, lack of general vitality—this is the price the animals pay for our desire to standardize their physical traits.

Years ago, Jerold Bell, D.V.M., clinical associate professor of genetics at Tufts University in Massachusetts, wrote: "The greatest threat to overall breed health and vitality is the popular sire syndrome …"

Dr. Bell was talking about the practice of breeding hundreds of bitches to the same, famous stud dog in the effort to conform to a breed standard. Alpaca farmers should carefully research the issue of breed standards before promoting a standard for alpacas. Human selection pressure can do considerable harm to an animal population.

"Oh, wait one minute," you may think now. "I've seen photos of large herds of vicuñas, and they all looked very much alike. No diversity there!"

Yes, that is true; I have seen those photos. There is one important difference. The vicuña population is wild, and survival of the fittest regulates reproduction. Because their numbers are quite large, vicuñas may be genetically diverse in areas—the immune system, for example—that are not visible.

Type

Outstanding fiber can be bred on any camelid phenotype. Some llamas have fiber of a quality that is comparable to fine alpaca fiber. As an alpaca farmer, however, I want my alpacas to be what dog breeders would describe as "typey." That means that the animals can be identified as alpacas—not llamas—at first glance. Key characteristics that set alpacas apart from llamas are the smaller size, spear shaped ears, a slight rise of the topline toward the loin, a more vertical pastern, and a shorter head. *Within these parameters, there is plenty of room for variation and healthy diversity.*

Soundness

Even a novice farmer can easily identify individual alpacas with obvious conformational faults—bowed legs and gopher ears come to mind. In their respective books, Dr. Fowler and Eric Hoffman present detailed drawings and descriptions of alpaca conformation.

"Why is all this stuff about conformation important?" more than one alpaca owner has asked over the years. "They are bred to produce fiber. Does it matter if their legs are crooked?"

When Eric Hoffman discusses conformation in his book, he talks about "quality of life" and reminds readers to pay attention to this concept when setting goals and making breeding decisions. I am very glad that he did. In their eagerness to reach production goals, livestock producers often ignore quality of life for the animals. An alpaca that moves painfully on crooked legs has little quality of life. In this section, I address several conformational issues to promote critical thinking as it applies to breeding goals and selection for specific traits.

Physical soundness should be important to all livestock farmers, particularly those who make breeding decisions. To evaluate and select for soundness, we must ask ourselves: What physical functions is the animal that we are breeding expected to perform?

Under normal management practices, alpacas graze extensively, cush to rest and chew their cud, pronk for exercise and the sheer joy of it, copulate, give birth, and nurse their young. In addition, males wrestle with one another to gain dominance. Which conformational traits are important for these activities?

Grazers are walkers. Always on the lookout for the next tasty mouthful of grasses, legumes, and herbs, alpacas are walking—at a slow but steady pace—for hours each day. Aside from finding palatable and nutritious plants, walking several miles each day keeps the alpacas toned and healthy. A female with good muscle tone will have a much easier time giving birth than a physically weak barn potato. As natural pacers, alpacas are well suited to cover long distances in this extremely efficient gait. In this type of locomotion, both legs on one side of the body are moved forward simultaneously. At very fast speeds, it looks as if the pacer is gliding over the ground. Pacing is made possible by a fairly narrow front that correlates with a slender body. Why are some alpaca farmers promoting heavy bone and wide chests?

Alpaca farmers who wish to breed for a dual-purpose camelid—fiber and meat—may have reason to prefer alpacas with heavy bone. Such a trait correlates with a heavier carcass weight. Years ago, when a prominent and influential alpaca owner promoted breeding for heavy bone, he never discussed the issue of meat production. In my opinion, the author's reason for heavy bone—survival in a harsh climate—was simply not valid.

In a published response, I explained why I considered this an ill-advised breeding objective. An Australian alpaca farmer supported my views. In private correspondence, the woman wrote: "I cannot see why they should need thick leg bones for coping with the severe environment of the Andes, when vicuñas do not seem to be heavy boned and yet cope just fine." I am in total agreement with her statement.

Of course, selecting against heavy bone does not translate into selecting for weedy animals that lack substance. There is, however, no good reason to produce the alpaca equivalent of the llamas that llama owner Lynd Blatchford once described as "oxen with banana ears."

Once you have observed a herd of alpacas pronking at dusk, you will be enchanted. The movement requires incredible strength. Farmers who never see their alpacas pronk should question their animals' health and their own management practices. What evolutionary advantages did the more athletic pronkers have over the pronkers with average ability or the non-pronkers? I imagine that it was the ability to elude predators. I have noticed over the years that the most athletic pronkers—showing superior height, speed, and endurance—are usually alpacas that resemble the vicuña in the ratio of their legs' length to the size of their trunk. Alpacas with vicuña-like proportions are definitely the soundest movers in a herd. I have also noticed over the years that the slender, long-legged females give birth with the greatest of ease.

It is generally accepted in the alpaca community that the distance from the soles of the front feet to the elbow, the distance from elbow to topline, and the distance from the topline to the head should all roughly measure the same. From my observations, those are *not* the conformational proportions of the longer-legged vicuña. Who decided that alpacas should differ in their proportions from their wild ancestors? Was it an arbitrary decision or one based on practical, sensible reasons?

Although I favor alpacas with vicuña-type proportions, in my herd, both body types are represented. I would like to see another inch or two of leg under my two favorite males, but I have no intention of selling them. Both have wonderful fiber, great temperament, and outstanding fertility and breeding behavior. A female alpaca in my herd with the body depth/leg length/neck length ratio as usually described in our industry's literature is much calmer and placid than her more elegant looking herd members. For that reason, I also consider her a "keeper." Breeding choices often involve compromises, and these are good examples.

Cattle farmers check for pelvic width because this measurement is an indicator of birthing ease or possible difficulties. I have never seen or heard anyone mention this practice in relation to female alpacas. Instead, several authors described the practice of transferring alpaca embryos to be carried to term by much larger llama females. This is, in my opinion, the height of foolishness as far as assessing and promoting alpaca reproductive health—particularly ease of birthing—is concerned.

Males wrestle with one another to gain dominance. Another objective is to damage the testicles and penis of the opponent, in effect gelding him and making it impossible for him to pass on his genes. The razor sharp male fighting teeth are formidable weapons. Nature's wisdom equipped alpacas with very thick skin. Human arrogance decides that nature be damned—let's breed for thin skin. Sure, fighting teeth can be filed or nipped off to prevent injuries. Their eruption can be sudden and is easily missed. I feel better knowing that my males have thick skins. I already discussed the difficulties that soft, "stretchy" skin poses at shearing time.

"I love those little apple heads," an owner gushed when we discussed conformation.

Due to clever marketing, head shape has become of extreme importance to many alpaca farmers. It should be, but not in the context that I see in our industry's advertisements. Dog breeders know that little apple heads are the cause of respiratory, neurological, and dental problems in canines. The wild vicuña does not have a little apple head. Rather, it has a functional head that allows for plenty of breathing space and to see approaching predators from a long distance—quite fitting for a prey animal.

All groups of livestock producers and pet breeders have knuckle heads in their ranks who breed for apple heads and other traits that prove to be harmful to the animals. It is difficult to swim against the stream when a knuckle head becomes a Pied Piper. A popular trend often starts with a famous stud. Should you follow it? Ultimately, if it involves the health of the animals, it's a moral decision.

Easy Keepers

Sheep breeders found out that large ewes with small stomachs, *though ideal for the show ring*, cannot consume enough dry matter to produce enough milk to support two young lambs. Lambed indoors and fed a hay/grain ration, the same ewes did well.

Although alpacas are not sheep and rarely have twins, this is another issue where I believe we can extrapolate from another species. Good hay, supplements, and grain are expensive. As alpaca farmers, we should strive for conformation that makes it possible for the animals to thrive and raise young on good pasture, with only minimal additions of other feed. This facet of breeding alpacas has received virtually no attention. There is, pun intended, considerable food for thought here!

There are numerous other examples of the show ring not rewarding functional traits in other species. We can take notice and learn from them. Far from being a "beauty contest," the purpose of a livestock show is to select individuals with conformation that is most advantageous for whatever it is we are asking the animal to do or produce. Do alpaca show judges always apply these selection criteria? Educate and judge for yourself!

Genetic Defects

Geneticists have determined that the individuals of all species carry on the average of between four to six genes coding for genetic defects. It is hard for me to fathom that some alpaca buyers and farmers think that alpacas are somehow exempt from these odds. *All* animals have skeletons in their genetic closets. Please don't expect every single one of your crias to be perfect. That includes those sired by famous, high priced champion males. A seller can control a lot of things, but not recessive defects produced by the roll of genetic dice. Once a gene coding for a genetic defect has been located on a livestock breed's genome, DNA testing can positively identify carriers. Until then, don't blame farmers for problems beyond their control. Although rare, spontaneous genetic mutations can also result in unpleasant surprises for farmers. Additionally, there is plenty of evidence that environmental conditions (toxic plants, lack of certain minerals, infectious disease) can produce defects in the offspring of all species, so genes coding for defects are not always the cause of deformities or other health problems in alpacas.

They're Alive!

Some farmers totally lose sight of the fact that they are purchasing livestock—literally *live* stock. With all their genetic "improving," shaping, and tweaking of physical traits, they seem to ignore or not care that the animals are live creatures, and drastically changing the alpacas' appearance will have consequences. Our alpacas need not be mirror images of their ancestor, the vicuña, but we should continuously remind ourselves that nature is the most efficient and sensible breeder. Natural selection does not tolerate dysfunctional traits that impair survival.

23

MARKETING AND SELLING ALPACAS

"Marketing alpacas is work, but it does not have to be expensive." Kristin Joyce

Why Now? Why Here?

"Selling Alpacas?" many readers will ask. "Why a chapter about selling alpacas now? You haven't even discussed buying alpacas."

That is true, and the choice is deliberate and has a purpose. What you learn in this chapter should further clarify how you wish to structure your farm business and the skills you need to succeed. Do you have sufficient parking space on your farm to host visitors? Enough to host workshops for large groups? Do you own a vehicle to transport alpacas to festivals? Will you use social media to market alpacas? Are you aware that many marketing strategies require you to have good writing skills? Ultimately, marketing plans should determine the size and scope of your enterprise.

Quite often, farmers who start out with tiny herds think of marketing and sales as far off in their future and give little thought to that aspect of breeding alpacas. People are often so smitten with the animals that they close their ears and eyes to the realities of farming. I think that's a serious mistake. Success in a business requires that you plan ahead. I have seen wonderful people—hard workers who produced great stock and took excellent care of it—fail financially because they lacked marketing skills or refused to make the effort to apply them to their agricultural business. If you wish to claim business expenses with the Internal Revenue Service, you must eventually show a profit. The IRS will not tolerate an agricultural business that shows only losses year after year. Agents are not interested in how much you love your animals and the "alpaca lifestyle." Do not describe your alpaca business as a hobby. If you are audited, the auditor will demand proof that you actively market your farm and its products in a professional manner.

The Marketing Pie

Not surprisingly, the experts in marketing and sales disagree with one another on the finer points of what defines marketing. In my research, I came across the work of Laura Lake, a marketing consultant; her explanation made the most sense to me. She encourages her clients to think of marketing as a pie. Inside this pie, you have slices of advertising, market research, public relations, customer support, product pricing, media planning, and possibly others. Marketing is therefore not just advertising your product but offering choices and excellent experiences to the customer.

Glitz and Glamour

Farmers with large herds and large budgets often spend thousands of dollars on glitzy marketing campaigns. They work. Many people equate sophisticated marketing with superior stock. It would be foolhardy for a frugal farmer on a limited budget to try and compete on such a level. The frugal alpaca farmer evaluates each option carefully and weighs expenses against results. No two farms are exactly alike. Common sense will tell a farmer that no two marketing programs should be exactly alike. Clearly defined goals help to develop successful strategies. The following marketing venues are not listed in order of importance.

Alpaca Owners Association (AOA)

The AOA combines the Registry and a marketing program. Its staff also oversees and manages the show division. You can show alpacas without an AOA membership but must pay a surcharge to do so. This is not cost effective if you wish to enter more than one show during one calendar year. Presently, most alpacas residing in the United States of America and used as breeding stock are registered with the AOA. To register an alpaca and receive a registration certificate, the owner must submit a blood sample for DNA testing to verify parentage. Strictly speaking, the test validates parentage rather than verifies it. This process is referred to as *exclusion DNA testing* and has an accuracy of 99.97 percent or higher. AOA testing is sophisticated, and testing requirements are stringent. Additionally, an owner may request that the blood sample is used to test for *Bovine Viral Diarrhea Virus* (BVDV). The blood sample consists of a few drops of blood placed on a specially designed blood card. Not much blood is needed, and the card can be mailed in a plain letter envelope. It is possible to register a non-breeder—for example, an alpaca exclusively used for its fiber—at a greatly reduced fee and later upgrade the registration to breeding status. The registration process for the non-breeder includes DNA validation of parentage. Both registration status and a negative BVDV test result may effectively be used for marketing purposes.

The AOA also administers a program that calculates data for various physical traits called *Expected Progeny Differences* (EPDs). Expected Progeny Differences provide estimates of the genetic value of an animal as a parent. We are not talking about parenting skills but, for example, traits such as birth weight, fiber comfort factor, or micron count. EPDs are used in all livestock industries. Scott P. Greiner, an Extension animal scientist, explains such a program in more detail on the Virginia Tech website.

All alpaca owners who registered an animal with the AOA are kept informed about the organization's activities. To become a voting member, you will need to pay an additional fee.

Unregistered Alpacas

Registered breeding stock usually sells for many times the amount of a non-registered animal. As with all other livestock, there is a market for unregistered alpacas. Ethical sellers of unregistered stock will disclose that, in contrast to other livestock produced in this country, unregistered alpacas cannot be "bred up" with the goal of registering the progeny after several generations of breeding to registered stock. The AOA requires registration for each generation in an alpaca's ancestral line-up. I have never marketed or sold unregistered alpacas and don't feel qualified to give more information or advice.

Regional and Local Affiliates

In addition to regional affiliates, most states have a state alpaca organization. There are also various livestock and grazing organizations you can join. As alpacas move more into the agricultural mainstream, a whole new world will open up to farmers without a background or experience in agriculture. Contact your local office of the *United States Department of Agriculture* (USDA) for information and suggestions. I have found the staff members in our local New Jersey office to be eager to help and pleasant to deal with. Analyze each organization's purpose and objectives. Some are strictly dedicated to education; others offer education as well as extensive marketing opportunities.

Volunteer Opportunities

National, regional, and local alpaca organization all offer plenty of opportunities to volunteer. There are three reasons to volunteer. The first is the pure enjoyment you get from the activity; the second is the promotion of your farm; the third is the educational value of a volunteer activity. If you don't care about the second reason, that's fine. If you *only* care about the second reason, you will soon be disappointed because volunteer work isn't automatically followed by name recognition. Don't spread yourself too thin. Don't take on so many obligations that you can't possibly do a good job at all of them. You will most definitely get name recognition but not in the positive way that you envisioned. Carry your weight, even if it's behind the scenes with a small contribution of your time and energy. Sometimes, volunteer work can turn into a paid job. It will certainly give you valuable insight into organizational details. Your volunteer experience may help you to better market and manage events on your own farm.

Farm Name

Marketing experts stress the importance of developing a brand—products, graphics, a name, and a slogan all define a business. Although there is no hard and fast rule, I think it makes sense to choose a farm name first and coordinate the other components with the name. The name should help your business stand out from the rest. Because people often have strong reactions to words and the images associated with them, make your selection carefully.

Herd Identifier

For a fee, you can register your farm's name with the AOA. Only you will be permitted to register an alpaca with that name as a herd identifier. You will often see the identifier in front or at the end of an alpaca's call name. Examples are: *Panda Bear of Stormwind Farm* and *Stormwind's Lorena*. If you purchase and later decide to breed two alpacas from another farm, you are the breeder and should use your own identifier. In contrast, if you purchase a pregnant female alpaca, you are not the breeder of its cria and therefore should not feel free to use your herd identifier when naming this baby without asking the farmer who bred it for permission. Please don't feel insulted if permission is denied. The breeding of animals is a scientific as well as a creative process. You should no more think of using another farmer's herd identifier than you would consider buying a painting and passing it off as your own creation. You may want to question the motives of those farmers who choose to use legally unprotected North American or even South American identifiers. Most farmers are proud of their "cria-tions" and list their own identifier in front of the name of an alpaca bred by them.

Logo

A logo gives your farm brand recognition. You will pay a lot of money for a logo if you don't have at least a basic vision of what you want. Before you commission an artist, look through trade magazines for logos you like as well as those you positively dislike. Share both categories with the artist.

When David and I commissioned a graphic artist to design our logo, we used this strategy. We described in fairly specific terms what we wanted. The very first logo design the artist sent us hit the spot. We loved it. The logo's creator was quite taken aback by this and feared we were too polite to express our desires for changes. That was not the case. As the result of careful preparatory work on our part, her first design met with our total approval.

Farm Slogan

A business slogan further defines what a farm and its owners are all about. Take the time to think about what message you wish to send to your customers. Check for mistakes. I have seen a few business slogans with spelling, grammatical, and punctuation errors. The most common mistake is a misplaced apostrophe.

Farm Sign

A farm sign can be effective if you get plenty of traffic exposure. Choose colors and location of your sign for easy visibility. Surroundings should be attractive. Most townships have specific requirements for business signs. There are usually restrictions on size, height, and location of a sign. On a modest budget, I would not pay for a high-end product in this marketing category. Despite a well-traveled location, our sign has brought us surprisingly little walk-in traffic. It shows only our business name and logo. No specific services or goods are advertised. We plan to add information that will clarify what we have for sale: Breeding Stock and Fiber. Additionally, we use our sign as a landmark when giving directions to visitors. When we opened our retail store a few years ago, I added inexpensive lawn signs to alert potential customers that they can find alpaca products and local honey for sale in the *Stormwind Alpacas Farm Store.*

Business Cards

Business cards with all pertinent contact information are almost a necessity. The information should be easy to read. Expensive stationery can wait if you are on a very tight budget.

Websites

It is almost impossible these days to sell anything without being connected to the Internet. A website and an e-mail address are minimum components of an effective marketing program. Since the majority of alpaca farmers have both, you'll hoe a hard row without these marketing tools. Not everybody has the skills to create a website. If you must hire a designer, be as precise in your directions as possible. Designers are not mind readers. You should be ready to give the designer a list of design details: colors, fonts, titles of website pages, and text. There is a whole science to designing websites so the sites will be picked up by search engines. If this is all foreign to you, research the subject in the library before you hire a designer and possibly sabotage his or her efforts to create an effective marketing site for you. Website advertising doesn't end with the initial design of the site. Updating your site is important. Discuss this with your designer so there are no financial surprises down the road. Building the site with a feature that allows you to easily update your sales list would be my priority on a modest budget. Cooperative websites can be effective. In my opinion, they can only supplement—not replace—your own customized site.

E-Mail

"Who doesn't have e-mail?" you may ask now.

I've had calls from several people who did not and had no access to a computer or a smart phone. All lived in remote, rural areas. It will be difficult to make sales without an e-mail address. It's just as hard to make sales if you have e-mail but won't respond to inquiries. I have heard this complaint again and again from potential buyers. People leave e-mail messages for farmers, and nobody responds to their questions. I try to respond to a message the same day. When I visit my family in Germany, I program the computer to leave an auto response that gives information about my return.

Social Media Networking

Young people judge business owners who don't participate in at least one media networking venue as marketing dinosaurs. I am sure that these venues are effective for many farmers. They are not without risk for those who lack the knowledge to protect their computers from viruses and hackers. Although I did not wish to spend more time at my desk, I realized that it is important to be flexible in business. Over time, I added several social media features to my marketing program. With Carol's help, I taught myself the computer skills that are required to participate in such programs.

The Phone

My next statement may come as a shock to those of you raised with computers. Phone calls sell alpacas! Not relentless canvassing—that's a turn-off to many potential customers. I am talking about a friendly, informal phone conversation without any sales pressure. Many people who are ready to spend several thousand or even several hundred dollars on a living creature want the opportunity to ask spontaneous questions and receive spontaneous answers. They want to hear the seller's voice and get a sense of his or her character. Give them a connection with a live person, not an unknown entity hiding behind e-mail! Articles about agritourism stress that the farmers who do well selling their products are those who enjoy talking to their customers.

Print Advertising

There are many options. Some print ads are free and will allow you to advertise a sales event on your farm. They may attract many people who have no intention of buying alpacas and may get upset if they are not permitted to pet your animals. Advertising in the classified section of an agricultural publication can be very effective and is usually not expensive. More sophisticated print advertising calls for expertise that most of us don't have. The fee for a graphic designer will have to be factored into the price. I have seen great print ads: informative yet not cluttered, with attractive photos that did not overwhelm the text. I have also seen many terrible print ads: cluttered, missing pertinent information, and background so dark that the text was unreadable.

Photos

Aside from sharing photos with friends and family, photos are an important aspect of marketing. Photos enhance print ads as well as website advertising. If you are a novice at evaluating conformation, you will be at a distinct disadvantage when it comes to selecting photos. Dog breeders train their dogs to "stack" and hold the pose that they consider desirable. This is very hard to accomplish with alpacas. What's more, until you've developed an eye for conformational strengths and weaknesses, you won't recognize a poor pose when you see it. A photo taken at an unfortunate moment can make your animal look deformed. A friend of mine, who could ill afford to waste marketing dollars, once took out an expensive ad in *Alpacas Magazine* for a stud she co-owned. Had I not seen this gorgeous male alpaca on the farm, I would not have recognized it in the photograph. The alpaca appeared to be oddly short in the loin, and its rear looked at least a foot too high. Nobody with any knowledge of conformation would have contracted for a breeding based on this advertisement.

If you don't have a fellow alpaca farmer to advise you, contact your local Kennel Club. Yes, I know, most dog breeders don't know much about alpacas. Get a hold of a drawing of an alpaca skeleton from Eric Hoffman's book and show it to them. Experienced dog breeders and show handlers will recognize an unattractive and distorted alpaca pose when they see it. As you look at your own and other farmers' alpacas over the years, your ability to discern conformational differences will improve drastically.

Please don't describe your alpacas' *conformation* as confirmation in your advertisements. A person confirms an appointment; an alpaca's physiology conforms to a standard imposed by evolutionary and human selection pressure. For example, the spear shaped ears of an alpaca conform to the picture we have of correctly shaped alpaca ears as opposed to the banana shaped ears of a llama.

Banners

Banners help to identify your farm when you're at a show or festival. Instead of paying for a commercially produced vinyl banner, a creative fiber artist can easily construct a very attractive, unique banner from alpaca fiber. A felted sheet can be decorated in various ways to display your farm's name. It is not only a frugal but also an eye-catching choice.

Cleanliness

While your farm need not be fancy, it should be neat and presentable. Although quality alpacas can be found on ramshackle properties, don't count on many buyers to recognize value against the background of a virtual dump site. Potential buyers will draw conclusions about the level of care that your alpacas receive from how your property looks. Such observations may in fact not be based on reality. A fellow farmer known to me purchased a beautiful looking male from a rather fancy and spotless looking ranch. Upon arrival at her farm, the animal received a body score of 1—out of a possible 10—from the attending veterinarian. The alpaca was totally emaciated and had obviously been starved. The woman had only seen the meticulously cared for property and had felt the fine fiber – a winning combination in her novice eyes. Obviously, cleanliness and excellent care do not always go hand in hand, but often they do, and they are certainly perceived to do so by many people.

Many visitors to our farm have remarked on the cleanliness of our premises. I remove manure from pastures on a daily basis (except, of course, when the stuff is literally frozen to the ground). I keep the barns picked up and the grassy paths leading to them neatly mowed.

Landscaping

Make an effort to have attractive landscaping. Because nursery plants are expensive, choose carefully and slowly add to your collection. Gardeners with established perennial beds are often happy to share their riches. Some perennials such as Black-eyed Susans can be started from inexpensive seeds. The colorful Zinnias grow like weeds. They're annuals, so collect their seeds each fall and store them in a cool place until spring. Sunflowers make stunning displays and will attract birds to your property. Flowering plants such as geraniums add eye-catching color to hanging baskets. You don't have to buy the baskets already planted but can assemble them yourself at a much lower price. Marigolds need very little care, thrive in fairly poor soil, and their seeds are easily harvested. Find out which plants do well in your particular soil and then resist the temptation to buy those that must be babied. Composted alpaca manure makes great fertilizer for flower gardens and lawns.

The Farm Office

Do you worry that your small home and farm can't compete with the mansions and huge barns that you see in some ads? Don't! Worrying about things that you can't change is fruitless and creates negative energy. The kind of customer who is attracted by status symbols will not seek you out, that is true. There are still plenty of people who are more interested in how you care for your animals than the size of your house or your bank account, including those who are wealthy but have a good grip on priorities. It's your hospitality and professional knowledge that count, not fancy rooms and decorating schemes.

With modest facilities, you may not have a separate office area for entertaining potential customers. I don't view that as a negative. You can store all farm paperwork in a file cabinet or several of the large plastic containers available in most department stores. A great solution are storage containers that can serve double duty as a bench. Your choice of storage is less important than a well organized filing system. Customers who wish to see what a histogram looks like should not have to wait while you hunt around for it in nooks and crannies all over the house.

Marketing Cooperatives

It is sometimes difficult to motivate customers to travel to a farm where only a few animals are offered for sale. Joining a marketing co-op is therefore an excellent way to market your alpacas and products. By banding together with others, you can offer potential buyers a "visit" to several farms at one convenient location. Participating farms share expenses from rental fees for a portable toilet to printing costs for promotional literature. Analyze the goals and venues of such a group carefully before committing any funds and time. Although diversity can be a good thing, it can also lead to conflicts.

Auctions

Auctions offer an opportunity for marketing your farm in the auction catalog as well as a direct sale on the day the auction is held. Purchase prices at an auction don't reflect pure profit for the seller. You will have to pay a commission. There are travel expenses, including veterinary fees for tests and certificates in compliance with regulations that govern the transportation of livestock. If an animal doesn't sell, you will not receive a refund of your initial sign-up fee. You should also have a biosecurity area for the unsold alpacas returning to your farm.

Shows

Another marketing venue is attendance at an alpaca show. Show wins will attract customers. Years ago, I believed that the concept of small, well organized, and fairly inexpensive one day shows for alpacas would become popular. I was wrong. Those who loved attending the small, certified shows that I superintended *really* loved them, but it was a struggle each year to get enough entries to stay within our modest budget. The cost of showing alpacas—when compared to other livestock shows—is, in my opinion, ridiculous. The fancy accommodations at many alpaca shows are a far cry from the down-to-earth atmosphere you'll find at most livestock shows. The exhibitors' show fees pay for the rented panels, the sod put in the pens, rental of completely enclosed show buildings, and many other costly amenities.

You'd like to try anyway? Unless you are willing to waste tons of money, you better become a professional handler. In the alpaca world, this doesn't mean you are officially certified or accredited. It means that you are knowledgeable about all the nuances of producing a show winner. Of course, you may enjoy beginner's luck. More likely, you will encounter a learning curve much steeper than you anticipated.

AOA certified shows require you to get a *Certificate of Veterinary Inspection* (CVI) for each animal and have the alpaca micro-chipped. Additionally, it must test PCR negative for BVDV. If you must cross state lines, the simple CVI is not enough. Your alpacas must also be tested for infectious diseases such as tuberculosis and brucellosis. Some shows may require a Rabies inoculation.

You must weigh the expense of showing—entries, veterinary services, meals, and travel—against potential income. Is showing alpacas cost effective? Only if you win or attend very small shows where marketing opportunities are not diluted by too many exhibitors in one place. Another, much more affordable, option is a fleece show. Preparing a show fleece requires special shearing, skirting, and storing techniques. It's best to attend a workshop where show fleece preparation is taught in a hands-on manner. I think that shows serve an important purpose. Nobody has time to make annual pilgrimages to many other farms for the sole purpose of viewing animals. Seeing alpacas other than your own helps you to evaluate your breeding program and prevents you from becoming barn blind. Attend as a visitor if showing is not in your budget.

Fairs and Festivals

Health requirements may also apply to fairs and festivals. Choose your venues wisely. Analyze your objectives for attending and only attend those that serve your marketing purpose. Depending on time of the year and location, you may only want to bring fiber and fiber products for sale. Of course, the animals themselves are a big attraction and will help to bring customers to your booth. We learned to rope off an area around the livestock panels to deny the public direct access to the alpacas. This protects the animals, reduces their stress level, and also protects you from frivolous lawsuits.

Be prepared to hear hundreds of times: "Do they spit?" My answer is always: "Of course they will spit—if you spit at them first."

Most people "get" the joke and laugh. I then explain that properly raised alpacas do not spit on people. After attending dozens of fairs with our alpacas, I came to the conclusion that people in general have lost an emotional connection with animals to a frightening degree. Attending fairs and festivals requires lots of stamina, patience, and tolerance. It will rarely result in a sale of alpacas.

Berserk Males

No, this section is not about my husband after he discovered that our Whippet puppy, Diesel, hid and partially devoured a wad of cash in her sleeping crate. I am thinking about a potential alpaca farmer's marketing nightmare. This issue, which seems to crop up all the time, is the perception of potential customers as to what constitutes great alpaca temperament and behavior. It's very, very difficult to convince some folks that this year's super friendly male cria is next year's berserk male.

Before we discuss undesirable behavior, let's talk about how a male alpaca *should* behave. Normal males are mildly curious with strangers and trust people known to them. Despite this trust, they remain aloof and only seek brief or no contact with human beings. They tolerate handling and training for normal maintenance procedures. Sexually mature male alpacas will neither attack nor challenge in any way the people who enter their pastures and barns.

Under certain circumstances, very young alpacas may constantly seek human attention. This may happen because they were or are being fed with a bottle or are bored due to lack of playmates. Dealing with such babies requires iron self-discipline. It is all too easy to respond to the advances of these adorable creatures. Crias imprinted on human beings quickly begin to act like fluffy, cuddly camelid "puppies." This behavior appeals to novice buyers who are totally unaware of future repercussions. Unfortunately, once sexually mature, these "puppy" males are extremely dangerous. I don't think it's hyperbole to state that a fully grown alpaca suffering from *Berserk Male Syndrome* could kill a frail, elderly person or a child. To sell a super friendly male alpaca cria, knowing darn well that it will morph into a dangerous animal, is unethical.

Although it is not common, these issues may arise with females as well. Quite a few years ago, the author of an article in a camelid publication described the purchase of a female alpaca that had been handled extensively as a cria due to the loss of a leg. A prothesis had been fashioned for it. The stump was cleaned on an almost daily basis, adding to the already existing behavior problem. The author seemed to be proud of and amused by the fact that her "spirited" alpaca rammed and butted her in the pasture whenever she let down her guard. My husband, David, after hearing about the article, mumbled that "P.T. Barnum was right."

Why am I addressing this issue in the chapter on marketing? Because these little future berserk males are so adorable and appealing as youngsters, you may have to face an uncomfortable situation while marketing your own, properly behaved male alpacas. For example, a couple with two small children visited our farm a few years ago. The rambunctious little boys—hey, I raised one myself—chased the alpacas. When I politely but firmly requested that they stop this, their mother became quite defensive.

"We were at the L's farm this morning," she told me pointedly. "They had the most precious, little male. My children ran after him, and then he chased them and knocked their sun hats off. It was so adorable to see them play and run after one another."

There obviously was a message here for me, the old meany, who had spoiled her children's fun. I didn't reply. After they left, I thought about strategy, since this was not the first time such an incident had occurred. Should I have told my visitor that the "precious" male will most likely and not too gently knock her sons on their little behinds when they visit that farm two years from now? Should I have explained that this male will probably try to jump on and trample her should she be so foolish as to enter its pasture? It sounds like sour grapes and smacks of trying to badmouth another farmer. Not a good idea! Not saying anything like I did was also not a good marketing strategy.

A better plan is to educate a potential buyer that the techniques—frequent handling and interaction— we use with a puppy to socialize it will have the opposite effect on alpaca crias. Initially, the effects of extensive handling will be identical. The puppy will be your attentive companion in house and yard; the cria will be your attentive companion in the pasture. Things change when they reach sexual maturity. With proper discipline, the adult dog will continue to be a loving companion. If anything, it will be more obedient and attentive. The adult male alpaca will view you as a fellow herd member. What do male alpacas do with their pasture buddies? That's right, they wrestle with one another; they try to pin the other fellow to the ground; they try to slash its skin open with their fighting teeth. Alpacas, especially sexually mature males, have enormous strength. Even if you could wrestle one to the ground, why would you want to look over your shoulder each time you enter the pasture? Why would you run the risk of your family members and farm visitors—potential buyers perhaps—being slammed to the ground and attacked? It's so much nicer to raise alpacas the correct way—to handle them only briefly and rarely when they are crias and delay halter training until they are close to a year old.

I now copy a few pertinent quotes from Marty McGee Bennett's articles and books and include information on the sources of the quotes. I hand the buyer the sheet with a friendly smile and say, "You may want to do some serious research on this matter since your safety and the safety of your children is at stake."

I believe that plans to reverse the process are wishful thinking on the part of owners who refuse to face the only truly safe solution to the problem: euthanasia. Although it may be possible to "fix" the problem if it is caught very early and owners create an environment that minimizes the alpaca's interaction with and exposure to human beings, don't hold your breath while waiting for positive results.

Marty McGee Bennett objects to the *Berserk Male Syndrome* label. She prefers to call it *Novice Buyer Syndrome*. She is right. Berserk males were not born with their dangerous behavior traits. The ignorant or selfish actions of their owners made them that way.

The editor of the *Premier Equipment Catalog* discussed livestock behavior in the 2002 edition and told his readers never to trust a "ram/bull/stallion/or buck goat." Compared to many intact males of these species, *properly raised alpaca males are extremely mild-mannered*. Regardless, it doesn't hurt to teach your children to exercise special caution in the presence of intact male animals.

The behavior issues of berserk males do not extend to their alpaca herd members. They are quite respectful of the dominant *alpaca* in their pasture.

Good Behavior

In sharp contrast to the farmers who raise berserk males, there are those who don't handle their alpacas except at shearing time. The areas of handling and training offer a level marketing playing field. If anything, the farmer with few crias has an advantage over owners with large cria populations. Handling sessions and training will not make a dent in your budget, and they're not terribly time consuming. Well-mannered alpacas with correct temperament and good behavior may help you to make sales. Although I am constantly amazed that new buyers often totally disregard behavior issues, those who have a background in raising or breeding animals do appreciate alpacas that respect their human handlers.

Buyer Profile

Buyers choose sellers. That is true, but you should also develop a profile of the kind of buyer you wish to target for marketing and sales. Your marketing strategies should be tailored to fit that customer profile. Maybe you have small children and will target customers with youngsters. It will be beneficial to identify the customer profile most suited to your personality and what you plan to offer. For example, I enjoy the mentoring that I feel must be offered to new buyers. I don't object to a little or even a lot of "hand holding." On the opposite side of the coin, I knew a farmer who dropped the buyers that she identified as "needy" like hot potatoes.

Odd Reasons for Making a Sale

Occasionally, you will sell alpacas for odd reasons. Early on in our alpaca days, I met a farmer who sold a white male sight unseen because she had named it Whitey Herzog. The buyer was an avid baseball fan. Some buyers purchase animals because the alpacas' birthdays fall on the same day as that of a close family member. One farmer sold two alpacas because the buyers discovered that the husband's parents were born in the same Italian village as the seller's father.

Pricing

I sometimes have fellow farmers ask me, "With prices for alpacas all over the place, how do you set a fair price?"

Unfortunately, pricing alpacas is like pricing art, designer clothes, and collectibles. Prices are all too often a reflection of clever marketing, not true value. If you think for one minute that, as a frugal farmer with a small marketing budget, you can financially compete with a farm spending thousands of dollars on a single ad, you are setting yourself up for failure. The belief that "bigger is better" is just too entrenched in the American mind. Buyers are all too often willing to pay more for an image. Although the boutique concept doesn't easily translate into the livestock market, it works well for unusual and beautiful alpaca fiber products.

"You are so negative," a novice farmer told me when we discussed pricing.

I disagree. I am realistic. Farmers who are realists sell alpacas. Dreamers go bankrupt or have fifty pets on their farms. There is nothing wrong with maintaining fifty pasture companions on your farm if you can afford to do so and enjoy it. When I retire from farming, I would like to keep two or three alpacas—not forty or fifty—for my private enjoyment. In the meantime, I have a very simple way of pricing my animals. I ask myself: "How much would I be willing to pay for this alpaca?" This honest approach has worked well for me and has attracted the kind of people I enjoy doing business with. I don't price individual animals at two or three times what I realistically expect to get. Some farmers do this when they don't really wish to sell an alpaca. I find this an annoying and dishonest practice. It has worked for some individuals.

Time Is Money

Time is money. Don't allow yourself to be used by farmers who want to sell alpacas but not educate their buyers. I admit this makes my blood boil and feel there should be an *Alpaca Farmer's Hall of Shame* for such people. Their favorite trick is to tell perspective buyers to "visit farms A and B so you can learn about barn design, pastures, and alpaca care." This very nicely gets the seller off the hook as far as educating new owners, a rather time consuming activity. This is especially true if the buyers have no previous livestock experience. Friends of ours had a fellow visit their farm on five consecutive Saturdays to learn everything they could teach him about raising alpacas. The sixth Saturday, their visitor called and gleefully informed them that he just bought five alpacas from a farm in a neighboring state.

All farmers should freely answer *general* questions about alpaca ownership. On *Stormwind Farm*, we reserve *unlimited* time for our customers. They pay for it as part of their purchase price; they deserve it. Casual visitors are offered a brief farm tour, our sales list, and an honest explanation of my policy. My comprehensive consulting service starts with a purchase or a non-refundable deposit. Consultation without a purchase is not a problem with a mutually agreed upon consulting fee schedule. I have literally spent hundreds of hours with some customers and am glad to do so. I don't, however, give away my time and knowledge for free. That's simply bad business. Of course, a policy of not giving much time to people who bought elsewhere becomes very difficult to enforce when you know that animals are suffering. A llama owner close to us has been swamped by people who bought their animals at auctions, with absolutely no follow-up support system in place.

"How can I not help?" she asked. "I can't stand the thought of the llamas being neglected and suffering."

Several alpaca farmers have reported similar experiences. There is no perfect solution to this dilemma. You can only hope that your help will yet convince one more person to expect and demand support from the farmer they purchase their next animal from. Of course, there's the other extreme. People who bought from us were treated quite rudely by the owner of a neighboring alpaca farm when they introduced themselves.

"Go ask the breeder you bought from for advice," the wife snapped at them.

They hadn't asked for any advice; they merely tried to get to know a fellow alpaca owner. Rejecting friendly advances from fellow farmers is boorish behavior and will only hurt you socially and financially. People don't have an obligation to buy from you just because they visited your farm unless you make that a stipulation of their visit.

"I hate marketing," a friend told me once. "I do too," I heartily agreed at the time.

Later on, after reflecting on our conversation, it occurred to me that this was not true at all. I *do* dislike sitting behind my computer, but marketing is also about communicating and connecting with people. I enjoy making new friends and widening my horizon.

Serious Commitment to Marketing

Farmers with small herds don't always treat raising, marketing, and selling alpacas as a serious business. You would be amazed how many people have told me that they called farms, left messages, and never received a return call. Too many farmers seem to be under the impression that alpacas "sell themselves." Nothing sells itself! Marketing is work! Your attitude toward fulfilling commitments or taking care of things should not be casual if you wish to succeed.

Can You Part With Them?

I have spent nearly two decades observing marketing programs as well as critically analyzing my own efforts. I have come to the astonishing conclusion that quite a few alpaca farmers sabotage their own efforts to make a sale.

"That's ridiculous," you may say now. "Why would anybody do that?"

Alpacas are very appealing creatures. Despite their naturally reserved temperament, they respond well to kind and gentle treatment. An alpaca is intelligent and quickly accepts handling and management routines if an owner makes the effort to teach the animal properly. The crias are adorable, resemble stuffed toys, and are entertaining to watch. Does it come as a surprise then that owners find it impossible to part with an alpaca? This is especially difficult in cases where the animal has been born and raised on the seller's farm. For the kind of person who has trouble parting with any belongings, this is an important consideration. If it's difficult for you to give away or sell clothing, household goods, and cars that have been in your possession for years, imagine selling a living, breathing creature that you've become attached to. Hoarders make poor livestock sellers. I know; I am married to one. Every sale resulted in a fight until I clearly spelled out the rules: "If you try to stop me from selling alpacas, I will dissolve the business."

Although I am fine with selling as long as I like and respect the buyer, and I've satisfied myself that the animal will be well taken care of, I admit that parting with alpacas can be a wrenching experience.

What Do They Want?

Marketing experts tell you to give customers what they want. Although that is good marketing advice, it should be applied with reservations where live creatures are involved. Customers may want traits—woolblindness comes to my mind—that compromise the health and overall quality of life of the alpacas. I draw the line there, even if it means losing a sale.

Be Creative

Do you feel a little discouraged right now because I told you more negative aspects about marketing alpacas than you wanted to hear? You may not have *wanted* to hear them, but you *needed* to hear them. A realistic attitude going into a business will help you to succeed.

Marketing programs should be very much tailored to the individual's personality as well as his or her budget. If you feel uncomfortable touting your alpacas' virtues over the phone, then mail out cards or brochures instead. If the thought of a formal presentation to a group of buyers is enough to have you break out in nervous hives, schedule an informal *Open Farm Day* instead. This is another marketing activity where several farmers can get together and share expenses. In part, people will buy from you because they feel comfortable with your personality. Don't pretend to be somebody you're not.

Let's conclude on a positive note. There is something about alpacas that gets one's creative juices flowing. I've seen this again and again in the industry. People grow and expand their horizon in ways that are truly amazing at times. If you love the alpacas and the lifestyle that you must adopt to raise them, you too will find innovative ways to succeed. Not all marketing strategies will result in sales. If you have realistic expectations, you will be a lot more relaxed, and isn't that one of the reasons you started raising alpacas in the first place? With all your busy marketing and selling, don't forget to hang out in the barn and pastures and simply appreciate your alpacas.

The Sale

Once you and a prospective buyer agree on purchase price and details such as health and reproductive guarantees, it is time for both parties to sign a contract. You should have a blank contract prepared well ahead of a sale. Adjustments and changes can be made, of course, but the basic document should already be available to study and discuss. If you have no legal or business experience, your money is not wasted on a consultation with an attorney to review a sample contract for each of several different possible transactions: maiden female, bred female, proven stud, unproven male, and alpacas sold without reproductive guarantees. Paying for and following the advice of a professional may just be the most frugal business decision you will make.

Farm Hospitality

Once a buyer has purchased an alpaca from us, I offer private mentoring sessions. Sometimes, buyers have traveled several hours to reach *Stormwind Farm*, and lunch or snacks are very much appreciated. This is one aspect of raising and selling alpacas that you absolutely must discuss with your family. Although my husband does not feel comfortable in large crowds, he shares my feeling about hospitality and takes an active role in helping me. After a meal, while I remain seated to talk shop with alpaca customers, he clears the table and cleans the kitchen. Neither one of us has "privacy issues" where we do not wish strangers to enter our home. You and your family may feel differently. It makes sense to discuss this before you even buy your first alpacas. You can certainly try to market and sell your alpacas exclusively off the farm, but it will be more difficult and further strain your budget.

If you share our philosophy of welcoming people into your home and life, you may want to try my recipe for my signature tart German apple cake. You can serve it to your customers or at a meeting of your fellow alpaca farmers.

Stormwind's Apple Cake

Dough Ingredients: 2 ⅔ cups unbleached flour, ¾ cup sugar, 1 pinch salt, 2 eggs, 3 ½ sticks cold butter

Filling Ingredients: 1 cup raisins, 9-10 large Granny Smith apples, juice of 1 lemon, 1 cup apple juice, 2 teaspoons cinnamon, 1 ½ packages vanilla pudding (not instant), 3 cups half & half cream, 1 tablespoon vanilla extract

Dough: Mix flour, sugar, and salt. Add eggs and butter (cut butter in small pieces). Knead until dough is smooth and all ingredients are blended. Form a ball with the dough, wrap it, and refrigerate for 30 minutes. Divide dough into two portions. Butter a casserole dish. Roll out one portion of the dough and spread it evenly across the bottom of the casserole dish.

Filling: Cut apples in half and remove cores. Simmer apples, apple juice, and raisins. Apples should remain fairly firm. Drain juice. Pour lemon juice over apples. Cover rolled out dough with apple/raisin mixture. Cook pudding (using the 3 cups of half & half). Add vanilla extract. Pour mixture over apples.

Finish: Roll out second portion of dough, cover filling, and seal edges. Cut vent holes in the top. Preheat oven to 375° F. Bake cake for 60-70 minutes. Brush egg yolk over top about 15 minutes before cake is finished. Cover and keep in a cool place but do not refrigerate. Serve the next day with whipped cream. Enjoy!

24

PRODUCTS AND SERVICES

"Small service is true service while it lasts:
Of humblest Friends, bright Creature! Scorn not one;
The Daisy, by the shadow that it casts,
Protects the lingering dew-drop from the Sun." William Wordsworth

Hardworking Tourists

"Hmm—" My sister, visiting *Stormwind Farm* in 1997 for the first time from her home in Germany, surveyed our property with a thoughtful look on her face. "You have a potential goldmine here."

"Yes, I know, we were lucky to be able to buy this little farm, and hopefully the alpacas will give us extra retirement income," I agreed.

"Forget selling the alpacas." Karin eyed our pastures and barn speculatively. "You keep the alpacas. They're too cute to sell. Make money by turning your house into a bed-and-breakfast."

"Too much work," I groaned.

"No, no," my sister replied. "You cater to German tourists. You know how the Germans love to work. Turn it into a 'Make your own bed and breakfast'."

I raised my eyebrows. "What?"

Karin giggled. "Yes, and you'll allow them to scoop poop, dust the barn, help with shearing, dig up the vegetable garden—"

We both laughed, knowing fully well that her silly sounding ideas were not all that silly, and that our own father would have been my first happy customer. Agritourism—combining agriculture with tourism—has grown by leaps and bounds over the last few years. For energetic, hardworking, and creative farmers with the right kind of infrastructure, income from agritourism can support a family. Of course, it's not as easy as my sister made it sound.

Fiber Products

The scope of products you may want to offer for sale can vary to a great degree. Although some alpaca farmers only offer raw fiber for sale, others add rovings, felted sheets, and yarn to their product list. Some branch out into finished products like clothing or toys—either made on the farm, outsourced to local fiber artists, or imported from South America. The very ambitious ones expand their inventory to include farm products like honey, dried herbs, or craft items such as handmade soaps, quilts, and wreaths.

Retail Locations

When I still worked off the farm, I didn't have the time to develop a retail program as part of our farm business. Visitors to the farm asked to buy products made from alpaca, and I had nothing to offer them. We found a great solution. One of our boarders prepared and regularly restocked her own retail kit for us. The products were stored in a large container. When visitors expressed an interest in seeing finished products made from alpaca fiber, we had something to show and sell them. Although she missed the opportunity to see her animals every day, managing her little retail business kept my boarder connected with the alpaca world. It was a win-win situation for both parties.

When I started farming full-time, I opened my own retail business and attended festivals, farm markets, and craft shows. My booth and displays were simple and low budget. I stored and carried the products in small suitcases that I purchased in thrift shops. Attending these events can be profitable but is always a lot of work. If it was an outdoor event and the weather turned nasty, my profits were zero for the day. Worse, I had paid the vendor fee and so lost money. Because I was slowly but surely wearing down from working at off-farm retail events, my husband and I decided to take the next step. We opened a seasonal retail business on the farm.

If you plan to sell products on the farm, research the matter carefully. Make sure that your infrastructure is in compliance with all building codes. That includes state as well as local requirements. Additionally, your state may have regulations for a retail business such as annual fees and quarterly sales tax filings. Your location and the socio-economic status of surrounding communities will impact a retail business to a great extent. Unless your farm is located in a very popular tourist area, don't count on a big income from a retail business. With strangers walking—and possibly tripping and falling—on your property, there are issues of liability. Discuss this with your insurance agent.

Meat and Pelts

Alpaca mortality is high on the Andean mountain plateaus. South American alpaca farmers routinely eat camelid meat and sell the pelts of any deceased crias. Because prices for all alpacas, even geldings, were very high in the decades following the first importations, nobody thought of slaughtering alpacas in North America. Many North American alpaca farmers—totally smitten with their animals—still have difficulty with the concept of alpacas being slaughtered for meat consumption and pelts. As of this writing, I am aware of several North American farms with large herds where alpacas—mostly the surplus males—are slaughtered and the meat is sold. The sale of meat for human consumption is governed by strict laws. If you plan to sell meat, get in touch with your state's veterinary office and the USDA to make sure that you are in compliance with all regulations. You should be able to find instructions on slaughtering livestock in a library or on the Internet. Most books about raising sheep also include a chapter on pelt preparation. Although many people would consider the expression *humane slaughter* a contradiction in terms, I'll use it for lack of better words. If you slaughter, you owe the animals a death that is as humane—quick and painless—as you can make it. Dr. Temple Grandin, an undisputed authority on the humane treatment of livestock, believes that fear is worse for animals to endure than physical pain. I agree. Reading Dr. Grandin's books will give you new insights into the issues.

Services—Their Multiple Purposes

Before you decide to offer services, it's smart to first analyze your objectives. Is your purpose to strictly generate immediate income or is marketing for future sales your primary objective? Stacking a thousand bales of hay for a fellow alpaca farmer will generate income but more than likely will have no marketing value. Offering a free seminar on your farm will not result in immediate income but is a great marketing strategy that may translate into selling alpacas. At times, the categories overlap. This book, for example, is a product but also a service that I will use as part of my marketing program to sell alpacas. I am well aware that the financial rewards will more than likely not justify the time, energy, and money spent on this project. Because I also have other objectives for writing the book, I won't be disappointed if its publication does not turn out to be a highly successful marketing strategy.

If your time and financial resources are very limited, it's important to carefully evaluate how you will spend them.

Seminars and Workshops

Hosting seminars and workshops is a lot of work. Advertising, food, and possibly speaker fees can quickly add up to a large expense. You should prepare a budget and analyze its components as to financial feasibility. Will the event be held outdoors or indoors? Will you be the speaker or presenter, or will you bring in an outside speaker? Well known speakers command high fees. Free seminars will only work for you if last minute cancellations will not upset you. Don't offer food at a free seminar. If people cancel, you are not out the money you spent in the supermarket. For legal reasons, think twice before you offer food that you prepared yourself at any event you sponsor or attend. Is your house large enough to accommodate a group of people? I started to host seminars and workshops in our second barn once it was finished. David purchased Adirondack style plastic chairs, and we set up a table for coffee and displays. Our seminar area can comfortably seat fifteen people. I love hosting seminars but admit that, at the end of the day, I am usually exhausted.

Shearing

There is a need for willing and able shearers. Initially, you may want to volunteer your services as an apprentice to experienced shearers. The second year, you should shear your own alpacas. The third and fourth years, if you find you have a knack for it, offer your services to farmers with small herds. By the fifth year, you'll have people booking you by December. If you add shearing llamas to your service options, you may have more customers than you can service.

Beware though! Remember, we discussed earlier that it's not just a matter of hacking off the fiber any old way. Alpaca farmers as well as some llama owners sell their fleeces to handspinners who demand a quality product. The fleece of an improperly shorn alpaca is close to worthless. Discussing the issue with an experienced handspinner will help you understand what must be done to produce a superior fleece that a farm owner can sell with pride. Better yet, skirt several fleeces before you offer shearing services. You will be surprised how your perspective will change.

There are alpaca owners who don't use or sell their fiber. They're not fussy about how the fleece looks once it is off the animals. They do care about the appearance of their shorn alpacas. Such a client is ideal for a novice shearer, particularly if, in addition to shears, you own clippers and can give the animals a nice finish job.

Shearing is backbreaking and potentially dangerous work. Before you shear for others, consider legal liabilities.

Husbandry Services

Plenty of people buy alpacas only to find out that they have neither the time nor the interest to perform all farm chores themselves. Aside from shearing, fellow farmers may hire you to cut nails, halter train crias, and perform other husbandry services. If you're a nurturing kind of person and enjoy nursing duties, consider offering your services to farmers whose animals need special nursing care. This may include crias that need to be bottle-fed or are ill. Be sure the animals do not have an infectious disease. Raising a bottle-fed cria is an awesome and time-consuming responsibility. Educate yourself thoroughly about how to care for such a baby. Caring for a bottle-fed cria will restrict your freedom to leave your farm for more than a few hours. Investigate the possibility of being charged with performing veterinary services without a license if you administer medical treatments such as inoculations for payment.

Midwife Duties

Another market niche is taking over birthing duties. I know of several farmers who work very long hours away from their farms. When the time comes for one of their females to give birth, they board it at a facility where the owners are home around the clock. There are quite a few details that must be discussed and ironed out for such an arrangement. Will the animals be picked up the day after the female has given birth? What if there are complications? If the owners can't be reached in an emergency, will you be authorized to call your veterinarian? Will the owners pay the bill no matter how high? Will you be authorized to order immediate euthanasia for a severely deformed cria? Be prepared to deal with problems such as bottle-feeding a cria. Will you charge extra for that? It's best to plan ahead and discuss your policies. It is important that you share your care protocols with your boarder.

Farm Maintenance Services

If you don't feel comfortable working with another farmer's alpacas, you can offer your services taking care of the many other chores that must be completed on a livestock farm. They may include maintaining and cleaning pastures, stacking hay, repairs, and a hundred things more.

Farm Sitting

Your own herd may be tiny and leave you with time on your hands. If your spouse, partner, or children are willing and able to care for the alpacas in your absence, farm sitting for other farmers can be a great way to earn additional income. My advice is not to take on more than you can comfortably handle. I am not so much discussing the physical work load but the expertise and knowledge needed in an emergency. Carefully consider any legal issues before offering this service.

Boarding Services

Boarding alpacas is another way to generate income. You will not become rich. If you're ethical and caring, you will work hard for your money. I suggest not to offer full boarding services until you have cared for alpacas for a few years. If you plan to attach special fees for certain services, make sure to clearly spell them out in your contracts. This will protect both you and the boarder from unpleasant surprises. It gets a little tricky if you're boarding for people who have no background in animal care. To protect yourself financially, put all mutually agreed upon decisions in writing, date them, and insist that the owners sign them.

Does your boarder wish to show? The health of your own alpacas will be compromised if the animals that are boarded with you are taken to shows where biosecurity is non-existent. Does your boarder plan to send her females all over the country to be bred? Will your farm have a biosecurity area in place for the alpacas when they return?

In addition to loving alpacas and hard work, you should also be a "people person." The owners of boarded animals will want to visit them. They will need to use your bathroom facilities and should be offered refreshments. Boarding is not a suitable business for those who greatly value their privacy.

Aside from the monthly income, the presence of other people's animals may help you to sell your own. It will be easier to attract potential buyers to your farm if you can offer more than one or two animals for sale. Don't "push" the sale of your own animals at the expense of those owned by your boarders. This will definitely backfire if their owners hear about it—and they will! Aside from that, it's just not the right thing to do. Some farmers charge a commission for sales made from their farm. This needs to be addressed with your boarder ahead of time.

The boarding business ceases to be fun if you do not receive the agreed upon monthly compensation. Find out what the laws are in your state before you take on boarders. You have to consider that expenses for the animals don't stop just because their owner stopped paying. A boarder's large, unpaid veterinary bill may sour the good relationship you have with your veterinarian. Will you be able to lovingly care for the animals under those circumstances? It's not their fault that their owner is a deadbeat or has fallen on hard times. On the other side of the coin, I feel the farm's owner should show consideration and compassion. For example, I could no more charge a boarder for burying a dead cria than I would charge a friend for a meal at my house. Several farmers whom I talked to didn't realize that exclusively boarding insured animals will not necessarily protect the proprietor of a boarding facility. As with all business matters in this country, consult your insurance agent and an attorney.

"This is all a little more complicated than I thought," a friend recently admitted to me after I touched on some of the issues.

She had plans to go into the boarding business. The day before we discussed the pitfalls of boarding for others, she had just had to call the owner of a female that had been brought to her farm for breeding. Upon carefully checking the alpaca, my friend discovered a thick, whitish pus oozing from its vulva. She sent it home to be treated. When the owners returned it several weeks later, the cria at the mother's side had all hair missing from its ears. Nasty looking, crusty scabs covered the skin. Back they went!

On *Stormwind Farm*, we offer six months free board for any alpaca purchased from us. I halter train the weanlings as part of our standard free boarding service and do not charge for extras like giving vitamins, trimming nails, deworming, and assisting a veterinarian. Free board for purchased alpacas does not include veterinary services and shearing. Although I have very strong opinions on just about any aspect of alpaca care, I believe in allowing owners to make certain choices as long as the choice does not harm my own alpacas. For example, I present the pros and cons of a CD&T booster inoculation given to a pregnant female or product choices for dipping a newborn's umbilical cord. The owners must decide, and I'll abide by their decisions. I will not accommodate a boarder if my action would result in harm or unnecessary discomfort to the animal. For example, I would not agree to skip annual shearing. I also would not agree to forcefully wean a baby and separate it from its mother before the age of six months without a compelling reason. Anyone boarding with us has to agree to my parasite management program. Not to do so would jeopardize the health of my own animals.

Stud Service

You can call a male alpaca a stud, or you can call it a herdsire. The alpaca won't care either way. A healthy, virile male can service several females each day. There are several options to generate income. The first is to have a female alpaca brought to your farm. It will stay there until proven pregnant. Since many alpacas slip their pregnancy during the first three months, I would not send one home before that time is up. When you decide on a stud fee, consider that the female alpaca may come to your farm with a cria at its side. The second option is what is commonly called a drive-by breeding. You will take your male to the female's location and take it home again that day. The third is a drive-by breeding in reverse. The female is brought to the male on your farm and taken home immediately following the breeding. If great distances are an issue, both parties may agree to meet somewhere in the middle. Although all options may result in a pregnancy, the drive-bys are less likely to be successful.

A main concern with any breeding should be biosecurity issues. These include sexually transmitted diseases. The other big concern is heat stress followed by temporary or even permanent sterility. For various reasons, I have scheduled breedings during the summer but with precautions. The actual breedings took place early in the morning or in the late evening, and the male was hosed down with cold water from head to toes right afterward.

Find Your Niche

Although the alpaca community already has fiber artists who produce wonderful alpaca products, there is always room for more. Aside from selling finished products from your own fiber, you can offer spinning and knitting classes. I believe that the areas that still have lots of room for growth are for the artists who paint, draw, sculpt, make jewelry, and create pottery pieces.

You have no artistic talent? Then sit down and assess the talents you do have. Analyze how they can be applied to alpaca farming to fill a need in the industry. Running an inn, transporting alpacas for other farmers, building websites, selling mineral mixes, handling animals at shows, managing events, consulting services, halter training crias, selling hay, building farm signs, selling chutes—there are lots of opportunities to make extra money. Some businesses call for a large sum of start-up money. Others can be launched on a modest budget or even without investing a penny. Once you own alpacas, you'll discover a wide variety of products and services you can provide to the general public, other members of the alpaca community, and fiber fanatics. I mentioned a few in this chapter, but the list is as long as your creative thinking can stretch it. If you don't see an existing need, you may want to *create* one.

Meantime, my German relatives enjoy their vacations on *Stormwind Farm's Make Your Own Bed and Breakfast*. They adore the alpacas and complain about my coffee.

"Never mind the coffee," I tell them. "Your work is waiting for you. Those pastures better be spotless when you're done with them!"

25

HEALTHY OWNERS RAISE HEALTHY ALPACAS

"Use common sense. Don't be afraid to ask for help when you need it." Jane Marks

Keeping Fit

By now, it should be clear to all readers that—to a great extent—profits from an alpaca business are based on the animals' health. With a holistic approach, the alpacas' wellness begins with your own. How so? It takes dedication, discipline, and physical stamina to run a successful alpaca farm on a modest budget. Frugal alpaca farmers do not pay a farm manager or other hired help to perform physical labor that they have the time to do themselves. Don't underestimate the strength you'll need to take care of chores without help.

"I used to be such a weakling," a breeder of Belgian draft horses told me years ago, "that I was exhausted after just cleaning out one stall." She flexed her arm muscles with pride. "You should see me now. I throw twenty bales of hay around like they're cotton." She added, with a little self-conscious smile, "My husband loves how my body has shaped up."

She needed that strength. You had to see the size of those draft horses to appreciate their requirements on housing and feed. My husband and I admired a two-week-old foal during our visit. It looked big enough to squash us like bugs. Of course, as an alpaca farmer with great pastures, you will only fling flakes of hay around on a daily basis, not entire bales. Nevertheless, strength and stamina are needed to accomplish the many other tasks necessary to run a smooth operation and maintain a farm's infrastructure.

Country living is not necessarily healthier than life in a city or suburb. One study that I read about found that women in rural areas are more likely to be overweight than their suburban counter-parts. I am a living example of that statement. Seven years after moving to our small farm, I weighed thirty pounds more than on the day we left our house in town. I had been working physically harder than ever. Certainly, my strength had increased due to all the heavy lifting and carrying I had done. My endurance, always my greatest asset, had not diminished to any great degree. My eating habits, always pretty healthy, had not changed. So where did all that weight come from?

Exercise

In town, I had walked vigorously for at least forty minutes each night. On the farm, sustained cardiovascular exercise had been replaced with gardening and caring for the alpacas. I very much dislike driving. In town, I had started my walks by simply stepping outside and onto the sidewalk in front of our house. After moving to the farm, I found a different excuse each night not to hop in my car for a quick drive to our township's municipal park. Although my intense enjoyment of the alpacas and a deep sense of responsibility prevented any cutting of corners, the added weight was not easy to carry around. My blood pressure and cholesterol level were up considerably. This was not good! I took stock of the situation. One thing was clear: I loved my alpacas and our life on the farm more than ever. When my legs became painful from lack of circulation, I knew that if I wanted to continue owning and breeding alpacas, I had to increase the amount of cardiovascular exercise. All the walking I did between house and barns obviously wasn't enough. Equally important, the weight had to come off.

Hiking with the Boss

It has been several years since I read *Eat to Live*. The author, Dr. Joel Fuhrman, changed my approach to nutrition and eating in a meaningful way. In *Hiking with the Boss*, I describe how I took back my health and eventually—in 2012 at the age of sixty-two— hiked 221 miles in fifteen days from my sister's house to the German village where I was born.

Nutrition

Food fuels our bodies. Even genetically favored individuals will eventually see their health decline with poor nutrition. That's true of alpacas as well as their owners. Luckily, there is no need to join an expensive health club or pay for costly dietary plans. If, for whatever reason, you won't read Dr. Fuhrman's book, at least try the *Frugal Alpaca Farmer's Program for Better Nutrition*:

Stop drinking all soda and juices and switch to plain water and unsweetened herbal teas. Drink coffee black and restrict yourself to no more than two cups per day. Replace juices with whole fruit. Remove all processed foods from your kitchen. That eliminates virtually 90 percent of all "food" you find in a normal supermarket. It's all unhealthy garbage and expensive on top of it. Any time a middleman mixes ingredients or adds to a basic food, you are paying for the labor and adding unhealthy chemicals to what you're putting in your mouth. Instead of boxed cereals, purchase plain rolled oats. They can be eaten cooked or raw with fruit, raisins, and nuts. Eliminate white foods: White flour, white rice, and white bread/rolls are all nutritionally nearly worthless and full of empty calories. Instead of buying expensive small fruit yogurts, buy a large container of plain yogurt and add it to fresh fruit—cheaper and less calories. Decrease your consumption of meat and increase your consumption of beans for protein. Educate yourself about organic gardening practices and grow your own vegetables. Cultivate a small herb garden near your kitchen. Not only do herbs add tasty flavors to your meals, they contribute healing vitamins and minerals. Good food is tasty in itself. Learn to appreciate its basic flavors and textures, without the addition of refined sugar, emulsifiers, artificial coloring, and all the other evil additives concocted by the food industry.

During cold months, use a crock pot to make soups and stews. This is especially nice if you entertain farm visitors and want to devote time to them rather than bustle around the kitchen Without sauces, fillings, and other fancy handiwork, preparing meals is quick and simple, but of course it's more work than buying pre-packaged meals in the supermarket or at a fast food establishment. Chopping of vegetables and fruit is the most time consuming part.

Join the alpacas in taking a swig of apple cider vinegar each day. Those of you who suffer from almost chronic heartburn may just see it disappear completely. Wean yourself from alcohol and cigarettes. Our friends know that we don't keep any in stock; they are welcome to bring their own.

Do not think of this program as a diet but a permanent change for a healthier and cheaper lifestyle. If you're addicted to refined sugar, the first few days will be tough. After a while, expect great things to happen. For the last few years, my apple cake and other sweets have been rare treats in our household.

Avoid Chemicals

Try to avoid the use of harmful chemicals on your farm, especially around young children, teenagers, and pregnant women. The following information highlights the important points in an article published in *Lancaster Farming* (2006) and is based on concerns raised by Sandra Steingraber, an internationally known expert on the environmental links to cancer and reproductive health. Steingraber was the keynote speaker at a conference sponsored by the *Pennsylvania Association of Sustainable Agriculture*. She spoke about the dangers of toxic substances—such as pesticides—to the agricultural community.

- Farmers who use pesticides are at an increased risk of bearing children with birth defects such as cleft palate, undescended testicles, and malformed limbs.
- Pesticides have the ability to disrupt embryo implantation, shorten gestation periods, cause spontaneous abortions, and cause numerous birth defects.

- Toxic chemicals can make their way into the fluid that surrounds a growing, delicate fetus and the milk that nourishes a baby.

You have every reason to be concerned. Humans and alpacas are both mammals. Exposure to toxic chemicals compromises fertility and the health of the offspring in both species. Adults are also not safe from the harmful effects of pesticides, herbicides, and other chemicals routinely used on farms. Farmers must educate themselves on how to protect their families and livestock. The organic farming community can and will help.

Other Hazardous Materials

Medications, dewormers, syringes, and poisons—all hazardous materials must be kept locked up or safeguarded in such a way that children and pets cannot access them. I already addressed the use of hormones in a previous chapter. There is no breeding result that would be important enough to me to utilize hormonal treatments on my farm. If an alpaca should ever not be able to get pregnant without the injection of hormones, it'll just have to remain barren.

In *Alternative Treatments for Ruminant Animals* (2004), Dr. Dettloff wrote:

"The next debacle in veterinary medicine that will spill over into human health will be a hormone-related problem in our food that will affect the next generation of people via the endocrine system by an imbalance. If there is ever a reason to return to the natural ways of animal husbandry, hormones are the reason."

I agree. Even if we don't slaughter alpacas for food, we should heed Dr. Dettloff's warning. Adding hormones to the already harmful cocktail of hazardous materials in our environment for the sole purpose of alpaca reproduction is, in my opinion, insane.

Infectious Diseases

Many infectious diseases are species specific. Those that can infect humans are labeled zoonotic. For example, animals can transmit *Rabies* as well as *Brucellosis* to humans. Pregnant women should never handle aborted crias. If that is not an option, every possible care—protective gloves and clothing—must be taken to protect the unborn human fetus. The best protection is a good biosecurity protocol. This starts with testing alpacas for disease during a pre-purchase examination and being careful about purchases in general.

Mental Health

Your mental health can have a huge impact on the level of care your alpacas will receive. Daily physical activity and fresh air will go a long way to release tensions. Unfortunately, that's sometimes not enough. The February 19, 2005 issue of *Lancaster Farming* included two articles on mental health. One was the story a Pennsylvania dairy farmer who overcame a period of depression with the help of his family and John Shearer, a licensed counselor. The farmer pointed out that it was difficult for him to admit to others that he was depressed. Depression can have many reasons, from a genetic predisposition to learned behavior. Diet can be one cause.

Shearer stressed that people who suffer from depression tend to belittle themselves, are often guilt ridden, and have perfectionist tendencies. These personality traits can easily lead to emotional problems for anyone who raises livestock. People who devote all of their time and energy to caring for others, including animals, often experience a physical breakdown and depression when the deep well of their care and devotion has finally run dry. Alpaca health impacts human health. Caring for a sick animal is time consuming and debilitating to the human caretaker. Disease and death due to ignorance can be prevented. I already addressed housing, nutrition, and general care in previous chapters. Continue to educate yourself on these subjects so your own health is not compromised by chronic illness in your herd. A healthy herd of alpacas is a joy to care for and will enhance your own sense of well-being.

Accepting Death

In all my years of talking to prospective buyers, only one asked me how we handle the disposal of dead animals. I gave this visitor high marks for her realistic attitude and put her immediately in the "Very likely to succeed as an alpaca farmer" category. Because disease and death cannot be entirely avoided when raising alpacas, how to deal with death should be part of every livestock producer's mental health program.

There must be a plan on how to dispose of the body. Because paying for removal from your farm is expensive, the frugal farmer only has two options. The first is burial on your own property. You must make sure that the hole is deep enough to prevent wild animals from digging up the remains. The second option—and one that is becoming popular with many livestock farmers—is composting. We keep a pile of saw dust on our property for that purpose. Garden mulch also works well. With only one animal composted at a time, there is no need for heavy equipment to turn the pile. The body is simply covered and left alone for nature to do its job. If any animal, wild or domesticated, dies on your farm and you choose to bury or compost it, who will do that?

Several years ago, I came downstairs in the morning and found a typewritten note posted on the kitchen door: "Ingrid, I think the dogs killed something last night. Go out the door to the little tree. From there, take approximately twenty steps to your left. Make a right turn and go another five steps. I think it's a cat."

It turned out to be a groundhog. Roughly a year later, another note with even more detailed instructions greeted me before I had my morning coffee. Why the notes? You see, my husband finds it very hard to bury an animal. I have taken over this chore. I certainly don't like it, but somebody has to do it.

"How weird is this?" you may ask now. "This chapter is supposed to address an alpaca farmer's health, and you've taken up a big section of it talking about death and burials."

The issue of death on a livestock farm can have a very negative impact on human mental health if family members are not prepared to face it. This includes children who cannot and should not be insulated from this farming reality.

Safety Alert!

Sometimes, the cause of an alpaca's death may be your fault. If that happens, acknowledge it, don't dwell on your mistakes without ever forgiving yourself, but seek to rectify the situation to prevent future problems. Formulate a plan on how you can make your farm a safer place. That includes the prevention of accidents that may result in severe injuries—or worse—to the human caretakers. This past winter, three of my friends from the alpaca community reported injuries. Two fell on the ice on their walk to the barn. One broke his shoulder; the other one suffered a concussion. The third sustained severe injuries when the brakes on her tractor failed and it careened down her farm's slope. The ride ended with the tractor ramming into a fence post, and my friend was thrown twenty-five feet. The results weren't pretty. Each year, many farmers are injured while handling livestock or working with machinery. Limbs are mangled or severed, head injuries lead to brain damage, and death is not uncommon.

Old farms often have areas where garbage is buried. Years ago, rural areas did not have weekly garbage pick-up. Residents had to either cart their trash several miles to the nearest dump or bury it on their property. The contents of an old farm dump site may surface in a pasture. The ingestion of metal debris is a common problem on farms. Dairy farmers call it hardware disease. To ward off expensive surgery, farmers have their cows swallow small cylinder shaped magnets. Nails or other metal debris will attach themselves to the magnet. No, you city slickers, I'm not making that up! Fortunately, alpacas don't seem to be interested in swallowing every little object they find. Your toddler or a visiting child might. Keep your fields clean and free of debris! Why tempt fate when it's easy and prudent to take precautions.

My husband often accuses me of being a "worry-wart" who sees safety hazards lurking in every nook and cranny. That same husband was very thoughtful and very silent after reading a post on an alpaca Internet site. "I wish I had listened to my wife...," the post started. The exact details escape me, and I do not wish to contact this farmer to bring back painful memories. Suffice it to say that, when he entered the barn that morning, he found that one of his male alpacas had sustained fatal injuries on an object his wife had begged him to remove from the barn. If you're raising alpacas with a spouse or a partner, it's all too easy to assume that "the other one" checked for and removed potential safety hazards. Discuss which member of your family—it may be one of the children—is the most observant and concerned about safety for humans as well as alpacas and put that individual in charge of checking pastures, fences, and barns with his or her eyes wide open on a regular schedule. Daily pasture walks should be part of a farm's safety protocol.

Child Safety

I grew up in post-war Germany. With a severe shortage of men, small boys were often expected to do a man's job. Tiny girls helped with milking, weeding, collecting eggs, feeding swine, and various household tasks until they virtually fell asleep on their feet. The lives of farm children—not just in Germany but all over the world—were filled with grinding toil and hazardous working conditions.

Although they are still expected to do farm chores, on many farms today in the USA, children are also encouraged to have fun at fairs and are permitted to keep the money they've raised from farm projects. Their off-farm activities are often as varied as those of children growing up in cities and suburbs. The lives of these American farm children present a physically and emotionally healthy balance between the grinding work pace suffered by previous generations and the low expectations many non-farming parents have for their offspring.

There is an increased emphasis on safety for children working on farms, at least in this country. Do not permit your little ones to operate heavy equipment. I would not allow small children in a breeding pen, particularly while behavior testing a female. Male alpacas that are spurned by pregnant females are usually not happy campers. While they normally would not attack a child, their desire and insistence to mount a female can easily result in a toddler being knocked down and trampled.

Shearing Festival? Maybe Not...

One of the most dangerous times for people and alpacas alike is shearing day. Many farm owners sponsor and hold shearing festivals, opening their farms to the public for an exciting event. The opportunities for injuries and general mayhem are great during such a festival. You better attend a few of them with a very critical eye before holding one on your own farm. If you wish to make the fiber harvest a social event, it is far safer to do so after the shearing has been completed and the barn has been cleared of all shearing supplies.

We keep the number of people in attendance at shearing days to a minimum and proceed with slow caution. The help of one or two competent people in addition to my husband and myself works for us. Friends and fiber customers who try to invite themselves are told a friendly but firm, "No, thank you."

Stepping Up to the Plate

Your children or partner may not share your passion for raising alpacas. Much stress can be avoided if this issue is discussed well before alpacas are actually purchased. If family members are not eager to pitch in with farm chores, they should step up to the plate in other areas. I always find it amusing that modern parents consider it normal that their children know how to work a computer but consider the same children incapable of cooking, baking, ironing, or cleaning. It should be understood by the entire family that the primary alpaca caretaker need not feel guilty spending reasonable amounts of time with the animals. The only child especially benefits from parental time shared with pets or livestock. It doesn't hurt children to hear, "Not now, you'll have to wait until I have taken care of the animals." If you introduce your children to alpacas in a fun, patient way, odds are that they'll come to appreciate the animals and will want to be active participants in their care.

The team approach works on our own farm. My husband has little interest in farming. He shouldn't spend much time outdoors because of a pre-cancerous skin condition. David sees how hard I work on the farm and has stepped up to the plate by taking over food shopping, cooking, and other household chores. Neither one of us has ever worried about what is gender appropriate when it comes to work. Managing a farm without employees calls for a true partnership and a fair division of labor.

H. D. (David) Wood

A Holistic Approach

The take home lesson in this chapter is: If you expect to take care of the alpacas' physical and emotional needs, you must take care of your own as well. These very observant creatures will pick up on your emotions. If you are tense and angry while handling them, they will fear your touch. If you are impatient due to exhaustion, count on them not to cooperate. If you neglect their care because you are ill, they will not thrive. If your health and fitness are poor, working on your farm—however small—will be difficult and may become impossible. Exhausted and sickly farmers are apt to cut corners. Water buckets may not be kept quite so clean anymore; manure is left on the pastures for a week rather than picked up on a daily basis; going out hourly in 90° heat with 90% humidity is just too tiring—once a day seems good enough. Eventually, neglect will take its toll. This is unfair to the alpacas.

Think of everything on your farm—you, your family, your animals, the soil and the plants it supports—as physically and spiritually connected. That is truly a holistic approach to raising alpacas. It is, in my opinion, the only approach that will give a frugal alpaca farmer on a small budget a chance to be financially successful.

26

HOW MUCH HAY CAN ONE HORSE EAT?

"Don't make it all work. Sometimes, sit down with the alpacas and enjoy their company." Jane Marks

From Horses to Alpacas

No, I didn't suddenly change species. We are still discussing alpacas. For you to appreciate the title of this chapter, I must share a true story with you. Not far from our little farm is the *Deborah Heart and Lung Center*. Years ago, David's regular physician referred him to the center to be examined by a specialist. My husband discovered that salaries were not in line with those paid by other—for profit—hospitals.

"Why do you stay?" my husband asked a cardiologist on staff one day.

The doctor shrugged, and then a smile lit up his face. "I make plenty of money," he answered. "How much hay can one horse eat?" he asked with a twinkle in his eye.

Why am I telling you this story? Well, you read *The Frugal Alpaca Farmer*. You may possibly now want alpacas more than ever but think that your budget is just too small. Or the money is there, but you still wonder about the scope of your farming venture.

Unnecessary Hay

If you belong to the first group, sit down and try to determine where and how the unnecessary "hay" is being gobbled up in your household. Americans live in a society of consumers. Many often buy without thinking. Money is spent on gadgets nobody really needs. Families—children and adults— acquire toys that hardly anybody plays with for any length of time; clothing is discarded after a few months of wear. The list could go on and on. Many of the "wants" in this country are fueled by clever advertisements. Learn to ignore them and reduce your exposure to lessen temptation. Let's explore several ways to save money.

Bargain Shopping

Great bargains can be found in thrift shops and at yard sales. Once you make it known to extended family, friends, and neighbors that you are willing to take hand-me-downs, you will be surprised at the items that will be offered to you. I still wear a winter jacket that belonged to my brother. He was perfectly happy with it but his wife, the fashion police, decided after one season of wear that the color was outdated.

"Why don't you go shopping with us from now on," my brother suggested with a laugh. With his wife glaring at him, he added, "That way, you can see what you'll be wearing next year."

I laughed with him, happy with my new treasure. Quality clothes wear like iron. I will never have to replace the pricy Italian merino wool coat a friend gave me. Too bad that it's not alpaca.

Holiday Spirit

Many families plunge themselves into debt during buying sprees for occasions such as Christmas or other holidays. My husband and I both refused to get caught up in the annual Christmas present buying frenzy when we simply could not afford to do so. We had very little money when Benjamin, our four-month-old son, celebrated his first Christmas. I bought him a nice stainless steel cooking pot for a Christmas present. The baby generously allowed me to cook in it each night.

"You are shameless," said my husband.

"I am a wise woman," I said, "and you don't know how lucky you are that you married me."

Money was still scarce when our son was old enough to realize that most adult people in a family exchange gifts. I think I presented my husband with six pairs of socks, and he gave me a pack of shower caps in a show of "Look what mommy and daddy gave each other for Christmas." We had a tree and good food and enjoyed the holidays immensely. One of my co-workers announced proudly that she and her husband decided to follow our example.

"I told myself," she burst out with glee, "if Ingrid Wood can do it, so can I."

She added that it was the best Christmas she has ever had, with homemade cookies and a relaxed, happy family.

It is wonderful to give and receive gifts, but not when a family is still paying off debt for purchased Christmas presents six months later.

Family Celebrations

Because they bring special energy and valuable long-term goals to the alpaca community, I am glad to see young people become interested in farming with alpacas. Several couples I talked to were planning to get married and worried about wedding expenses derailing their dream to own a farm. I was not surprised by those comments. Over the years, I often felt incredulous and sad as I observed young people and their parents totally stressed out over preparing and paying for elaborate weddings. I also attended wonderful wedding parties in backyards. They were comfortable, happy gatherings of family and friends, with home cooked food that was plentiful and far more varied and delicious than the catered dinners I ate at formal and very expensive weddings.

Pioneer Spirit

Mainstream Americans don't realize that a small segment of the American population still has their ancestors' pioneer spirit flowing through their veins. A subscription to *Countryside & Small Stock Journal* will open your eyes to all kinds of ways to save money. This bi-monthly publication offers a truly astonishing and educational mix of practical advice, life histories, and opinions. Many readers who contribute articles live off the grid—meaning their homesteads are not hooked up to public electricity and water supplies.

While many people may be quick to dismiss old-fashioned advice—planting and harvesting by the moon's phases, for example—offered in the publication as hokey nonsense, others acknowledge that there is merit in what observant generations of farmers learned over centuries of working the soil and raising livestock. Think of how harmful many modern practices are to the environment and all its creatures! Many farmers are returning to grazing their livestock and other old-fashioned practices.

More than just receiving practical advice on everything from raising rabbits to canning vegetables, you will be exposed to a philosophy of "less is more." Adopting this lifestyle may make it possible for you to one day own a farm and alpacas.

How Much Hay Can One Horse Eat?

What about the future frugal farmer with an ample budget? If you are fortunate not to have to worry about start-up expenses, examine your motives as to why you want to own and raise alpacas before you decide on the size and scope of your alpaca farm. Unlike the frugal farmer with a small budget, you have more options.

What is your definition of the "alpaca lifestyle?" I heard people exult over having escaped the stress of city life only to see them try to re-create that very environment in the rural communities they moved to. This phenomenon can also be observed among alpaca farmers. Many express joy over having left the corporate rat race. Some then set out to build up their farm into a large corporate entity with similar pressures to what they faced in their previous professions. These type of farms require large staffs. The farmers who own them spend much of their time in front of their computers and on their phones. I imagine that there are long meetings with lawyers and accountants. For sure there is aggravation with employees who don't show up for work or bungle an important job. When very successful people are interviewed, they invariably claim that "free time" to enjoy life is their most precious commodity and how, unfortunately, they don't have enough of it. That complaint always strikes me as utterly ridiculous. There's a very simple solution to their dilemma, and anybody with half a brain can figure out what it is. How much hay can one horse eat? How much money does it take to feel content? I know many people who feel that there can never be enough "hay." Some pay a heavy price for that.

My own vision of farming was never sitting at a desk for hours each day to take care of the mountain of paperwork generated by big business deals. Because our society does not amply reward people in agriculture who perform menial tasks, I was realistic about potential income. I knew quite well that what I enjoy doing most—hard, physical work—would not translate into great profits. I have never regretted my choices. My vision, however, does not have to be shared by any of my readers. Maybe you will *enjoy* planning a large operation and supervising a staff to manage it. There are as many business models as there are farms.

Goals and Objectives

If you are serious about becoming an alpaca farmer, discuss the scope of your planned business with your family. Clarify and write down your goals. What are your objectives? What will make you happy? How much "hay" does your family need to feel content? More important, what is your definition of "good hay?"

It is finally time to reach into the desk drawer where you stashed that little slip of paper describing the kind of farm you planned to purchase as well as your vision of the perfect alpaca. Go ahead, take it out and read it. Your goals and objectives haven't changed? Well, then I either didn't do a very good job or—when you purchased this book—you knew much more about raising livestock than the majority of people who plan to start an alpaca farm or ranch. Odds are that you've changed your mind about several or perhaps many issues.

Alpacas Ain't Horses

All the talk about equines in this chapter gives me the opportunity to remind my readers that alpacas are not horses. Alpacas are not kept in stalls. The design of many horse barns' interiors without modifications is neither practical nor wise for an alpaca herd. Adopting most horse breeders' birthing protocols—confinement of the mare, extensive handling of the foal after birth, imprinting of the foal on human beings—can have disastrous results on your alpaca farm. Don't even look at how horses wear halters when it comes time to place halters on your alpacas!

27

PURCHASING YOUR ALPACAS

"You are not just buying alpacas; you are buying a different way to live. Choose carefully!" Kristin Joyce

You Decide to Become a Farmer

Years ago, a buyer arrived at a friend's farm and waved a bundle of computerized spreadsheets in his face.

My friend told him bluntly, "Take your spread sheets and beat it! The action is in the barns and on the pastures, not on the computer screen."

You may consider such an attitude a little harsh. Keep in mind that my friend had suffered through a long parade of buyers who all seemed to view raising alpacas as no different than investing in stocks and bonds or purchasing a warehouse full of stuffed toys for resale.

"I've reached my limit with armchair farmers," he confessed.

We decided that part of the blame should be assigned to an article published in a local newspaper. Several of the interviewed farmers had described breeding alpacas as an extremely lucrative business. "Anybody can do it," assured one fellow. "It's the perfect retirement job." This kind of nonsense unfortunately turns off knowledgeable, experienced livestock farmers who would have much to contribute to our industry. Even worse, it attracts the kind of people who come to resent the work involved in raising alpacas, or their farming venture ends in a financial fiasco.

Last week, a woman rang our doorbell. I stepped out on the porch to greet her and was astonished to hear my visitor tell me that she had no farming experience but planned to grow lavender and raise alpacas.

"You can make millions with lavender," she informed me. "It's easy to grow, and it grows anywhere. And alpacas are a good investment."

So there, I thought, the lavender farmers have joined us in attracting the dreamers. I candidly told my visitor that neither growing lavender nor raising alpacas is an easy or a quick way to become wealthy. I could tell that my words fell on deaf ears.

After you have read *The Frugal Alpaca Farmer*, you know only a fraction of what is involved in alpaca farming, but the knowledge you gained should be sufficient to keep your feet firmly planted in reality. If you take your responsibilities to our "speechless brothers" seriously, raising alpacas will be a drastic lifestyle change for most of you. Will you be capable to do the physical work demanded of a frugal alpaca farmer? Are you ready to make the sacrifices that come with owning *live*stock? Are you tough enough to weather the inevitable disappointments that every farmer must face sooner or later? Does the thought of canceling your attendance at a fancy party because an alpaca shows signs of impending birth delight you? Is the latest livestock supplies catalog your bedtime reading material? If you're a female, does the word *stud* evoke images of alpaca males instead of the man of your dreams? If the answer is a firm "Yes!" to all of the above, we are ready to move forward.

Many Options

It's easy for a farmer with lots of money to buy alpacas. Financial losses due to poor choices are easily absorbed and forgotten. When every dollar counts, any purchase must be viewed from many angles. There are many questions you should ask yourself. Where will I go to buy my first alpacas? From a farm with a big herd or a small herd? Do I want to buy from a farmer close by or will it be better to look several states away or even farther afield? Should I buy huacayas, suris, or both? What minimum number will I need to start a breeding program? Is it better to start with an older female or a weanling? Are certain colors more desirable than others? Do I want show quality alpacas? What's the best time of the year to shop for alpacas? Several of the questions may have already been answered in previous chapters. This—the last— chapter should clarify things further and possibly address additional concerns. By the end of this chapter, you should have an outline—a blueprint so to speak—for what you are looking for. Your goals may not mesh with the desires expressed by other buyers. That's fine. Established farmers also differ in their specific breeding objectives and how to obtain them. If you search carefully, you will find a farmer whose stock and program are right for you.

Many Opinions

During your research, you will be confronted with a virtual mountain of information and opinions. If you come to the alpaca industry as a novice farmer, you will feel overwhelmed. Not just husbandry issues, but almost anything related to alpacas is subject to debate. Just about anything related to alpacas is subject to debate. In my opinion, that's what makes raising livestock so interesting and challenging. There is no one right way to purchase, raise, market, and sell alpacas.

It will take several years of serious study before your own breeding philosophy has crystallized. Along the way, you may find that your vision of the perfect alpaca changes. That's OK; we should not remain stagnant as farmers. That does not mean that you should chase every breeding trend that comes down the pike. You may also experience buyer's remorse and question the wisdom of your selection. Those are feelings experienced sooner or later by all intelligent livestock producers. Only the truly ignorant or very arrogant never doubt their decisions. Do your research but don't become so bogged down in the details that you lose sight of the bigger picture. Even more important, don't ever lose sight of the fact that you're dealing with *live*stock*!*

Time of the Year

Because alpacas are shorn once a year, some consideration should be given to the timing of your shopping and purchase. For many months after shearing, you will not be able to view the animals in their full fiber glory. The fleece of the alpaca you wish to purchase may already be sold.

In that case, you will have to rely on a fiber sample or a fiber histogram to judge fiber quality. Density and staple length are easier to judge when the alpaca is in full fleece. The upside to looking at a shorn alpaca is that it will be easier to evaluate conformation. A heavy fleece can hide many conformational faults. Remember that nutrition and stress can have a huge impact on fiber properties. Weather may have an impact on the fiber's handle. I noticed over the years that high humidity gives fiber a noticeably softer than normal handle.

Close or Far?

When we purchased our first two alpacas in 1996, there were about twenty alpaca farms in New Jersey. Most did not have animals for sale. Although we bought close to home and have always been happy that we did, other beginning farmers sometimes didn't have a choice to do this in those days. Many had to travel farther afield to purchase their foundation animals. This no longer applies to most areas of the country. Use this proliferation of alpaca farms to your advantage. Even if you're experienced with other livestock or pet breeding, you will still need a certain amount of hand holding. If you've never bred so much as a hamster, you will require more than hand holding. The farmer who sells to you will need to adopt you until you have learned the basics. This is difficult to put into practice if the two parties live many hours apart.

Purchasing alpacas from afar can result in other complications. If the animal proves to be reproductively unsound, which party is responsible for the expenses involved with a return trip? Who pays for the cost of the replacement animal being shipped to you? One farmer I know received two deathly ill alpacas from the other coast. She tried to refuse delivery. After a stand-off with the livestock transporter, a veterinarian was called in. He in turn refused to issue inter-state health certificates to return the animals to the seller. The sick alpacas stayed. Their inexperienced owner not only paid a king's ransom to nurse them back to health but spent many hours doing so. Another novice farmer, who selected a beautiful looking male from website photos, was attacked by the animal as soon as she led it off the trailer.

"It knocked me over, but I couldn't let go of its lead because we were in the driveway," the woman explained. "You should have seen us rolling around in the mud together." She added with wistful sadness, "Now I'm afraid of it. The seller never told me that the alpaca has that kind of temperament."

In a third example, a novice farmer entered a newly arrived male in a show only to be sternly told by the judge that the alpaca was emaciated—a one on a scale of one to ten—to the point of endangering its life.

"The judge was nice about it, but it was so humiliating," the man told me. As an inexperienced owner, he had not known how to body score.

Photos can be very deceiving. A photo of an alpaca in full fleece does not reveal body condition. A skilled photographer can also make a very mediocre or even poor quality animal look like a show champion.

The worst story was told to me by a couple who bought several alpacas, paid in full, and took possession. Close to a year later, the owners are still waiting for their registration certificates. Meantime, two of the original animals had their babies. None of these animals can be registered under these circumstances by the couple and are, financially speaking, virtually worthless compared to their purchase price. All of this after paying a hefty sum to travel across country as well as hotel and meal expenses to visit the seller's farm! Meantime, ethical, caring farmers lived within a few hours driving of the buyer's farm.

"Yes, we knew they were there," the wife admitted. "We were just taken in by all the sales hype. The absolute worst part is that these alpacas were hardly ever handled, and we can't get near them."

She told me that they've since befriended an alpaca farmer in their area and feel like crying when they see how trusting of people and tame his alpacas are.

Take my advice and only buy from a farmer across country after you have a few years experience under your belt. Additionally, the seller should be personally known to you and be someone whose judgment you can trust. After ten years in the business, I purchased a male from California. It was an unusual opportunity, the seller and I knew each other through circumstances unrelated to the sale, and he candidly discussed the animal's weak points as well as its strengths. Without having seen the alpaca, I knew I would not be facing unpleasant surprises. The male's strengths and weaknesses are exactly as described by the seller, and I am happy with my purchase.

Full-Time or Part-Time Farmer?

Occasionally, you will see ads promoting the fact that the seller is a full-time alpaca farmer. This implies that he or she is a professional versus the part-time amateur. Many, many family farms in this country are run successfully by part-time farmers. In some cases, one partner farms while the other one holds an outside job. Full-time farmers, unless they have other income, certainly will feel more pressure to make a sale. I do not believe that a full-time alpaca farmer will always be more supportive. If a seller is committed to support, you will get it. If he or she is only committed to making money, you won't, regardless of part- or full-time status. Ethical farmers fully expect to be contacted if animals that they sold have problems. Some farmers are too busy working with the next potential customer to worry about those who previously gave them their business. Some sellers "care" about the animals while buyers are making their monthly installment payments. As soon as that last check clears their bank, their buyer is dropped like a hot potato. It all depends on the individual. Good service has nothing to do with the seller's part-time or full-time farmer status.

One Seller or Several Sellers?

On a modest budget, you will more than likely start out with a minimum number of animals. Should you heed the old advice, only in reverse: "Don't take all your eggs from one basket"? If problems with a seller arise later on, it will be hard if all your animals were purchased from that one farm. There is the other side of the coin. I point out throughout the book that alpacas are herd animals and bond closely with their herd members. If, for example, you plan to purchase two females, they will be a lot happier on your farm if they already knew and liked each other prior to your purchase. Much will depend on individual alpaca personalities and, of course, the quality of the "basket"—the seller. Many alpaca farmers offer substantial discounts for multiple purchases. This makes purchasing from one farm attractive to a frugal buyer.

Big Herd or Small Herd?

Alpaca herds come in all sizes—from tiny farms offering only one alpaca for sale to huge operations with hundreds of animals to choose from. I will briefly list several advantages as well as the disadvantages for both.

"One stop" travel to a farm with a large herd will give you a large selection of many alpacas. That's easy on your travel budget. If an animal you purchased turns out to be reproductively unsound, it should be fairly easy to find a replacement at a farm with many animals to choose from. Of course, when it's the seller's decision which alpaca should replace the infertile one, you may not agree with the choice of the home farm and end up as an unhappy customer. The owners or staff of a big operation may not have sufficient time to devote to educating and advising a novice farmer. This should not be an issue if you have experience with livestock, especially other fiber species.

By visiting and buying from several farms with small herds, you will see a wide variety of infrastructures. This will be an invaluable education. Of course, it is also very time consuming. If you require or simply wish to have extensive and often immediate access to your mentors, sellers with small herds may be better able to meet such obligations than those with a large group of clients. Because they have a small inventory, farmers with small herds are more likely to refer future customers to farms where owners bought from them.

When we bought our first alpacas, Breeze was the only female for sale at *Serenity Alpacas* (located in Hunterdon County, New Jersey) at that time. Among other reasons, we bought Breeze because I sensed the sellers' total commitment to service. My instincts proved me right. Many years later, I still feel comfortable calling Hugh and Carol Masters of *Serenity Alpacas*, our original mentors in the alpaca community, for advice or help. They have been generous in more ways than I can count.

An important consideration may be to buy from a farmer who manages the kind of farm—acreage, size of herd, and end products—that you wish to own and manage. If you plan to eventually have a large breeding operation with hundreds of alpacas, purchasing your starter animals from a farmer with a very small herd and using him or her as a mentor may not be the best choice. In contrast, if you plan to farm on small acreage with a small herd, you would be smart to bypass the farm that is run like a corporation and buy your alpacas and get advice from the farmer whose only helpers are a spouse or partner and possibly a Livestock Guardian Dog.

Excellent as well as poor quality alpacas can be found in herds of all sizes. The same can be said for the owners' knowledge, professionalism, and honesty.

Honest Sellers

My final decision to purchase from *Serenity Alpacas* was based on Carol's practice of pointing out her animals' faults as well as their virtues. No other farmer we talked to had done that. I was accustomed to such blunt honesty from my dealings with fellow dog breeders. Carol's candid critiques made me feel comfortably at home. For two years prior to our visit, I had read the "feel good" articles published about alpacas with suspicion. I knew that no livestock could possibly be that perfect.

A dog breeder friend had scanned one issue of a popular alpaca publication and crowed, "What *is* this? The *World of Make-Believe*? You are nuts to even think of getting into this."

After meeting Carol and Hugh, I felt more confident about my decision to raise alpacas. The arrival of my first issue of *The Alpaca Registry Journal* confirmed that others approached raising alpacas with the serious concerns and realistic approach that I feel all farmers should bring to the business of "cria-ting." This outstanding publication, with Eric Hoffman and Fran Haselsteiner serving as the editorial staff, is unfortunately no longer published. (A current camelid publication that candidly addresses negative as well as positive aspects of farming with alpacas is *International Camelid Quarterly*.) In any case, it's a good policy to request from a seller: "Tell me this alpaca's faults, please." If he or she can't name a single trait that needs improvement in the alpaca you plan to purchase, you may want to consider buying elsewhere.

Auctions

Auctions are popular venues for selling and buying alpacas. I am so opposed to auction sales of live animals that I cannot offer the reader a balanced view. I discussed auctions with several old cattlemen. Without exception, they told me about the shenanigans that took place at cattle auctions they attended. Their stories opened my eyes to the deals that may be brokered behind the scenes, and the "ringers" that may be planted in the audience to bid up prices. Even if such deceptive practices do not go on at alpaca auctions, I don't see auctions as financially beneficial to the *majority* of farmers—buyers or sellers. Although I usually toss auction catalogs in the recycling bin without further ado, I once scrutinized a copy a little more closely. It offered a total of sixty-six alpacas to be auctioned. Fifty-six were females. Out of this number, only twenty-five came with a live-born cria guarantee covering twenty-four hours after birth. Additionally, quite a few of the sixty-six ads made claims as to the inheritance of color genes of the described alpacas that were, to put it mildly, bizarre. For example, one advertisement explained that the featured male alpaca "is loaded with black genes" from its sire as well as its grandsires. A black alpaca can only be $A^a A^a$ at the *Agouti locus*, no matter how many black ancestors it has. It is, of course, remotely possible that this black alpaca is $A^a A^a E^D E^D$. I am quite sure, however, that the seller didn't know an *Agouti locus* black from an *Extension locus* black any more than I know the difference between TCP/IP and EIDE (Transfer Control Protocol/Internet Protocol and Enhanced Integrated Drive Electronics). A friend provided those computer terms to me. I have no clue what they represent and certainly wouldn't write ad copy for a computer catalog. In any case, I would not describe *any* alpaca as "loaded" with black genes. This wasn't the only advertisement to reveal ignorance of basic genetic facts on the seller's part. Read those catalog ads with a healthy dose of skepticism!

There are additional concerns. Does the auction where you intend to buy alpacas provide the opportunity for detailed pre-purchase exams? I am not just talking about insurance exams to determine basic good health. A friend of mine attended an auction and inspected quite a few of the animals offered. An alarming number had crooked tails. This can be a sign of a spinal deformity. A few females had abnormally shaped vulvas. My friend reported that bidding was rather high and vigorous on these alpacas. It's bidder beware! Auctions often provide a poor environment for biosecurity. Since I devote an entire chapter to this subject, please read it again before heading to a livestock auction.

Many auctions serve food and alcohol. No surprise there! It is so much easier to entice buyers to bid up an animal while they're feeling no pain. As a frugal, novice alpaca farmer, stick to eating the free food and to drinking water, sit on your wallet, and watch the festivities unfold. Very knowledgeable, experienced farmers with a good eye for conformation and a good "hand" to assess fiber may indeed find great deals at a livestock auction. If my book is your first serious exposure to learning about alpacas, you are a long time away from belonging in that category.

Private Treaty Sales

In my opinion, the best venue for a novice farmer to purchase alpacas is at what is commonly referred to as a private treaty sale. It's simply a fancy term for a buyer visiting a single farm or co-op sale—several breeders at one location—and entering into a private treaty with the other party. There's none of the pressure to arrive at a quick decision that you encounter at an auction. To the contrary, there is ample time to discuss the many details that you are concerned with. You can sleep over your decision. Don't allow yourself to be rushed into signing contracts by a seller anxious to close a sale. Farmers who care about their animals will not want to sell under such circumstances.

Retirement Sales

Be skeptical of retirement sales. Not all are legitimate. I knew of one camelid farm where the owners held a retirement sale for more than a decade. Sellers have come up with truly clever ad campaigns to entice people to buy. When an alpaca farmer sells most of his herd at a retirement sale due to heart problems, a hangnail, or a receding hair line (pick one), and two months later announces the purchase of dozens of animals, it gives you cause to wonder. People do retire from farming or get sick and can no longer care for their animals. When there is a true desire or need to sell animals as quickly as possible, you may be able to pick up quality alpacas at bargain prices.

Country of Origin?

Some sellers market animals whose ancestors were supposedly from a particular South American country as especially desirable. The first fact that a buyer should know is that country of origin identifies the country the alpaca was imported from, not necessarily where it was bred. In *The Complete Alpaca Book*, Eric Hoffman explains that many alpacas that were exported from Chile—and are described as *Chilean* in this country—were in fact born and raised in either Peru or Bolivia. There was a good reason for this. Chile was free of foot-and-mouth disease (FMD) for most of the 1990's. It was easier and less expensive for North American farmers and livestock brokers to import alpacas from Chile rather than from Peru or Bolivia. Eric Hoffman, who screened thousands of South American alpacas selected for export to North America, is very clear about the fact that animals of high quality as well as poor specimens were found in all countries of export.

After two decades in the business, I find the subject of country of origin tiresome and annoying. It was created and funded by marketing hype and has been, genetically speaking, extremely damaging to the wider alpaca population. There is beauty and purpose found in alpacas of all genetic backgrounds. More than thirty years of observing, studying, and researching breeding programs (dogs and alpacas) taught me that genetic diversity is of grave importance to any population. Detailed explanations of my premise go well beyond the scope of this book. I discuss the subject in *A Breeder's Guide to Genetics—Relax, It's Not Rocket Science*. The book, written with coauthor Denise Como, is suitable for readers without a background in science or knowledge of genetics. I can't speak for other farmers, but on *Stormwind Farm*, we breed North American alpacas and don't judge an alpaca's quality based on where its ancestors lived many years ago.

Does Behavior Matter?

Another issue is temperament, or, to be more accurate, behavior. I make a distinction between the two. An animal can have a naturally difficult temperament but behave in an acceptable manner due to correct handling and training. In contrast, an alpaca with an inherently pleasant temperament can easily be turned into a fearful, aggressive lunatic by an ignorant or mean spirited owner. I believe that genetic make-up (temperament) and environment combine to shape an alpaca's behavior.

Selection for temperament or behavior should very much depend on your personal objectives and individual circumstances. Are you young and strong? Do you remain unruffled when animals or children do not behave to your expectations? By all means purchase the gorgeous female alpaca that wasn't handled much or roughly and acts as if every human being will slit its throat. Are you in your fifties and have difficulty carrying a large bag of feed more than a 100 feet? Do your family members expect you to cut nails, behavior test, and give inoculations without their assistance? Would you, at least occasionally, enjoy being able to hug your alpacas and have them submit calmly to your embrace? Then you may want to pay attention to temperament and behavior! In that case, you are well advised to narrow your choice of farms to operations where the owners spend quality time on training and handling. Not all farmers care about shaping behavior. The attitude that alpacas are livestock and should therefore be forcefully restrained still exists in our industry. Owners may lack the knowledge, the skill, the motivation, or—in the case of large herds—the staff to handle and train crias as outlined in the *Camelidynamics* program.

Weanlings or Adults?

When you purchase adults, especially adult females, you accelerate the speed of herd expansion. If you are new to livestock and feel a little intimidated by the size of an adult alpaca, starting alpaca farming with weanlings will give you confidence. An added bonus to buying a very young animal is the opportunity for you to handle and train it to your satisfaction. While you're waiting for your babies to grow up, you should explore other venues for making money from your business. It also gives you plenty of time to shop around for a breeding male and attend seminars on reproductive topics. There is no one right way to approach this choice. A lot will depend on purchase prices and your response to individual animals. I have not hesitated to purchase weanlings when a particular animal seemed especially desirable to me and the price was right.

The Alpacas
of Stormwind Farm

by Ingrid Wood

The Starter Herd

Alpacas feel most comfortable as members of a herd. A starter herd of four to five alpacas should satisfy the novice livestock farmer. What if you plan to start out with a single bred female because your budget does not allow the purchase of a second breeding animal? An ethical seller will not allow you to keep only one alpaca on your farm. There are several excellent choices you can make to provide it with a companion. One choice is a barren female alpaca that is otherwise healthy. Because it is never pregnant, it may very well behave more like a pet. It will be easy to take the alpaca to fairs or on walks around your property by prospective customers. A friend of mine owns a middle-aged, infertile female. Because this alpaca does not mind being bred, my friend uses it to give young male alpacas their first positive experience as a stud. An older female past breeding age will also do nicely as a companion. Technically speaking, female alpacas are never past the age where they can be bred. There comes a time, however, when pregnancy, birth, and nursing are simply too hard on an old girl's body. Learn about the care of a geriatric alpaca before you accept such a female. For example, teeth are a major concern in all aging mammals. The downside to having an open—non-bred—female on your farm is that the male alpacas will know it is open. This can lead to an increase in fighting among them. I wish there was an inexpensive way to spay a female alpaca.

Another choice is a proven gelding to accompany a single female to your farm and share its pasture and barn. What's a *proven* gelding? Quite simply, it's a castrated male without any sex drive. Not all geldings lose the desire to breed or at least chase females. Request to see proof that the gelding offered to you does not chase and overpower your female like an intact male would.

Herdsires

A whole book could be written about selecting a stud or, as alpaca farmers call a breeding male, a herdsire. A very young, unproven male will often be more affordable than an experienced—a proven—male. Of course, you won't know whether it is fertile. Request a reproductive guarantee. An older male with a proven track record—crias on ground—may be a better choice, but it may be infected with a venereal disease. It all depends on price and many other variables. If you desire total control over your product, the breeding of livestock or pets is not for you. A certain amount of risk is involved in all your choices. If you try to make up your mind between a young and an older male, please remember that fiber coarsens with age. We discussed that in more detail in a previous chapter. Making a direct fiber comparison between a one-year-old youngster and a five-year-old veteran is foolish.

It's amazing how many buyers fail to check the one piece of equipment that is absolutely necessary for a male to qualify as a productive stud. Lawsuits have been filed over missing alpaca testicles. Because there is a high incidence of cancer in undescended testicles, a male with a retained testicle should be gelded. A genetic component may be the cause of this defect. Not all farmers agree that such a male should not be bred. I would pass up a monorchid, especially if it will be your only breeding male. A show championship or expensive advertising campaigns are not proof that a male is anatomically correct. At the request of a friend, I once checked out a very prominent and widely used male alpaca. There was positively only one testicle in its scrotum. When I remarked on this, the farm manager commented that I was "the first person to ever check on them," as if that somehow made the lack acceptable. It's important to know that reproductively sound male alpacas have an uncanny ability to temporarily "suck up" both testicles. This protective behavior no doubt evolved in answer to the alpaca's fighting style. Keep in mind that purchasing proven studs is not a fool-proof guarantee of future reproductive success. Fertility can be permanently lost due to disease or heat stress.

The AOA data base can be used to extensively research information on individual alpacas. "I would never buy an alpaca male without researching its record on the Internet," a fellow farmer told me. Research is always recommended on any topic, but let me give you the other side of the coin. Let's assume that the first male cria born on your farm is three years old, and you'd like to sell it. Since your herd is tiny, you don't have a female to prove it on. As a fledgling farmer without a proven track or show record, other farmers are not interested in breeding their females to your unproven male. Your beautiful male may be four or five years old, and potential buyers will still not see any offspring listed if they search the AOA database.

Is that proof that it is genetically less valuable than males with several or many offspring to their credit?

As a frugal farmer on a small budget, you should study basic genetic principles and learn to think outside the box. You will not be able to afford to purchase or breed to one of the superstars. You don't need to. There are plenty of very nice males available for a fraction of the cost.

Co-Ownership

Co-ownership, another way to own an excellent male, can be very tricky. It's not a choice I would recommend to a novice farmer. There are more than a few possible pitfalls. What happens if one of you moves? How about if the animal becomes injured or ill and you disagree at which point to cut off medical support? One of you wants to take it to a show or fair; the other one fears stress and exposure to infectious diseases. You find out that you disagree on choice of feed and bedding. Your partner allows the male to be used by a farmer you do not wish to be associated with. A serious illness breaks out on your partner's farm just as you're ready to pick up the male to breed to one of your females. There are all kinds of potential problems. Can they all be covered in a written contract? Not likely.

Many friendships have been ruined over co-ownerships gone sour. I know of at least two prominent alpaca farmers who were embroiled in a nasty lawsuit over co-ownership problems. After a rather unpleasant experience, I will never again contract for a breeding to a male that travels between co-owners. A friend and I discussed swapping breedings if it fits into our breeding plans— with no money exchanging hands. That may well be a very workable program with people whom you trust. As a frugal farmer on a modest budget, it's good business to network with and support other farmers who will return the favor.

Huacayas or Suris?

Although the alpaca phenotype is unmistakable, there are differences in size, conformation, fiber quantity and quality, and temperament among individual alpacas. First learn to distinguish between the two varieties— huacaya and suri. Huacayas have a fluffy, sponge-like fleece with crimp.

Suri fiber drapes flat against the body in long ringlets and has no crimp. Although the two varieties are normally very distinct from each other, farmers report seeing fiber that combines characteristics of both types.

Huacayas breed true. Two huacaya parents always produce— with exceptions so rare that you need not concern yourself with them—huacaya offspring. Two suri parents or a parental suri/huacaya combination may produce a phenotypical huacaya cria. I discuss the subject in more detail in *A Breeder's Guide to Genetics – Relax, It's Not Rocket Science.* The chapter devoted to the inheritance of alpaca fiber varieties explains theories and observations by other farmers and scientists in a way so a lay person can understand them. If your heart is set on suris, don't shy away from buying them because of this issue. Discuss a clause in your purchase contract concerning the birth of a huacaya cria. Some farmers sell huacaya offspring from suri parents at very reasonable prices. I would not hesitate one second to buy such an animal if I liked its qualities.

Years ago, a prominent farmer with dual herds advised others to crossbreed the two varieties for quick financial gain. Before you adopt his scheme, educate yourself on what the genetic probabilities of such a breeding program are. The program is a little more complicated than breeding a $3,000 huacaya dam to a $5,000 suri sire and finding a $4,000 suri cria sitting in your pasture. Although there is nothing inherently dishonest about breeding a huacaya to a suri, for those who don't have a clear understanding of genetics, it's best to stay away from crossbreeding the two varieties.

It may not be practical for a farmer on a very modest budget to develop two parallel breeding programs. Make your selection—huacaya or suri—and admire the other from afar until your business is financially stable. If you can afford it, then by all means enjoy owning and breeding both varieties. I have several friends who do, and I love visiting their farms.

I think the existence of two alpaca varieties is a genetic gift and adds to the appeal of these interesting and delightful animals.

Flavor of the Month

Beware of often short-lived breeding trends. As a farmer with limited financial resources, you can't possibly hope to catch up with rapidly changing tastes and hyped-up breeding schemes. Recognize the fact that those who breed strictly for profit and without regard for the animals' welfare must constantly offer "new and improved" stock to create an artificial demand that cannot be satisfied by their competitors. What's worse, sometimes conformational faults are advertised as desirable. A non-functional trait such as wool blindness is thus promoted to fuel sales. Both the pet and livestock industries offer numerous examples of such follies.

Novice farmers rarely appreciate the fact that trendy animals only remain in vogue while being pitched by influential owners. Let's assume that you decide to ignore frugality and stretch your budget to purchase a female alpaca that was bred to the newest "flavor of the month" herdsire. By the time your female has produced the offspring sired by Super Stud one year later, Super Stud's owner may have created a totally different, lucrative bandwagon for people to jump onto. You are then at a loss to explain why buyers aren't storming your farm to purchase your cria at an exorbitant price. After all, hadn't *you* paid an exorbitant price for its dam?

A highly advertised stud may in fact have superior conformation and fiber. The purchase of one of its highly priced offspring *may* be a good investment. However, the sire's high industry profile is not a guarantee for *your* financial success. Keep in mind that hundreds of females were bred to it, a lucrative business for the male's owner but not necessarily—as I already pointed out—for the owner's customers.

I know that the uncertainty of what is a superior alpaca is a source of great frustration to novice farmers. Many, having been successful in other businesses, think they can use a manufacturing type of approach to breeding alpacas. Some people treat animals like fashions in the garment trade. What is in today will be out tomorrow. As a frugal farmer, you will have to select stock with a less simplistic mindset.

Choosing for Color

One of the attributes that attracted me to alpacas is the amazing variety of colors and patterns—a visual smorgasbord! There is truly something for everybody's taste. If you make a particular color one of your top selection criteria, your search will become more difficult. If superfine fiber is important to you, it will be easier to find such an animal in white, beige, or light fawn. Darker color fleeces are often coarser, but please don't generalize this statement. Black is a very popular color. Don't pay more money because a farmer tells you that his black alpaca is a 10th generation black. I already mentioned that, genetically speaking, there is no difference between a first or 100th generation black. This is true for all alpacas that carry a recessive allele coding for black at the *Agouti locus*. Grey is a popular color, and prices for grey animals can be higher in comparison to other colors. In reality, "grey" alpacas are roans: a mixture of red/white or black/white fiber. Many blue-eyed white alpacas are what I call "greys in disguise." Years ago, a smart, young friend of mine purchased a blue-eyed, white female alpaca—its sire was a rose-grey—for a nominal price. To the great delight of its owner, the alpaca has produced a string of grey crias that have all been sold at a profit.

Commercial producers and some fiber artists favor white fleeces because they are easily dyed. Others prefer the natural fawns and browns. Keep in mind that selection for color or patterns is often subject to fleeting whims. As a farmer with modest financial resources, you have more important issues to concern yourself with. My advice is to not limit your initial selection by absolutely insisting on a particular color or pattern. After you have a deeper understanding of the industry in general and have studied the inheritance of color genes, you can always breed and select for the color or pattern of your choice. The most informative and extensive description on camelid color genes is a chapter in Eric Hoffman's book. It was written by Dr. Sponenberg, an undisputed authority in this very specialized and complex area of livestock breeding. The *Alpaca Research Foundation* has funded and reported on several studies on this subject. Familiarizing yourself with the scientific facts of color inheritance will help you to make smart and financially advantageous choices.

Health and Breeding Records

Conscientious farmers maintain detailed health and breeding records. Inoculations, deworming, weight, shearing date, fecal checks, veterinary exams, and reproductive data etc. should all be documented. Record keeping can run to extremes. On one side, there are farmers who keep no written records at all. On the other side, there are the data freaks who produce reams of paper on a single alpaca for a single year. When I purchase an animal, I prefer to see a common sense approach. One record sheet for each animal per year should be sufficient for all health information. Likewise, one record sheet per year should tell you at a glance about a female's reproductive history.

Registry Research

A friend of mine is a great advocate for researching an alpaca's reproductive history on the AOA website. I emphatically disagree with exclusively making purchases based on registry data and have already outlined my reasons in the section on the purchase of a breeding male. What about females? Decisions that have nothing to do with an alpaca's reproductive soundness can easily present a distorted picture here as well. For example, friends of ours are presently keeping all their females open—not bred—because the husband plans to have major knee surgery next year. Those females will show a gap in their breeding history. Another example is a suri farmer whom I know who only breeds her females every other year. She travels extensively and does not wish to worry about breeding and birthing during her absences.

Environmental conditions as well as human error can distort the picture. I described in an earlier chapter how one of my alpacas spent almost an entire year at another farm without a pregnancy to show for it. It was bred and became pregnant immediately after we moved it to *Serenity Alpacas*. If your research shows that this female alpaca didn't get pregnant until it was three years old, will you consider it reproductively unsound?

Here is another example for your contemplation. Alpaca female Lucy was bred and gave birth to her first cria, a female, without any problems. Her owner sends Lucy—with baby at side—to another farm for breeding. The new farm manager is not very knowledgeable about alpaca reproductive issues. She exposes Lucy four days in a row to a very aggressive male with low sperm count that overpowers the fearful, young alpaca and breeds it each time. Predictably, Lucy doesn't get pregnant but develops a uterine infection which remains undiagnosed. She is bred repeatedly over a span of several weeks. Months later, a veterinarian diagnoses Lucy with uterine scar tissue. Lucy never becomes pregnant again. Will you turn down her daughter for purchase?

Increasingly, farmers do not register males sold as geldings. Such a practice can totally distort a female's breeding history. Crias die due to an owner's neglect, ignorance, or sheer stupidity. Their deaths are no reflection on their dams' reproductive soundness. Additionally, reproductive soundness is not a highly heritable genetic trait. Checking out a female alpaca's breeding history will not tell you much about the reproductive health of its yearling offspring.

Old-Fashioned Leg Work

"Hard data" can sometimes be pretty soft. Health records don't necessarily reflect true genetic potential. For example, low IgG levels can be due to environmental conditions; so can a male's fertility problems. Nutritional levels can distort the numbers on a fiber histogram. I'm afraid there is no good substitute for doing old-fashioned leg work. You must visit farms, talk to farmers, and ask questions about the information presented in health and breeding records.

In many livestock industries, farmers base their breeding decisions on production records. Those records can be deceptive as well. In the dairy industry, for example, data on milk production does not reflect the ultimate bottom line: profit! An innovative New York dairy farmer who spoke at an organic farming conference in New Jersey told his audience that—after switching to grass based, rotational grazing dairying—his production is down, but his profits have increased due to lower feeding and veterinary bills. If you decide to base your purchase decisions on alpaca EPD statistics, keep this story in mind.

AOA Certificates

Demand to see proof that the seller *owns* the animals you wish to buy by producing the *original* AOA certificates. If you're interested in a young cria that has not been registered yet, ask to see the sire's and dam's certificates and take note of the owners' names printed on top of the documents. You have been told that it is normal in the alpaca industry to purchase animals from farmers who don't fully own one or both of the parents? You may want to study two very sad case histories. I did not know the wronged parties and was not involved in their cases in any way. They called for advice, and I did not ask why they chose me. It didn't matter.

Case 1: A bought several alpacas from B on time payments. While in arrears to B with his payments, A sold these animals to C. The alpacas remained on A's farm because C also had only put a deposit on them. (Are you following so far?) B eventually repossessed the alpacas, but refused to enter into any negotiations with C. The latter, honest but naive, lost his money and may be facing years of legal entanglements to re-coup his losses.

Case 2: X bred two females to Y's stud. Y was still making payments to Z on the male but did not disclose this fact to X. After the crias were born, Z refused to sign off on their registration papers. Once again, an innocent party who entered into a contract with good faith is facing a legal ordeal with financial losses.

Many Canadian alpacas are dual registered with the AOA as well as with the CLAA (Canadian Llama and Alpaca Association). Others are not. Several U.S. buyers lost substantial sums of money when they purchased CLAA registered breeding stock, only to find out that crias from these alpacas were not eligible for registration in the USA. Such financial entanglements can and will effectively put a farmer on a very modest budget out of business.

"My goodness," one buyer exclaimed to me after hearing about these cases, "I thought alpaca farmers were all such nice people."

So are the vast majority of treasurers of youth sports leagues and volunteer firemen companies, but some of them steal the funds they were entrusted with. All business communities have their ethical members as well as their scoundrels. You should neither view every alpaca farmer as a potential inmate of his or her state penitentiary nor visit any farm wearing rose colored glasses. It's *"Buyer Beware!"* just like in any other business.

Lifetime Guarantees

During one of our initial contacts with alpaca farmers, a young couple used very high pressure sales techniques on us. Among other things, these sellers offered any female purchased from them with lifetime breed-back guarantees to any stud owned by them. How long is a lifetime? In the case of this couple, less than ten years. Another seller, also offering lifetime guarantees, left alpaca farming three years later. Since 1995, when my husband and I started our research into farming with alpacas, I have seen many farms come and go. Aside from the time issue, your breeding goals may change or, for whatever reason, you would not wish for your females to return to the farm you purchased them from. In our case, after hearing several reports from reliable sources about the maintenance practices of the couple that had pressured us to buy from them, leaving females— especially with babies at side— would have been out of the question.

Assistance with Marketing

Marketing can be expensive. It's unreasonable to expect a seller to do all your marketing for you without compensation. I think you should be able to get some assistance though. When I sell alpacas to a novice farmer who requests this service, I include a presentation and brainstorming session on marketing as part of my consultation. By asking questions to determine the buyer's talents and strengths, I help each customer formulate a customized marketing plan. Bringing each component of the plan to fruition is the buyer's responsibility.

Some farmers support their buyers by taking animals for sale on consignment. The offer to help with marketing by consigning your animals sounds great until you take all expenses into consideration. You will probably pay board and a commission. You will also miss much of the pleasure of handling your own animals. Additionally, you lose some or all control over who buys your alpacas.

Negotiations

Should you bargain with the seller? That depends entirely on you and the individual seller. Some sellers set unrealistically high prices if they don't wish to sell an alpaca. As a buyer, I find this practice highly annoying and deceptive. On my sales list, I prefer to set fair and competitive prices and then stick to them. I will, however, offer a generous discount from my listed prices for multiple purchases. In any case, it doesn't hurt to ask: "Will you come down in price if…?" Because a substantial number of buyers make time payments, a seller may gladly offer you a reduction in price if you pay in full. It may be cost-effective for you to consult with a financial adviser regarding payments.

Contracts

Although a seller should offer you a written contract, I have always believed that the integrity of the seller or stud owner is more important than any contract. Over the years, I had many experiences as an alpaca farmer to confirm this belief. If you feel the need to cover every possible outcome in a contract, it may be wise to decline to do business with that seller. Nevertheless, a written and signed contract is important and protects both parties. Read each contract carefully and don't be shy about asking many questions before you decide on the purchase of a particular animal. During the excitement of a purchase, important details are easily overlooked or misinterpreted. If your knowledge and comprehension of legal language is limited, you may want to ask an attorney to go over the contract and discuss it with you. Visiting several farms and collecting a blank contract from each seller will give you a basis for comparison.

Pre-Purchase Exam

A pre-purchase exam may be required before you can insure an alpaca. If you decide not to insure your animals, you nevertheless have the right to insist on such an exam as part of your contract. This means that a veterinarian is called in to inspect the animal for obvious defects. Eyes, heart, testicles/vulva, teats, and skin should be examined. Additionally, the veterinarian can check for spinal deformities, crooked tail, limb deformities, bite, and whatever else you consider important. An insurance exam may not require such a detailed report, so you will need to initiate this on your own. You may also want to order tests that diagnose infectious diseases such as Brucellosis, Johne's, Bovine Viral Diarrhea Virus, and possibly others depending on where the seller's farm is located. Your state's Department of Veterinary Medicine can assist you in this matter. For example, Arizona, Texas, and New Mexico frequently have issues with vasicular stomatitis on livestock farms. During an outbreak, your state may not permit any alpacas to enter from those states unless certain quarantine requirements are met, even if not a single alpaca from the above mentioned states was diagnosed with the disease. What if you purchase your alpacas in April but do not plan to bring them to your farm until November? There are no guarantees, but it will help if the seller's farm has no incoming animals during that time frame. If it does, a fecal check for internal parasites can be repeated prior to arrival. Repeating other tests would be quite costly.

You also have the option of requesting a test for IgG levels to assure yourself that the alpaca has a highly functioning immune system. Many farmers advertise the high IgG level enjoyed by their crias. These tests are normally performed twenty-four hours after birth. They tell you that transfer of immunity took place, meaning that the dam had adequate to high levels in her colostrum, and that the cria nursed shortly after birth. Is there a correlation between high IgG levels at twenty-four hours of age and those of the adult alpaca? I have not seen any research done on this. When you study alpaca physiology, you learn that, within several weeks after birth, the cria's own immune system must kick in to protect it from disease pathogens. We must therefore question the relevance of cria IgG levels on future health. Alpaca crias may have initially extremely low IgG levels due to environmental reasons such as the dam's death or an alpaca's refusal to nurse its baby. Such crias, if they survive due to human intervention, can certainly have high functioning immune systems as adults if they are so genetically programmed. You can see that the issue is a little more complicated than basing your purchase strictly on cria IgG levels.

Who pays for these exams and tests? That depends on the agreement you have with the seller and needs to be spelled out in the agreement. Test expenses can run into hundreds of dollars. Is it financially prudent to pay for them? Should you take your chances and elect to skip the tests? Your decision may be based on purchase price, the seller's track record, your willingness to take a gamble, and possible other variables. For obvious reasons, it would be best for the buyer to contract with a veterinarian not known to the seller for these services. Because veterinarians who are familiar with camelids can be quite rare in certain areas, this may not be a realistic option. In any case, the blood tests are usually run at independent laboratories. You can insist on that no matter who actually draws the blood.

Insurance

Insuring alpacas is quite costly—up to 3.25 percent of the purchase price. Nobody should try to tell you how to handle this issue. It depends entirely on how much of a risk taker you are. A veterinary exam prior to a purchase is no guarantee that the animal will not die. If the uncertainty of it all stresses you out, the price of the insurance premium will be worth it. Insuring the animal for a portion of the purchase price may be a workable compromise. If you pay on an installment plan, expect that the seller demands that you insure the animal. For example, if the price is $3,000 and you make a down payment of $1,000, you will be expected to insure the alpaca for $2,000 and name the seller as the co-beneficiary. When we first encountered this requirement during contract talks, we did not fully understand the reason for this arrangement. Why were we asked to pay an insurance premium for an animal before taking possession? If the alpaca died before it arrived on our farm, shouldn't that be the seller's problem? After some thought, we realized that our deposit effectively took the animal off the market. The seller therefore no longer had the opportunity to find a buyer who was willing and able to pay full price at that particular point in time. It was only reasonable then for us to protect him from a potential loss.

Agisting

What if the thought of owning alpacas appeals to you but you don't live on a farm? You have the option to agist your animals. Agisting is another word for boarding. You don't necessarily have to board at the farm where you purchased your animals even though that may be the most sensible solution.

Paying another farmer to care for your alpacas can work out very well, or it can have a negative outcome. It's best to make a written plan stating your expectations. How do you envision your participation? Exactly what role will you play in caring for your alpacas? Consult your written plan before and during a visit with prospective facilities. Keeping written notes is an effective strategy whether you intend to agist or bring the alpacas to your own farm or ranch. There are so many details to remember. If you visit several farms, they all will blend into one blur after a while. Start a separate folder for each facility. In addition to the factual information you are given, write down your impressions while they're still fresh in your mind.

If you plan to eventually have a farm of your own, you should make every effort to agist within a reasonable driving distance of your home. You will want to work closely with the owners of the boarding facility to learn all the facets of alpaca farming. Be prepared to initially perform menial jobs such as removing dung piles, loading hay, scrubbing water buckets, and similar tasks. Discuss visitation policies and to what extent the boarding facility will permit you to handle your animals. We know of one boarder who shears his own animals. Because there are liability issues involved, don't get annoyed if a farm's owner does not go along with such a plan.

Agisting for a limited period of time to learn the business is, in my opinion, a good plan. If you are lucky, you will find a boarding facility where you'll learn a lot and you and your alpacas are considered part of the family, including long after your animals have been moved to your own farm. The right mentor can save you much money as you set up your own facilities and care protocols. You may view the money spent on agisting as a paid apprenticeship. Make sure that you have a contract that spells out exactly what you will be paying for. Expect to pay a late fee if you're tardy with your payments. Finally, discuss the financial implications of boarding your alpacas with your accountant. As a boarder, you will not be able to claim the full tax deductions that farm owners are entitled to take.

Permanent agisting makes careful selection of a boarding facility even more important than a short-term arrangement. Agisting was a financially viable and even lucrative option for many owners when the alpaca industry was in its infancy and sales prices were uniformly high. That is no longer the case. If you plan to make a profit, I would not advise permanent or even long-term agisting.

A Fiber Herd

There are people who do not wish to deal with the work and stress involved with breeding alpacas but would still like to approach alpaca ownership as a business. I know that there are fiber artists who keep a fiber herd and make a profit. Many who truly support themselves with such a business are living off the grid. They are rugged individuals who, by modern standards, live a Spartan existence. In most areas of the country, you have to work very hard to make a profit—never mind a living—off a fiber herd.

Alpacas as a Hobby

If you find the complexities of farming with alpacas as a business simply overwhelming, then consider owning alpacas as a hobby. Your children can participate in 4-H activities, you can use the fiber to spin, knit, and felt, or you may want to simply enjoy watching a few alpacas graze in your pasture. Of course, the alpacas must be properly maintained, but that will be a walk in the park compared to running a breeding operation or fiber business. Quite frankly, I have known a number of business owners—breeding and selling alpacas—who would have been much happier living with a few of their animals as their beloved pasture companions. If you maintain alpacas strictly as a hobby, there will be no tax deductions for any of your expenses.

Rescue Programs

"If I decide to keep pasture pets, I'd rather rescue alpacas than buy them," a visitor to our farm told me.

Over the years, I have become highly disillusioned with many pet and livestock rescue programs. Unfortunately, there are morally corrupt people who, under the rescue umbrella, put profits in their own pockets while neglecting the animals that they "rescued." Some reward themselves with lavish lifestyles. If you plan to get your alpacas through a rescue group, check it out carefully. Speak to the veterinarian who treats the alpacas maintained by the group. Be equally cautious if you deal with an individual who places rescued alpacas for a fee.

Many well-meaning animal lovers who purchase "rescue" pets, horses, and livestock are—regrettably so—what I call enablers. They feel sorry, for example, for the puppy crammed into a tiny cage at a pet shop or the alpacas kept in a filthy enclosure with sun-bleached "hay" and fetid water in a dirty tank. Moved by pity and compassion, these people buy the animals, often paying much higher prices than a reputable pet breeder or livestock producer would charge.

What follows their purchases? The pet shop owner immediately dials the number of his favorite puppy mill owner.

"Hey, Harry, bring me another one of those Goldendoodles. They're selling like hot cakes."

The owner of *Alpaca Hell* gives a shout to her spouse.

"Jack, put the halter on Princess. I'll breed her right now."

Are there legitimate rescue missions? Of course. Illness, unexpected financial hardship, accidents, death—there are situations that deserve an open heart and generous financial assistance. What do you do to help the animals that are neglected or abused at bogus "rescue" farms? You report their owners to the proper authorities to make sure that they cannot continue to profit from the animals' misery.

Support! Support! Support!

If you have no or very little livestock experience, you should strongly consider buying from the farmer who promises to be the most supportive. Don't automatically assume that a farm run with staff is a guarantee for support. On some farms, the service is only as good as the present farm manager. Determine what is important to you. Will the farmer visit your premises before contracts are finalized? Beware of the seller who doesn't ask detailed questions about your facilities. If a farmer is not interested enough to find out how the alpacas he or she sells will live, the chance of generous support are slim indeed. Will he sit down with you and help you to draw up a shopping list of necessary items? Will she teach you maintenance procedures such as trimming nails? Does he offer help with shearing? Can you feel free to call her day or night in an emergency? Will assistance be offered in finding a veterinarian? What about transporting your female for that promised free breeding? If you are interested in showing, will you be given lessons in how to train your alpaca for the show ring? Is a follow-up visit to your farm planned to show you techniques to move the animals with minimal stress? Are well-defined plans in place to assist you with formulating a marketing plan? Will you be taught how to skirt a fleece? What exactly *can* you expect from the seller? It wouldn't hurt to make a written list of expectations and compare notes after a farm visit. Listen carefully to what a seller tells you. If all he talks about are *his* accomplishments and success stories, open your ears wide. A good seller should inquire as to *your* plans, *your* desires, *your* needs, and what will make *you* a happy alpaca owner.

Ask how many customers the farm services each year. If the sales volume is large, is there sufficient staff to respond to your needs? Will you be truly valued as a client or be just one in a crowd? How do you prefer to communicate? For example, one farmer lost us as potential customers in 1996 when her children would not allow her to have an uninterrupted phone conversation with me. They weren't toddlers, so I was not willing to make allowances. As novice buyers, the seller's support was important to us. You may prefer to communicate via e-mail. When you sent an e-mail inquiry, how long did it take for the seller to get back to you?

Although many buyers claim that support is important to them, it always amazes me just how low their expectations are. Many years ago, I learned an important lesson. A woman once spent a long afternoon on our farm, learning and absorbing lots of information, only to tell me at departure time that she had recently bought alpacas from Farm X. A little angry, I inquired why she had not asked the seller for all this information.

"Well," my visitor said, quite astonished by my question, "X is much too busy. She doesn't have time to explain all that stuff to me."

As you make the rounds of the alpaca farms, please be honest. Don't ask a farmer for time consuming consultations *after* you purchased alpacas from someone else. I don't object to anyone interested in alpacas to come for a brief visit and view my facilities. Additionally, when I issue an invitation to a free *Alpacas 101* seminar on my farm, it would be unreasonable to expect everybody or even anybody in attendance to buy from me. Under such circumstances, my knowledge is freely shared with participants. If a buyer chooses to purchase alpacas from another farmer, however, I do not expect that buyer to come to my farm after the purchase for an extended visit requesting the benefit of my expertise. Such service is reserved for *my* customers. Additionally, I do not wish to give advice on alpaca husbandry protocols for animals not sold by me and owned by virtual strangers without compensation and a contract.

Not everybody has the personality to be a good and willing mentor. What one seller views as pleasant service, another one will resent as a pain in the neck and a chore to be avoided. Of course, if a seller doesn't promise education, guidance, and support, don't expect it. If you buy alpacas from such a person, you are well advised to pay another experienced farmer a consultation fee for such services.

Arrival

Finally, the big day is here! The alpacas arrive on your farm. What should you do with them once they have settled in? For at least a month: nothing! Just feed them and, if possible, leave them alone. Observe them quietly and allow them to become accustomed to your presence. Resist the urge to touch, handle, train, and hug. A move is stressful for the animals. Those who had emotional bonds with herd members will miss their buddies. Your barn will not immediately feel comfortable to them. Unfamiliar pets and wildlife threaten their peace of mind and keep them at constant high alert. Your looks and smell are strange to the animals. Alpacas don't like pushy people. Give them space. Turn your back to them—literally— and allow them to check you out. Read Marty McGee Bennett's books over and over again and with full concentration. Better yet, attend a *Camelidynamics* clinic if you haven't done so already.

After several weeks, calmly and gently begin to use the learned techniques. After working with your animals for a few sessions, you may want to change the location of catch pens and the spatial arrangements in your barn to better suit your needs. This is where the moveable livestock panels and advice from your mentor are invaluable. Your alpacas will thank you, your bank account—well, by now you know the equation: less stress equals less expense equals more profits.

Welcome!

I believe that alpacas are here to stay. Alpaca farmers and their animals have entered the mainstream agricultural community. Like farmers everywhere, you will have to work hard, be flexible, tough, and willing to make sacrifices. With such a program, raising alpacas may change your life in ways you can't as yet imagine. Be realistic in your expectations! A little luck doesn't hurt, but it's not luck that will keep your alpacas healthy and generate your farm's profits. Only extensive knowledge, old-fashioned work ethic, and—yes, you guessed it—a commitment to frugality will accomplish that. Welcome to the community of frugal alpaca farmers!

Afterword

"There is such a steep learning curve in this business," a fellow farmer marveled. She added, "It's not as easy as I was told. I didn't realize how much there is to know."

Along the way, I certainly had my share of disappointing setbacks. I learned from each and took steps not to repeat my mistakes. Although it is nearly impossible for an individual to become an expert on all aspects of breeding and raising alpacas, general knowledge of a fairly broad scope is a necessity if you wish to create and maintain a profitable enterprise.

Please remember: *The Frugal Alpaca Farmer* serves as an introduction to alpaca ownership and breeding practices. For much more extensive information, I highly recommend Eric Hoffman's *The Complete Alpaca Book*, Dr. Fowler's book, *Medicine and Surgery of South American Camelids*, Marty McGee Bennett's *The Camelid Companion* and, if you plan to breed alpacas, *Llama and Alpaca Neonatal Care* (B. Smith, DVM, K. Timm DVM, P. Long, DVM). These books should be the foundation of your personal library, and you would do well to read them cover to cover.

In several chapters, I mentioned additional books that will broaden the knowledge and enhance the education of any alpaca farmer. It is wise to initially read any material that addresses soil assessment, soil improvement, and a specific soil's suitability for your intended purposes. The soil is the foundation of your farm. I believe that people who don't appreciate, protect, and nourish the soil on their land do not deserve to call themselves farmers. When it is time for my husband, David, and me to leave *Stormwind Farm*, its soil will be in better condition than it was in 1995, the year we took ownership of the land.

Over the past few years, we changed the focus of our own farm business from breeding and boarding alpacas to managing a small fiber herd and our seasonal farm store. When David had back surgery, we started to employ a shearer for our fiber harvest. Fortunately, we are still able to complete daily chores on the farm without help. I did not see any reason to discuss these changes in the pertinent chapters of the book. *The Frugal Alpaca Farmer* is not about me, but how my knowledge and experience can help and benefit my readers and their alpacas.

Writing this book turned out to be far more time consuming than I anticipated when I started the project. Despite the demands on my time and energy, I felt driven to complete *The Frugal Alpaca Farmer* and see it published. Why? Our small farm has been described as alpaca paradise by many visitors.

"Your alpacas have a good life." "This is a peaceful place." "Lucky alpacas!"

I hear these comments while we walk on our farm's green pastures and see the alpacas graze and play. I wish for all alpacas to spend their lives in an environment that enhances their sense of well-being and hope that my book will help to accomplish that.

There will also be readers who—wiping their brows in relief—will say, "Thank God that I read this book. There is no way that I will ever have a livestock farm."

For those readers, *The Frugal Alpaca Farmer* also served a good purpose. If you are one of them, you may nevertheless enjoy a visit to an alpaca farm near you.

Farming with alpacas has not made me rich, at least not in the financial sense. It gives me modest profits but a wealth of opportunities to engage in healthy, physical activities. I wish all my readers success as well as joy and contentment.

2017
Springfield Township, New Jersey

About the Author

Ingrid Wood was born and raised in Germany. Her life-long fascination with farming and breeding livestock traces back to wonderful childhood vacations spent with relatives on their farms. One of her grandfathers was a beekeeper. An uncle tended the family's vineyards; a great-aunt kept dairy cows. Others raised pigs, chickens, and small flocks of sheep. All were hard workers and inspiring role models for a young girl.

In 1970, Ingrid followed her American-born husband, David, to the United States of America. After raising their son, Benjamin, in the historical town of Mount Holly, New Jersey, the Woods moved a few miles from their suburban home to a small farm they purchased in Springfield Township (Columbus). The first alpacas arrived on Stormwind Farm in 1997.

After breeding and boarding alpacas for many years, the focus of the farm's activities has changed. *Stormwind Alpacas Farm and Farm Store* is now a popular tourist attraction. In addition to caring for the alpacas and managing the farm store, Ingrid enjoys spending time with her family and friends, playing with her grandchildren, writing, reading non-fiction books, gardening, and knitting.

Ingrid's articles have been published in several camelid publications in the USA, Canada, and Germany. Published books include *A Breeder's Guide to Genetics – Relax, It's Not Rocket Science* (2004), *The Alpacas of Stormwind Farm* (2011), *Hiking with the Boss* (2013), and *The Frugal Alpaca Farmer—A Holistic Approach to Success* (2017).

Index

agisting, 378
Agri Dynamics Company, 33, 45, 119
anatomy, 22
Anderson, David E, 162-163, 165,
AOA, 208, 302, 373
apple cider vinegar, 104, 121, 122
auctions, 313, 361
backyard, 11, 317
Balch, Phyllis A., 118, 125
barn, 54-58, 60
behavior, 23-24, 364
berserk males, 315
biosecurity 235, 242
birth, 202
blood, 113, 176
blue-eyed, 279
boarding, 331
breed standard, 294
breeding, 181, 192-193, 200
Brown, Alice, 24, 110, 238
Bruford, Michael, 20
Brunetti, Jerry, 46, 52, 97
buckets, 70-71
BVD virus, 177
BVDV, 210, 237, 241, 303
camelids, 19, 23
choke, 106, 177
chute, 74
clippers, 75

Colby, Pat, 122
color, 278-279, 370
colostrum, 239
contract, 200, 376
crimp, 277
de Baïracli Levy, Juliette, 45-46, 51, 96, 117
Dettloff, Paul, 99, 122, 124, 178, 339
dewormer, 123, 141, 163
disease prevention, parasites, 165
dogs, 24, 115, 180, 221, 231
drainage, 41, 43
dung, 165
Eagle Peak Herbals, 123
electricity, 62-63
embryo transfer, 199
emotions, 25, 131
equipment, 9, 81, 86
Ewing, Barbara, 13
FAMACHA, 164
fans, 72
fecal, 163, 165
feeders, 68
feeding, 137
fencing, 89-90
fertilizer, 37
fiber, 36, 267, 271, 288
fighting teeth, 175, 298

follicles, 183, 185, 272
Fowler, Murray E., 19, 23, 26, 30, 35, 44, 47, 103, 106, 110, 169, 182, 209
frugal, 3, 287
Fuhrman, Joel, 337
fungus, 45
Gerken, Marina, 20
grain, 60, 103, 105
Grandin, Temple, 131, 328
grazing, 31, 48
guardians, 217, 219
halters, 142, 251
hay, 44, 65, 99, 106, 348
hedgerows, 96
Hellman, Doug and Lori, 259
herbs, 116, 117
herd identifier, 305
herding, 139
herdsire, 333, 366
hierarchy, 133
Hiking with the Boss, 285, 337
hobby, 380
Hoegger Supply Company, 123
Hoffman, Eric, 20, 26, 44, 47, 271, 363
holistic, 4, 118, 145, 345
honeybees, 231
horse, 12, 25
huacaya, 20-21, 368
humus, 34
hydrant, 72
immune system, 113, 294
imprinting, 211
inoculations, 141
instincts, 129
insurance, 378
International Camelid Quarterly, 226, 360
investment, 7, 9

Jorritsma, Leslie, 276
Joyce, Kristin, 29, 113, 217, 253, 301, 353
Kadwell, Miranda, 20
Kinsey, Neal, 34, 41
labor, 206
Labrecque, Wini, 271, 276
Larson, Jovi, 255, 256
llamas, 20, 219
Logsdon, Gene, 31, 45
manure, 37-39
marketing, 284, 301, 312, 321
Marks, Jane, 53, 81, 89, 201, 335, 347
Masters, Carol, 8, 40, 127, 285, 359
Masters, Hugh, 40, 71, 127, 187, 245, 252, 257, 359
McGee Bennett, Marty, 27, 75, 134, 143, 317
McKelvie, Scott and Kate, 172
Mellott, Diann, 67, 83, 157, 181
meningeal worm, 172
micron count, 274
milk, 108, 168
minerals, 34-35, 70, 102
mower, 50, 83
nails, 142, 175
nursing, 108
organic, 34, 41, 339
orgling, 189
paddock, 91
parasites, 162
pasture, 29, 43, 45, 48, 50, 204
permits, 64
physiology, 22
pioneer, 350
placenta, 206-207
predators, 90
pregnancy, 195
products, 325

profit, 14
protocols, 159
pyramid scheme, 11
Quality Llama Products, 75-76
receptive, 185
registry, 372
Reigh, Carol, 220
reproductive system, 182
rescue, 380
resources, 26, 124, 145
restraint, 144
safety, 259, 343
scale, 73
second cuts, 268
seconds, 268
senses, 147
services, 325
shearing, 253, 329, 343
skirting, 280, 282
Smith, Bradford B., 27
soil, 32-36, 43
spit, 14, 314
start-up expenses, 9
storage, 69, 283
Stormwind Alpacas Farm Store, 327
stress, 127, 129, 136, 142
stud service, 333
supplements, 103
suri, 20, 22, 368
temperament, 23
The Merck Veterinary Manual, 40, 47, 65, 103, 111
tools, 82, 85
toxic, 47, 96
trailers, 247
travel, 245
trees, 51
USDA, 304, 328
veterinarian, 14, 157, 209
vitamins, 34-35

water, 63, 70, 111, 249
weaning, 137, 213
weeds, 45-46
Wheeler, Jane, 20
Wood, Benjamin, 349, 387
Wood, Grace, 19
Wood, H. D. (David), 1, 127, 345
Wood, Kaitlin, 19
Wood, Rioghnan, 19
Yocom-McColl, 277
zoning, 11

Made in United States
Troutdale, OR
11/23/2023